STRATEGIES FOR IMPLEMENTATION

STRATEGIES FOR IMPLEMENTATION

MAGDA EL-SHERBINI

An imprint of the American Library Association
CHICAGO 2013

Magda El-Sherbini is head of cataloging at The Ohio State University Library. For the last few years she has been on the faculty of the Kent State University School of Library and Information Science. Throughout her library career she has been involved in all aspects of cataloging. Magda is an active member of the Association for Library Collections & Technical Services (ALA/ALCTS) and has served as chair of numerous ALCTS committees. She has also been a member of the ALA RDA Advisory Board. She was vice chair/chair-elect of the Program of Cataloging Policy Committee. In 2010, she was awarded a Fulbright grant to visit the Bibliotheca Alexandrina in Egypt to conduct research and teach cataloging. She currently serves on the Fulbright Regional Peer Review committee.

Printed in the United States of America

17 16 15 14 13 5 4 3 2 1

ISBNs: 978-0-8389-1168-6 (paper); 978-0-8389-9645-4 (PDF). For more information on digital formats, visit the ALA Store at alastore.ala.org and select eEditions.

Library of Congress Cataloging-in-Publication Data

El-Sherbini, Magda.
RDA : strategies for implementation / Magda El-Sherbini.
pages cm
Includes bibliographical references and index.
ISBN 978-0-8389-1168-6
1. Resource description & access. I. Title.
Z694.15.R47E42 2013
025.3'2—dc23 2012036380

Cover design by Karen Sheets de Gracia. Images © Shutterstock, Inc.
Text design by Kimberly Thornton in the Minion Pro and Brandon Grotesque typefaces.
Composition by Dianne M. Rooney.

∞ This paper meets the requirements of ANSI/NISO Z39.48–1992 (Permanence of Paper).

CONTENTS

PREFACE

HE IDEA FOR THIS BOOK CAME FROM CHRISTOPHER L. Rhodes, acquisitions editor, ALA Editions, who saw the need for an RDA handbook that would address some of the basic precepts of RDA theory and implementation. I was delighted to accept his invitation to author this manuscript. Although the topic is very broad, my task was to present a practical compendium of necessary information that would enable a starting RDA practitioner to begin the process of implementation of the new standard.

This book is an introduction to RDA, and is not intended to cover every aspect or discuss every nuance in detail. It is rather a practical handbook addressed to those who have heard of RDA but are not sure what to think of it. I hope that it will shed some needed light on the new code and help to bring about the transition from AACR2 to RDA.

My own involvement with RDA goes back to ALA's 2007 Midwinter Conference, when I joined the ALA RDA Publisher Advisory Group. Later, my own library became a beta test site for RDA Toolkit. When the RDA Code was released in June 2010, OSUL was part of the US national test. I conducted training for my staff on the RDA Code and the use of RDA Toolkit. At the same time, I conducted workshops and webinars in Ohio to familiarize librarians with the new product. This handbook is a result of my involvement with RDA over the last few years.

As I developed the outline for this book and started to research the topic, I discovered a wealth of material on the Internet. The library community has been debating many of the issues involved with RDA at its various stages of development, and I am grateful to all those librarians who were willing to share their thoughts and observations through conferences, discussion groups, and the Web.

This book describes the status of RDA as of January 2012. Many of the issues have not been settled yet, and many are likely to change as we go forward. The actual RDA implementation will take place in the first quarter of 2013, when all the revisions and rewriting of RDA Toolkit will be completed. From now until 2013, libraries will need to make plans for RDA implementation. It is my hope that this book will set the stage for implementation and provide some guidelines for the decision making process.

I would like to acknowledge many colleagues for their contributions to this book. Although it is impossible to thank everyone who made a contribution, I would like to thank Adam L. Schiff, principal cataloger at the University of Washington, and Judy Kuhagen and David Reser at the Library of Congress Policy and Standards Division for their comments and valuable feedback.

I also would like to acknowledge Barbara B. Tillett, Chief, Policy and Standards Division, Library of Congress, for making her RDA and FRBR presentations available to the library community. Many thanks go to the Library of Congress for making all the RDA test documentation accessible. I also would like to thank the cataloging staff at The Ohio State University Libraries for providing me with title pages of materials. Special acknowledgment and thanks to my husband, George Klim, for editing the final copy and providing valuable comments. Most of all, I would like to thank my son, Adam Klim, for being patient, kind, and supportive throughout this process.

CHAPTER ONE

FROM AACR2 TO RDA

ESOURCE DESCRIPTION AND ACCESS (RDA), THE NEW cataloging code, has been one of the hot topics of discussion on library forums and at professional conferences since 2005. Because the Internet emerged as an important tool for accessing information and electronic publications became increasingly difficult to catalog, classify, and describe, libraries were confronted with the need to examine their traditional tools for description in order to address the challenges of describing the new electronic and digital resources.

The second edition of the *Anglo-American Cataloguing Rules* (AACR2) remained the dominant cataloging standard, but it presented growing challenges when attempts were made to apply it to Internet-based materials. Cataloging the Internet became an emerging trend in libraries and a major concern for catalogers.

The first edition of the *Anglo-American Cataloguing Rules* (AACR) was published in 1978. Since that date, there have been many updates and revisions generated from the revision process established by the Joint Steering Committee for the Development of RDA (JSC) of the American Library Association. AACR2 was developed for an environment dominated by the card catalog. The International Conference on the Principles and Future Development of AACR held in Toronto in 1997 identified substantive problems with AACR2. Although the updates issued in the years following that conference addressed some of these problems, it eventually became clear that a fundamental rethinking of AACR2 was required to respond fully to the challenges and opportunities of the digital age.

Recognizing the need to update AACR2, the JSC strategic plan included a new edition of AACR which was scheduled for publication in 2008. In December 2004, a draft of part I of AACR3 was made available to the constituency for review, and the responses were discussed at the April 2005 meeting. Following that discussion, and in response to the constituency's review of the draft of part I, the JSC and the Committee of Principals decided to take a different approach to the new edition. Because the third edition was a radical departure from preceding editions, a decision was made to use the new working title "Resource Description and Access" (Joint Steering Committee for Development of RDA 2009).

The library community has been waiting for the release of the new standard since April 2005, and predictions and speculation about the new code are reflected in professional library literature. Medeiros (2005) discussed the goals of RDA and described its potential uses by a large community of information professionals. The same author (Medeiros 2006) gave a brief discussion at the RDA Forum that was held at the 2006 ALA Midwinter Meeting in San Antonio, Texas. A number of practical problems that are likely to arise with the implementation of RDA were discussed by Intner (2006). The author pointed out two main problems: (1) "materials collected by libraries have become more varied and sophisticated since [AACR] first appeared in 1978," and (2) "catalogers as a group have not developed greater inclination to take risks." Intner speculated that "great challenges await the third millennium's new cataloging rules." Hillmann (2006) expressed concerns about transcription and specified sources of information, reliance on notes, and multiple versions.

As RDA continued to develop, the library community offered its opinions and commentary on the proposed changes. Librarians wrote articles about the new code and shared information in order to enhance awareness of the changes among the library community. Duszak (2006) presented general information on the RDA cataloging code, including the scheduled publication dates and major organizations that were involved in the development of the code. In addition, the author provided readers with a list of 15 important facts about RDA.

Bowen (2005) became one of the key contributors to the discussion of RDA as the new code grew and developed. She presented questions and answers related to RDA as a standard designed to replace the *Anglo-American Cataloguing Rules,* Second Edition (AACR2). In her RDA Update, she contributed updated information on the results of a Joint Steering Committee (JSC) meeting held in Ottawa, Ontario, from April 24 to 28, 2006 (Bowen 2006). She also provided information about other conferences and forums related to the development of RDA.

Moore (2006) presented an overview of the history and processes involved in creating the new cataloging rules. She discussed the structure and the content of RDA and the possibility of non-library and non-MARC information communities, as well as librarians, using the codes. Weiss and Molly (2006) provided the context for this new standard and explained the work that had been done by the JSC. They covered the rationale behind the new standard, the process of developing the first draft, reactions to that draft, and the current direction of the JSC's work.

Much of the early work on RDA consisted of descriptions of the changes, as well as predictions about the future of the new standard. As the publication date approached, authors began to focus their attention on the implementation and various practical aspects of using RDA.

This text has been prepared for catalogers and technical services staff to assist them in making the transition from AACR2 rev. to RDA. It will focus on addressing the differences between RDA and AACR2 rev., understanding the International Federation of Library Associations and Institutions (IFLA) *Functional Requirements for Bibliographic Records* (IFLA Study Group on the Functional Requirements for Bibliographic Records 1988), explaining RDA Toolkit (2010–) and how it works, and highlighting the key adjustments that catalogers will need to make initially as they undertake the transition process to RDA. Examples illustrating key features will be presented throughout the book and practice questions will be included with key answers.

This book

- Is a comprehensive overview of RDA.
- Is intended for all library cataloging staff in all types of libraries, with special emphasis on academic.
- Provides tips on how to make the transition from AACR2 to RDA seem less difficult.
- Describes the Functional Requirements for Bibliographic Records (FRBR) in relation to RDA.
- Explains the structure of RDA and how RDA Toolkit works.
- Provides many examples from various resources.

This book is a discussion of key issues related to RDA. The author's objective is to help prepare catalogers for the implementation of RDA.

Chapter 1 is an introduction that discusses the history and background of AACR2, the need for a new cataloging code, the objectives and principles of RDA, the benefits to users and catalogers, and collaboration with other communities and standards.

Chapter 2 provides a detailed comparison between RDA and AACR2 in order to illustrate the similarities and differences between the two standards.

Chapter 3 discusses RDA implementation strategies and includes the following topics:

- General tips for catalogers
- Selecting the type of RDA description
- Transcribing data elements from the source
- Decision-making by catalogers
- Integrating new RDA records with the legacy records and making a decision to re-catalog a set of manifestations
- Exporting RDA-based bibliographic records from the Online Computer Library Catalog (OCLC) into your Online Public Access Catalog (OPAC)
- RDA and the PCC participants
- RDA's effect on OPAC displays
- Strategy for implementing the new MARC 21 fields to accommodate the new RDA elements
- Adjusting the online system to accommodate the new MARC 21 fields
- Authority processing using vendor services and RDA
- Accessing RDA records from OCLC and LC

Chapter 4 offers an explanation of the Functional Requirements for Bibliographic Records (FRBR) and Functional Requirements for Authority Data (FRAD). In this chapter, the reader will find an explanation of FRBR Group 1, Group 2, and Group 3 entities. A section is devoted to the FRBR user's tasks, FRBR-group relationships, basic principles of FRAD, FRAD's impact on RDA application, and RDA structure.

Chapter 5 provides descriptions of manifestation and item. It includes discussions about pre-cataloging decisions, language and script, transcription, preferred source of information, and mandatory elements of description.

Chapter 6 discusses works and expressions for specific library materials. This includes recording the primary relationship between manifestation and work embodied in the manifestation, constructing the authorized access point, and recording relationships.

Chapter 7 provides tips for using RDA Toolkit, and includes instructions on how to search and browse RDA Toolkit, how to create a workflow, how to use AACR2 rule numbers to search RDA, and how to search using RDA elements versus the table of contents.

Chapter 8 provides RDA examples of specific types of library materials. Most of the examples are taken from the Library of Congress catalog, The Ohio State University catalog, and the University of Chicago catalog. Some examples were created to illustrate specific situations in cataloging.

Chapter 9 includes three checklists: a copy cataloging checklist, an original cataloging checklist, and an authority records checklist. These are based on checklists created by several libraries, with some modifications and additions that are appropriate for a more general discussion.

This book also includes a comprehensive list of readings and references.

I. HISTORY AND BACKGROUND

The history of AACR2 is well documented. The Joint Steering Committee (JSC) of the American Library Association (ALA) offers a good, brief description on their website (Joint Steering Committee 2009). Development of cataloging rules goes back to when Panizzi (1841) recorded rules for the catalogs of the British Museum. In 1883 the "Condensed Rules for an Author and Title Catalog" were published by the American Library Association in *Library Journal*. About a decade later, the United Kingdom Library Association (LA) (1893) published the *Cataloguing Rules*. Between 1904 and 1967, ALA and LA tried to consolidate their efforts and publish a single set of cataloging rules. The first international cataloging code was published in 1908 in an American edition in two separate versions, North American and British (American Library Association 1908). In 1949 the Library of Congress created rules for descriptive cataloging for their own use. The American Library Association adopted these rules.

The 1949 rules went through several developments, revisions, and editing, which led to publication of two versions of the *Anglo-American Cataloguing Rules* (AACR) in 1967: a North American text and a British text (American Library Association 1967).

All texts of the AACR consisted of three parts:

Part I, Entry and Heading
- Based on the Paris Principles, the 1949 ALA rules, and Lubetzky's 1960 draft

Part II, Description
- Consisted of revised rules from the 1949 Library of Congress rules

Part III, Non-Book Materials
- Contained rules for both entry and description of non-book materials.
- Consisted of revised rules from the 1949 Library of Congress rules, and supplementary Library of Congress rules.

A program of International Standard Bibliographic Description (ISBD) was developed at the International Meeting of Cataloguing Experts in Copenhagen in 1969. The ISBD organizes the description of an item into distinct areas: title, statement of responsibility, edition, resource specific information, publication, physical description, series, notes, and standard number identifiers (ISBD (M)).

In 1974 the Joint Steering Committee for the Revision of AACR (JSC) was established and was charged with incorporating the North American and British texts into a single version. In 1978, the *Anglo-American Cataloguing Rules,* Second Edition (AACR2) was published in one version unifying the two sets of rules, and made them consistent with the ISBD (American Library Association 2002).

The second edition of AACR2 was divided into two parts:

Part I, Description

- Is based on the ISBD framework
- Includes a general chapter (chapter 1) and chapters for individual formats, including new chapters for machine-readable data files (chapter 9) and three-dimensional artifacts and realia (chapter 10)
- Bases rules for non-book materials on alternative codes that were published in the 1970s

Part II, Entry and Heading

- Brings rules more closely in line with the Paris Principles

Key principles of AACR include cataloging from the item "in hand" rather than inferring information from external sources, and the concept of a chief source of information that is the preferred source where conflicts exist.

The Library of Congress, the National Library of Canada, the British Library, and the Australian National Library adopted AACR2 in 1981. Since its publication in 1978, AACR2 has undergone many amendments and revisions (in 1988, 1998, and 2002) that reflect changes in entry procedures and the development of new formats, particularly emerging formats such as electronic resources (Adamich 2008).

With the advent of new publishing formats, especially electronic versions of original paper documents, catalogers found that the AACR2 rules were either too specific or difficult to use in describing this new content (Huthwaite 2001).

In 1997 the Joint Steering Committee (JSC) for the Development of RDA held an International Conference on the Principles and Future Developments of AACR in Toronto, Canada. The participants identified a number of issues of concern with AACR. These included the principles of AACR2, content versus carrier, the logical structure of the AACR2 rules, the way to handle serials, internationalization of the rules, amendments to the rules revision process, and incorporating FRBR terminology and concepts (Manning 1998). To address some of these concerns, a draft of part I of the third revised edition of AACR2 was issued in 2003 under the name of AACR3 to address rules for description (Chapman 2006). This draft was made available to the library community in 2004 and comments were solicited. Based on comments and feedback, the JSC changed their direction and decided to adopt a new title that would reflect a move away from Anglocentrism. The words "Anglo-American" and "cataloguing" were removed. The new title, Resource Description and Access, was considered to be more appealing and more easily understood by other metadata communities (Rhodes 2010).

The first RDA draft was made available to the library community for comments in 2008. It was released in June 23, 2010, as the web-based RDA Toolkit. RDA was tested by the Library of Congress, National Library of Medicine, National Agricultural Library, and 20 other libraries across the country for 6 months after its publication. The British Library, Library and Archives Canada, and the National Library of Australia monitored the US national libraries' tests, but did not conduct testing at the same level (Library of Congress 2009).

The following chart shows the time line of the development of AACR2 and RDA.

AACR2		RDA	
1839	Panizzi's British Museum Rules		
1853	Jewett's Rules		
1876	Cutter's Rules		
1883	American Library Association		
1893	United Kingdom, Library Association		
1908	Anglo-American Rules		
1941	ALA Draft		
1949	LC Rules		
1967	AACR 1st edition		
1978	AACR 2nd edition		
1988	AACR2 2nd edition revision		
		1997	International Conference on the Principles and Future Development of AACR
1998	Revision		
2002	Revision		
2003–5	Updates	2003	AACR3 draft
		2005	Move to RDA
		2010	RDA release

II. THE NEED FOR A NEW CATALOGING CODE

New types of publications, such as PDF files and digital content, were being created. AACR2 does not provide guidelines for cataloging these materials. Users have different expectations of what a library catalog is and what it can do. The growing popularity of the Internet and the ease of accessing data through the Web created the need for a response from libraries. Library catalogs had to improve their functionality and their interfaces to provide users with an easy way of searching and retrieving information with a single search.

It was imperative that libraries create a new code that covers the rapidly expanding range of information packages, especially electronic and online resources (Huthwaite 2001). Some of AACR2's limitations are:

- Limitations of the class of material concept when describing materials that belong to more than one class of materials

- Alteration in recording data to save space by using abbreviations and the rule of three. Space limitation has been eliminated in RDA and no adjustment is necessary. This change allows libraries to use metadata from publishers or from digital objects without changing this data
- Inadequate rules for the description of continuing resources

Libraries have developed a new set of principles—FRBR and FRAD—that provides the underlying basis for cataloging rules. This set of principles (IFLA 2008) supports

- User tasks (find, identify, select, obtain)
- A better understanding of the range of relationships in the bibliographic universe
- The clustering of bibliographic records to show relationships between works and their creators to make the user more aware of the work's different editions, translations, or physical formats
- New methods to record information that improve search, navigation, and retrieval of appropriate sets of records

In the last few decades, technology has made great strides in the delivery of digital information. Information technology systems now have the capacity to store these resources and to manage them in different ways.

Catalogs and cataloging rules and indexes have enabled improved management of information encompassed in physical items (books, serials, videos, etc.). Many new communities recognize the need for metadata. There are multiple metadata standards that are attempting to define various new formats and resources (MARC, Dublin Core, ISBD, EAD, MARCXML, etc.). AACR2 and RDA are also metadata standards.

Using RDA will help to ensure consistency and interoperability, which will only improve and strengthen the library's position in the information environment. It will enable libraries to keep pace with other information providers, including Amazon, Indigo, Library Thing, etc.

AACR was perceived as having a strong Anglo-American bias (despite being translated into many other languages). The new standard attempts to base cataloging code on internationally agreed principles and to remove this bias. Its goal is to create something completely international, and to extend it beyond the library world to others (museums, archives, and publishers in particular) (Cossham 2009).

There are some basic problems with the current rules, as shown by the regular revisions of the Library of Congress Rule Interpretations. Examples of problems with AACR2 include the "class of materials" concept and the shortcomings of the rules for general (GMD) and special material designations (SMD), outdated and complex terminology, deficiencies in the rules for cataloging digital resources, and the retention of a card-catalog focus. The rules are also complex, and need simplification if they are to work as an international content standard for metadata (Rhodes 2010).

DESIRE FOR A PRINCIPLE-BASED SET OF GUIDELINES

AACR is case-based (and based on convention, e.g., ISBD); RDA aims to be more principle-based, so that catalogers can use more judgment rather than have to learn so many different rules (Kiorgaard and Kartus 2006).

III. RDA OBJECTIVES

Cost efficiency. Descriptive data should meet the functional requirements in a cost-effective manner.

A flexible framework for describing all resources—analog and digital. The data function independently of the format, medium, or system used to store or communicate them. Descriptive data is amenable to use in a variety of environments. There is no reference in the main rules to ISBD or MARC; rules simply state what should be recorded, not how to record it. No attempt is made in the examples to show how the element is recorded.

Continuity. Descriptive data is compatible with existing records in the online library catalog. It will integrate existing files with a minimum of retrospective adjustment to those files.

Blended conceptual models of Functional Requirements for Bibliographic Records (FRBR) and Functional Requirements for Authority Data (FRAD) help users find information more easily.

IV. RDA PRINCIPLES

Differentiation. Descriptive data provided should serve to differentiate the resource described from other resources represented in the file.

Sufficiency. Descriptive data should be sufficient to meet the needs of the user with respect to selection of an appropriate resource.

Relationships. Descriptive data should indicate significant bibliographic relationships between the resource described and other resources.

Representation. Descriptive data should reflect the resource's representation of itself.

Accuracy. Descriptive data should furnish supplementary information to correct or clarify ambiguous, unintelligible, or misleading representations made by the resource itself.

Common usage. The guidelines and instructions for recording data elements other than those transcribed from the resource itself should reflect common usage.

Uniformity. Guidelines and instructions provided in the appendixes on capitalization, numerals, abbreviations, order of elements, punctuation, etc., should serve to promote uniformity in the presentation of descriptive data.

V. RDA'S IMPACT ON CATALOGING

- RDA will not affect classification systems or call numbers; Dewey and LC can be used as before.
- It can be used with MARC 21 and many other formats.
- Authority records will be affected. The MARC 21 authorities formats will include new fields to deal with RDA details.
- Bibliographic records will no longer fall under RDA's auspices because abbreviations are no longer used and new MARC 21 fields are introduced.
- New MARC 21 fields are created; for example, General Material Designation (GMD) will be replaced by three new terms:

  Content type: MARC 21 tag 336 (336 two-dimensional image $2 rdacontent)
  Media type: MARC 21 tag 337 (337 video $2 rdamedia)
  Carrier type: MARC 21 tag 338 (338 videodisc $2 rdacarrier)

REFERENCES

Adamich, Tom. 2008. "Resource Description and Access (RDA): The New Way to Say AACR2." *Knowledge Quest: Visual Literacy* 36 (3): 72–76. http://librarystaffdevelopment .wikispaces.com/file/view/RDA+The-New-Way-to-Say.pdf.

American Library Association. 2002. *Anglo-American Cataloguing Rules,* Second Edition, 2002 revision. Chicago: Canadian Library Association; Chartered Institute of Library and Information Professionals; American Library Association.

———. 1978. *Anglo-American Cataloguing Rules,* Second Edition. Chicago: Canadian Library Association; Library Association; American Library Association.

———. 1967. *Anglo-American Cataloguing Rules.* Chicago: Canadian Library Association; Library Association; American Library Association.

———. 1908. *Catalog Rules; Author and Title Entries.* Chicago: American Library Association; London: Library Association.

American Library Association. 1908. *Cataloguing Rules; Author and Title Entries.* London: Library Association; Chicago: American Library Association.

———. 1883. "Condensed Rules for an Author and Title Catalog." *Library Journal* (8) 251–54.

Bowen, Jennifer. 2005. "What's after AACR2?" ALCTS Newsletter Online 16 (6): 1. www.ala.org/alcts/ano/v16/n6/nws/rdaqs.

———. 2006. "RDA Update." *ALCTS Newsletter Online* 17 (4): 51. www.ala.org/alcts/ano/v17/n4/evnt/rda.

Chapman, Ann. 2006. "RDA: A New International Standard." *Ariadne* 49: 2. www.ariadne .ac.uk/issue49/chapman.

Cossham, Amanda. 2009. "Introducing RDA: The New Kid on the Block." Paper presented at RDA/FRBR Workshops, LIANZ A, CatSig, and the National Library, March 2009. http://repository.openpolytechnic.ac.nz/bitstream/handle/11072/455/Cossham

%2c%20A.%20F._2009-national%20Presentation-Introducing_RDA__Amanda _Cossham_.pdf?sequence=1.

Duszak, Thomas. 2006. "Goodbye AACR2rev, Hello RDA: The New Cataloguing Code." *Catholic Library World* 76 (3): 198–99.

Hillmann, Diane I. 2006. "RDA for Who?" *Technicalities* 26 (3): 8–10.

Huthwaite, Ann. 2001. "AACR2 and Its Place in the Digital World: Near-Term Solutions and Long-Term Direction." Paper presented at the Bicentennial Conference on Bibliographic Control for the New Millennium, November 15–17. www.loc.gov/catdir/bibcontrol/ huthwaite_paper.html.

International Federation of Library Associations and Institutions. 2008. "Functional Requirements for Bibliographic Records: Final Report." http://archive.ifla.org/VII/s13/ frbr/frbr_current2.htm.

———. 1997. *The Principles and Future of AACR: Proceedings of the International Conference on the Principles and Future Development of AACR: Toronto, Ontario, Canada, October 23/25, 1997.* Ottawa: Canadian Library Association; London: Library Association Publishing; Chicago: American Library Association.

International Federation of Library Associations and Institutions Cataloguing Section. 1974. *International Standard Bibliographic Description for Monographic Publications.* Berlin: De Gruyter Sauer.

International Federation of Library Associations and Institutions Study Group on the Functional Requirements for Bibliographic Records. 1988. *Functional Requirement for Bibliographic References,* 2nd ed. Munich: Saur. www.ifla.org/en/publications/functional -requirements-for-bibliographic-records.

———. 1967. *Functional Requirement for Bibliographic References.* Munich: G. K. Saur. www.ifla.org/en/publications/functional-requirements-for-bibliographic-records.

Intner, Sheila. 2006. "RDA: Will It Be Cataloger's Judgment or Cataloger's Judgment Day?" *Technicalities* 26 (2): 1–12.

Joint Steering Committee for Development of RDA. 2009a. "List of Changes to AACR2 Instructions." 5JSC/Sec/7/Rev; July 2, 2009. www.rda-jsc.org/docs/5sec7rev.pdf.

———. 2009b. "A Brief History of AACR." July 1. www.rda-jsc.org/history.html.

Kiorgaard, Deirdre, and Ebe Kartus. 2006. "A Rose by Any Other Name?: From AACR2 to Resource Description and Access." www.valaconf.org.au/vala2006/papers2006/83 _Kartus_Final.pdf.

Library Association. 1893. *Cataloguing Rules 1. of the British Museum 2. of the Bodleian Library 3. of the Library Association.* British Museum Department of Printed Books, Bodleian Library. London: Simpkin, Marshall, Hamilton, Kent and Company.

Library of Congress. 1949. *Rules for Descriptive Cataloging in the Library of Congress.* Washington, DC: Library of Congress.

Library of Congress Bibliographical Control Working Group. 2009. Testing Resource Description and Access. www.loc.gov/bibliographic-future/rda.

Manning, Ralph W. 1998. "Anglo-American Cataloguing Rules and Their Future." Paper presented at the 64th IFLA General Conference, August 16–August 21. http://archive.ifla .org/IV/ifla64/083-126e.htm.

Medeiros, Norm. 2006. "On the Dublin Core Front: Metadata in a Global World." *OCLC Systems and Services* 22 (2): 89–91.

———. 2005. "On the Dublin Core Front: The Future of the Anglo-American Cataloguing Rules." *OCLC Systems and Services* 21 (4): 261–63.

Moore, Julie Renee. 2006. "RDA: New Cataloging Rules, Coming Soon to a Library Near You!" *Library Hi Tech News* 23 (9): 12–17.

Panizzi, Anthony. 1841. *Rules for the Compilation of the Catalogue: Catalogue of Printed Books in the British Museum,* vol. 1: v–ix.

RDA Toolkit. 2010– . Chicago: American Library Association; Ottawa: Canadian Library Association; London: Chartered Institute of Library and Information Professionals. www.rdatoolkit.org.

Rhodes, Chris. 2010. "Chris Oliver on RDA and the Future of Cataloging." *ALA Editions (blog).* www.alaeditions.org/blog/categories/cataloging-and-classification.

Weiss, Paul J., and R. T. Molly. 2006. "AACR3 Is Coming: What Is It?" *Serials Librarian* 50 (3/4): 285–94.

CHAPTER TWO

DIFFERENCES BETWEEN AACR2 AND RDA

T FIRST GLANCE. A BIBLIOGRAPHIC RECORD THAT WAS produced according to RDA instructions gives the impression of being quite similar to a record based on the rules of AACR2. One of the reasons for this similarity is the simple fact that the new RDA instructions are based on the old AACR2 rules. This is not to say that the new standard simply copies the old. Rather, the new RDA instructions follow established cataloging patterns and practices. In this sense, the RDA instructions have remained substantially the same as the AACR2 rules.

What the new RDA standard offers are many options and alternatives that allow catalogers to use their own judgment in rule interpretation. This feature of RDA is also similar to AACR2, although it is greatly expanded, allowing the cataloger even more flexibility and independence.

There are numerous instances where the AACR2 rules have been changed significantly; these changes and enhancements are discussed in the following sections. Although these changes have an impact on the final product, they do not change the cataloging procedures too drastically. Catalogers will be able to continue coding records in MARC and they will still fit into the ISBD structure that we are all accustomed to:

- Many RDA instructions are derived from AACR2. Therefore, most RDA instructions did not change and maintain compatibility with the legacy data of AACR2.
- Some RDA instructions are similar to AACR2 rules but have been reworded. The following example illustrates this point.

  AACR2

  1.6B1 If an item is issued in a series, transcribe the title proper of the series as instructed in 1.1B.

  RDA

  2.12.2.3 If the resource is issued in a series, record the title proper of the series applying the basic instructions on recording titles given under 2.3.1.

- Both AACR2 and RDA provide options, omissions, and additions.
- Records created using either AACR2 or RDA will still be coded in MARC 21 and will fit into the ISBD record structure.
- Both AACR2 and RDA include codes to access instructions.
- Both AACR2 and RDA include examples and appendixes to provide catalogers with instructions on capitalization, abbreviations, initial articles, etc.
- Both discuss description and access.
- Some RDA instructions are similar to those of AACR2, but employ different terminology. For example, the AACR2 rule reads "determining the main

entry," whereas RDA changed that same statement to "identifying the work or naming the work."

DIFFERENCES BETWEEN AACR2 AND RDA

In general terms, RDA is different from AACR2 in a number of ways. It provides a theoretical framework that is based on data models instead of the piece in hand approach AACR2 uses. The new RDA standard adheres to the following criteria:

- Builds cataloger's judgment based on principles
- Focuses on content, not on display. Its emphasis is on what should be recorded, not on how it is recorded.
- Is independent of any particular syntax or structure encoding schema so that it can be applied to whatever conventions or encoding standards a cataloger follows. This in particular will make the data that libraries create more adaptable and sharable in the digital environment (Stephens 2010).
- Provides a set of guidelines rather than rules
- Provides mandatory and optional elements based on FRBR
- Focuses on describing what is being cataloged
    - Describes the type of resource (how is it issued: single or multipart, ongoing, integrating, etc.?)
    - Describes the type of description (comprehensive versus analytical)

RDA Toolkit is a fully web-based, interactive tool. It provides flexible searching capabilities; links between sections within the tool; and mapping to other external tools, such as AACR2 and MARC 21. It provides links from the RDA instructions to the LC Policy Statement (LCPS) (Stephens 2010).

- RDA Toolkit is not intended to be read as a linear document, but to lead the cataloger to the instructions that are needed.
- RDA instructions focus on recoding data that will help users by providing the information they need to find, identify, select, and obtain information resources.
- RDA supports integration of library catalog records with those produced by other metadata communities.

The following section will provide more details about the differences between RDA and AACR2, with examples that illustrate these differences (Joint Steering Committee 2009; Schiff 2010).

The list of changes addressed in this chapter is not comprehensive and does not include all the changes from AACR2 to RDA. It will provide some idea about what to expect when implementing RDA. It also does not address changes in MARC 21 fields that were created to accommodate RDA elements. (This topic will be covered in chapter 3, "Tips for Implementation.")

I. GENERAL DIFFERENCES

DIFFERENCE IN SCOPE

AACR2	RDA
Description is based on • ISBD elements • Classes of materials • Mode of issuance • Type of description	Description is based on • Attributes of FRBR entities • Types of content and carrier • Mode of issuance • Type of description
Access is based on • Choice of access points • Form of headings • Reference	Access is based on • FRBR relationships • Attributes of FRAD entities • FRAD relationships • Subject relationships

DIFFERENCE IN DESCRIPTION

RDA employs new terms that replace some of the familiar AACR2 terms. These new terms are derived from the Functional Requirements models and the International Cataloguing Principles.

AACR2	RDA
Areas	Elements
Heading	Authorized access point
Main entry	Authorized access point for creator + preferred title
Author, composer, etc.	Creator
See reference	Variant access point
See also reference	Authorized access point
Added entries	Access points
Physical description	Carrier description
Chief source	Preferred sources
Uniform title	Preferred title +other information to differentiate ; conventional collective title
Notes	Describing content or recording relationships
GMD	Replaced by: Media type Carrier type Content type

USE OF SQUARE BRACKETS

AACR2 1.0C1	**RDA D.1.2.1**
When adjacent elements within one area are to be enclosed in square brackets, they are enclosed in one set of square brackets.	Each adjacent data element that requires square brackets is enclosed in its own set of square brackets. Square brackets are used only for information *not found* in the item, regardless of source within the item.
260 $a [Maryland : $b Scarecrow Press, $c 2007]	260 $a [Maryland] : $b [Scarecrow Press], $c [2007]
260 $a [S.l. : $b s.n., $c 2006]	260 $a [place of publication not identified] : $b [publisher not identified], $c [2006]

RECORDING INACCURACIES

Catalogers will transcribe errors as they appear on the manifestation and will provide access points for the correct form.

AACR2 1.0F1	**RDA 1.7.9, 2.3.1.4**
In an area where transcription from the item is required, transcribe an inaccuracy or a misspelled word as it appears in the item. Follow such an inaccuracy either by [sic] or by i.e., and the correction within square brackets. Supply a missing letter or letters in square brackets.	When instructed to transcribe an element as it appears on the source of information, transcribe an inaccuracy or a misspelled word as it appears on the source, except where instructed otherwise. Make a note correcting the inaccuracy if it is considered to be important for identification or access (see 2.20). If the inaccuracy appears in a title, record a corrected form of the title as a variant title (see 2.3.6) if it is considered to be important for identification or access.
245 14 $a The Hitsory [sic] of Egypt / $c by John Miller. 246 3 $a The History of Egypt	245 14 $a The Hitsory of Egypt / $c by John Miller. 246 1 $i Title should read: $a The History of Egypt
245 14 $a The unfinished journey : $b American [i.e., America] since World War II. 246 34 $a The unfinished journey : $b America since World War II	245 14 $a The unfinished journey : $b American since World War II. 246 1 $i Title should read: $a The unfinished journey : $b America since World War II
245 14 $a The world of Internet and the n[e]w generation / $c Adam Mousa.	245 14 $a The world of Internet and the nw generation / $c Adam Mousa. 246 1 $i Title should read: $a The world of Internet and the new generation
AACR2 12.1.B1: For serials, correct obvious typographic errors when transcribing the title proper and give the title as it appears on the resource in notes. (In case of doubt about whether the spelling of a word is incorrect, transcribe the spelling as found.)	Exceptions: 2.3.1.4 Inaccuracies. When transcribing the title proper of a serial or integrating resource, correct obvious typographic errors, and make a note giving the title as it appears on the source of information (see 2.20.2.4). (In case of doubt about whether the spelling of a word is incorrect transcribe the spelling as found.)
245 00 $a Zoology studies. 246 10 $i Title appears on no. 1: $a Zooology studies	245 00 $a Zoology studies. 246 10 $i Sources of information on number 1 reads: $a Zooology studies
245 00 $a Housing starts. 246 10 $i Title appears on v.1, no. 1 reads: $a Housing sarts	245 00 $a Housing starts. 246 10 $i Sources of information on volume1, number 1 reads: $a Housing sarts

ABBREVIATIONS

Catalogers will no longer abbreviate elements unless abbreviations appear on the source.

AACR2 APPENDIX B9	RDA 1.7.8
AACR2 allows abbreviations to be used in certain transcribed elements (e.g., edition statement, numbering, place of publication, distribution, etc., series).	Abbreviations in transcribed elements permitted only if abbreviations appear on the source.
100 10 $a Brookbank, Joseph, $c b. 1612. 130 0 $a Bible. $p O.T. 250 $a Rev. ed. AACR2 1.0C1: When an element ends with an abbreviation followed by a full stop or ends with the mark of omission and the punctuation following that element either is or begins with a full stop, *omit* the full stop that constitutes or begins the prescribed punctuation. 250 $a 5 ed. *(Edition is abbreviated on the sources of information.)*	100 10 $a Brookbank, Joseph, $c born 1612. 130 0 $a Bible. $p Old Testament. 250 $a Revised edition. *(Source of information reads "revised edition".)* RDA D.1.2.1: When an element ends with an abbreviation followed by a full stop or ends with the mark of omission and the punctuation following that element either is or begins with a full stop, *include* the full stop that constitutes or begins the prescribed punctuation. 250 $a 5 ed.. *(The first full stop is for the abbreviation and the second one is for the ending punctuation.)*
260 $b Springer Pub. Co.,	260 $b Springer Publisher Company *(Source of information reads "Springer Publishing Company".)*
260 $b University of Leeds, Dept. of Spanish,	260 $b University of Leeds, Department of Spanish *(Source of information reads "Department of Spanish".)*
260 $a [Ashland, Or.] : $b Blackstone Audio, $c p2009.	260 $a [Ashland, Oregon] : $b Blackstone Audio, $c [2009], ℗2009. *(Source of information reads "Ashland, Oregon".)*
260 $a [S.l : $b s.n]	260 $a [place of publication not identified] : $b [publisher not identified] *(The Latin abbreviations S.l. [sine loco "without place"] and s.n. [sine nomine "without name"] are eliminated and will not be used in cataloging.)*

AACR2 1.0C1 (cont.)	**RDA D.1.2.1** (cont.)
260 $a Belmont, CA $b Brooks/Cole, $c 2012 [i.e., 2010]	260 $a Belmont, California : $b Brooks/Cole, $c 2012 [that is, 2010] *(In RDA, the abbreviation "i.e." is replaced with "that is".)*
300 $a 234 p. : $b col. ill.; $c 20cm.	300 $a 234 pages : $b colored illustrations; $c 20 cm. *("cm." is not an abbreviation, it is a symbol- [RDA B.5.1].)*
300 $a 2 v.; $c 23 cm.	300 $a 2 volumes; $c 23 cm.
300 $a 86, [21] p. : $b ill., 1 folded map ; $c 24 cm.	300 $a 86 pages, 21 unnumbered pages : $b illustrations, 1 folded map ; $c 24 cm.
300 $a 1 videocassette (approx. 120 min.); $c	300 $a 1 videocassette (approximately 120 min.); $c *(The abbreviation "approx." is replaced with "approximately".)* *(Abbreviations for measurements of duration [RDA 7.2] should be used: For example, min. [for minutes] and sec. [for seconds].)*
300 $a [11], 303, 232, [28], 993 [i.e. 299] p.; $c 30 cm.	300 $a 11 unnumbered pages, 303, 232, 28 unnumbered pages, 993 [that is, 299] pages; $c 30 cm.
300 $a 1 videodisc (ca.75 min.); $c *(The abbreviation "ca." means "circa".)*	300 $a 1 videodisc (approximately 75 min.); $c *(The abbreviation "ca." is replaced with "approximately".)*
490 1 $a University of Texas bulletin ; $v no. 544 (Nov. 22, 1925)	490 1 $a University of Texas bulletin; $v number 544 (November 22, 1925) *(Source of information reads "number 544 [November 22, 1925"].)*
504 $a Includes bibliographical references (p. 389-448) and index.	504 $a Includes bibliographic references (pages 389-448) and index.

CAPITALIZATION

<table>
<tr><th>AACR2 APPENDIX A.4A1, A.4D1, A.4E1, A4F1</th><th>RDA 1.7.2</th></tr>
<tr><td>Capitalize words in the title according to AACR2 Appendix A. Always capitalize the first word in the title. Capitalize other words according to the language of the piece (AACR2 A.4A1).
• When the title is the main entry and the first word is an initial article, capitalize the second word (AACR2 A.4D1).
• When the title consists of a common title and the section title, capitalize the first word in the section title (AACR2 A.4F1). If the first word in the section title is an article, do not capitalize the second word. If a designation ($n) begins with a word, capitalize the word.
• Capitalize the first word of a title embedded within another title.
• If the serial is the result of a merger of two serials, however, and both titles are represented in the title proper, do not capitalize the title of the second serial (AACR2 A.4E1).
• Capitalize the first word in an alternative title.</td><td>RDA specifies that capitalization be transcribed exactly as it appears on the resource being cataloged.
Option:
• Apply RDA's guidelines for transcribing those aspects of typography.
• If the agency creating the description has established in-house guidelines for capitalization, punctuation, numerals, symbols, abbreviations, etc., use those guidelines.
• If the agency creating the description designated a published style manual, etc. (e.g., The Chicago Manual of Style) as its preferred guide, use those guidelines or that style manual.
• Take what you see, especially when capturing digital data.</td></tr>
<tr><td>245 10 $a April 1865 : $b the month that saved America / $c Jay Winik.</td><td>245 10 $a APRIL 1865 : $b The Month That Saved America / $c Jay Winik.</td></tr>
<tr><td>245 04 $a The World almanac.</td><td>245 04 $a The world almanac.
(On the source of information "world" is not capitalized.)</td></tr>
<tr><td>245 00 $a Journal of chemistry. $p Organic chemistry.</td><td>245 00 $a Journal of chemistry. $p organic chemistry.
(On the source of information "organic" is not capitalized.)</td></tr>
<tr><td>245 00 $a Farm chemicals and crop life.</td><td>245 00 $a Farm chemicals and Crop life.
(On the source of information "Crop" is capitalized.)</td></tr>
<tr><td>250 $a 1st ed.</td><td>250 $a FIRST EDITION.
(Capitalize the first word in a Numeric and/or alphabetic designation of first issue or part.)</td></tr>
<tr><td>490 1 $a . . . . $v v. 1, no. 4</td><td>490 1 $a . . . . $v Vol. 1, no. 4
(On the sources of information "Vol." is capitalized.)</td></tr>
</table>

DECIDING WHEN TO CREATE A NEW RECORD

AACR2 21.2 AND 21.3	RDA 1.6
AACR2 requires a major change in the title proper and changes of persons or bodies responsible for a new work. It also specifies when it is necessary to create a new description for serials.	RDA lists some additional situations where a new description is needed for multipart monographs, serials, and integrating resources: • "Mode of Issuance" (RDA 2.13) • "Media type" (RDA 3.2) • "Major change in the title proper for serials" (RDA 2.3.2.13) • "Change in responsibility for serial" (RDA 6.1.3.2) affecting the primary access point. • "Change in edition statement for serial" (RDA 1.6.2.5) • "Re-basing for integrated resource" (RDA 1.6.3.3)

LEVEL OF DESCRIPTION

AACR2 1.0D	**RDA 0.6, 1.3**
AACR2 has three levels of description: • 1st level description • 2nd level description • 3rd level description	RDA has core elements and other elements: **Core elements:** Elements that you must record to be minimally compliant with RDA. **Core if elements:** Elements you must record if certain core elements are missing or if needed to distinguish.
First level as an example: Title proper First statement of responsibility Edition statement Material specific details First publisher, etc. Extent of item Notes Standard number	Core element: Title proper First statement of responsibility Designation of edition Designation of a named revision of an edition Numbering of serials Scale of cartographic content First place of publication First publisher's name Date of publication Title proper of series/subseries Numbering within series/subseries Identifier for the manifestation Carrier type Extent
Per AACR2 rule 1.0D2, the following elements are required when preparing a second-level description • Title proper • Parallel title • Other title information	In RDA, only title proper is core element. Parallel title and other title information are optional 245 00 $a Strassenkarte der Schweiz mit Namenliste, 1:200 000. *or*
245 10 $a Strassenkarte der Schweiz mit Namenliste, 1:200 000 = $b Carte routière de la Suisse avec index des noms, 1:200 000 = Carta stradale della Svizzera con indice dei nomi, 1:200 000.	245 10 $a Strassenkarte der Schweiz mit Namenliste, 1:200 000 = $b Carte routière de la Suisse avec index des noms, 1:200 000 = Carta stradale della Svizzera con indice dei nomi, 1:200 000 = Charta da vias da la Svizra cun glista dals nums, 1:200 000.
246 31 $a Carte routière de la Suisse avec index des noms, 1:200 000	246 31 $a Carte routière de la Suisse avec index des noms, 1:200 000
246 31 $a Carta stradale della Svizzera con indice dei nomi, 1:200 000	246 31 $a Carta stradale della Svizzera con indice dei nomi, 1:200 000
	246 31 $a Charta da vias da la Svizra cun glista dals nums, 1:200 000

SOURCE OF INFORMATION

AACR2 1.0A3	RDA 2.2.2
Chief source of information for each class of materials: Books, pamphlets, and printed sheets Cartographic materials Manuscripts Music Sound recordings Motion pictures and video recordings Graphic materials Electronic resources Three-dimensional artifacts and realia Microforms Continuing resources	Sources of information have been condensed to the three categories: • Resources with pages, leaves, sheets, or cards (or images of one or more pages, leaves, sheets, or cards) • Moving images, and • All other resources

II. DIFFERENCES IN DESCRIPTION

TITLE PROPER

AACR2 1.1B1	RDA 1.7.3
If the title proper as given in the chief source of information includes the punctuation marks "..." or [ ], replace them by—and ( ), respectively.	Transcribe punctuation as it appears on the source, omitting punctuation on the source that separates data to be recorded as one element from data to be recorded as a different element, or as a second or subsequent instance of an element.
245 00 $a Information Retrieval (Z39.50).	245 00 $a Information Retrieval [Z39.50]. *(Source of information reads [Z39.50].)*
245 10 $a Patriotism is a hollow word if—/ $c Kak Dee.	245 10 $a Patriotism is a hollow word if . . . / $c Kak Dee. *(Source of information reads "if . . .".)*
245 10 $a Memory power : $b you can develop a great memory—American's grand master shows how / $c Scott Hagwood. 245 04 $a — and that is how it all began.	245 10 $a Memory power : $b you can develop a great memory . . . American's grand master shows how / $c Scott Hagwood. *(Source of information reads "memory . . .".)* 245 04 $a - - and that is how it all began. *(Source of information reads "- - and".)*

PARALLEL TITLE

AACR2 1.1D1	**RDA 2.3.3**
AACR states that parallel titles are to be transcribed from the chief source of information.	RDA states that parallel titles are NOT core elements in RDA. Parallel titles proper may be taken from any source within the resource. There are no limits on how many parallel titles should be recorded.
245 10 $a Dionysos kai he dionysiake tragoidia = $b Dionysus und die dionysische Tragödie = Dionis I dionisiĭskaia tragedii͡a : Vi͡acheslav Ivanov : filologicheskie i filosofskie idei o dionisiĭstve / $c Filip Vestbruk.	245 10 $a Dionysos kai he dionysiake tragoidia = $b Dionysus und die dionysische Tragödie = Dionisi dionisiĭskaia tragedii͡a : Vi͡acheslav Ivanov : filologicheskie i filosofskie idei o dionisiĭstve = Dionysus and Dionysian tragedy : Vyacheslav Ivanov : philological and philosophical ideas on Dionysiasm / $c Filip Vestbruk.
246 31 $a Dionysos kai he dionysiake tragoidia	246 31 $a Dionysos kai he dionysiake tragoidia
246 31 $a Dionysus und die dionysische Tragödie	246 31 $a Dionysus und die dionysische Tragödie
246 31 $a Dionis i dionisiĭskaia tragedii͡a : Vi͡acheslav Ivanov : filologicheskie i filosofskie idei o dionisiĭstve	246 31 $a Dionis i dionisiĭskaia tragedii͡a : Vi͡acheslav Ivanov : filologicheskie i filosofskie idei o dionisiĭstve
	246 31 $a Dionysus and Dionysian tragedy : Vyacheslav Ivanov : philological and philosophical ideas on Dionysiasm *(On page 295 there is another title "Dionysus and Dionysian tragedy : Vyacheslav Ivanov : philological and philosophical ideas on Dionysiasm".)*
AACR2 1.1D2: In preparing a second-level description, give the *first* parallel title. Give any subsequent parallel title that is in English.	**RDA 2.3.3.3**: There are no limits on how many parallel titles should be recorded "If there is more than one parallel title proper, record the titles in the order indicated by the sequence, layout, or typography of the titles on the source or sources of information."
245 10 $a International meteorological vocabulary = $b Vocabûlaire météorologique international = ezhdunarodnyĭ meteorologicheskiĭ slovar' = Vocabulario meteorológico internacional.	245 10 $a International meteorological vocabulary = $b Vocabulaire météorologique international = Mezhdunarodnyĭ meteorologicheskiĭ slovar'= Vocabulario meteorológicointernacional.
246 31 $a Vocabulaire météorologique international	246 31 $a Vocabulaire météorologique International
	246 31 $a Mezhdunarodnyĭ meteorologicheskiĭ slovar'
	246 31 $a Vocabulario meteorológico Internacional

STATEMENT OF RESPONSIBILITY

AACR2 1.1A2	RDA 2.2.4
When the statement of responsibility is taken from outside the chief source of information, the statement of responsibility must be enclosed in square brackets.	Enclose the statement of responsibility in square brackets only when it is taken from a source outside the resource itself.
245 14 $a The doctor in the Victorian novel : $b family practices / $c [by Tabitha Sparks] *(Statement of responsibility is taken from the verso of the title page.)*	245 14 $a The doctor in the Victorian novel : $b family practices / $c by Tabitha Sparks. *(Statement of responsibility is taken from the verso of title page where RDA considers it part of the resource being cataloged.)*
In AACR2 1.0D2, the 2nd level description requires that all statements of responsibility be recorded.	RDA 2.4 states that only the statement of responsibility relating to title proper is core. All others (e.g., parallel statement of responsibility relating to the title proper, statement of responsibility relating to the edition) are "optional."
AACR2 1.1F1 instructs to enclose in square brackets statements of responsibility from source other than chief source.	In RDA 2.4.2.2 the sources for statement of responsibility have been expanded; only those from outside resource must be bracketed.
245 10 $a . . . / $c [by Barry Campbell]. 500 $a statement of responsibility is taken from cover	245 10 $a . . . / $c by Barry Campbell.

STATEMENT OF RESPONSIBILITY AND COLLABORATIVE WORKS

RDA instructs the catalogers to transcribe what is on the resource being cataloged, with some options.

AACR2 1.1F5, 21.6B AND 21.6C	RDA 2.4.1.5
If a single statement of responsibility names more than three persons or corporate bodies performing the same function, or with the same degree of responsibility, omit all but the first of each group of such persons or bodies. Indicate the omission by the mark of omission (. . .) and add et al. (or its equivalent in a non-roman script) in square brackets.	Record a statement of responsibility naming more than one person, etc., as a single statement regardless of whether the persons, families, or corporate bodies named in it perform the same function or different functions. Record the first-named person, family, or corporate body with principal responsibility (or the first-named if principal responsibility not indicated).
245 00 $a Internet technology / $c by Nancy Drew . . . [et al.].	100 10 $a Drew, Nancy, author. 245 10 $a Internet technology / $c by Nancy Drew, Bess Marvin, George Frayne, and Ned Nickerson. *Alternative:* Optional omission (RDA 6.27.1.3) 245 10 $a . . ./ $c by Nancy Drew [and three others].
245 04 $a The Laval and Viking cases : $b freedom of services and establishment v. industrial conflict in the European Economic Area and Russia / $c editor, Roger Blanpain ; guest editor, Andrzej M. Świątkowski ; contributors, Nikitas Aliprantis . . . [et al.]	245 04 $a The Laval and Viking cases : $b freedom of services and establishment v. industrial conflict in the European Economic Area and Russia / $c editor, Roger Blanpain ; guest editor, Andrzej M. Świątkowski ; contributors, Nikitas Aliprantis [and seventeen others]. 700 10 $a Blanpain, Roger, $e editor.
245 00 $a Parkinson's disease : $b a guide to patient care / $c Paul J. Tuite . . . [et al.]	100 1 $a Tuite, Paul J., author. 245 10 $a Parkinson's disease : $b a guide to patient care / $c Paul J. Tuite, Cathi Thomas, Laura Ruekert Pharmd, Hubert Fernandez. 700 10 $a Thomas, Cathi, $e author. 700 10 $a Pharmd, Laura Ruekert, $e author. 700 10 $a Fernandez, Hubert, $e author.

AACR2 1.1F5, 21.6B AND 21.6C (cont.)	**RDA 2.4.1.5** (cont.)
	100 10 $a Armitage, Henry.
245 10 $a A report on the recent events in Dunwich / $c Henry Armitage . . . [et al.].	245 10 $a A report on the recent events in Dunwich / $c Dr. Henry Armitage, Librarian, Miskatonic University, William H. Mudge, Professor of Metaphysics and Director of the Institute for Paranormal Studies, Miskatonic University, Reverend J.M. Harris, King's Chapel, Arkham, Massachusetts, and the late Curtis Whateley, Dunwich, Massachusetts. *or* 245 10 $a A report on the recent events in Dunwich / $c Dr. Henry Armitage, Librarian, Miskatonic University, [and three others].

TITLE AND ABBREVIATIONS OF TITLES OF NOBILITY, ADDRESS, HONOR, ETC.

AACR2 1.1F7	**RDA 2.4.1.4**
Lists categories of information not to be transcribed in statements of responsibility (only to include the titles of nobility, address, honour and distinction, initials of societies, etc. otherwise, omit all such data from statement of responsibility).	Transcribe as found, with an option to omit certain information or abridge a statement of responsibility only if it can be abridged without loss of essential information.
245 10 $a . . . / $c by Harry, Smith. 245 10 .../ $c by the Library Association.	245 10 $a . . . / $c by Harry, Smith. *(Source of information reads: by Dr. Smith Harry.)* 245 10 .../ $c by the Library Association. *(On source of information: Sponsored by the Library Association [founded 1877]).*

NOUN PHRASE OCCURRING WITH A STATEMENT OF RESPONSIBILITY

AACR2 1.1F12	RDA 2.4.1.8
AACR2 treats a noun phrase occurring in conjunction with a statement of responsibility as other title information.	RDA treats a noun phrase occurring in conjunction with a statement of responsibility as part of the statement of responsibility.
245 10 $a Pacazo : $b a novel / $c Roy Kesey.	245 10 $a Pacazo / $c a novel by Roy Kesey. *(Source of information reads "Pacazo, a novel by Roy Kesey".)*
245 10 $a Special education for today's teachers : $b an introduction / $c by Michael S. Rosenberg, David L. Westling, James McLeskey. 245 10 $a as ... / $c by Colin Barham.	245 10 $a Special education for today's teachers / $c an introduction by Michael S. Rosenberg, David L. Westling, James McLeskey. *(Source of information reads "Special education for today's teachers an introduction by Michael S. Rosenberg, David L. Westling, James McLeskey".)* 245 10 $a as ... / $c research and text by Colin Barham. *(Source of information reads "research and text by Colin Barham".)*

EDITION STATEMENT

AACR2 1.2.B1, C.2B1 C.3B1	**RDA 2.5.1.4, B.4, 1.8.1**
Transcribe the edition statement as found on the item. Use abbreviations as instructed in appendix B and numerals as instructed in appendix C.	Transcribe an edition statement as it appears on the source of information.
250 $a 2nd ed., rev.	250 $a Second edition, revised. *(Source of information reads "Second edition, revised".)*
250 $a 3rd ed., rev. and augm.	250 $a Third edition, revised and augmented. *(Source of information reads "Third edition, revised and augmented".)*
250 $a 5 ed. *(Source of information reads "5 ed".)*	250 $a 5 ed.. *(Source of information reads "5 ed." Notice the first period is for the abbreviation and the second one is for punctuation.)*
250 $a Version 7.	250 $a Version VII. *(Source of information reads "Version VII".)*
250 $a Nouv. Éd.	250 $a Nouvelle édition. *(Source of information reads "Nouvelle édition".)*

PLACE OF PUBLICATION

AACR2 1.4B4	**RDA 2.8.1.4, 2.8.2.4**
AACR2 specifies the use of abbreviations in Appendix B.	Transcribe places of publication and publishers' names in the form in which they appear on the source of information. There will be no abbreviations unless found in the sources of information.
260 $a Charlotte, N.C. : $b	260 $a Charlotte, North Carolina : $b *(Source of information reads "Charlotte, North Carolina".)*
260 $a Peterborough, Ont. : $b	260 $a Peterborough, Ontario : $b *(Source of information reads "Peterborough, Ontario".)*
260 $a New Delhi [Ind.] : $b *(AACR2 1.4B6, 1.4C2, 1.4C3, 1.4C4 all specify the addition of information in square brackets.)*	260 $a New Delhi : $b 500 $a Publisher in New Delhi, India. *(2.20.7.3 Make notes on details relating to place of publication, publisher, or date of publication not recorded in the publication statement element, if they are considered to be important for identification or access.)*
AACR2 rules state that if two or more places in which a publisher, distributor, etc. have offices that are named in the item, give the first named place. Give any subsequently named place that is given prominence by the layout or typography of the source of information. If the first named place and given prominence are not in the home country of the cataloging agency, give also the first of any subsequently named place that is in the home country. Omit all other places.	RDA instruction 2.7.2.4, 2.8.2.4, 2.9.2.4, and 2.10.2.4 instructs to record the place names in the order indicated by the sequence, layout or typography of the names on the sources of information. There is no "home country" provision.
260 $a Toronto : $b *(Source of information reads "Toronto-Buffalo-London. Cataloging agency is Canada" and the record was created by Canadian library.)*	260 $a Toronto ; $a Buffalo ; $a London : $b *(If applying core element, only the place first recorded is required.)* 260 $a Toronto : $b

UNKNOWN PLACE OF PUBLICATION

AACR2 1.4C6	RDA 2.7.2.6, 2.8.2.6, 2.9.2.6, 2.10.2.6
If no place or probable place can be given, use the Latin abbreviation *S.l.* (sine loco), or its equivalent in a non-roman script.	RDA uses [Place of publication not identified] or [publisher not identified]
260 $a [S.l.] : $b Royal Geographical Society, $c 2001.	260 $a [Place of publication not identified] : $b Royal Geographical Society, $c 2001.

PUBLISHER INFORMATION

AACR21.4B4	RDA 2.8.4.5, 2.9.4.5, 2.10.4.5
AACR2 specifies the use of abbreviations found in Appendix B when recording the publisher's name. 260 : $b University of Leeds, Dept. of Spanish,	RDA does not use abbreviations. 260 : $b University of Leeds, Department of Spanish,
AACR2 Rule 1.4.D2 provides instruction to use the name of publisher in its shortest form. 260 : $b Penguin, $c 260 : $b Da Capo, $c	RDA 2.8.1.4 instructs to transcribe in the form found on source (do not abbreviate unless source abbreviates). 260 : $b Penguin Books, $c *(Source of information reads "Penguin Books".)* 260 : $b Da Capo Press, Inc., $c *(Source of information reads "Da Capo Press, Inc".)*
AACR2 1.4D4 instructs to record more than one publisher only in certain cases (e.g., when second-named publisher is in "home country" of cataloging agency and the first is not). 260 $a Montréal : $b Infopresse, $c	RDA 2.8.4.5 instructs to record more than one publisher in order indicated by sequence, layout, and typography. However, 2.8.4 notes that only the first publisher's name is CORE; listing other publishers is optional. 260 $a Montréal : $b Éditions Infopresse; $a Paris : $b Pyramyd, $c *(If applying core element, only the name of the publisher first recorded is required.)*

UNKNOWN PUBLISHER'S NAME INFORMATION

AACR2 1.4D6	RDA 2.8.4.7, 2.9.4.7, 2.10.4.7
If the name of the publisher, distributor, etc., is unknown, use the Latin abbreviation *s.n.* (sine nomine) or its equivalent in a non-roman script.	RDA uses [publisher not identified].
260 $a Columbus, Ohio : $b [s.n.], $c 1998. 260 $a [S.l. : $b s.n., 2007]. *(All elements are enclosed in one square bracket.)*	260 $a Columbus, Ohio : $b [Publisher not identified], $c 1998. 260 $a [Place of publication not identified] : $b [Publisher not identified], $c 2007. *(Each element is enclosed in its own set of square brackets.)*

APPROXIMATE DATE

AACR2 1.4F7, 2.16G	RDA 1.9.2
AACR2 provides a format for supplied dates.	In RDA 1.9 a different format is specified. Ranges of years will be recorded using the format "[between XXXX and XXXX]," and if the dates are probable, a question mark will be added. If the earliest and/or latest possible dates are known, "not before" and "not after" will be used.
260 , $c [1951 or 1952] One year or the other	260 , $c [1951 or 1952]
260 , $c [1960?] *(Probable date.)*	260 , $c [1960?]
260 , $c [between 1906 and 1912] *(Use only for dates fewer than 20 years apart.)*	260 , $c [between 1906 and 1930] *(The 20-year limit between the two dates is no longer in RDA.)*
260 , $c [198-] *(Decade certain.)*	260 , $c [between 1980 and 1989]
260 , $c [198-?] *(Probable decade.)*	260 , $c [between 1980 and 1989?]
260 , $c [18-] *(Century certain.)*	260 , $c [between 1800 and 1899]

AACR2 1.4F7, 2.16G (cont.)	**RDA 1.9.2** (cont.)
260 , $c [18-?] *(Probable century.)*	260 , $c [between 1800 and 1899?]
260 , $c [not after February 27, 2011] *(Approximate dates ("ca.") will be indcated in the same way as probable dates, using a question mark.)*	260 , $c [not after February 27, 2011] *(Approximate dates (formerly indicated using "ca.") will be indicated in the same way as probable dates, using a question mark.)*
260 , $c [ca. 1965?] 260 , $c [n.d.]	260 , $c [approximately 1965?] 260 , $c [date of publication not identified.] *(Try to supply a probable date whenever possible. If you REALLY cannot supply a probable date and you are cataloging a single-part monograph, then give the explanation "[date of publication not identified]".)*

COPYRIGHT DATE

AACR2 1.4F6	**RDA 2.8.6.6**
If the dates of publication, distribution, etc., are unknown, give the copyright date or, in its absence, the date of manufacture.	If no approximate date of publication can be supplied, the date of publication element will contain *date of publication not identified*. If dates of distribution, copyright, or manufacture are known they will be recorded in the respective elements. Precede the date by the copyright symbol (©) or the phonogram symbol (℗), or by copyright or phonogram if the appropriate symbol cannot be reproduced. Always give a copyright date if found on the resource.
260 $a Springville, Utah : $b Sweet water Books, $c c2011.	260 $a Springville, Utah : $b Sweet water Books, $c [date of publication not identified], ©2011. 260 $a Woodland Hills, CA : $b Disa Records, $c [date of publication not identified], ℗2008. 260 $a Mainz : $b Schott, $c [2010], ©2010.

DATE OF MANUFACTURE

AACR21.4F6	RDA 2.10.6
If the copyright date is not available and the date of manufacture is present, give the date of manufacture.	If neither the date of publication nor the date of distribution *nor copyright date* is identified and manufacture information is on the resource, record the date of manufacture.
260 $a Venice, California : $b Holly ridge Press, $c 2009, printing.	260 $a Venice, California : $b Hollyridge Press, $c [date of publication not identified], $g 2009.

EXTENT

AACR2 1.5B1, 1.5B2	RDA 3.4
Record the extent of the item by giving the number of physical units in Arabic numerals and the specific material designation as instructed in sub rule .5B in the chapter dealing with the type of material to which the item belongs. Describe a single-part printed text item as instructed in 2.5B.	Record the extent of the resource by giving the number of units and an appropriate term for the type of carrier as listed under 3.3.1.3. Record the term in the singular or plural, as applicable. In extent, description of the element is based on: • Terms of pages or leaves • No bracketing for unnumbered pages, instead use "unnumbered pages." • No abbreviations of pages and volume. Instead, use "pages" or "volumes." • Use the term "approximately" instead of "ca." • Use "that is" instead of "i.e." • Bibliographic volumes are not recorded, only physical volumes (5 *volumes*, not *8 volumes in* 5). *(For instructions on using other terms to designate the type of unit see 3.4.1.5.)*
300 $a xxii, 232 p.	300 $a xxii, 232 pages
300 $a 432 p.	300 $a 432 pages
300 $a 3 film.	300 $a 3 films
300 $a v.	300 $a volume

AACR2 1.5B1, 1.5B2 (cont.)	**RDA 3.4** (cont.)
300 $a 345 p : $b ill., col. 300 $a xv, 234 p., [10] p. of plates : $b ill. (some col.), maps (some col.) ; $c 23 cm.	300 $a 345 pages : $b illustration, color 300 $a xv, 234 pages, 10 unnumbered pages of plates : $b illustrations (some color), maps (some color) ; $c 23 cm.
300 $a 140 p., 12 p. of plates	300 $a 140 pages, 12 pages of plates
300 $a 7 v. in 4; $c 28 cm.	300 $a 4 volumes; $c 28 cm.
300 $a 4 v. (xxii, 1120 p.)	300 $a 4 volumes (xxii, 1120 pages)

UNCORRECTED PAGE OR LEAF AND THE TERM "I.E."

AACR2 2.5B4	**RDA 3.4.5.5**
AACR2 indicates that if the number printed on the last page or leaf of a sequence does not represent the total number of pages or leaves in that sequence, you should record the uncorrected information and supply corrections in square brackets.	RDA indicates that when correcting the wrong pagination number; record the wrong number as it appears on the last page or leaf followed by "that is" and the correct number of pages.
300 $a 232 [i.e. 223] p.	300 $a 232, that is, 223 pages.

UNNUMBERED PAGES AND THE TERM "APPROXIMATELY"

AACR2 2.5B7	**RDA 3.4.5.3**
AACR2 instructs to specify an estimated number of unnumbered pages, preceded by "ca.," or to enclose the exact number in square brackets.	In RDA 3.4.5.3 the word *approximately* will be used instead of "ca.," or it will be stated explicitly that the pages are unnumbered.
300 $a [194] p. 300 $a ca. 456 p.	300 $a 194 unnumbered pages *or* 300 $a 1 volume (unpaged) *(Per RDA 3.4.5.3.)* 300 $a Approximately 456 pages
300 $a ca. 267 p. : $b chiefly ill. (some col.) ; $c 30 cm.	300 $a approximately 267 pages : $b illustrations (some color) ; $c 30 cm. *(Notice here that "ca." is spelled out as "approximately".)*

UNNUMBERED LEAVES OR PAGES OF PLATES

AACR2 2.5B9	RDA 3.4.5.9
AACR requires the cataloger to count or estimate the number of leaves or pages of plates when these are unnumbered.	If the leaves or pages of plates in a resource are separate from the sequence or sequences of pages or leaves of text, etc., record the number of leaves or pages of plates at the end of the sequence or sequences of pagination, etc.
300 $a xv, 234 p., [10] p. of plates : $b ill. (some col.), maps (some col.) ; $c 23 cm.	300 $a xv, 234 pages, 10 unnumbered pages of plates : $b illustrations (some color), maps (some color) ; $c 23 cm.

EXTENT FOR MUSIC

Significant changes in terminology for cataloging music were made. (Paradis 2010; Saunders 2010; Gerhart 2011).

AACR2 5.5B1, 5.5B2	RDA 7.20.1.3, 3.4.3.2
AACR2 provides a list of specific material designations to be used when recording the extent of music.	RDA does not include some of these terms:
Score	Score
Condensed score	Condensed score
Close score	Condensed score
Miniature score	Study score
Piano[violin. etc.] conductor part	Piano conductor part Violin conductor part
Vocal score	Vocal score
Chorus	Chorus score
Part	Part
p. of music v. of music leaves of music	Score
Sound Sound cassette Sound disc [name of instrument] roll Sound cartridge Sound tape reel Sound track film reel	Audio Audiocassette Audio disc Audio roll Audio cartridge Audiotape Soundtrack reel

ACCOMPANYING MATERIALS

<table>
<tr><th>AACR2 1.5E</th><th>RDA 27.1</th></tr>
<tr><td>Describe accompanying materials in MARC 21 field 300 $e</td><td>RDA provides options:
Describe accompanying materials in MARC 21 field 300 $e
or
in a second 300 field, whichever seems most appropriate.
or
Describe the accompanying materials in a 500 note</td></tr>
<tr><td>300 $a 1 computer disc (2 text files. 27 image files) : $b CD-ROM, PDF, JPEG, color illustrations; $c 4 ¾ in., in pocket enclosure (22 cm.) + $e 1 press release (1 page; $c 30 cm.)</td><td>300 $a 1 computer disc (2 text files. 27 image files) : $b CD-ROM, PDF, JPEG, color illustrations; $ 4 ¾ in., in pocket enclosure (22 cm.) + $e 1 press release (1 page; $c 30 cm.)
or
300 $a 1 computer disc (2text files. 27 image files) : $b CD-ROM, PDF, JPEG, color illustrations; $ 4 ¾ in., in pocket enclosure (22 cm.)
300 $a 1 press release (1 page; $c 30 cm.)
Use the name of a carrier type from RDA 3.3.1.3 unless it is a booklet or some other material not on that list.
336 $a text $2 rdacontent
336 $a still image $2 rdacontent
337 $a computer $2 rdamedia
337 $a unmediated $2 rdamedia
338 $a computer $2 rdacarrier
338 $a sheet $2 rdacarrier
or
500 $a Accompanied by 1 press release (1 page ; $c 30 cm.)</td></tr>
</table>

CATEGORIZATION OF RESOURCES VERSUS GENERAL MATERIALS DESIGNATION

RDA developed three new fields to replace the AACR2 GMD:

336—Content Type (RDA 6.9): form of communication through which a work is expressed; e.g., performed music, two dimensional moving image and text.
337—Media Type (RDA 3.2): general type of intermediation device required to view, play, run, etc., the content of resources; e.g., audio, computer microform, video and unmediated.
338—Carrier Type (RDA 3.3): format of the storage medium and housing of a carrier; e.g., audio disc, online resource, microfiche, videocassette and volume.

AACR2 1.1C	RDA 3.2, 3.3, 6.9
Categorization of resources by GMD Cartographic material Music Text Filmstrip Motion picture Slide Transparency Electronic resource Microform Sound recording Video recording	Categorization of resources by media type, carrier type and content type. These fields are repeatable. **Content Types (New MARC 21 field 336):** Form of communication through which a work is expressed. *Examples:* cartographic dataset, notated music, sound, text, two-dimensional moving image. **Media Types (New MARC 21 field 337):** General type of intermediation device required to view, play, run, etc., the content of a resource. *Examples:* audio, computer, microform, unmediated, video. **Carrier Types (New MARC 21 field 338):** Format of the storage medium and housing of a carrier. *Examples:* computer disc, audio disc, sheet, volume, online resource, videodisc, microfiche.
245 00 $a Civil War symposium $h [videocassette]. 246 10 $i Title on container: $a Dilemma of interpretation 260 $a West Lafayette, IN : $b C-Span Archives, $c 2001. 300 $a 1 videocassette (133 min. : $b sound, color ; $c 1/2 in.	245 00 $a Civil War symposium. 246 10 $i Title on container: $a Dilemma of Interpretation 260 $a West Lafayette, IN : $b C-Span Archives, $c 2001. 300 $a 1 videocassette (133 min. : $b sound, color ; $c 1/2 in. 336 $a two-dimensional moving image $2 rdacontent 337 $a video $2 rdamedia 338 $a videocassette $2 rdacarrier

NUMBERING WITHIN SERIES

AACR2 1.6G.	**RDA 2.12.9.3**
The numbering of the item within a series is recorded in the terms given in the item. Use abbreviations as instructed in Appendix B and numerals as instructed in Appendix C.	The numbering of the resource within a series is recorded as it appears on the source of information.
490 1 $a Recent scientific research; $v Jan. 1996	490 1 $a Recent scientific research; $v January 1996 *(Source of information reads, "January1996".)*
490 1 $a Recherches en linguistique étrangère, $x 0999-9752 ; $v v. 25	490 1 $a Recherches en linguistique étrangère, $x 0999-9752 ; $v Volume XXV *(Source of information reads, "Volume XXV".)*
490 1 $a Travaux d'humanisme et Renaissance, $x 0082-6081 ; $v no. 14	490 1 $a Travaux d'humanisme et Renaissance, $x 0082-6081 ; $v number XIV *(On the source, "number XIV".)*
490 1 $a Archiv zur Weimarer Ausgabe der Werke Martin Luthers ; $v Bd 10	490 1 $a Archiv zur Weimarer Ausgabe der Werke Martin Luthers ; $v Band 10 *(Source of information reads, "Band 10".)*

III. DIFFERENCES IN ACCESS POINTS

ACCESS POINTS—PERSONS AND CORPORATE BODIES

A detailed explanation of access points is provided in chapter 6 of this book, "Identifying Works and Expressions."

AACR2 21.6B AND 21.6C	RDA 6.27.1.3, 19.2.1.3
If the statement of responsibility in the source of information contains more than three persons or corporate bodies, the main entry will be under title, and only the first person named will be recorded in the statement of responsibility, followed by . . . [et al.].	If two or more persons, families, corporate bodies are collaboratively responsible for creating the work, construct the authorized access point representing the work using the authorized access point representing the first-named person, family, or corporate body, followed by the preferred title for the work. **19.2.1.3** Record the creator applying the general guidelines on recording relationships to persons, families, and corporate bodies associated with a resource given under 18.4.
	100 1 $a Jackson, Brian A., $d 1972-
245 00 $a Evaluating novel threats to the homeland : $b unmanned aerial vehicles and cruise missiles / $c Brian A. Jackson . . . [et al.]	245 10 $a Evaluating novel threats to the homeland : $b unmanned aerial vehicles and cruise missiles / $c Brian A. Jackson, David R. Frelinger Michael J. Lostumbo, Robert W. Button.
700 1 $a Jackson, Brian A., $d 1972-	700 1 $a Frelinger, David R.
	700 1 $a Lostumbo, Michael J.
	700 1 $a Button, Robert W.

RELATIONSHIP DESIGNATION

AACR2 21.0D	RDA APPENDIX I
AACR2 provides a short list of relationship designations of function, and there is reference to designations used in other rules. AACR2 adds the designation in an abbreviated form: Function performed — Designation Compiler — comp. Editor — ed. Illustrator — ill. Translator — tr.	In Appendix I, RDA provides a list of relationship designators for relationships between a resource and persons, families, and corporate bodies associated with the resource.
700 1 $a Hindley, Becky, ed. 100 1 $a Reichardt, Johann Friedrich, $d 1752-1814.	700 1 $a Hindley, Becky, $e editor. 100 1 $a Reichardt, Johann Friedrich, $d 1752-1814, $e composer.

BOOKS OF THE BIBLE

AACR2. 25.18A2	RDA 6.23.2.9.1 AND 6.30.2
Enter the Old Testament as *Bible. O.T.* and the New Testament as *Bible. N. T.*	For the Old Testament, record *Old Testament* as a subdivision of the preferred title for the Bible. For the New Testament, record *New Testament* as a subdivision of the preferred title for the Bible. Old and New Testament should be spelled out, not abbreviated.
130 0 $a Bible. $p O. T 130 0 $a Bible. $p N. T	130 0 $a Bible. $p Old Testament 130 0 $a Bible. $p New Testament

PARTS OF THE BIBLE

AACR2 25.18A1	RDA 6.23.2.9.2 AND 6.30.2.2
Enter a book of the Catholic or Protestant canon as a subheading of the appropriate Testament.	Access points for individual books of the Bible should use the name of the book immediately following "Bible." Omit the name of the Testament in the preferred title for individual books or groups of books.
130 0 $a Bible. $p O.T. $p Pentateuch	130 0 $a Bible. $p Pentateuch

AUTHORIZED ACCESS POINT REPRESENTING AN EXPRESSION OF THE BIBLE

AACR2 25.18A.10	RDA 6.30.3.2
If the item is in three or more languages, add the word "polyglot." 130 0 $a Bible. $l Polyglot	If the resource described contains more than one language expression of the work, create authorized access points for each of the expressions.
245 14 $a The interlinear Bible : Hebrew, Greek, English.	245 14 $a The interlinear Bible : Hebrew, Greek, English. 730 0 $a Bible. $p Old Testament. $l Hebrew. 730 0 $a Bible. $p Old Testament. $l Greek. 730 0 $a Bible. $p Old Testament. $l English. *(Notice that there is no "Polyglot" in 130. Instead, an access point is added for each expression.)*

TREATIES WITH MORE THAN THREE SIGNATORIES

AACR2 21.35A AND 25.16B1	RDA (RDA 6.19.2.7–6.19.2.8)
AACR2 makes a distinction between treaties and formal agreements between two or three governments on the one hand, and those between four and more governments on the other.	For treaties or any other formal agreements between two or more national governments, give first-named signatory with preferred title "Treaties, etc." as the authorized access point for the work (RDA 6.29.1.15).
245 00 $a Treaty of cooperation between Denmark, Finland, Iceland, Norway and Sweden signed in Helsinki on March 23rd, 1962 as amended on February 13th, 1971.	110 1 $a Denmark. 240 10 $a Treaties, etc. $d 1971 February 13 245 10 $a Treaty of cooperation between Denmark, Finland, Iceland, Norway and Sweden signed in Helsinki on March 23rd, 1962 as amended on February 13th, 1971. 710 1 $a Finland. 710 1 $a Iceland. 710 1 $a Norway. 710 1 $a Sweden. *(The 710s are cataloger's judgment or a library's policy decision where there are three or more signatories.)*

IV. RECORDING THE PREFERRED TITLE FOR A COMPILATION OF WORKS (Nicholson 2011)

COMPILATIONS OF TWO OR MORE WORKS

AACR2 25.7	RDA6.2.2.10.3
If an item consisting of two works is entered under a personal and a corporate heading, use the uniform title of the work that appears first. Make a name title added entry using the uniform title of the second work.	For compilations of two or more works, record preferred title for each of the works in the compilation. *or* Using alternative provision, record "conventional title" + "Selections."
100 1 $a Lopate, Phillip, $d 1943- 240 10 $a Stoic's marriage 245 10 $a Two marriages : $b novellas / $c Phillip Lopate. 505 0 $a The stoic's marriage—Eleanor, or, The second marriage. 700 12 $a Lopate, Phillip, $d 1943- $t Eleanor.	100 1 $a Lopate, Phillip, $d 1943- 240 10 $a Novellas. $k Selections 245 10 $a Two marriages : $b novellas / $c Phillip Lopate. 505 0 $a The stoic's marriage—Eleanor, or, The second marriage. 700 12 $a Lopate, Phillip, $d 1943- $t Stoic's marriage. 700 12 $a Lopate, Phillip, $d 1943- $t Eleanor. *(The second 700 is optional—RDA 17.8 [Work Manifested] requires that only the first work in a compilation be given.)*

COMPILATION BY ONE CREATOR—COMPILATION OF THREE OR MORE WORKS IN DIFFERENT FORMS BY ONE CREATOR

AACR2 25.9	**RDA 6.2.2.10.1–2**
AACR2 rules instruct to use the term "Selections" as a collective title for items consisting of three or more various works by an author.	RDA does not use "Selections" alone as a collective title; the term is always appended to a preferred or a collective title.
240 10 $a Selections	240 10 $a Novels. $k Selections *(Two or more, but not all of the works of one person, family, or corporate body in a particular form—in this case novels.)*
240 10 $a Selections	240 10 $a Works. $k Selections *(Two or more, but not all of the works of one person, family, or corporate body, in various forms.)*
	RDA constructs analytical access points for all the parts individually (700 . . . $t); A conventional collective title (240) can be used in addition to the titles of individual works in the volume which are listed in the 700 fields (240 . . . $a Works. $k Selections. . .); Date in the 240 field is to refer to a particular expression.
100 1 $a Twain, Mark, $d 1835-1910. 240 10 $a Selections. $f 2001 245 10 $a Two novels and favorite essays / $c Mark Twain. 260 $a St. Louis : $b CJK Pub. Co., $c 2001.	100 1 $a Twain, Mark, $d 1835-1910. 240 10 $a Works. $k Selections. $f 2001 245 10 $a Two novels and favorite essays / $c Mark Twain. 260 $a St. Louis : $b CJK Pub. Co., $c 2001. 505 0 $a Tom Sawyer—Connecticut Yankee in King Arthur's court—Selected essays. 700 12 $a Twain, Mark, $d 1835-1910. $t Adventures of Tom Sawyer. 700 12 $a Twain, Mark, $d 1835-1910. $t Connecticut Yankee in King Arthur's court. *(The second 700 is optional per RDA 17.8 [Work Manifested] which requires that only the first work in a compilation be given.)*

COMPILATIONS LACKING A COLLECTIVE TITLE

AACR2 21.7C1	RDA 6.27.1.4
When a compilation of works by different creators lacks a collective title, enter it under the heading for the first work in the compilation. Make added entries for editors/compilers and for the other works (if no more than three works in the compilation) as instructed in 21.7B1, insofar as it applies to works without a collective title.	If the compilation lacks a collective title, construct a preferred access point for the compilation. Create separate access points for each work (and/or devised title for the compilation).
100 1 $a Baden, Conrad. 240 10 $a Symphonies, $n no. 6 245 10 $a Sinfonia espressiva $h [sound recording] / $c Conrad Baden. Symphony no. 3, op. 26 / Hallvard Johnsen. Symphony no. 2 / Bjarne Brustad. 700 12 $a Johnsen, Hallvard. $t Symphonies, $n no. 3, op. 26. 700 12 $a Brustad, Bjarne. $t Symphonies, $n no. 2.	245 00 $a Sinfonia espressiva / $c Conrad Baden. Symphony no. 3, op. 26 / Hallvard Johnsen. Symphony no. 2 / Bjarne Brustad. 700 12 $i contains (work) $a Baden, Conrad. $t Symphonies, $n no. 6. 700 12 $i contains (work) $a Johnsen, Hallvard. $t Symphonies, $n no. 3, op. 26. 700 12 $i contains (work) $a Brustad, Bjarne. $t Symphonies, $n no. 2. *or* Construct an authorized access point for the compilation using a devised title (MARC 21 field 245). 245 00 $a [Three Norwegian symphonies]. 500 $a Title devised by cataloger. 505 0 $a Sinfonia espressiva / Conrad Baden—Symphony no. 3, op. 26 / Hallvard Johnsen—Symphony no. 2 / Bjarne Brustad. 700 12 $i contains (work) $a Baden, Conrad. $t Symphonies, $n no. 6. 700 12 $i contains (work) $a Johnsen, Hallvard. $t Symphonies, $n no. 3, op. 26. 700 12 $i contains (work) $a Brustad, Bjarne. $t Symphonies, $n no. 2. *(Notice that in the second example, the devised title is in 245, the note is in 500, the relationship term is in MARC 21 field 700 from appendix J.)* *(The second and third 700s are optional. RDA 17.8 [Work Manifested] requires that only the first work in a compilation be given.)*

COMPILATIONS OF DIFFERENT EXPRESSIONS OF THE SAME WORK

AACR2 25.5C1	RDA 17.10
Name a compilation with different language versions (expressions) of the same work with the title of the work + the languages of the two versions in subfield $l. If the item is in three or more languages, use the term "polyglot."	Provide access points for each version (expression). Only the access point for the first-named or predominant expression is required.
041 1 $a gerlat $h lat 100 1 $a Caesar, Julius. 240 10 $a De bello Gallico. $l German & Latin 245 14 $a Der Gallische Krieg : $b lateinisch-deutsch / $c C. Iulius Caesar ; herausgegeben von Otto Schönberger. 500 $a Contains De bello Gallico in Latin with German translation; commentary in German. 700 1 $a Schönberger, Otto.	041 1 $a ger $a lat $h lat 100 1 $a Caesar, Julius. 245 14 $a Der Gallische Krieg : $b lateinisch-deutsch / $c C. Iulius Caesar ; herausgegeben von Otto Schönberger. 500 $a Contains De bello Gallico in Latin with German translation; commentary in German. 546 $a German and Latin. 700 1 $a Schönberger, Otto. 700 12 $a Caesar, Julius. $t De bello Gallico. $l German. 700 12 $a Caesar, Julius. $t De bello Gallico. $l Latin.
041 1 $a per $a eng $a ara $h per 100 1 $a Khalīlī, Khalīl Allāh. 240 10 $a Rubāʻīyāt. $l Polyglot 245 10 $a Quatrains of Khalilullah Khalili / $c Khalīl Allāh Khalīlī. 246 $a Persian, English, and Arabic.	041 1 $a per $a eng $a ara $h per 100 1 $a Khalīlī, Khalīl Allāh. 245 10 $a Quatrains of Khalilullah Khalili / $c Khalīl Allāh Khalīlī. 246 $a Persian, English, and Arabic. 700 12 $a Khalīlī, Khalīl Allāh. $t Quatrains of Khalilullah Khalili. $l Persian. 700 12 $a Khalīlī, Khalīl Allāh. $t Quatrains of Khalilullah Khalili. $l English. 700 12 $a Khalīlī, Khalīl Allāh. $t Quatrains of Khalilullah Khalili. $l Arabic.

REFERENCES

Gerhart, Cate. 2011."RDA Changes for Music Materials." http://tinyurl.com/Gerhart2011.

Joint Steering Committee for Development of RDA. 2009. "List of Changes to AACR2 Instructions." 5JSC/Sec/7/Rev. www.rda-jsc.org/docs/5sec7rev.pdf.

Nicholson, Joseph. 2011. "RDA in MARC." www.llaonline.org/ne/lla2011/RDApreconference.pdf.

Paradis, Daniel. 2010. "Significant Changes for Cataloging Music: AACR2 vs. RDA." Paper presented at the Music Library Association Annual Conference, San Diego, CA, March 2010. www.rda-jsc.org/docs/10_3_24_MLAannmtg_SignificantchangesforcataloguingmusicAACR2vsRDA.pdf.

Saunders, Sharon. 2010. "Summary of MARC Coding Changes." www.abacus.bates.edu/~ssaunder/homepage/RDA_and_music.pdf;Differences between RDA and AACR2.

Schiff, Adam L. 2010. "Changes from AACR2 to RDA: A Comparison of Examples." Paper presented at the British Columbia Library Pre-Conference, Penticton, BC, April 22, 2010. http://faculty.washington.edu/aschiff/BCLAPresentationWithNotes-RevMay2011.pdf.

Stephens, Jenny. 2010. "From AACR2 to RDA: The Purpose and Structure of RDA." RDA Background Information, Staff Training Presentation Sessions. Canberra, NSW: National Library of Australia. http://tinyurl.com/Stephens2010.

ACKNOWLEDGMENTS

Most of the examples used in this chapter are originally created by the author, but some have been taken from other sources and modified. Sources used include presentations by the Library of Congress staff including Tom Delsey, Adam Schiff, Chris Todd, Janess Stewart, Charlotte Stretton, and many others. The following list of works in particular shaped the understanding of the differences between AACR2 and RDA.

ADDITIONAL RESOURCES

Davis, Renette. 2010. "RDA Serials Cataloging: Changes from AACR2 to RDA." http://tinyurl.com/Renette2010.

Delsey, Tom. 2009. "AACR2 Versus RDA." Paper presented at the Canadian Library Association Pre-Conference, May 29, 2009. http://tsig.wikispaces.com/file/view/AACR2_versus_RDA.pdf.

Gallwey, John. 2010. "How Are You Getting On with RDA? (or, How *Will* We Get On with RDA?)." Paper presented at the Special Libraries Association Annual Conference, June 13 to 16, 2010, New Orleans, LA. http://s36.a2zinc.net/clients/sla/sla2010/Custom/Handout/Speaker243_Session71_1.pdf.

Glennan, Kathy. 2006. "From AACR2 to RDA: An Evolution." Paper presented to the Music Library Association Conference, February 26, 2006. http://bcc.musiclibraryassoc.org/Descriptive/RDA_Evolution.pdf.

Intner, Sheila S., Joanna F. Fountain, and Jean Weihs, eds. 2010. *Cataloging Correctly for Kids: An Introduction to the Tools,* 5th ed. Chicago: American Library Association.

LeGrow, Lynne. 2010. "RDA Is On the Way!" (Unpublished presentation, February 2010).

Library of Congress. 2010. "Documentation for the RDA Test: Examples for RDA: Compared to AACR2." www.loc.gov/catdir/cpso/RDAtest/rdaexamples.html.

Manning, Ralph W. 1998. "Anglo-American Cataloguing Rules and Their Future." Paper presented at the 64th IFLA General Conference, August 16–August 21. http://archive.ifla.org/IV/ifla64/083-126e.htm.

MARC 21 Changes for RDA, see: www.loc.gov/marc/RDAinMARC29.html and see the lists of changes in the formats themselves as announced in the MARC 21 updates: www.loc.gov/marc/marcginf.html#naa.

OCLC Technical Bulletin 258 lists all of the MARC changes OCLC implemented in May 2010: www.oclc.org/support/documentation/worldcat/tb/258/default.htm.

Oliver, Chris. 2010. "Demystifying RDA Similarities and Differences between AACR and RDA." June 2nd, 2010 CLA Preconference. http://tinyurl.com/ChrisOliver2010.

"RDA (Resource Description and Access) and School Libraries—Where Are We Going, and Why Can't We Keep AACR2?" 2009. www.opal-libraries.org/resources/cataloging/CAT_Technicalities_29_2_RDA_handout.pdf.

Stewart, Richard A. 2010. "Cataloging with RDA: What's Similar? What's Different?" Paper presented at the Indian Trails Public Library District, Wheeling, IL. http://tinyurl.com/Stewart2010.

Tillett, Barbara B. 2010. "Changes from AACR2 for Texts." Paper presented for LC Digital Futures and You, January 2, 2010. http://tinyurl.com/Tillett2010.

CHAPTER THREE

RDA IMPLEMENTATION STRATEGIES

HIS CHAPTER PROVIDES IDEAS AND SUGGESTIONS FOR implementing RDA in your library. The tips that are included here are not all-inclusive, but they do provide first steps to becoming familiar with RDA and are intended to help you determine what you will need to do in the first few months of implementation. The following topics will be discussed here to help catalogers make the transition to RDA seamless and trouble free:

- General tips for catalogers
- Decision making by catalogers
- Integrating new RDA records with the legacy records and making the decision to re-catalog a set of manifestations
- Exporting an RDA-based bibliographic record from OCLC into your OPAC
- RDA and the PCC participants
- RDA's effect on OPAC displays
- Strategy for implementing new MARC 21 fields to accommodate the new RDA elements
- Adjusting the online system to accommodate the new MARC 21 fields
- Authority processing vendor services and RDA
- How to access RDA records from the Library of Congress Catalog and OCLC

Catalogers who have extensive experience in using AACR2 should have little difficulty in implementing RDA. As you begin the process, keep in mind that RDA is based on AACR2. A number of introductory steps are suggested before starting to use RDA.

I. GENERAL TRAINING TIPS FOR CATALOGERS

FAMILIARITY WITH THE CONCEPTS AND PRINCIPLES OF THE FUNCTIONAL REQUIREMENTS FOR BIBLIOGRAPHIC RECORDS (FRBR) AND FUNCTIONAL REQUIREMENTS FOR AUTHORITY DATA (FRAD)

- Start with FRBR and FRAD to familiarize yourself with the concepts, terminology, objectives, and the principles of FRBR and FRAD.
- RDA chapters are aligned with FRBR entities and user tasks. It is very important to become familiar with FRBR and FRAD and to understand that RDA chapters are aligned with FRBR entities. Group 1 entities (work, expression, manifestations, and items); Group 2 entities (person, family, and corporate body); and Group 3 entities (subject content, which includes Group 1 and 2

in addition to concept, object, place, and event). RDA is also aligned with the FRBR user tasks (find, identify, select, and obtain). Familiarity with these concepts will make it easier to understand and apply the RDA instructions. Please keep in mind that although the terminology has changed in RDA, the same information is being used to describe resources.

- Make sure that all catalogers in your section understand the meaning of all FRBR terms.
- Include FRBR terminology.
- Address FRBR relationships.
- Use FRBR tasks as the basis for core data elements.

A good overview of FRBR and FRAD concepts and principles can be found in chapter 4 of this publication. Starting with this chapter will help in establishing solid foundations for a better understanding of RDA concepts and instructions.

FAMILIARITY WITH RDA TERMS AND SIMILARITIES AND DIFFERENCES BETWEEN RDA AND AACR2

Some training in RDA will be required of all catalogers working with the new system. If the cataloger is currently using AACR2, this training should be simple and easy. The following points need to be addressed in cataloger training:

- Become familiar with the new terminology and new organization of information.
- Become familiar with RDA terminology, e.g., work, expression, manifestation, preferred title (which is called "main entry" in AACR2), authorized access points (called "headings" in AACR2), creator (called "author, composer, illustrator" in AACR2), etc.
- Emphasize that the same information is used to describe resources, even if the terminology has changed.
- Start using the new terminology on a daily basis.
- Provide orientation to the underlying conceptual models and principles.
- Study the rule changes between AACR2 and RDA.

Detailed information about RDA terms, and similarities or differences between AACR2 and RDA, are provided in chapter 2.

KNOW THE RDA INSTRUCTIONS

- Become familiar with the structure and the organization of RDA.
- RDA structure is very different from that of AACR2. Understanding how RDA is organized is very important, especially if you will be using the print version of RDA, where searching for instructions will require checking in multiple places.

- Chapters in RDA are no longer based on formats, but on elements of description for each FRBR entity.
- Chapters in RDA are no longer based on ISBD areas of description.
- Internal organization of each chapter is very different from AACR2 and should also be highlighted.
- For special-materials catalogers, it might be useful to map the frequently used MARC 21 rules to RDA.
- RDA Toolkit maps the AACR2 rules to RDA. It might be useful to consult this tool at the beginning of the implementation to familiarize yourself with RDA.

Chapter 7 of this book provides detailed information about the organization of RDA.

FAMILIARITY WITH RDA TOOLKIT

RDA Toolkit is a dynamic, interactive online cataloging tool and not just a static electronic text. In this interactive environment, catalogers will be able to customize the cataloging instructions to create their own workflows. They will also be able to access workflows and cataloging policies created by other institutions.

Catalogers will have the ability to create a customized view of RDA instructions. For example, they will be able to limit the instructions to show only the core element or to show only those instructions that are related to integrated resources or serials. These options offer the kind of flexibility that will help catalogers be more efficient in their work. For those catalogers who prefer to work with the print version, the RDA publisher will provide a few print copies.

Become familiar with RDA Toolkit. The online RDA Toolkit is much easier to search than the print version. You can use keyword searching and browse by going directly to the elements from the table of contents. You can also gain access to RDA instructions by searching AACR2 by rule number. The *RDA Resources* tab provides access to two significant documents that are essential to all catalogers: AACR2 and the Library of Congress Policy Statements.

RDA Toolkit provides a series of teaching and training courses as well as webinars on RDA. Some of the training and webinars are free of charge and are easily accessible. These tools provide essential information that will help users to become more familiar with RDA. (See the Training Calendar in RDA Toolkit.) The website also provides links to RDA archived webinars and presentations.(RDA Toolkit 2010–).

When using RDA Toolkit, it is good to practice creating your workflows. Another suggestion is to move your "cheat sheet" information from your paper to the online environment. RDA provides you with the capability to do this through the workflows, where you can create documents and interlink them to other RDA Toolkit documents and other resources. Documents in this set are searchable and customizable. It is good practice to share your workflows with the library community. This will help other catalogers create and customize their own workflows.

RDA Toolkit includes an embedded glossary and an index that will be very helpful in searching for specific instructions.

Chapter 7 of this book provides a description of RDA Toolkit.

TIPS FOR PREPARING IN-HOUSE TRAINING

When designing in-house training for a group of catalogers, plan to train all the catalogers in the organization at the same time and at roughly the same level. Use RDA Toolkit to familiarize the catalogers with the process of creating workflows and looking up instructions. The following are some tips for creating a plan for the training:

- Determine your implementation target date.
- Create a checklist of cataloging policy decisions that need to be made.
- Take the training one step at a time—start with cataloging books and then gradually move to other formats.
- Create a train-the-trainers group. After receiving initial training, these individuals will help to train other catalogers and serve as resource persons to answer questions or solve cataloging issues.
- Divide the training materials into small modules. For example, create a module for identifying manifestation and item, and another one for identifying work and expression, or recording relationships.
- There are many webinars and webcasts available through the Internet. You can select some of these to be used in informal training sessions such as brown bag lunches.
- Prior to training, prepare brown bag lunch sessions for all the participants. It is good to use RDA webcasts, webinars, and any other media tools that will help catalogers to assimilate the main principles and concepts of RDA. These sessions are very important and will help to prepare catalogers for actual in-house training. During the brown bag lunches, serve something light that will encourage catalogers to attend and not feel obligated. Popcorn is ideal in this situation.
- When conducting training, try to limit each session to no more than three hours. Allow some time for exercises, questions, and answers.
- When you move from one module to another, make sure to remind the participants of what you covered in the previous session and how this is related to the current session.
- Create a spreadsheet of all the catalogers in your organization who will need RDA training.
- Divide the training groups into original cataloging and copy cataloging.
- Try to limit the size of each training group to no more than eight participants.
- Determine the target dates for the training sessions and send the schedule to all catalogers so they can sign up for the training based on their schedules. Avoid training sessions on Mondays and Fridays.

- Make sure that you plan for make-up sessions for those catalogers who will not be able to attend their scheduled sessions.
- After completing the introductory training sessions, plan for hands-on training for all catalogers. These sessions should be in a computer lab with access to OCLC Connexion. If this is not possible, you could use offline workforms.
- Prepare resources to be cataloged. The individuals who participated in the train the trainer session can help oversee the hands-on training and answer questions.
- Discuss each bibliographic record and highlight the major points in each bibliographic record.
- During training, the catalogers should be given an opportunity to work together, discuss each other's work, and share comments and feedback.
- After completing the training, create a graduation certificate to be awarded to everyone who participated in the training. Invite the head of your department or associate director to present the certificates to honor the participating catalogers. Last but not least, celebrate the completion of training with a small reception for all catalogers.
- Create RDA resources for catalogers that point the catalogers to additional information. For example:
  - Create an online tutorial or a web-based electronic learning tool. This online learning should be focused and brief. It is useful for beginning catalogers to go over the online learning tool before the actual training session.
  - RDA Toolkit Blog (2011) website lists several US RDA–tester interviews. By reading these, the cataloger trainees will learn about what other libraries have experienced in testing RDA (see www.rdatoolkit.org/blog/category/46).
  - LC's Resource Description and Access (RDA) web page is an important site to consult. It includes documentation, training modules, time lines, and a frequently asked questions section. It also provides many links to the community, including the PCC, OCLC Policy Statement, Joint Steering Committee (JSC) for Development of RDA, and presentations on RDA from JSC, etc.
  - In September 2011, the Library of Congress launched a new website containing information about their preparation for RDA, including training documents, presentations, exercises, and examples of records. Links from the page originally created for LC documentation related to the US RDA Test will be migrated to this LC Resource Description and Access website over time, as appropriate (www.loc.gov/aba/rda).
  - Check the National Library of Australia's website describing their implementation of the "Resource Description and Access (RDA) in

Australia" (www.nla.gov.au/acoc/resource-description-and-access-rda -in-australia).

- Follow up and make sure that the implementation is going smoothly.

PREPARE LOCAL RDA DOCUMENTATION

Create a new manual or website that will be devoted exclusively to RDA documentation. This manual should include the following documents and links:

- All in-house training materials
- Examples of bibliographic records that handle specific issues, such as the rule of three, compilation, reproduction, bound with, etc.
- Comparisons between RDA and AACR2. There are many online presentations that illustrate this comparison. Reviewing them will help you in determining what to do in specific cataloging situations. (Chapter 2 of this book provides a comparison between AACR2 and RDA.)
- Comparisons of RDA and AACR2 records that highlight some of the key differences between them. (Chapter 8 provides many examples of records that were created using RDA.)
- Lists of the new RDA terminology and vocabulary
- Links to documentation and best practices of other libraries and institutions
- Decisions related to your local cataloging policy

Make your RDA documentation available to others, especially the policy decisions that are related to selecting the elements (full versus core), policies related to using non-RDA records from other cataloging agencies, and policies for changing existing records in your OPAC to RDA (when/what/and how). Sharing this documentation will help catalogers learn from each other's experiences.

CHANGING CATALOGERS' HABITS

One of the most important elements of training will be the task of changing the catalogers' habit of memorizing the rules and relying on their experience. It is important for trainers to emphasize this point. Catalogers will need to consult the new instructions frequently, even if they have many years of cataloging experience behind them. It is important to keep pace with changing cataloging rules to avoid using invalid rules.

Another area that needs to be addressed is the use of "cataloger's judgment." In addition to following cataloging rules and filling in required fields, the catalogers are asked to judge independently how the record they are creating can be enhanced and made more accessible. The term "cataloger's judgment," empowers a cataloger to make thoughtful decisions about the data they record in a bibliographic record. This calls for greater cataloger awareness of users' tasks and needs.

CONTINUING EDUCATION

There is a wealth of information about RDA available on the Internet. Catalogers may want to browse Google or Google Scholar to look at the PowerPoint presentations, webinars, articles, blogs, webcasts, and electronic forum postings related to RDA. The Library of Congress is making its RDA training materials, policies, and decisions available through its Resource Description and Access website. Subscribing to Listservs such as AUTOCAT, OCLC-Cat, and RDA-L, and reading journal articles related to research on RDA is always useful.

The Association for Library Collections and Technical Services (ALCTS) offers a variety of opportunities for continuing education that focuses on technical services issues. The following three are of particular interest:

- ALCTS e-Forum is intended to be a moderated discussion of timely issues for a particular period of time. It is available to ALCTS members and nonmembers free of charge. (See the e-Forum website for subscription information: www.ala.org/ala/mgrps/divs/alcts/confevents/upcoming/e-forum/index.cfm.)
- ALCTS offers educational webinars on various topics related to librarianship, including technical service issues. These webinars are offered for a fee and require registration. (See the webinar website at www.ala.org/ala/mgrps/divs/alcts/confevents/upcoming/webinar/index.cfm.)
- ALCTS provides web-related courses in their Fundamentals series. These courses provide an excellent introduction to the principles and procedures of collection management, technical services, and preservation of library materials. Catalogers have the option to take a course individually or as a series. (Check for the ALCTS web courses at www.ala.org/ala/mgrps/divs/alcts/confevents/upcoming/webcourse/index.cfm.)

ALCTS is but one of many sources of information and training for librarians interested in RDA and related technical service issues. Other print and online resources are available on an ongoing basis:

- Attending conferences such as ALA, ASIST, MLA, and AALL will help you in keeping up with new developments and sharing ideas/concerns related to RDA. The ALA Wiki Site (http://wikis.ala.org/readwriteconnect/index.php/ALA_wikis) provides links to many presentations about RDA from ALA conferences. These presentations are available at no cost.
- Participate in webinars on RDA. These are becoming an increasingly useful tool, as the cost of travel to the sites of workshops is becoming prohibitive.
- Journals like *Library Resources and Technical Services* (LRTS), *Cataloging and Classification Quarterly* (CCQ), *OCLC System and Services*, and *Library Collections, Acquisitions, and Technical Services* provide articles on various aspects of cataloging.

- As always, attending workshops and presentations will assist in addressing your concerns and answering your questions. In addition, you will find free RDA webcast presentations by Barbara Tillett on the LC RDA Webcast website (www.loc.gov/catdir/cpso/rdawebcasts.html).

TIPS FOR LIBRARIES

Each library must decide whether to implement RDA or continue using AACR2. Some of the following tips and suggestions may make this process a little less onerous.

- Consider the budgetary impact of licensing RDA.
- Assess the budgetary impact of continuing education, e.g., attending workshops, conferences, and webinars for catalogers.
- Consider the impact on productivity during the implementation period.
- Form an RDA implementation working team in your library to serve as a link between users and the cataloging team.
- Anticipate your staff's needs. RDA is a flexible tool that provides many options and choices. User needs will help to determine which RDA elements to use and what type of description will be appropriate.
- Financially support the creation of a web-based training tool.
- Encourage catalogers who are experienced using RDA to take the initiative in organizing workshops and training at the local, regional, or national levels.

TIPS FOR INFORMING PUBLIC SERVICE DEPARTMENTS AND END USERS ABOUT RDA AND THE NEW LOOK OF THE BIBLIOGRAPHIC RECORD

It is important to arrange an informational meeting about RDA for public service librarians to inform them about the changes in the bibliographic record. Prepare some examples to demonstrate the changes and ask about how these changes will affect the search process and information retrieval. For example:

- With RDA, every author's name will be recorded in the bibliographic record as an authorized access point regardless of how many names appear on the source of information.
- The new MARC 21 fields 336 to338 will allow categorization of information in a more user-friendly manner than the former general materials designation (GMD).
- RDA does not encourage abbreviations. All data must be spelled out unless it is recorded in an abbreviated form on the source of information.
- In some instances, catalogers might need to consult public service librarians about making cataloging policy decisions that will impact information access.

II. DECISION-MAKING BY CATALOGING AGENCY

SELECTING THE TYPE OF DESCRIPTION

RDA includes many instructions that refer to cataloging agency decisions. It is important for cataloging departments to create local policies to handle specific cases. One of the decisions that should be made prior to the implementation is to select the type of RDA description. There are three types of description indicated in RDA chapter 1.5:

Comprehensive description: The whole unit (a single-part unit, a multipart monograph, a serial, an integrating resource, a collection) (RDA 1.5.2)

Analytical description: A part or parts (a part contained within a larger resource issued as a single unit, a part of a multipart monograph, volume in a series, a chapter, a part of an integrated resource) (RDA 1.5.3)

Hierarchical description: Multilevel description of the whole and of each part (RDA 1.5.4)

RDA provides sufficient flexibility to enable catalogers to make decisions about the type of description they will use based on the collection they are cataloging. Some collections, such as special collections and archival materials, will require analytical description. Other materials will require a comprehensive description.

TRANSCRIBING DATA ELEMENTS FROM THE SOURCE

Catalogers need to make decisions about how RDA elements will be transcribed. RDA provides options to record the elements (RDA 1.7.1):

- Transcribe elements as they appear in the source of information
- Alternatives:
    - Follow in-house guidelines or preferred style manual
    - Accept data from scanning, downloading, etc.

If the cataloging agency chooses to apply RDA's guidelines, then apply the RDA general guidelines on capitalization, punctuation, symbols, abbreviations, etc., as they are given under RDA instructions 1.7.2 to 1.7.9. These instructions should be used in conjunction with the RDA appendixes; when applicable, the following should be applied (RDA 1.7.1):

Examples:

- Transcribe capitalization in title (RDA appendix A4).
    - Capitalize the first word of title information, except for:
        - Other title information
        - Parallel other title information
        - Other title information of series
        - Parallel other title information of series

Other title information of subseries
Parallel other title information of subseries
Arabic or Hebrew article

- Transcribe a compound term with unusual capitalization as it appears in the source without capitalizing a lowercased first letter, e.g., "eLerning."
- Transcribe an Internet address (or part of one) as it appears in the source, without capitalizing a lowercased first letter, e.g., "gmail.com."
- Do not capitalize the first word if the title begins with punctuation indicating an omission, e.g., " . . . if elected."
- Use the following capitalization for other elements:
    - Capitalize the first word in a numeric and/or alphabetic designation of first issue or part, e.g., "Vol. 1, no. 6."
    - Capitalize other words in numbering of serials only if normal usage in the language capitalizes them, e.g., "June 2006" in Bd. 2, in German.

Other useful documents that you should consult are the RDA Joint Steering Committee's documents "Book Workflow" (JointSteering Committee 2008a) and "Transcribing Workflow." (JointSteering Committee 2008a). These two documents will provide a step-by-step workflow and will show how to transcribe the elements. (Chapter 5 of this book provides information about the type of description in the section entitled "Transcription").

CHOICES IN RDA

RDA provides a great deal of flexibility in cataloging. In describing the core elements and full elements, RDA offers variations to the general rules that can accommodate exceptional situations. Many of the RDA instructions include subheadings that are labeled "alternative" (RDA figure 1), "optional omission" (RDA figure 2), "optional addition" (RDA figure 3), or "exception" (RDA figure 4), which explains how to handle exceptional situations when they are encountered. These instructions require creating local policies or following the LC Policy Statement (LCSP). Another decision that needs to be made is related to the use of core elements or core plus. Making a checklist of all the decisions that need to be made prior to training will be helpful. (Chapters 5 and 6 of this book provide more information about these policies.)

In figure 3.1, "alternative" suggests to the cataloger to do "something different" from what the previous instructions indicated.

In figure 3.2, the "optional omission" instructions direct the cataloger to do less than what the previous instruction said to do.

In figure 3.3, the "optional addition" instructions direct the cataloger to do more than what the previous instruction indicated.

Figure 3.4 illustrates how the note labeled "exception" refers the cataloger to another RDA instruction.

2.2.2.3 Resources Consisting of Moving Images

If the resource consists of moving images (e.g., a film reel, a videodisc, a video game, an MPEG video file), use the title frame or frames, or title screen or screens, as the preferred source of information.

Alternative

Use an eye-readable label bearing a title that is permanently printed on or affixed to the resource (excluding accompanying textual material or a container) in preference to the title frame or frames, or title screen or screens.

Figure 3.1: Subheading labeled "alternative"

2.7.1.4 Recording Production Statements

Record a production statement or statements for a resource that is in an unpublished form (e.g., a manuscript, a painting, a sculpture, a locally made recording).

Transcribe places of production and producers' names in the form in which they appear on the source of information. Apply the general guidelines on transcription given under **1.7** RDA.

Optional Omission LC-PCC PS

Omit levels in a corporate hierarchy that are not required to identify the producer. Do not use a mark of omission (...) to indicate such an omission.

Figure 3.2: Subheading labeled "Optional Omission"

6.2.1.6 Diacritical Marks

Record diacritical marks such as accents appearing in a title for a work as they appear on the source of information.

Optional Addition

Add diacritical marks such as accents that are not present on the source of information. Follow the standard usage for the language of the data.

EXAMPLE

Études juives

Figure 3.3: Subheading labeled "Optional Addition"

2.3.1.3 Facsimiles and Reproductions

When describing a facsimile or reproduction that has a title or titles relating to the original manifestation as well as to the facsimile or reproduction, record the title or titles relating to the facsimile or reproduction. Record any title relating to the original manifestation as a title pertaining to a related manifestation (see **27.1** RDA).

Exception

If the title of the original manifestation appears on the same source of information as the title of the facsimile or reproduction, apply the instructions given under **2.3.2.3** RDA.

Figure 3.4: Subheading labeled "Exception"

Choices and options that are available in RDA will lead the catalogers through an explicit, logical decision-making process in addition to building the cataloger's judgment based on principles that focus on content and not on display. LC documents on RDA alternatives, optional omissions, and optional additions can be found on the LC website under "RDA Alternatives and Options—LC Proposed Practice for the RDA Test." It is a useful document that can be used by all catalogers. (Library of Congress 2010a).

If the library is a member of consortia or other governing bodies, such as OCLC or Program for Cooperative Cataloging (PCC), it has to make a decision about which alternatives and options should be applied within the consortia. The important point is that all libraries will be required to use the core elements of RDA. (See Section VII for PCC decisions below.)

OTHER CHOICES THAT ARE NOT LABELED

There are other non-labeled instructions that offer more than one approach to a situation. For example, as a result of the internationalization of RDA, it is no longer assumed that the instructions are being used in an Anglo-American context. The cataloging agency preparing the description needs to make a decision regarding:

- Language of additions to access points
- Language of supplied data
- Script and transliteration
- Calendar
- Numeric system

"RDA Instructions Referring to Choices by 'Agency Creating the Data'" will aid in the decision-making process. It includes the RDA instruction number, the topic, and the LC recommendation (Library of Congress 2010b).

LIBRARY OF CONGRESS AND OTHER CATALOGING AGENCIES

The Library of Congress replaced their Rule Interpretations (LCRIs) with Policy Statements (LCPS). This tool has been added to RDA Toolkit and linked to the RDA instructions (see figure 3.5). Catalogers will need to decide whether to use the LC policy or to follow their own institutional policy.

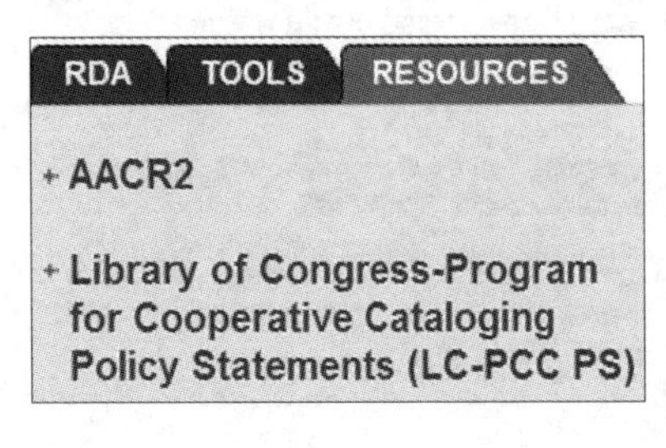

Figure 3.5: RDA Tabs (Resources tab)

III. INTEGRATING THE NEW RDA RECORDS WITH LEGACY RECORDS AND DECIDING TO RE-CATALOG A SET OF MANIFESTATIONS (Locally or Through OCLC)

One important point that needs to be emphasized is that this change is not new to the library catalog, as many have been made throughout history. In the past, libraries adopted these changes and made the transition easily. Until today, records based on AACR1 are still displayed in our online systems. It is the library's choice to sort out what is important to their users. Having said that, there are two issues for implementing RDA on the institutional and national level that have to be addressed.

ON THE INSTITUTIONAL LEVEL

RDA was designed to be compatible with internationally established principles, models and metadata standards and to be compatible with legacy records with little or no retrospective conversion. Therefore, re-cataloging will not be a major factor in implementing RDA.

The decision to re-catalog a collection is the library's decision. For example, the library can issue a policy statement with specific instructions: "from x date, library materials will be cataloged using RDA. Records that were created prior to this date using AACR2 will not change to RDA."

A library can choose to re-catalog a specific collection which has become difficult to search in the new display environment. For example, if a collection of literary works is affected by using RDA in terms of display and "FRBRization," the library may decide to re-catalog this collection.

Other changes and adjustments in local cataloging can be accomplished by using online system's functionalities such as global updates. For example, the headings for "Bible" will need to be adjusted to change the "O.T." and "N. T." to spell out the form "Old Testament and New Testament." Another example is the omission of the name of the Testament in the preferred title for individual books or groups of books of the Bible. In this case, there will be a change in the preferred title from "Bible. N.T. Gospels" to "Bible. Gospels." These are simple changes that can be performed using the OPAC's global update capability.

ON THE NATIONAL LEVEL

Catalogers are now in an excellent position to work together cooperatively and to share their work with each other. Local editing is a time consuming, costly process. When a library decides to re-catalog a collection, it is important to make the changes in the OCLC database. This will help to prevent other libraries from cataloging the same materials again. Catalogers can form a re-cataloging team and work with each other dividing among themselves the collection that needs to be re-cataloged. Each cataloger can work on one collection and share it with others through OCLC. Before making the decision to re-catalog a collection and make an update to OCLC records, catalogers must consult the OCLC Policy Statement (Section VI provides information on the OCLC Policy Statement during the RDA test. This policy might change in the future and it is advisable to keep up-to-date with OCLC regarding these policy changes).

IV. EXPORTING RDA-BASED BIBLIOGRAPHIC RECORDS FROM OCLC INTO YOUR OPAC

There are many RDA-based records in the OCLC database and many more will be created as you move forward with RDA implementation. If your online system is not prepared to accept RDA records, you will still be able to export the record from OCLC into your own system, but all the new MARC 21 fields will be stripped from your records.

In some cases, integrating the RDA records into your system may cause a problem in display, because the RDA instructions are very different from AACR2. One example is RDA instruction 6.2.2.10 for "Recording the Preferred Title for a Compilation of Works," where the rules for cataloging these materials are different from the AACR2 rules. (Chapter 6 of this publication provides many examples.) In this case, catalogers can either accept these records as is or change them to the AACR2 format. OCLC policy for the RDA test was not to change records automatically in OCLC WorldCat (OCLC 2011). OCLC issued a recent discussion paper on "Incorporating RDA Practices into WorldCat" (OCLC 2012). Highlights from the discussion paper include:

- Catalogers are not required to update or upgrade existing records to RDA.
- Catalogers may re-catalog an item according to RDA if it is considered useful. Such re-cataloging should only be done with access to the item. All descriptive fields would need to be reconsidered and revised to conform to RDA instructions. The revised record would then be changed to Desc (Leader/18) coded as *c* or *i* as appropriate with 040 $e rda added.
- Catalogers may update individual fields in pre-RDA records to reflect RDA practices if it is considered useful. Fields involving the transcription of data require access to the item in order to change transcribed data. The partially changed record would retain the indication of the rules under which it was initially cataloged, i.e., no changes would be made to the coding of Desc (Leader/18) and 040 $e would not be added or changed.
- Catalogers should use access points as established in the authority file, whether those forms are coded as RDA or AACR2.

In "Incorporating RDA Practices into WorldCat" (OCLC 2012), OCLC also provides specific instructions for changing the pre-RDA records. Because this is a discussion paper, this statement might change or be modified in the future, but it is important to know now what to expect when implementing RDA.

LC catalogers continued to produce RDA records and created a checklist for when and when not to edit an OCLC record (Library of Congress 2012a). (Checklist 1: Converting an AACR2 Record to RDA and Checklist 2: Using an Imported RDA Record.)

It will be useful for other libraries to create their own checklists and to make sure that they will not spend a great deal of time editing records to convert from AACR2 to RDA and vice versa. Following OCLC policy statements is important for the integration of the bibliography records.

V. RDA AND PCC PARTICIPANTS

The Library of Congress Program for Cooperative Cataloging (PCC) was the first agency to endorse the US RDA Test Coordinating Committee's decision to implement RDA. Immediately following the announcement, the PCC Policy Committee (PoCo) began to prepare for the implementation. To address the issues that might affect the PCC participants, the PCC PoCo formed three task groups (Library of Congress 2012b) on RDA to begin preparing for this transition:

- The PCC RDA-Decisions-Needed Task Group was formed to review the document "PCC RDA Policy and Practice Decisions Needed if RDA is Adopted" (Library of Congress Program for Cooperative Cataloging 2011a), prioritize and make recommendations for follow-up action. The Task Group created a spreadsheet to include the issue ID from the original document; RDA issues; priority rank; questions and decisions for this issue; and what group within PCC should be responsible for making each decision, be it PoCo, the Cooperative Online Serials (CONSER/BIBCO), one of the standing committees, or a subgroup of any of those. The charge and the final report of this Task Group are available from the PCC website (LC PCC 2011a).
- The Task Group on AACR2 and RDA Acceptable Heading Categories has to deal with the LC Authority File. The Task Group was requested to identify the types of headings currently existing within the LC name authority file (LC NAF) that were constructed under AACR2 and valid under RDA, therefore usable as-is; headings constructed under AACR2, in need of change to be used as valid RDA headings; and grey areas, where the need for change is uncertain. The Task Group was also asked to identify specifications for writing a report that can be used to collect all of a given type of heading. The final report and the recommendations are available from the PCC RDA website (LC PCC 2011b).
- The PCC Task Group on Hybrid Bibliographic Records was asked to investigate the use of hybrid records and make recommendations for best practices (LC PCC 2011c). The final report provides general guidelines for working with RDA and AACR2 records during the transition period from AACR2 to RDA. For example, it provides instructions for editing and enhancing monographic and continuing resources and directing catalogers to what is or is

not allowed to be changed in an existing record. The tables in the final report provide catalogers with instructions for each MARC 21 field that is related to monographs and continuing resources. Examples in the final report will guide catalogers to what to edit in the bibliographic record (LC PCC 2011c).

PCC POST-RDA TEST GUIDELINES (INTERIM PERIOD)

PCC has issued guidelines on the use of an authorized access point established in an RDA authority record for the PCC catalogers who will continue to create RDA bibliographic and authority records after the RDA test period. One of the important parts of the guidelines is asking catalogers not to change AACR2 records to RDA or change RDA records to AACR2. PCC is discouraging catalogers from creating hybrid AACR2/RDA authorized access points in establishing new headings or in making additions to existing headings.

If a cataloger is making additions to AACR2 headings or is creating a new heading based on existing AACR2 records, that cataloger will follow the AACR2 rules and the Library of Congress Rules Interpretations (LCRIs). If the cataloger is making additions to RDA headings or is creating new headings based on existing RDA records, that cataloger will follow RDA instructions (LC PCC 2012d).

MARC 21 ENCODING TO ACCOMMODATE THE NEW RDA ELEMENTS 046 AND 3XX IN NARS AND SARS

New MARC 21 fields were created to be added to the authority records, to accommodate the new RDA elements. These are fields 046 and 3XX and they are added to the Name Authority Records (NARs) and Subject Authority Records (SARs) as appropriate (LC PCC 2012e).

Section VII of the current chapter, "Implementing the New MARC 21 Fields to Accommodate RDA Elements," discussed all the new MARC 21 field authority records that were created to accommodate the implementation of RDA. The PCC created interim procedures on when to provide MARC 21 fields 046 and 3XX data in NACO authority records. These recommendations are incorporated in Section VII (B) of this chapter.

PCC DAY ONE FOR RDA AUTHORITY RECORDS

The PCC issued a document to explain to catalogers what to expect on "day one" of RDA implementation. One of the highlights of the PCC RDA Task Group on AACR2 and RDA Acceptable Heading Categories Report was a set of instructions on what should be done on the first day of implementation. The PCC made a distinction between *day one* issue for authority work and bibliographic record creation. Because no major issues were identified for day one for bibliographic records, day one instructions apply only to authority records. When new authority records are contributed to the Library of Congress Name Authority Cooperative (LC/NACO), they must be coded RDA and all access points included in the bibliographic record that are coded PCC must be established using RDA instructions (LC PCC 2012f).

The Task Group on AACR2 and RDA Acceptable Heading Categories issued a report that concludes that about 95.1 percent of the AACR2 authority records with MARC 21 fields 1XX can be used in the RDA environment without further modification. The Task Group proposed that these records be recoded as RDA records, as close to the PCC Day One for RDA Authority Records as possible, so that catalogers can clearly identify them. The remaining 4.9 percent are records that require review.

The Task Group suggested adding MARC 21 field 667 as a note in the authority records to alert catalogers that the headings cannot be used in an RDA bibliographic record after PCC Day One for RDA Authority Records (LC PCC 2012f).

The *PCC Day One Plan* document is very important for catalogers to consult as they begin to create authority records. Catalogers have to keep in mind that PCC does not support AACR2 or answer questions related to AACR2 after the release of RDA. The PCC AACR2 support for documentation will be discontinued and no longer updated (LC PCC 2012g).

PCC'S FREQUENTLY ASKED QUESTIONS FOR RDA

This is a useful document that will answer many of the catalogers' questions in regard to RDA implementation. It is important to consult this document from time to time as it is updated frequently (LC PCC 2012f). In addition, catalogers should consult the Library of Congress Policy and Standards Division RDA FAQ (Library of Congress 2012) and the Library of Congress Documentation FAQ for the RDA Test (Library of Congress Cataloging and Acquisitions. 2010). For more information about the RDA implementations, consult the official PCC RDA: Resource Description and Access (Library of Congress Cataloging and Acquisitions. 2012). This website includes a wealth of information and links to other PCC RDA documentation.

VI. RDA'S EFFECT ON OPAC DISPLAYS

One of the objectives of RDA is to change the way bibliographic records are displayed. Today's users have different expectations of what a library catalog is and what it can do. Growing familiarity with search engines and their apparent ease of use means that catalog functionality must be improved and coverage expanded. Users also want the ease of a Google-style search interface that retrieves everything with a single search.

Adoption of the principles of FRBR and FRAD is most important at this stage. FRBR and FRAD concepts emphasize the relationship between a person's work, the expression, manifestation of this work, and the work's physical copy (item).

Presenting these relationships will not be possible until the OPAC interface changes its display of records. Adopting RDA will not a have dramatic impact on the OPAC interface, but it will allow OPAC designers to transform the ways in which search results are displayed (Hider and Huthwaite n.d.).

Yee (2006) indicates that what needs to change in the OPAC is the display. She continued that the online catalog should be able to:

> Display context (all scope notes, broader and narrower term references, earlier and later name references, etc.), and to create displays that allow users to include or exclude the following, based on the existing MARC 21 tagging that differentiates:
>
> A. Expressions of the work itself, including expressions that are contained within other works
>
> B. Works about the work
>
> C. Works related to the work

Designing new OPACs based on the FRBR model is important for a number of reasons. For catalogers and system administrators, they improve the efficiency of data creation and maintenance. One example of this efficiency is allowing data for works and expressions to be created and stored once only and reused as needed. Furthermore, FRBR-based database structures will improve the ease and effectiveness with which users are able to access the data and navigate the database (Kiorgaard 2009).

RDA will definitely have an impact, not only on cataloging workflows, but on integrated library systems (ILS) as well. A few of the ILS vendors have taken the initiative to produce an online system that will support RDA and FRBR concepts. **V**isionary **T**echnology in **L**ibrary **S**olutions (VTLS) has designed Virtua® which has adopted FRBR concepts. In addition, VTLS added the new MARC 21 fields that will accommodate RDA elements. The Primo® system from Ex Libris designed an interface based on the FRBR concepts.

VTLS has long experience with FRBR and linked data. Through the design of their Virtua interface, users have the ability to place holds at any level of work, expression, or manifestation. VTLS created a workflow scenario that shows how the FRBR concept is applied in the VTLS catalog and how the records are displayed (Espley and Chachra 2010).

Figure 3.6 shows how VTLS uses the FRBR concept to display the title and the author of the work *Harry Potter and the Prisoner of Azkaban*. Different expressions are displayed in a clustered form. Each manifestation is displayed under the expression where it belongs. From this display, users will be able to see the work, related expressions, and manifestations in a single screen display. The record display is also better organized and less cluttered.

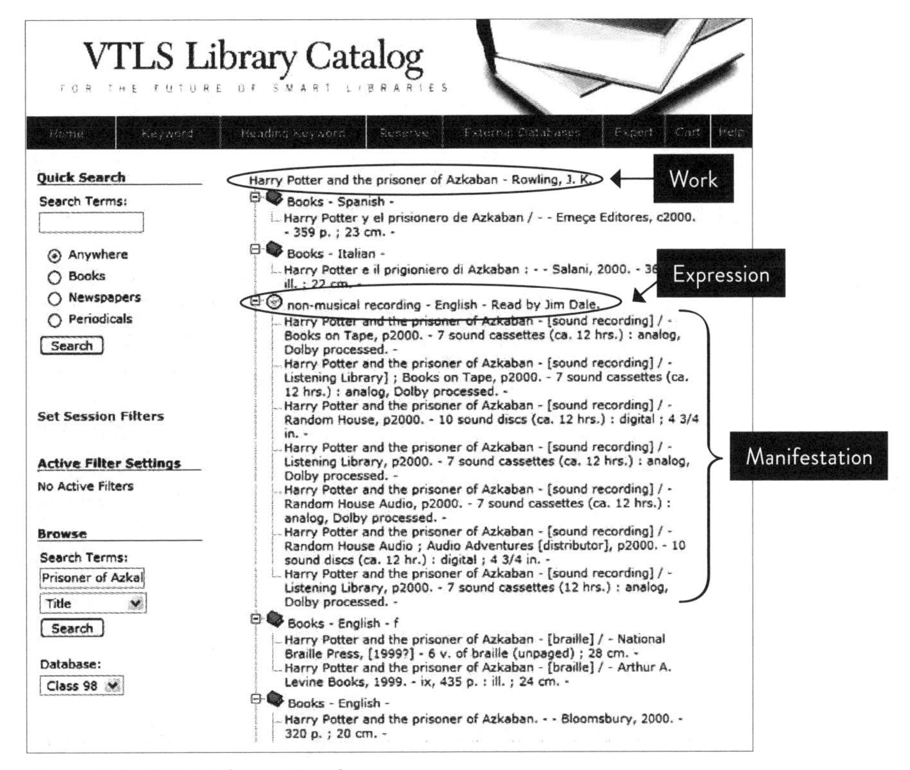

Figure 3.6: VTLS Library Catalog

This slide is taken from RDA: Resource Description and Access by Deirdre Kiorgaard.

OCLC WorldCat.org provides an example of a catalog which has been "FRBRized." To illustrate the clustering concept, search WorldCat.org under "Introduction to Cataloging and Classification." In the left-hand column there are 346 titles in all formats and then a breakdown by individual format is provided (figure 3.7).

To view "Introduction to Cataloging and Classification" by Arlene G. Taylor and David P. Miller, click on the title that is authored by Arlene G. Taylor and it will display all related editions and other expressions of this particular title (figure 3.8).

To see various manifestation of this title, click on "View all editions and formats" (#4) in figure 8. This will display all related editions (figure 3.9).

To view a specific edition, click on that edition and you will see the bibliographic description and holdings information or information about how to purchase this edition (figure 3.10).

To find a copy of this title in a library or to buy a copy, click on "borrow/obtain copy or buy" (figure 3.11).

OCLC WorldCat.org dramatically changes the way information is displayed. It links to book reviews, adds tags, creates citations, links to e-mail, online book shops, and provides help like "did you mean . . ." when you mistype. It also provides for interaction between the users and the bibliographic records through tagging, entering a rating, and writing reviews. In addition, users can now add tables of contents and can delete or modify their own reviews. These are features that go well beyond

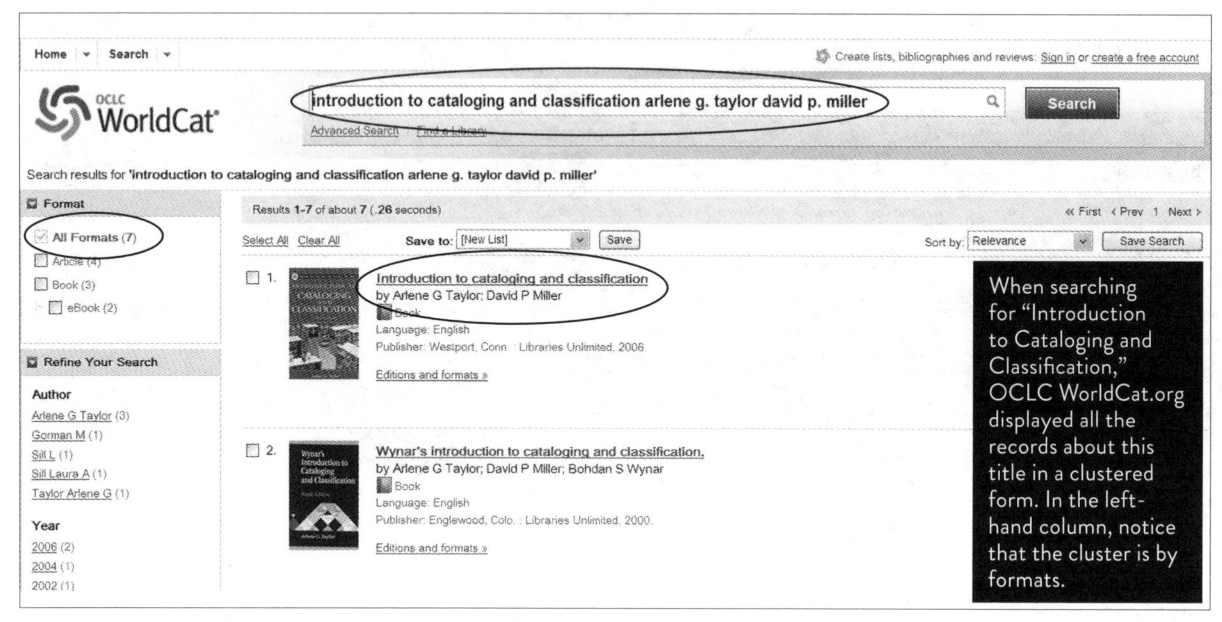

Figure 3.7: OCLC WorldCat.org—Searching for the title "Introduction to Cataloging and Classification"

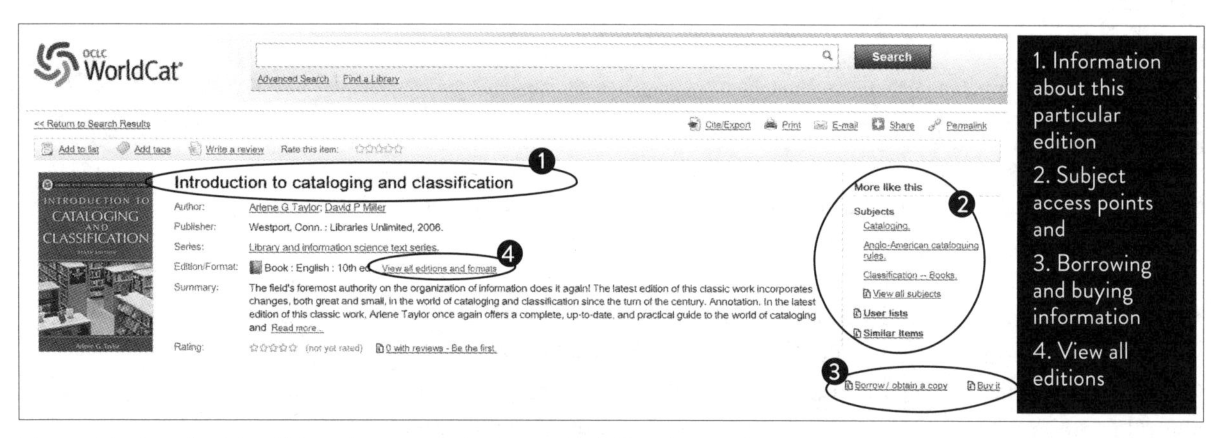

Figure 3.8: Specific title of "Introduction to Cataloging and Classification"

the bibliographic description and will allow the user to easily find, identify, select, and obtain library materials.

OCLC has also experimented with "FRBRizing" a set of records related to fiction. This prototype is named the OCLC Fiction Finder (http://fictionfinder.oclc.org). A screen shot from the OCLC Fiction Finder's website shows how the works of Mark Twain are displayed. First, the page provides an overview of his works, genres, subject headings, his roles, and classification (figure 3.12). Figure 3.13 is a display of clustering of works about him and by him. Figure 3.14 shows related works and other useful links. These three figures are all displayed in a single summary page. In addition, the page includes various forms of the author's name. The OCLC Fiction Finder display is a model that the Integrated Library Systems vendors can adopt to provide effective library catalog display.

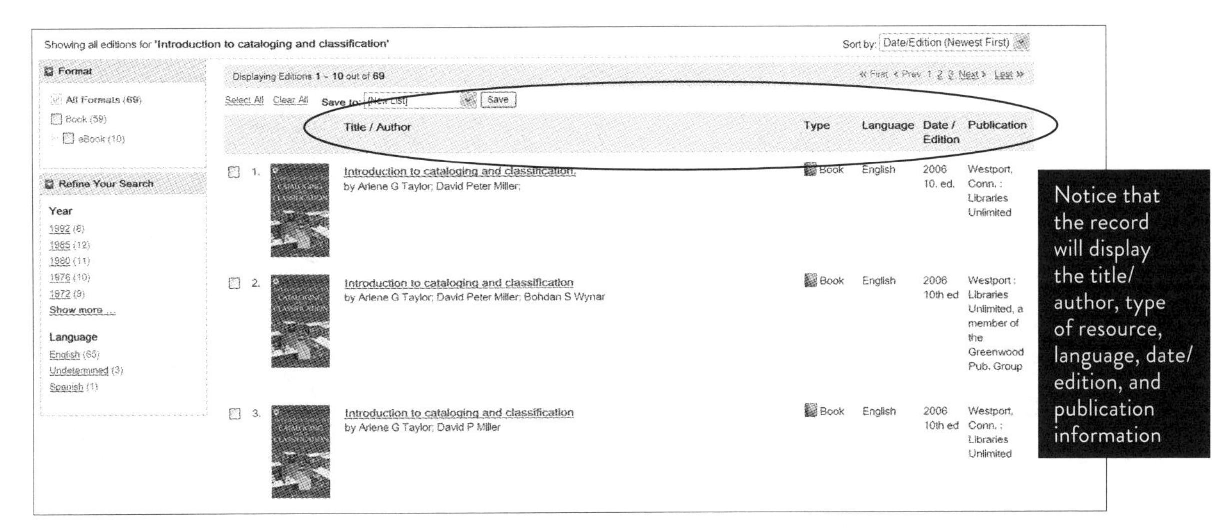

Figure 3.9: All editions and formats

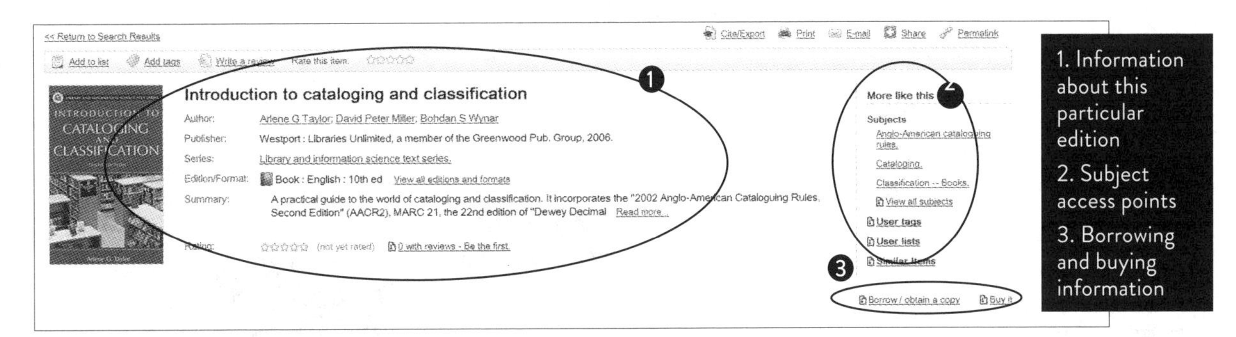

Figure 3.10: Bibliographic information about a particular edition

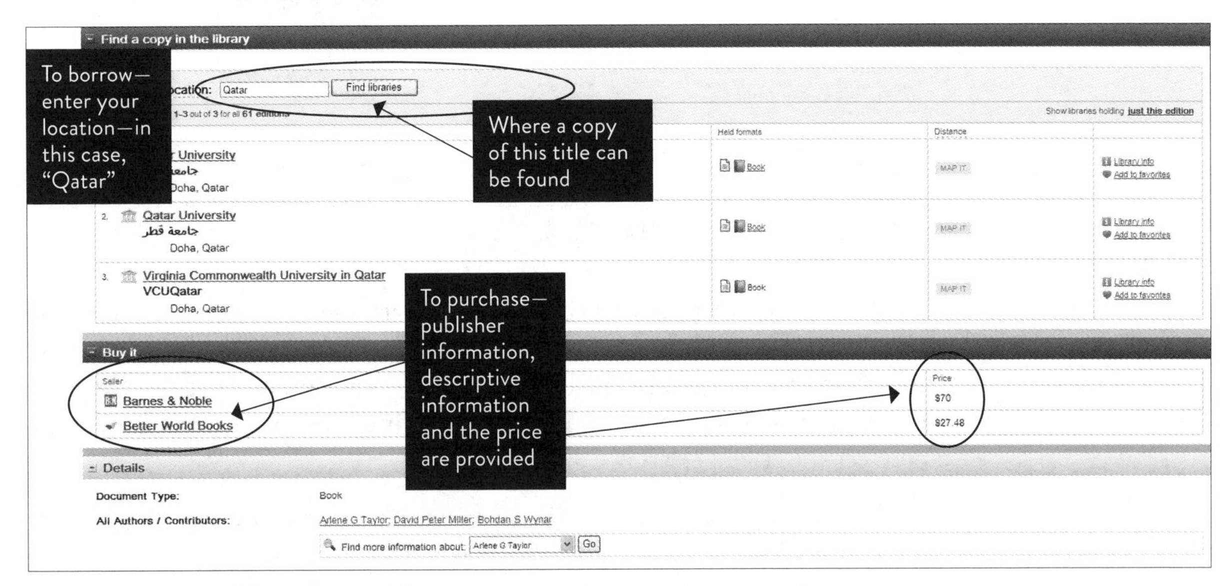

Figure 3.11: Borrow/obtain a copy or buy

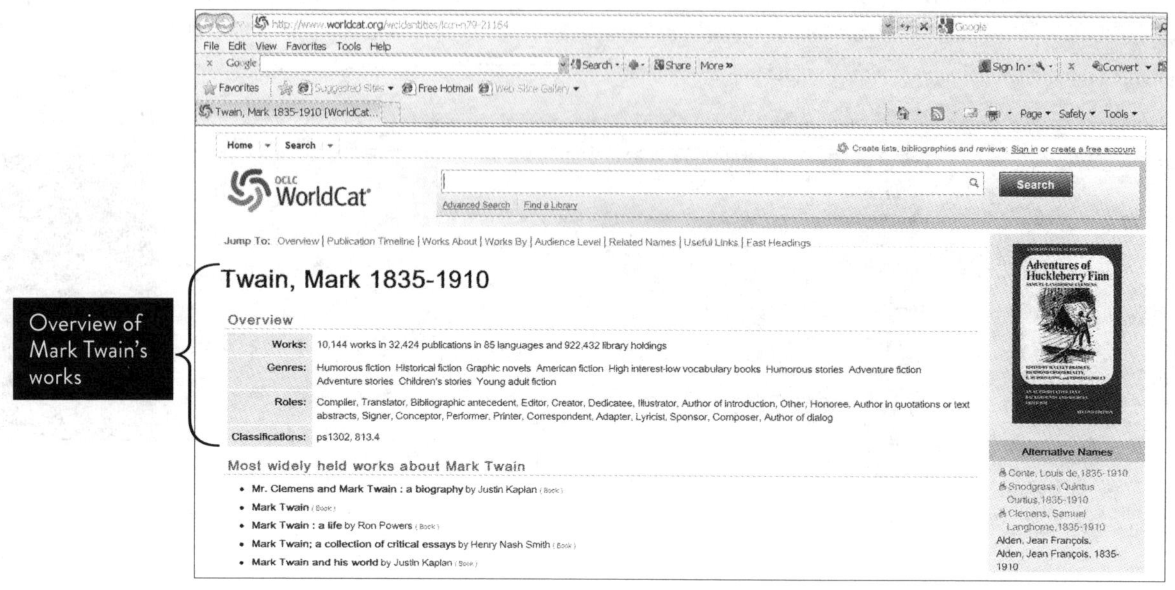

Figure 3.12: Overview of Mark Twain

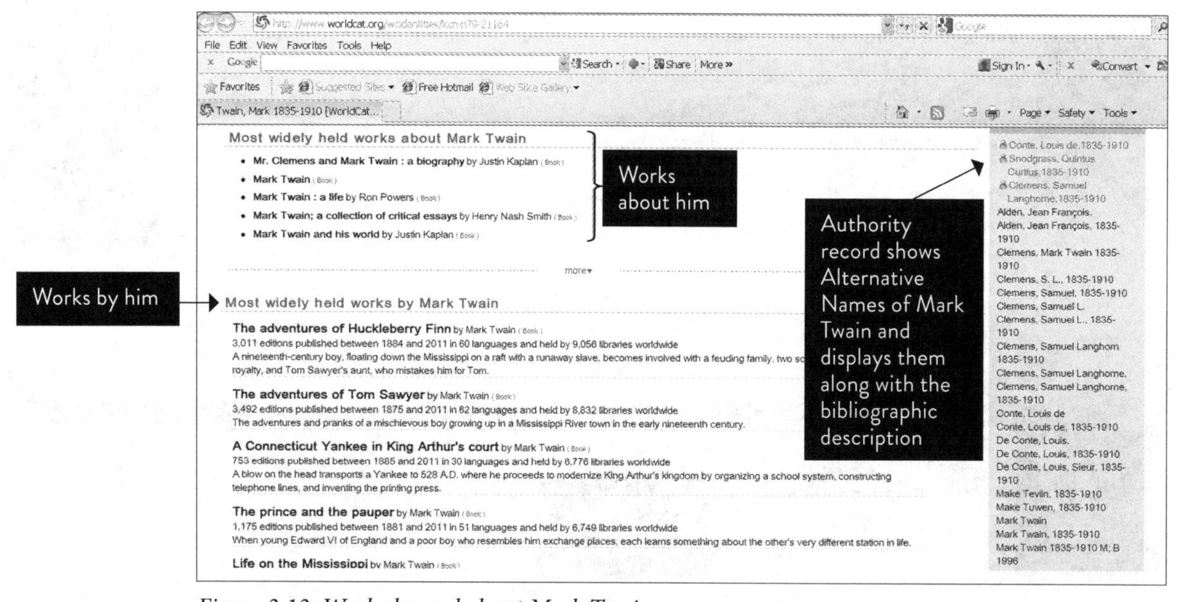

Figure 3.13: Works by and about Mark Twain

RDA editor Tom Delsey drafted three RDA database implementation scenarios for the RDA Joint Steering Committee (JSC). The scenarios are intended to illustrate some of the potential implementations of RDA data in various database structures. The document shows graphic representations of three possible database implementation scenarios (Joint Steering Committee 2007).

- Scenario 1: Relational/object-oriented database structure
- Scenario 2: Linked bibliographic and authority records
- Scenario 3: "Flat file" database structure (no links)

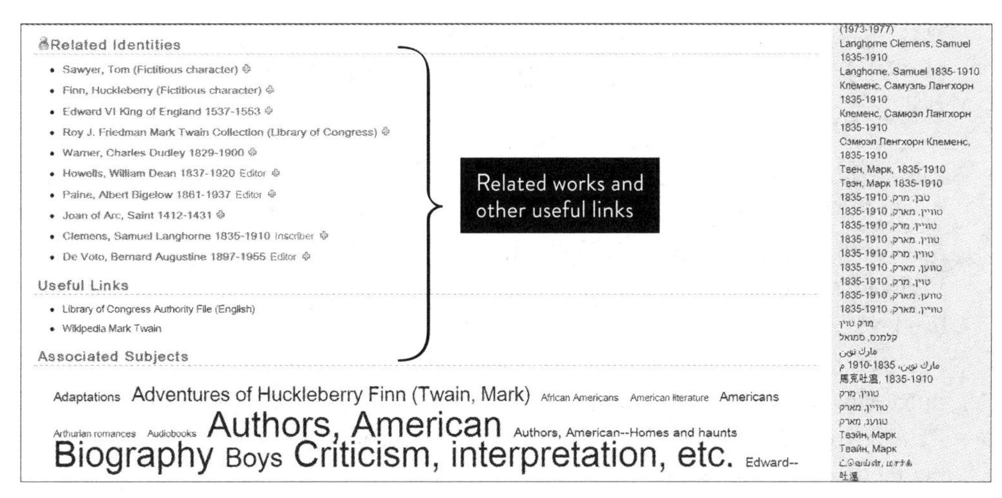

Figure 3.14: Related works

Scenario 3 is the flat-file structure of today's ILS. Scenario 2 adds links between bibliographic and authority records. Scenario 1 is a relational database structure representing the full FRBR implementation of RDA, including records for the work, expression, manifestation, and item (WEMI), which are all linked. It is important to note that each scenario includes the same data elements (or attributes) but different data structures are used to store the data and to reflect the relationships between the data elements (entities).

These scenarios are important for vendors to consider when designing the new generation of ILS systems that will support the objectives that RDA is designed to fulfill. For the transition to RDA, most libraries will continue for now to create bibliographic records with linked authority records (Scenario 2 of the JSC/Editor).

An important key to the implementation of RDA is to have an open dialogue with ILS vendors. RDA as a cataloging code emphasizes relationships among works, expressions, manifestations, and items, to allow for better clustering of records. ILS vendors who are working on interface design are faced with deciding when and how to take advantage of the possibilities offered by RDA. Vendors would do well to consider a redesign of their automation systems in order to incorporate new functionality of bibliographic and authority data. They also need to consider how and when to add the new RDA fields to MARC records. To take full advantage of RDA, vendors must consider redesigning their systems in order to incorporate the new RDA functionality for bibliographic and authority data.

Your ILS vendors should communicate their plan on how they will update your online catalog to accommodate the needs of RDA and how much this update will cost. Will there be a different version of the online system and how much will that cost? If the ILS does not have a plan to accommodate the needs of RDA, the library needs to look at the options. One option is to look for a new ILS vendor. These are just a few questions to ask about the ILS services. This is an important step that will help in making the decision to adopt or not adopt RDA.

VII. STRATEGY FOR IMPLEMENTING THE NEW MARC 21 FIELDS TO ACCOMMODATE RDA ELEMENTS

RDA can be used with a variety of metadata, including MARC 21encoding. Changes to MARC 21 are being made to accommodate the new RDA data elements. The good news is that most of MARC 21 fields and tags can be used to code RDA elements. Very few MARC 21 fields have been added and only a few fields and subfields have been redefined.

A summary of all the changes made to MARC 21 to accommodate RDA instructions can be found at the LC MARC 21 Standards website (www.loc.gov/marc/RDAinMARC29.html) under "RDA in MARC: January 2011." RDA Toolkit provides mapping for the following:

- RDA to MARC 21 Bibliographic
- MARC 21 Bibliographic to RDA
- RDA to MARC 21 Authority
- MARC 21 Authority to RDA
- RDA to MODS (figure 3.15)

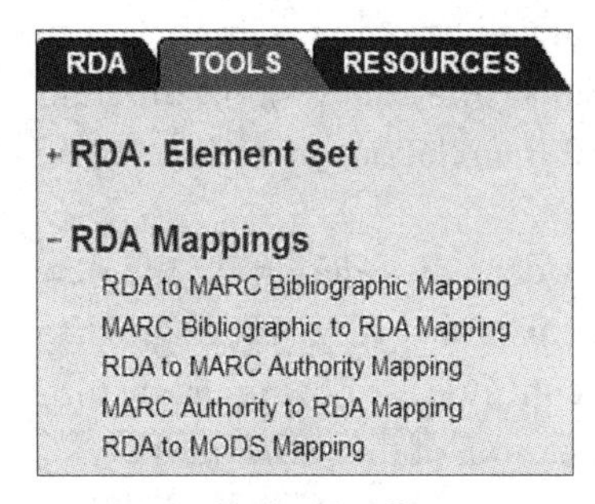

Figure 3.15: RDA Toolkit: (Tools Tab) Mapping

This mapping can help catalogers find the correlations between MARC 21 and RDA and vice versa. (Chapter 7 of this publication provides a detailed explanation of how to use the RDA mapping features from RDA Toolkit.)

The following section will address changes that are made most frequently in the MARC 21 field when coding RDA elements in MARC 21.

A. CHANGES/EXTENSIONS IN MARC 21 FOR THE BIBLIOGRAPHIC FORMAT

FIXED FIELD—LDR 18 "DESC" DESCRIPTIVE CATALOGING FORM (Figure 3.16)

Use "I" (contains ISBD punctuation) or "c" (ISBD punctuation omitted).

Example:

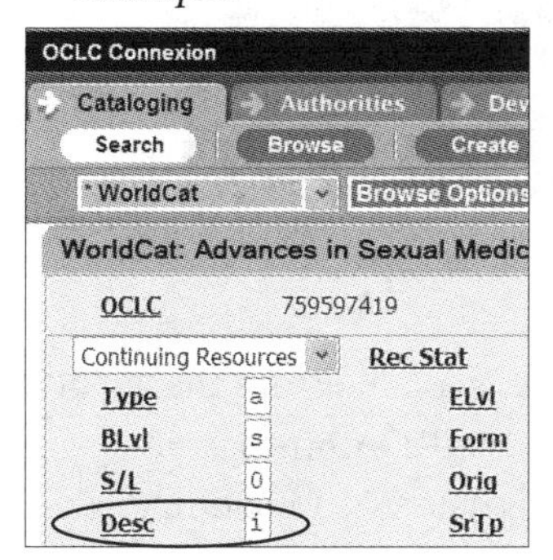

Figure 3.16: LDR 18

007 PHYSICAL DESCRIPTION FIXED FIELD (Figure 3.17)

Some extensions are made to MARC 21 fields 007 and 008 to accommodate RDA terms. For example, new codes have been added to MARC 21 field 007, such as "s"; "d"; "sg"; and "sd". These new codes may be also used in MARC 21 field 337 as a code in $b in addition to the Media type term in $a, and in MARC 21 field 338 as a code in $b in addition to the Carrier type term in $a,

Example:

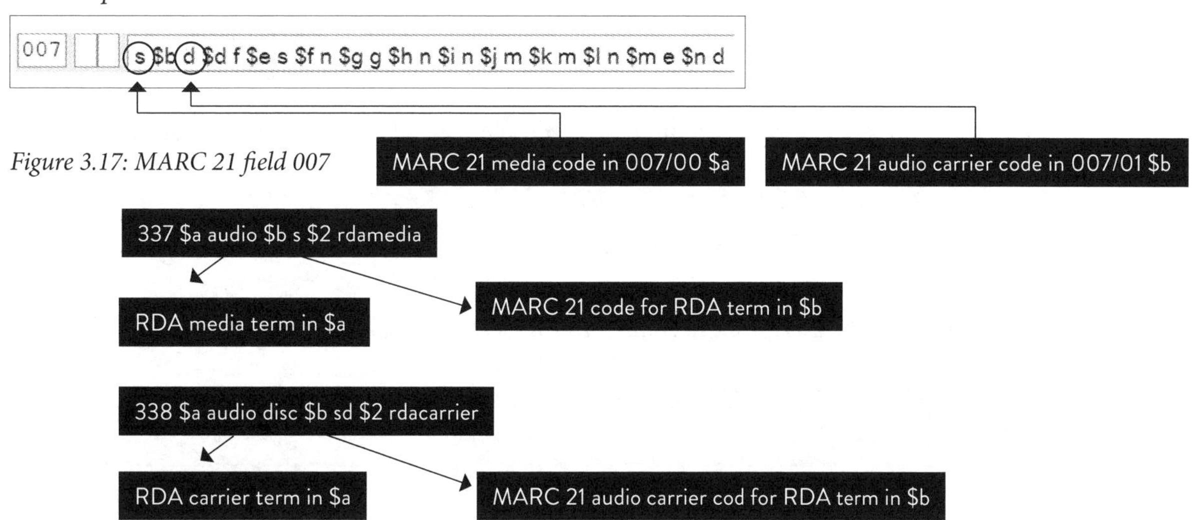

Figure 3.17: MARC 21 field 007

MARC 21 FIELD 008 FIXED-LENGTH DATA ELEMENTS (Figure 3.18)

New codes are added in MARC 21 fields 008/23 and 008/29 for form of item:

Code o—online
Code q— direct electronic

Example:

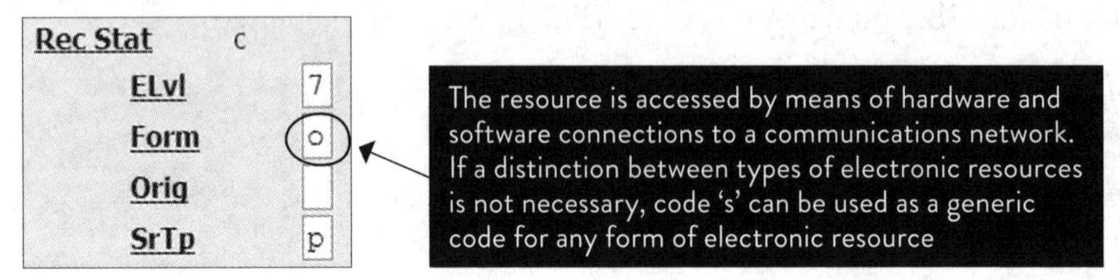

Figure 3.18: MARC 21 field 008

All the new codes in MARC 21 fields 007 and 008 are available from the MARC 21 Standards website (www.loc.gov/marc/007008changes-RDA.html) and from OCLC *Technical Bulletin* 258, "OCLC-MARC Format Update 2010 including RDA Changes."

MARC 21 FIELD 040 CATALOGING SOURCE (Figures 3.19, 3.20, and 3.21)

Two major changes are made to MARC 21 field 040:

$b Language of Cataloging (Not Repeatable)

If the record is produced in France, use "$b fre." For other language codes, consult the *MARC Code List for Languages.*

Figure 3.19: MARC 21 field 040

In records produced in the US, the language of cataloging will be $b eng.

Figure 3.20: MARC 21 field 040

$e RDA Description Recommendations (Repeatable) (Figure 3.21)

Figure 3.21: $e

When catalogers use the RDA convention in subfield "e" of MARC 21 field 040, the code in Leader 18 should be "i," to indicate the use of the ISBD's punctuation (see figure 3.16).

336, 337, 338 NEW MARC 21 FIELDS FOR CATEGORIZATION (REPEATABLE)

Content type—MARC 21 field 336 (more information about this field is in MARC 21 [www.loc.gov/marc/bibliographic/bd336.html]). Use controlled terms from RDA 6.9.1.

SUBFIELD 2

- Will be used to indicate the source of the term or code used to record the information.

  Example:

  336 $a two-dimensional moving image $2 rdacontent

- *Media type*—MARC 21 field 337 (more information about this field is in MARC 21 [www.loc.gov/marc/bibliographic/bd337.html]). Use controlled terms from RDA 3.2.1

SUBFIELD 2

- Will be used to indicate the source of the term or code used to record the information

  Example:

  337 $a video $2 rdamedia

- *Carrier type*—MARC 21 field 338 (more information about this field is in MARC 21 [www.loc.gov/marc/bibliographic/bd338.html
  - Use controlled terms from RDA 3.3.1.3

SUBFIELD 2

- Will be used to indicate the source of the term or code used to record the information.

  Example:

  338 $a computer disc $2 rdacarrier
  (MARC 21 fields 336–338 are discussed in chapters 2 and 5 of this publication.)

MARC 21 FIELDS 380–384

MARC 21 Field 380 (Form of Work) (Repeatable) (RDA 6.3)

"A class or genre to which a work belongs. May be used to differentiate a work from another work with the same title" (MARC 21, Field 380).

Example:

130 0 $a War of the worlds (Television program)
380 $a Television program

MARC 21 Field 381 (Other Distinguishing Characteristics of Work or Expression (Repeatable) (RDA 6.6)

"Any characteristic that is not accommodated in a special field that serves to characterize a work or expression. Examples are an issuing body, arrangement statement of music, version, or a geographic term. May be used to differentiate a work from another work with the same title" (MARC 21, Field 381).

Example:

130 0 $a Bible. $l English. $s Authorized. $f 2004
381 $a Authorized
046 $k 2004
(Attributes of an expression)

MARC 21 Field 382 (Medium of Performance) (Repeatable) (RDA 6.15)

"The instrumental, vocal, and/or other medium of performance for which a musical work was originally conceived or for which a musical expression is written or performed. May be used to differentiate a musical work or expression from another with the same title" (MARC 21, Field 382).

Example:

100 1 $a Stravinsky, Igor, $d 1882-1971.
240 10 $a Symphonie de Psaumes
383 $a mixed voices $a orchestra

MARC 21 Field 383 (Numeric Designation of a Musical Work) (Repeatable) (RDA 6.16)

"A serial number, opus number, or thematic index number assigned to a musical work by the composer, publisher, or a musicologist. May be used to differentiate a musical work from another with the same title" (MARC 21, Field 383).

MARC 21 Field 384 (Key) (Repeatable) (RDA 6.17)

"The set of pitch relationships that establishes a single pitch class as a tonal centre for a musical work or expression. May be used to differentiate a musical work or expression from another with the same title" (MARC 21, Field 384).

Example:

100 1 $a Mahler, Gustav, $d 1860-1911. $t Symphonies,
$n no. 2, $r C minor.
382 $a soprano $a alto $a mixed voices $a orchestra.
383 $a C minor.
384 $a C minor.

MARC 21 FIELD 490 SUBFIELD $x—ISSN (REPEATABLE)

- ISSN of subseries must be recorded, if it appears in the resource (RDA 2.12.16.3).
- If ISSN of both main series and subseries are present on the resource, give both.
- Optional omission: record only ISSN of subseries, and omit the ISSN of the main series.

MARC 21 FIELD 502—DISSERTATION NOTE (REPEATABLE)

- New subfields for RDA sub-elements to enhanced 502 Dissertation note (RDA 7.9). More information about MARC subfields for dissertation can be consulted from www.loc.gov/marc/bibliographic/bd502.html.

  $b Degree type
  $c Name of the granting institution
  $d Year degree granted
  $g Miscellaneous information
  $o Dissertation identifier

  Example:

  502 $b Ph.D. $c University of Louisville $d 1997.
  502 $b M.A. $c McGill University $d 1972 $g Inaugural thesis.

MARC 21 FIELDS 033 AND 518—DATE/TIME AND PLACE OF AN EVENT (RDA APPENDIX D.2.1)

"Note on the date/time and/or place of creation, capture, recording, filming, execution, or broadcast associated with an event or the finding of a naturally occurring object." Field 033 (Date/time and place of an event) contains the same information in coded form.

Generally give information in field 518, unless there is a compelling data manipulation need to use more standardized information as allowed in 033 (e.g., an ISO-standard date, a class number for place).

New subfields added to fields 033 and 518 (all are repeatable). More information about these fields can be accessed at www.loc.gov/marc/bibliographic/bd518.html.

Date/Time and Place of an Event
033 $p Place of event (controlled or uncontrolled form)
$2 Source of term (for $p only when it is from a controlled list)

Example:

033 00 $a 200008—$b 5754 $c L7 $p Abbey Road Studio 1, London $2 local.
(In $2 the source is locally assigned)

518 $d Date of event (controlled or uncontrolled form)

Subfield codes

$a Date/time and place of an event note (Not repeatable)
$d Date of event (Repeatable)
$o Other event information
$p Place of event (controlled or uncontrolled)
$0 Authorized record control number
$2 Source of term (for $p only) (Not repeatable)

Example:

518 $o Filmed on location $p Rome and Venice $d 1976 January through June.

Example of MARC 21 fields 033 and 518

518 $a Recorded April 9-10, 1975.
033 10 $a 19750409 $a 19750410.

MARC CODES AND TERMS TO REPRESENT RELATIONSHIPS

"Relationship designator is a designator that indicates the nature of the relationship between a resource and a person, family, or corporate body associated with that resource represented by an authorized access point and/or identifier" (RDA 18.5).

Name-to-Resource Relationship

In MARC 21, the relationship designator is added to fields1XX and 7XX in subfields $e or $4. The terms are selected from appendix I to express possible relationship between the resource and the person, family, and corporate bodies associated with works, expressions, manifestations, and items (MARC 21 fields 1xx and 7xx).

If the term is not in appendix I, the cataloger can assign one.

Examples:

710 2 $a Electronic Arts (Firm), $e publisher.

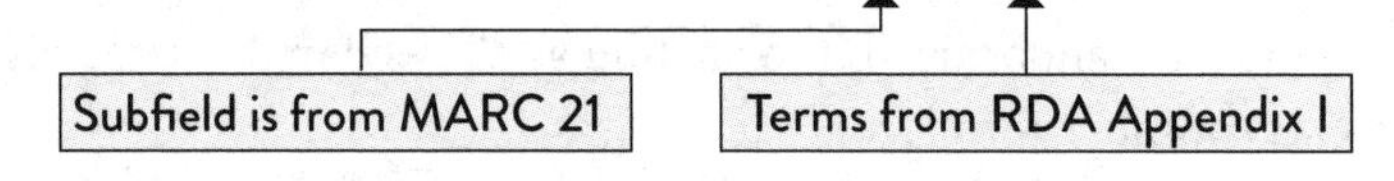

100 1 $a Winslet, Kate, $e actor.
700 1 $a Gallagher, Andrew, $d 1975- $e editor of compilation.
700 1 $a Gex, Nicolas, $e editor, $e author.
700 1 $a Arva, Aditya, $e photography.
700 1 $a Burstein, Mark, $d 1950- $e writer of added commentary.
710 2 $a Gens d'images (Society), $e sponsoring body.
710 2 $a National Museum (India), $e host institution.

$e is repeatable

700 1 $a Sacerdoti, Giorgio, $d 1943- $e editor of compilation, $e author.
710 2 $a Cincinnati Art Museum, $e curator, $e issuing body.
$4 Relator code (Repeatable)

"MARC code that specifies the relationship between a name and a work. More than one relator code may be used if the corporate name has more than one function. Take code from the *MARC Code List for Relators*. The code is given after the name portion in name/title fields."

Example:

110 2 $a J.H. Bufford & Co. $4 pop.
(Note—LC does not use relationship codes [$4])

100 1 $a Herman. Robert, $4 org.
100 1 $a Wood, Margaret, $d 1953- $e author.
245 10 $a Remembering Miss O'Keeffe: stories from Abiquiu / **$c** by Margaret Wood; photographs by Myron Wood; foreword by Miriam Sagan.
700 1 $a Wood, Myron, $e illustrator.
(In this example notice that the relationship designators "author" and "illustrator" are cataloger's judgment; second and third statements of responsibility are not core; also, it is not needed to justify recording field 700.)

Resource-to-Resource Relationship

Appendix J lists relationship terms that can be used to represent relationships between works, expressions, manifestations, and items. There are several methods that can be used to specify relationships described in MARC 21 fields 700–730 and resource described in MARC 21 fields 1xx/245 (RDA 24.5):

- Identifiers such as $o, $u, $x, $w, and $0
- Notes such as fields 5xx in bibliographic records and fields 6xx in authority records
- Structure description—MARC 21 fields 76x078x
- Structured access points—MARC 21 field 7xx in the bibliographic record and MARC 21 fields 4xx and 5xx in the authority record

Subfield "i" is used for presenting the relationship in the MARC 21 fields 7xx and 76x–78x in the bibliographic records and MARC 21 fields 4xx and 5xx in the authority record.

Whether to use an authorized access point or a description or both is the cataloger's judgment.

The following is a detailed description of each field:

MARC 21 FIELDS 700, 710, 711, AND 730 $I—(RELATIONSHIP DESIGNATION) (REPEATABLE)

Subfield "i" is newly defined to represent relationships between resources described in MARC 21 fields 7xx and resources described in MARC 21 fields 1xx/245. Appendix J (resource to resource) is used to select the appropriate term or terms.

Example:

100 1 $a Brown, Dan, $d 1964-
240 10 $a Digital fortress. $l French
245 10 $a Forteresse digitale.
700 1 $i Translation of: $a Brown, Dan, $d 1964- $t Digital fortress.
(The example is from the LC RDA documentation module 8: www.loc.gov/catdir/cpso/RDAtest/rdatraining.html.)

MARC 21 FIELDS 76X–78X SUBFIELDS $I AND $4 (RELATIONSHIP INFORMATION AND RELATIONSHIP CODE) (REPEATABLE)

Subfield "i" (relationship designators) and subfield 4 (relationship code) are newly defined to represent the relationship between resource described in MARC 21 fields 76X–78X and resource described in fields 1XX/245. Subfield "i" relationship information terms are taken from RDA Appendix J. Subfields "i" and 4 are repeatable in MARC 21 fields 76X–78X.

Example:

100 1 $a Li, Wenyuan.
245 10 $a Risk assessment of power systems : $b models, methods and applications / $c Wenyuan Li.
776 1 $i Electronic reproduction of: $z 047163168X $w (DLC) 2005295929 $w (OCoLC)56875811

Additional physical form entry

245 00 $a Archiv für Papyrusforschung und verwandte Gebiete.
246 1 $i Issues for 2010- have title: $a Archiv für Papyrus-Forschung und verwandte Gebiete
776 08 $i Online version: $t Archiv für Papyrusforschung und verwandte Gebiete $w (OCoLC) 564070198
776 08 $i Online version: $t Archiv für Papyrusforschung und verwandte Gebiete **$w** (OCoLC) 609805653

245 00 $a Analytic teaching and philosophical praxis
246 1 $a ATPP
776 08 $i Print version: $t Analytic teaching $x 0890-5118 $w (DLC)sf 93094816 $w (OCoLC)10813994
780 00 $t Analytic teaching (Online) $w (OCoLC)62460362 .

In the 780 field, the 2nd indicator 0 represents the "Continues" relationship

For more information on new MARC 21 fields that were created or adjusted to accommodate RDA implementation, see OCLC *Technical Bulletin* 258.

B. NEW MARC 21 AUTHORITY FIELDS FOR PERSON, FAMILY NAME, AND CORPORATE BODY

"Attributes of names and titles are typically information that has been recorded in name headings (e.g., date of birth) or in uniform title headings (e.g., key for music)—or they may have been included in a note in an authority record for the name or title. With RDA, they may be recorded separately from the heading or as part of the heading (or both). New fields for these attributes have been established for names and for resources (works and expressions)."

The following fields were selected from the MARC 21 standard "RDA in MARC 21." The RDA instruction for each attribute in these new fields was included. (For specific encoding information, consult the MARC 21 Format for Authority Data and the LC policy document "MARC 21 Encoding to Accommodate RDA Elements." Other examples can be found at www.loc.gov/aba/rda/pdf/Doc_G.PDF (MARC 21 RDA Authority Examples).

Note that these examples are either original or taken from MARC 21 Authority, with modification. September 29, 2010.

Chapter 6 of this book provides detailed information on person, family, and corporate body.

MARC 21 008/10 DESCRIPTIVE CATALOGING RULES

Use "z other"

MARC 21 FIELD 040 $e (REPEATABLE) DESCRIPTION CONVENTIONS

Use "rda"

MARC 21 FIELD 046 SPECIAL CODED DATES (REPEATABLE)

Dates that are associated with the entity described in the record. Date of work (RDA 6.4) and date of expression (RDA 6.10) are needed to differentiate a work from another work with the same title or from the name of a person, family, or corporate body or expression from another expression, work with the same title or from the name of a person, family, or corporate body.

Subfield codes:

- $f—Birth date (Not repeatable) (RDA 9.3.2)
- $g—Death date (Not repeatable) (RDA 9.3.3)
- $k—Beginning or single date created (Not repeatable)(date of work RDA 6.4—6.10 date of expression)

$l—Ending date created (Not repeatable) (date of work RDA 6.4—date of expression RDA 6.10)
$s—Start period (Not repeatable) (Start date for Period of activity RDA 9.3.4—Start date for Date associated with family RDA 10.4—Start date for Date associated with corporate body RDA 11.4.
$t—End period (Not repeatable) (End date for period of activity) RDA 9.3.4—End date for Date associated with family RDA 10.4—End date for Date associated with corporate body (RDA 11.4)
$u—Uniform Resource Identifier (Repeatable)
$v—Source of information (Repeatable)
$2—Source of date scheme (Not repeatable)
$6—Linkage (Not repeatable)
$8—Field link and sequence number (Repeatable)

This includes:

Date Associated with the Person (RDA 9.3) (core element)
Date Associated with the Family (RDA 10.4) (core element)
Date Associated with the Corporate Body (RDA 11.4) (core element)

Examples:

046 $f 1899 $g 1961
100 1 $a Hemingway, Ernest, $d 1899-1961
(Notice that the birth and death dates attributed to a person are recorded in 046 in addition to including them in the access point itself.)

046 $s 1977
110 2 $a Double Image (Musical group : 1977-)
(Notice that the date attribute of a corporate body is recorded in 046 in addition to including it in the access point itself.)

046 $s 1925 $t 1979
100 3 $a Pahlavi (Dynasty : 1925-1979)
(Notice that the date attribute of a family is recorded in 046 in addition to including it in the access point itself.)

046 $f 1694 $g 1778
100 1 $a St. Hiacinte, $c Mr., $d 1694-1778

For more examples, see MARC 21 Authority (MARC 21 2011).

PCC interim recommendations:

- Give subfields as applicable and if readily available.
- Use subfield $2 for certain dates.
- Source of information can be given in subfield $u, in subfield $v, or in field 670, whichever is most efficient.

Notice that the PCC Interim Recommendation can change when the actual implementation is ready. It is important to keep up-to-date with the PCC documentation and training.

MARC 21 FIELD 336—CONTENT TYPE (REPEATABLE) (RDA 6.9)

$a Content type term (Repeatable)
$b Content type code (Repeatable)
$2 Source (Not repeatable)
$3 Materials specified (Not repeatable)

Example:

110 2 $a System of a Down (Musical group). $t Hypnotize.
336 $a performed music $2 rdacontent
336 $a two-dimensional moving image $2 rdacontent
336 $a text $2 rdacontent

PCC interim recommendations:

- Apply only to NARs or SARs for expressions. Repeat field, not subfield $a, as needed.
- Give subfield $a, using term from RDA 6.9.
- If giving subfield $b instead of, or in addition to subfield $a, use the code from the code list in the MARC format.
- In subfield $2 give "rdacontent."

MARC 21 Field 370—Associated Place (Repeatable) Also see RDA Toolkit for recording these attributes:

Place of Birth (RDA 9.8)
Place of Death (RDA 9.9)
Country Associated with the Person (RDA 9.10) Place of Residence (RDA 9.11)
Place Associated with the Family (RDA 10.5)
Place Associated with the Corporate Body (RDA 11.3)
Location of conference (RDA 11.3.2)

Subfield codes:

$a—Place of birth (Not repeatable) (RDA 9.8)
$b—Place of death (Not repeatable) (RDA 9.9)
$c—Associated country (Repeatable) (place associated with the family RDA 10.5—Location of conference RDA 11.3.2—Location of headquarters RDA 11.3.3
$e—Place of residence/headquarters (Repeatable) (place associated with the family RDA 10.5—Location of conference RDA 11.3.2—Location of headquarters RDA 11.3.3

$f—Other associated place (Repeatable) (place associated with the family RDA 10.5—Location of conference RDA 11.3.2—Location of headquarters DA 11.3.3
$g—Place of origin of work (Repeatable) (RDA 6.5)
$s—Start period (Not repeatable)
$t—End period (Not repeatable)
$u—Uniform Resource Identifier (Repeatable)
$v—Source of information (Repeatable)
$0—Record control number (Repeatable)
$2—Source of term (Not repeatable)
$6—Linkage (Not repeatable)
$8—Field link and sequence number (Repeatable)

Example:

100 1 $a Singer, Isaac Bashevis, $d 1904-1991.
370 $a Radzimyn, Poland $b Surfside, Fla.
(Born in Radzimyn, Poland and died in Surfside, Fla.)

110 2 $a Republican Party (Calif.)
370 $e Calif.
(Place of residence/headquarters.)

PCC interim recommendations

- Do not give subfield $0 or subfield $2. Give other subfields, as applicable, if readily available.
- Give the RDA form of place it would have as an addition to an authorized access point.
- Source of information can be given in subfield $u, in subfield $v, or in field 670, whichever is most efficient.

MARC 21 FIELD 371—ADDRESS (REPEATABLE)

Also see RDA Toolkit for recording these attributes.

Address of the Person (RDA 9.12)
Address of the Corporate Body (RDA 11.9)

Subfield codes:

$a—Address (Repeatable)
$b—City (Not repeatable)
$c—Intermediate jurisdiction (Not repeatable)
$d—Country (Not repeatable)
$e—Postal code (Not repeatable)
$m—Electronic mail address (Repeatable)
$s—Start period (Not repeatable)
$t—End period (Not repeatable)

$u—Uniform Resource Identifier (Repeatable)
$v—Source of information (Repeatable)
$z—Public note (Repeatable)
$4—Relator code (Repeatable)
$6—Linkage (Not repeatable)
$8—Field link and sequence number (Repeatable)

Example:

100 1 $a Smith, Arthur
371 $a Box 1216 $b Barrière $d Canada $eV0E 1E0

PCC interim recommendations:

- Don't give subfield $4 or other subfields, as applicable, if readily available.
- Source of information can be given in subfield $u, in subfield $v, or in field 670, whichever is most efficient.

MARC 21 FIELD 372—FIELD OF ACTIVITY (REPEATABLE)

Also see RDA Toolkit for recording these attributes.

Field of activity of the person (RDA 9.15)
Field of activity of the corporate body (RDA 11.10)

Subfield codes:

$a—Field of activity (Repeatable)
$s—Start period (Not repeatable)
$t—End period (Not repeatable)
$u—Uniform Resource Identifier (Repeatable)
$v—Source of information (Repeatable)
$0—Record control number (Repeatable)
$2—Source of term (Not repeatable)
$6—Linkage (Not repeatable)
$8—Field link and sequence number (Repeatable)

Example:

100 1 $a Busan, Robert, $d 1963-
372 $a Music

PCC interim recommendations:

- Do not give subfield $0. Give other subfields, as applicable, if readily available.
- Capitalize the first word in subfield $a.
- Source of information can be given in subfield $u, in subfield $v, or in field 670, whichever is most efficient.

MARC 21 FIELD 373—AFFILIATION (REPEATABLE)—TO EXTEND THE FIELD TO CONTAIN NAMES OF ASSOCIATED INSTITUTIONS FOR CORPORATE BODIES AND RENAME THE FIELD ASSOCIATED INSTITUTION (UNDER DISCUSSION)

Subfield codes (see also RDA Toolkit for recording these attributes):

Affiliation (RDA 9.13)

$a—Affiliation (Repeatable)
$s—Start period (Not repeatable)
$t—End period (Not repeatable)
$u—Uniform Resource Identifier (Repeatable)
$v—Source of information (Repeatable)
$0—Record control number (Repeatable)
$2—Source of term (Not repeatable)
$6—Linkage (Not repeatable)
$8—Field link and sequence number (Repeatable)

Example:

100 1 $a Sukhomlin, N. B. $q (Nikolai Borisovich), $d 1945-2010
373 $a Independent University of Santo Domingo

PCC interim recommendations:

- Do not give subfield $0. Give other subfields, as applicable, if readily available.
- Source of information can be given in subfield $u, in subfield $v, or in field 670, whichever is most efficient.

MARC 21 FIELD 374—OCCUPATION (REPEATABLE)

Also see RDA Toolkit for recording these attributes:

Profession or Occupation of the Person (RDA 9.16)

Subfield codes:

$a—Occupation (Repeatable)
$s—Start period (Not repeatable)
$t—End period (Not repeatable)
$u—Uniform Resource Identifier (Repeatable)
v—Source of information (Repeatable)
$0—Record control number (Repeatable)
$2—Source of term (Not repeatable)
$6—Linkage (Not repeatable)
$8—Field link and sequence number (Repeatable)

Example:

100 1 $a Sukhomlin, N. B. $q (Nikolai Borisovich), $d 1945-2010
372 $a Independent University of Santo Domingo
374 $a Professor

PCC interim recommendations

- Do not give subfield $0. Give other subfields, as applicable, if readily available.
- Capitalize the first word in subfield $a.
- Source of information can be given in subfield $u, in subfield $v, or in field 670, whichever is most efficient.

MARC 21 FIELD 375—GENDER (REPEATABLE)

Also see RDA Toolkit for recording these attributes.

Gender (RDA 9.7)

Subfield codes:

$a—Gender (Repeatable)
$s—Start period (Not repeatable)
$t—End period (Not repeatable)
$u—Uniform Resource Identifier (Repeatable)
$v—Source of information (Repeatable)
$2—Source of term (Not repeatable)
$6—Linkage (Not repeatable)
$8—Field link and sequence number (Repeatable)

Example:

100 1 $a Busan, Robert, $d 1963-
372 $a Music
375 $a Male

PCC interim recommendations:

- Give subfields, as applicable, if readily available.
- Source of information can be given in subfield $u, in subfield $v, or in field 670, whichever is most efficient.

MARC 21 FIELD 376—FAMILY INFORMATION (REPEATABLE)

Also see RDA Toolkit for recording these attributes.

Type of Family (RDA 10.3) (core element)
Prominent Member of the Family (RDA 10.6) (core element)
Hereditary Title (RDA 10.7)

Subfield codes:

$a—Type of family (Repeatable)
$b—Name of prominent member (Repeatable)
$c—Hereditary title (Repeatable)
$s—Start period (Not repeatable)
$t—End period (Not repeatable)
$u—Uniform Resource Identifier (Repeatable)

$v—Source of information (Repeatable)
$0—Record control number (Repeatable)
$2—Source of term (Not repeatable)
$6—Linkage (Not repeatable)
$8—Field link and sequence number (Repeatable)

Example:

100 3 $a Nayak (Dynasty : $d 18th century : $c Madurai, India)
370 $a Madurai, India
376 $a Dynasty

PCC interim recommendations:

- Do not give subfield $0. Give other subfields, as applicable, if readily available.
- For names of prominent members, give the authorized access point form.
- Source of information can be given in subfield $u, in subfield $v, or in field 670, whichever is most efficient.

MARC 21 FIELD 377—ASSOCIATED LANGUAGE (REPEATABLE)

Also see RDA Toolkit for recording these attributes.

Language of the Person (RDA 9.14)
Language of the Corporate Body (RDA11.8)

Subfield codes:

$a—Language code (Repeatable)
$2—Source of code (Not repeatable)
$6—Linkage (Not repeatable)
$8—Field link and sequence number (Repeatable)

Example:

110 2 $a Joint Steering Committee for Development of RDA
377 $a eng

PCC Interim Recommendation:

- Give subfield $a if readily available.
- Use blank as 2nd indicator (use the MARC 21 language code list).
- Do not give subfield $2.

Figure 3.22 shows an example of an RDA authority record that includes the new MARC 21 fields. Note that Date attributes of a person (birth and death dates in this example) are recorded in field 046 in addition to including them in the access point itself. Notice that in this particular example, the month and day are added in field 049. In most cases, the special coded dates will be the same as in field 100.

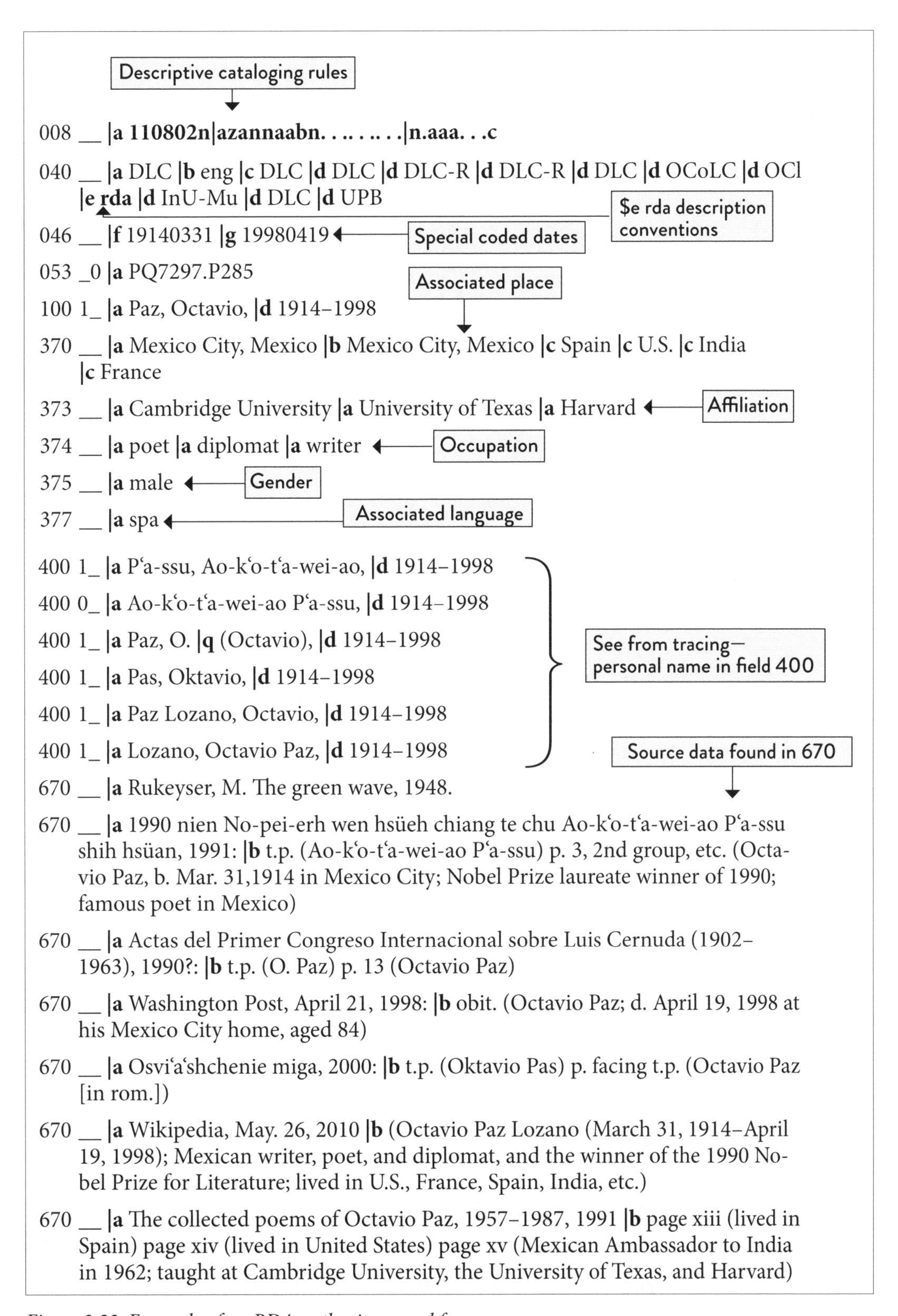

008 __ |a 110802n|azannaabn. . .. .|n.aaa. . .c

040 __ |a DLC |b eng |c DLC |d DLC |d DLC-R |d DLC-R |d DLC |d OCoLC |d OCl |e rda |d InU-Mu |d DLC |d UPB

046 __ |f 19140331 |g 19980419

053 _0 |a PQ7297.P285

100 1_ |a Paz, Octavio, |d 1914–1998

370 __ |a Mexico City, Mexico |b Mexico City, Mexico |c Spain |c U.S. |c India |c France

373 __ |a Cambridge University |a University of Texas |a Harvard

374 __ |a poet |a diplomat |a writer

375 __ |a male

377 __ |a spa

400 1_ |a P'a-ssu, Ao-k'o-t'a-wei-ao, |d 1914–1998

400 0_ |a Ao-k'o-t'a-wei-ao P'a-ssu, |d 1914–1998

400 1_ |a Paz, O. |q (Octavio), |d 1914–1998

400 1_ |a Pas, Oktavio, |d 1914–1998

400 1_ |a Paz Lozano, Octavio, |d 1914–1998

400 1_ |a Lozano, Octavio Paz, |d 1914–1998

670 __ |a Rukeyser, M. The green wave, 1948.

670 __ |a 1990 nien No-pei-erh wen hsüeh chiang te chu Ao-k'o-t'a-wei-ao P'a-ssu shih hsüan, 1991: |b t.p. (Ao-k'o-t'a-wei-ao P'a-ssu) p. 3, 2nd group, etc. (Octavio Paz, b. Mar. 31,1914 in Mexico City; Nobel Prize laureate winner of 1990; famous poet in Mexico)

670 __ |a Actas del Primer Congreso Internacional sobre Luis Cernuda (1902–1963), 1990?: |b t.p. (O. Paz) p. 13 (Octavio Paz)

670 __ |a Washington Post, April 21, 1998: |b obit. (Octavio Paz; d. April 19, 1998 at his Mexico City home, aged 84)

670 __ |a Osvi'a'shchenie miga, 2000: |b t.p. (Oktavio Pas) p. facing t.p. (Octavio Paz [in rom.])

670 __ |a Wikipedia, May. 26, 2010 |b (Octavio Paz Lozano (March 31, 1914–April 19, 1998); Mexican writer, poet, and diplomat, and the winner of the 1990 Nobel Prize for Literature; lived in U.S., France, Spain, India, etc.)

670 __ |a The collected poems of Octavio Paz, 1957–1987, 1991 |b page xiii (lived in Spain) page xiv (lived in United States) page xv (Mexican Ambassador to India in 1962; taught at Cambridge University, the University of Texas, and Harvard)

Figure 3.22: Example of an RDA authority record for person

NEW MARC 21 AUTHORITY FIELDS FOR WORK

MARC 21 Field 380—Form of Work (Repeatable)(RDA 6.3)

$a Form of work (Repeatable)
$0 Record control number (Repeatable)
$2 Source of term (Not repeatable)

Example:

130 0 $a Cinderella (Choreographic work)
380 $a Choreographic work

PCC interim recommendation:

- Do not give subfield $0. Give other subfields, as applicable, if readily available.
- Capitalize the first word in subfield $a.

MARC 21 Field 381—Other Distinguishing Characteristics of Work or Expression (Repeatable) (RDA 6.6; 6.12)

$a Other distinguishing characteristic (Repeatable)
$u Uniform Resource Locator (Repeatable)

Example:

130 0 $a Research paper (South African Law Commission)
381 $a South African Law Commission
(Attributes of a work.)

PCC interim recommendations:

- Do not give subfield $0. Give other subfields, as applicable, if readily available.
- Capitalize the first word in subfield $a.
- Source of information can be given in subfield $u, in subfield $v, or in field 670, whichever is most efficient.

MARC 21 Field 382—Medium of Performance (Repeatable) (RDA 6.15)

$a Medium of performance (Repeatable)
$0 Record control number (Repeatable)
$2 Source of term (Not repeatable)

Example:

100 1 $a Beethoven, Ludwig van, $d 1770-1827. $t Sonatas, $m piano, $n no. 14, op. 27, no. 2, $r C# minor
282 $a piano
383 $a no. 14, $b op. 27. 2
384 $a C# minor

PCC interim recommendations:

- Do not give subfield $0. Give other subfields, as applicable, if readily available.

MARC 21 Field 383—Numeric Designation of a Musical Work (Repeatable) (RDA 6.16.1.3.1; 6.16.1.3.2 ; 6.16.1.3.3)

$a Serial number (Repeatable)
$b Opus number (Repeatable)
$c Thematic index number (Repeatable)

Example:

100 1 $a Beethoven, Ludwig van, $d 1770-1827. $t Sonatas, $m piano, $n no. 14, op. 27, no. 2, $r C# minor
282 $a piano
383 $a no. 14, $b op. 27. 2

PCC interim recommendation:

- Give one or more subfields as appropriate.

MARC 21 Field 384—Key (Not Repeatable) (RDA 6.17)

$a Key

Example:

100 1 $a Beethoven, Ludwig van, $d 1770-1827. $t Sonatas, $m piano, $n no. 14, op. 27, no. 2, $r C# minor
282 $a piano
383 $a no. 14, $b op. 27. 2
384 $a C# minor

PCC interim recommendation:

- Give subfield $a if readily available, using 1st indicator of # (relationship to original unknown), 0 (original), or 1 (transposed) as appropriate.

The following example in figure 3.23 shows the new MARC 21 fields in the authority record for a Work.

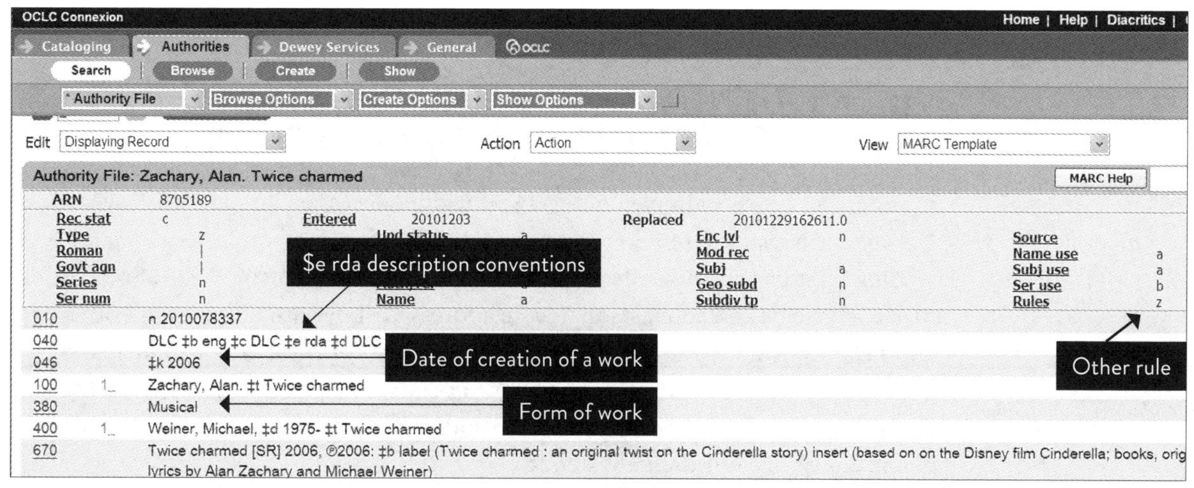

Figure 3.23: Example of using 38xs fields in RDA authority record

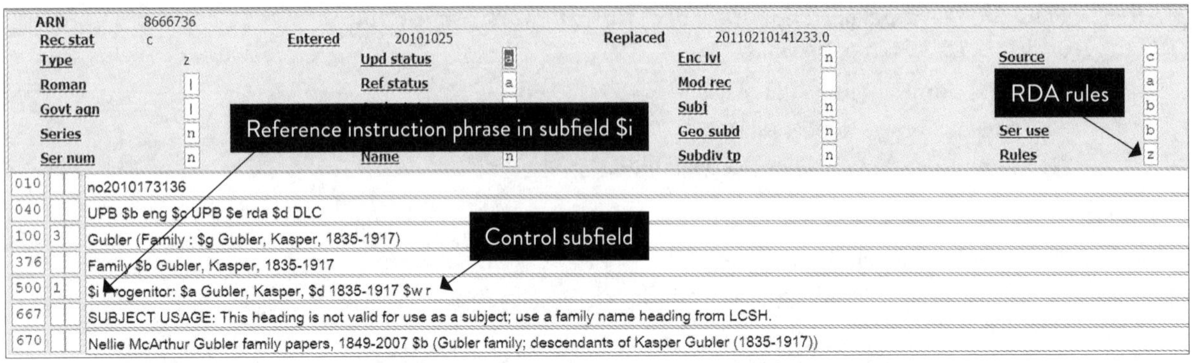

ARN 8666736
Rec stat c Entered 20101025 Replaced 20110210141233.0
Type z Upd status a Enc lvl n Source c
Roman | Ref status a Mod rec a
Govt agn | Subj n b
Series n Geo subd n Ser use b
Ser num n Name n Subdiv tp n Rules z

010 no2010173136
040 UPB $b eng $c UPB $e rda $d DLC
100 3 Gubler (Family : $g Gubler, Kasper, 1835-1917)
376 Family $b Gubler, Kasper, 1835-1917
500 1 $i Progenitor: $a Gubler, Kasper, $d 1835-1917 $w r
667 SUBJECT USAGE: This heading is not valid for use as a subject; use a family name heading from LCSH.
670 Nellie McArthur Gubler family papers, 1849-2007 $b (Gubler family; descendants of Kasper Gubler (1835-1917))

RDA rules
Reference instruction phrase in subfield $i
Control subfield

Figure 3.24: MARC 21 field 500 relationship designators

Three new subfields were added to MARC 21 fields 500–530 to represent relationships. These are:

$i Relationship information
$4 Relationship code
$w/0 Control subfield—special relationship

Guidelines to the use of these subfields can be found in "MARC 21 Encoding to Accommodate RDA Element: LC Practice for RDA Test: Original Cataloging."

Figure 3.24 shows an example of the MARC 21 field 500 relationship designators.

In this record, MARC 21 field 500 1 $i shows the relationship between a family and a person. The relationship designator is taken from RDA Appendix K.

When a tracing field contains a relationship designation in subfield $i, control subfield $w/0 contains code r (relationship designation in subfield $i or $4). Code r indicates that the generation of a tag related reference instruction phrase in a cross reference display should be suppressed. The content of subfield $i or $4 should be used to generate the reference instruction phrase that is used in a cross reference display (MARC 21, Field 500).

VIII. ADJUSTING THE ONLINE SYSTEM TO ACCOMMODATE THE NEW MARC 21 FIELDS

In order to be able to implement RDA, it will be necessary to determine what your ILS vendor is planning to do regarding RDA. This is a very important step for both loading records that are coded RDA and creating records using RDA. Some of the MARC 21 fields and subfields that were addressed above are not new, but others are and need to be added to your online system. Some of these fields/subfields can be added easily to your system by asking your IT staff to help you in the process. In some cases, it will be necessary to consult the vendor. The following suggestions will assist you in adjusting your online system.

Approach your vendor to obtain information about their plans for RDA implementation. RDA Toolkit blog (2011) provides interviews conducted with various ILS vendors. These interviews provide some indication of what the ILS vendors are planning in regard to RDA implementation.

You will need to make decisions about display and indexing of new fields in your local system. You will need to submit a "Requests for Enhancements" form to your vendor. Here are some examples of enhancements that you might need:

- MARC fixed field codes will be adapted for new content types developed by RDA and ONIX (publishing trade organization). These fields need to be updated in your online system. Integration of new content type codes into library systems will allow users to restrict searches to general or specific classes of content.
- RDA/ONIX framework is also being developed to allow publishers' metadata to be harvested to populate RDA records. This requires the vendors to integrate functionality and new content and carrier codes into the online system.
- "System vendors will have an easier time integrating RDA into their cataloguing modules, e.g., developing workflows, templates and context-sensitive help that utilize the functionality of the web-based RDA product." (Longo 2008).
- Talk to other libraries that use the same vendor and learn from their experience. Discuss your plans and your vision of "FRBRizing" the catalog and adding the new MARC 21 fields.
- Librarians in general and catalogers in particular need to research and discuss the impact that RDA will have on their practice and processes.
- Librarians, especially catalogers, need to be involved in the process by partnering with the ILS vendors in designing the new OPAC. They need to communicate to the ILS vendors their needs and requirements of the new system.
- Create a checklist to :
    - Review indexing and display configurations, for example, subfield $e in 7XX.
    - Add the new MARC 21 fields, such as 336 and 338, to accommodate the RDA core elements.
    - Make changes to validation tables.
    - Create new macros.
    - Configure import and export profiles to include new fields.
    - Test your online system to see that all the mechanisms are in place.

IX. VENDOR SERVICES AND RDA

Backstage Library Works, a professional provider of library services such as authority control processing, digitization, microfilming, cataloging, and other services, began to explore the idea of creating a crosswalk that would allow conversion of AACR2 records to RDA format or move RDA records to AACR2 format. Although this initiative is on target, there may be some cataloging issues that the vendor cannot resolve. Backstage Library Works identified a few issues that would be difficult to convert by machine without having the item in hand. For example, converting abbreviations in AACR2 records to their spelled-out form would be difficult. An abbreviation might be used on the source of information, but this can't be determined without looking at the manifestation itself. Mapping the general material designation (GMD) terms used in the AACR2 record to the new MARC 21 fields 336 and 337 would be difficult, because the terms in GMD were not used consistently (Backstage Library Works 2011).

Library Technology, Inc. (LTI), an authority control vendor, has announced their plan for the enhanced RDA options for authority control processing (Library Technology, Inc. 2011).

X. HOW TO ACCESS RDA FROM LC AND OCLC

You might be interested in looking at some RDA records in OCLC WorldCat, or in the LC catalog. Accessing RDA records in the LC catalog is easy. All you need to do is to follow these steps:

From the LC catalog home page, click on "Basic Search" (figure 3.25).
In the Search Text box, type 040e rda and click on "Expert Search" (figure 3.26).
Click on the *Begin Search* button.
To view the record, click on any title (figure 3.27).
You will be taken to the brief record display (figure 3.28).
To see the full MARC record, left click on MARC *Tags* tab (figure 3.29).
To access RDA records from OCLC:

In the OCLC Connexion Command Line Search, type in "dx:rda" and limit your search by type of materials, year, languages, etc., as is shown in the example below. You can also limit your records to only those held by your library or another library (figure 3.30).

Basic Search

Using a fill-in box, search by:

Figure 3.25: LC Catalog

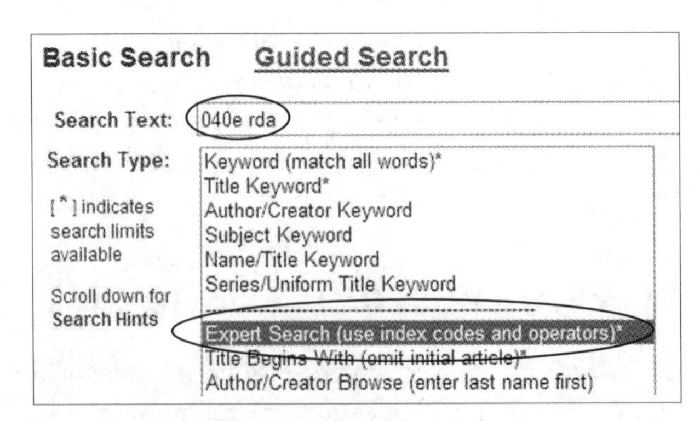

Figure 3.26: LC Basic Search Box

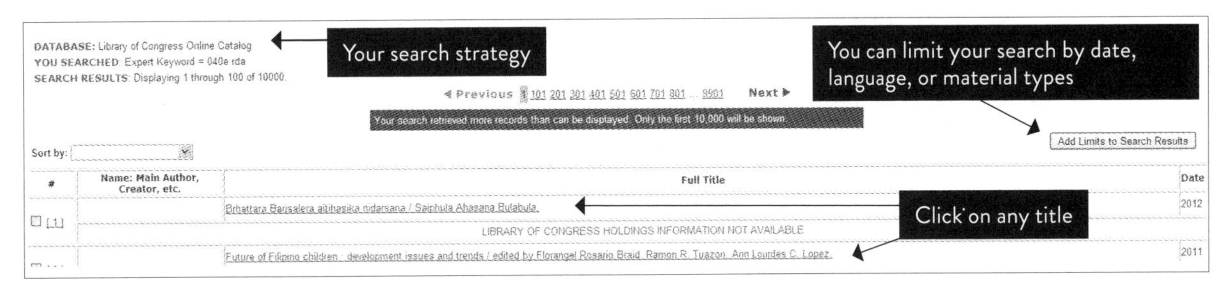

Figure 3.27: Result of searching

Brief Record | Subjects/Content | Full Record | MARC Tags

100 best resorts & retreats in India / editor-in-chief, Vinod Mehta.

LC control no.: 2010316756
LCCN permalink: http://lccn.loc.gov/2010316756
Type of material: Book (Print, Microform, Electronic, etc.)
Main title: 100 best resorts & retreats in India / editor-in-chief, Vinod Mehta.
Edition: First edition.
Published/Created: New Delhi : Outlook Publishing (India), 2009.
Description: 398 pages : illustrations, maps ; 21 cm + 1 map (57 x 44 cm folded into 19 x 11 cm)
ISBN: 8189449192

Figure 3.28: Brief display

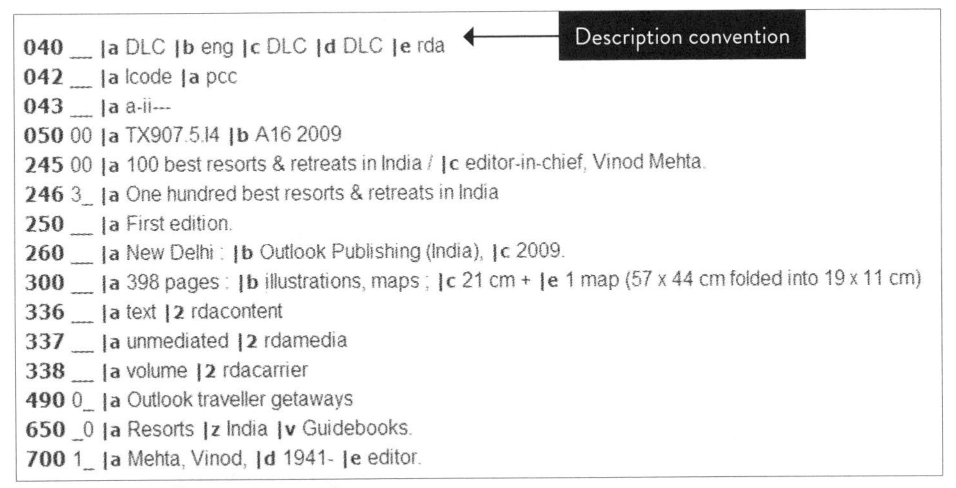

040 __ |**a** DLC |**b** eng |**c** DLC |**d** DLC |**e** rda
042 __ |**a** lcode |**a** pcc
043 __ |**a** a-ii---
050 00 |**a** TX907.5.I4 |**b** A16 2009
245 00 |**a** 100 best resorts & retreats in India / |**c** editor-in-chief, Vinod Mehta.
246 3_ |**a** One hundred best resorts & retreats in India
250 __ |**a** First edition.
260 __ |**a** New Delhi : |**b** Outlook Publishing (India), |**c** 2009.
300 __ |**a** 398 pages : |**b** illustrations, maps ; |**c** 21 cm + |**e** 1 map (57 x 44 cm folded into 19 x 11 cm)
336 __ |**a** text |**2** rdacontent
337 __ |**a** unmediated |**2** rdamedia
338 __ |**a** volume |**2** rdacarrier
490 0_ |**a** Outlook traveller getaways
650 _0 |**a** Resorts |**z** India |**v** Guidebooks.
700 1_ |**a** Mehta, Vinod, |**d** 1941- |**e** editor.

Figure 3.29: Full MARC Record

Command Line Search

Search For: dx:rda and mt:ser and yr:2011

Figure 3.30: OCLC Connexion Command Line Search

CONCLUSION

These strategies for implementing RDA are just the beginning of what is achievable. You might have more information or strategies of your own. Ideas presented here are intended to help beginning catalogers explore and learn about RDA. Finally, remember the following:

- Don't hesitate to ask questions that were asked many times before.
- Follow discussion lists and blogs for discussions and updates.
- Submit comments to the Joint Steering Committee. They welcome comments and suggestions.
- Keep in mind that most AACR2 rules do not change. This will make the training easy.
- Keep an open mind and do not panic. Remember you are not alone.

REFERENCES

American Library Association. n.d. ALA Wikis. http://wikis.ala.org/readwriteconnect/index.php/ALA_wikis.

Australian Committee on Cataloging, National Library of Australia. n.d. "Resource Description and Access (RDA) in Australia." www.nla.gov.au/acoc/resource-description-and-access-rda-in-australia.

Backstage Library Works. 2011. *RDA Crosswalk (blog).* June 20. http://ac.bslw.com/community/blog/2011/06/rda-crosswalk/#more-281.

Espley, John, and Vindo Chachra. 2010. "Insights and Processes from VTLS's 8 Years of Experiences with FRBR and RDA." Last modified June 25, 2010. www.slideshare.net/VisionaryTechnology/vtls-8-years-experience-with-frbr-rda-4755109.

Hider, Philip, and Ann Huthwaite. n.d. "The Potential Impact of RDA on OPAC Displays." Presentation. www.slideworld.org/viewslides.aspx/The-potential-impact-of-RDA-on-OPAC-displays-ppt-122562.

Joint Steering Committee for Development of RDA. 2008a. "Workflows—Book Workflow." (5JSC/RDA/Full draft/Workflows/Book; November 17, 2008). www.rda-jsc.org/docs/5rda-fulldraft-workflow-book.pdf.

———. 2008b. "Workflows—Transcription Workflow," 2008. (RDA 5JSC/RDA/Full draft/Workflows/Transcription; November 17, 2008); www.rda-jsc.org/docs/5rda-fulldraft-workflow-transcription.

———. 2007. Database Implementation Scenarios (5JSC/Editor/2 14; January 2007). www.rda-jsc.org/docs/5editor2.pdf.

Kiorgaard, Deirdre. 2009. "Resource Description and Access." National Library of Australia Staff Papers. www.nla.gov.au/openpublish/index.php/nlasp/article/viewArticle/1420.

Library of Congress. 2012. "RDA Transition: Frequently Asked Questions." www.loc.gov/aba/rda/pdf/rdaprep_faq_june21.pdf.

———. 2010a. "RDA Alternatives and Options, Proposed Practice for the RDA Test." Last modified April 26, 2010. www.loc.gov/catdir/cpso/RDAtest/RDA_alternatives.doc.

———. 2010b. "RDA Instructions Referring to Choices by 'Agency Creating the Data,'"

Proposed Practice for the RDA Test. Last modified March 22, 2010. www.loc.gov/catdir/cpso/RDAtest/RDA_agency.doc.

Library of Congress Bibliographic Control Working Group. "Testing Resource Description and Access (RDA)." www.loc.gov/bibliographic-future/rda.

Library of Congress Cataloging and Acquisitions. 2012. "2012 Resource Description and Access (RDA): Information and Resources in Preparation for RDA." www.loc.gov/aba/rda.

———. 2010. Library of Congress Documentation for the RDA Test: Frequently Asked Questions. www.loc.gov/catdir/cpso/RDAtest/rdafaq.html.

Library of Congress Program for Cooperative Cataloging. 2012a. "Importing Records for Textual Monographs: LC RDA Catalogers & Technicians Document R-4 , Rev. Oct. 26, 2011." http://tinyurl.com/LibraryofCongress2011.

———. 2012b. "CC RDA Task Groups Formed to Prepare for RDA." Last modified June 2012. www.loc.gov/aba/pcc/rda/RDA%20Task%20Groups.html.

———. 2012c. "RDA Policy and Practice Decisions Needed." http://tinyurl.com/LibraryofCongress2012.

———. 2012d. "PCC Post RDA Test Guidelines." Last modified September 12, 2012. www.loc.gov/aba/pcc/rda/PCC%20Post%20RDA%20Test%20Guidelines.html.

———. 2012e. "MARC 21 Encoding to Accommodate New RDA Elements 046 and 3XX in NARs and SARs." Last updated May 2012. http://loc.gov/aba/pcc/rda/PCC%20RDA%20guidelines/RDA%20in%20NARs-SARs_PCC.pdf.

———. 2012f. "PCC Day One for RDA Authority Records." Last updated January 13, 2012. http://tinyurl.com/LibraryofCongress2012f.

———. 2012g. "Frequently Asked Questions Program for Cooperative Cataloging and RDA." Last updated March 19, 2012. www.loc.gov/aba/pcc/rda/RDA%20FAQ.html.

———. 2011a. "RDA-Decisions-Needed Task Group." Last modified September 15, 2011. www.loc.gov/aba/pcc/rda/RDA%20Task%20groups%20and%20charges.

———. 2011b. PCC Task Group on AACR2 and RDA. 2011. "Acceptable Heading Categories: Final report." Accessed from the Index of /aba/pcc/rda/RDA Task groups and charges at www.loc.gov/aba/pcc/rda/RDA%20Task%20groups%20and%20charges.

———. 2011c. "Report of the PCC Task Group on Hybrid Bibliographic Records." www.loc.gov/catdir/pcc/Hybrid-Report-Sept-2011.pdf. www.loc.gov/aba/pcc/rda/RDA%20Task%20groups%20and%20charges/Hybrid-Report-Sept-2011.pdf.

Library Technology, Inc. 2011. RDA Options Enhanced. www.authoritycontrol.com/RDA110907.

Longo, Patricia. 2008. "Resource Description and Access: The Practical Impact of RDA." Paper presented at OLA Conference, February 2, 2008.

MARC Code List for Languages. 2007. www.loc.gov/marc/languages/langhome.html. www.oclc.org/us/en/support/documentation/worldcat/tb/258/default.htm.

MARC Code List for Relators. 2012. www.loc.gov/standards/sourcelist.

MARC Standards. 2011. "RDA in MARC." www.loc.gov/marc/RDAinMARC29.html.

MARC 21. Field 380: Form of Work (R). 2010. www.loc.gov/marc/bibliographic/concise/bd380.html.

———. Field 381: Other Distinguishing Characteristics of Work or Expression (R). www.loc.gov/marc/bibliographic/concise/bd381.html.

———. Field 382: Medium of Performance (R). www.loc.gov/marc/bibliographic/concise/bd382.html.

———. Field 383: Numeric Designation of Musical Work (R). www.loc.gov/marc/bibliographic/concise/bd383.html.

———. Field 384: Key (NR). www.loc.gov/marc/bibliographic/concise/bd384.html.

———. Field 500: See Also from Tracing—Personal Name (R). www.loc.gov/marc/authority/concise/ad500.html.

———. 2011. Authority Records Example. August 4, 2011. www.loc.gov/aba/rda/pdf/Doc_G.PDF.

———. 2010. "Encoding to Accommodate RDA Element: LC Practice for RDA Test: Original Cataloging." Training Document. Accessed September 10, 2012.

OCLC. 2011. "OCLC Policy Statement on RDA Cataloging in WorldCat for the U.S. Testing Period and Beyond." June 2011. www.oclc.org/us/en/rda/policy.htm.

———. 2012. "Incorporating RDA Practices into WorldCat: A Discussion Paper." www.oclc.org/rda/discussion.htm.

OCLC Fiction Finder. © 2010–2013 OCLC. http://fictionfinder.oclc.org.

OCLC WorldCat.org. www.worldcat.org. Accessed May 30, 2013.

Primo® System from Ex Libris. 2012. Ex Libris corporate website. www.exlibrisgroup.com/category/PrimoOverview.

RDA Toolkit. 2010– . Chicago: American Library Association; Ottawa: Canadian Library Association; London: Chartered Institute of Library and Information Professionals (CILIP). www.rdatoolkit.org/training.

RDA Toolkit Blog. 2011. "Testers Interviews." Last modified November 9, 2012. www.rdatoolkit.org/blog/285.

Tillett, Barbara. n.d. "Resource Description and Access (RDA) Webcasts." www.loc.gov/catdir/cpso/rdawebcasts.html.

Virtua. VTLS corporate website. www.vtls.com/products/virtua.

Yee, Martha. 2006. "Beyond the OPAC: Future Directions for Web-Based Catalogs." www.nla.gov.au/acoc/beyond-the-opac-future-directions-for-web-based-catalogues.

ADDITIONAL RESOURCES

In addition to the works cited in the text, the following works were consulted in writing this chapter. I am grateful to the authors of these works for making their work available to others. These are valuable resources and I hope that others will find them useful.

Cantello, Gillian, et al. 2009. "From Rules to Entities: Cataloging with RDA." Paper presented at the Preconference of the Canadian Library Association Conference, May 29, 2009. http://tsig.wikispaces.com/Pre-conference+2009+presentation+materials.

Delsey, Tom. 2009. "MARC 21, RDA, and the FRBR and FRAD Models: Making the Connections." www.rda-jsc.org/docs/td20090602.pdf.

Hart, Amy. 2010. *The RDA Primer: A Guide for the Occasional Cataloger.* Santa Barbara, CA: ABC-Clio.

Kiorgaard, Deirdre. 2008. "Resource Description and Access: Structure, Content and Development Process." https://www.nla.gov.au/openpublish/index.php/nlasp/article/viewFile/1418/1721.

Library of Congress. "Documentation for the RDA Test: Training Materials for RDA Test Participants." January 2010. Last modified December 23, 2011. www.loc.gov/catdir/cpso/RDAtest/rdatest.html.

Library of Congress Testing RDA Homepage. Contains testing information and documentation for training and cataloging with RDA Test Record Downloads. Last updated May 7, 2013.

Miksa, Shawne D. 2012a. *Introduction to Resource Description and Access: Cataloguing and Classification in the Digital Era.* London: Facet, 2012.

———. 2012b. "Preparing for Resource Description and Access." Last modified July 25, 2012. http://courses.unt.edu/smiksa/preparing_for_resource_descripti.htm.

Music Library Association. 2010. "Best Practice Guidelines for Using MARC 38X Fields in Conjunction with RDA in the Cataloging of Musical Works and Expressions: A Report to the Bibliographic Control Committee, MLA, Nov. 18, 2010." http://bcc.musiclibraryassoc.org/BCC-Historical/BCC2010/MARC38X_Best_Practice.pdf.

Oliver, Chris. 2010. *Introducing RDA: A Guide to the Basics.* Chicago: American Library Association.

Prager, George. 2010. "MARC 21 Changes for RDA," Presented at MARC and RDA: An Overview. July 12, 2010. www.aallnet.org/sis/tssis/annualmeeting/2010/handouts/g5-marcandrda-prager-handout.pdf.

Tillett, Barbara. 2012. "Examples for RDA—Compared to AACR2." www.loc.gov/acq/conser/rda_examples-rev04-15-2009.pdf.

———. 2009a. "Getting Ready for RDA: What You Need to Know." Massachusetts Library Association Conference, May 7, 2009. www.rda-jsc.org/docs/btmass-20090507.pdf.

———. 2009b. "Looking to the Future: Information Systems and Metadata."American Library Association Annual Conference, Denver, January 23, 2009.

Weber, Mary Beth, and Fay A. Austin. *Describing Electronic, Digital and Other Media Using AACR and RDA: A How-to-Do-It Manual.* London: Facet, 2011.

Welsh, Anne, and Sue Batley. 2012. *Practical Cataloguing: AACR, RDA and MARC 21.* London: Facet.

CHAPTER FOUR

FUNCTIONAL REQUIREMENTS FOR BIBLIOGRAPHIC RECORDS

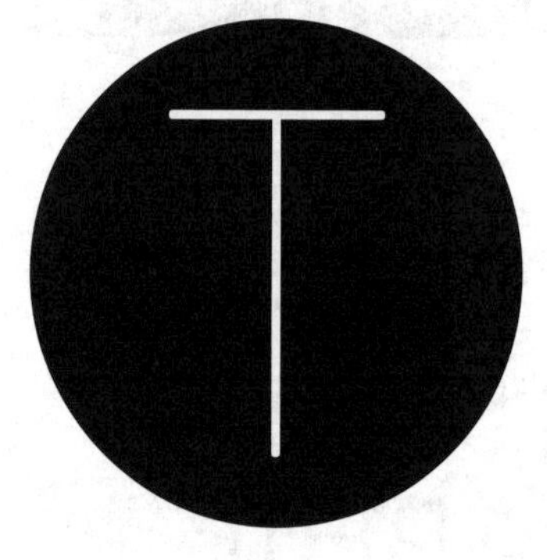

HE NEED TO IDENTIFY AND DESCRIBE THE FUNCTIONAL requirements for bibliographic records was first articulated in 1990 at the IFLA-sponsored Stockholm Seminar on Bibliographic Records. The meeting was called to address the issues and meet the challenges facing libraries at that time. The major challenge came from the increasing demands to catalog the emerging digital formats on the one hand, and the need to introduce fiscal control over cataloging, on the other. This entailed the need to scale down cataloging and introduced the concept of minimal level cataloging.

As the seminar participants worked to reconcile the two opposing trends, they developed a number of areas for future study. One of these was the idea of identifying the functions of the bibliographic record as it is applied to "various media, various applications and various user needs." Participants of the Stockholm Seminar commissioned a report which made its first appearance in draft form in 1995. After further consultation and rewriting, the Final Report on the Functional Requirements for Bibliographic Records, which came to be known by its acronym FRBR, was presented at the IFLA Meeting in Copenhagen in 1997 (Joint Steering Committee 2007).

Authors of the report endeavored to develop a conceptual model based on definitions of bibliographic entities, attributes, and the relationships among them that are related to specific user tasks. The study analyzed these entities in terms of their usefulness to the user, and further analyzed relationships among those entities as they are used to produce satisfactory search results. The user community that was considered extended beyond traditional library clients to include publishers and vendors as well as the general public. The study also incorporated a variety of traditional and new material formats, ranging from paper to digital. Final recommendations for a basic-level cataloging record were based on the analysis of the relative importance of relationships and attributes as they related to generic user tasks.

Three groups of entities have been identified and designated as key objects of bibliographic interest.

- The first group consists of what might be described as products of intellectual effort: work, expression, manifestation, and item.
- The second group consists of individual or collective entities, such as corporate bodies, that are responsible for the production of works and expressions.
- The third group of entities describes the subject of the intellectual endeavor, this being a place, an event, or an object.

I. WHAT IS FRBR?

The FRBR model represents a generalized view of the bibliographic universe. It is independent of any cataloging code or implementation. It is a conceptual model rather than an application or an implementation. It is not a data model, a metadata scheme, or a system design. but rather a conceptual model that can be used as the foundation for development of systems (Tillett 2004).

Carlyle and Fusco (2007) explained it in these terms:

> Conceptual models can model things, processes or abstractions—in other words, they can model almost anything at all. Of all of the things that a model can model, abstractions may be the most difficult. One reason is that the act of modeling, particularly the type of modeling that the creators of FRBR used, is often an attempt to make something that is abstract into something that is, at least in some senses, concrete.

The conceptual model is based on the entity-attribute-relationship model of analysis. Before we start exploring the model, some concepts need to be explained.

Entity—The bibliographic universe consists of several entities that are related to each other and can be described through data elements (or attributes). Entity can be described as a thing that can be identified in a database. In a bibliographic database, for example, an entity could be a work, an expression, a manifestation, an item, a personal name, a corporate body, an object, a concept, or a term, etc.

In a relational database, an association between two or more entities is called a relationship. In 1970, Edgar F. "Ted" Codd, an IBM programmer who worked at IBM's San Jose Research Lab in California, invented the relational database where the data could be organized according to principles based on identified relations between various kinds of data. The data item can be organized as a set of tables in which specific items in a table could be related to data located in other tables. Codd tried to reduce redundancy by accessing or reassembling data in many different ways without the need to reorganize the database tables. (Annab 2005).

In a bibliographic database, a relationship might exist between a work and a work, a work and an expression, expressions and work, manifestation and expression, manifestation and work, person and work, work and person, etc.

Attributes are characteristics that help define relationships and entities in a database. Each entity has a logically defined attribute. For example, the attribute of a work includes title of the work, date of the work, intended audience, etc. The attributes of a person might be the person's date of birth or death, the person's occupation, education, employer, political affiliation, etc. Attributes of an expression may include title of the expression, date of the expression, language of the expression, etc.

Entities that have been defined in the FRBR report represent the key objects of interest to users of bibliographic data. The entities have been divided into three groups. In this model, entities that are of interest to users of bibliographic systems are identified. Attributes that are of interest to users are identified for each entity. Relationships that form links between entities are also specified.

Figure 4.1 shows that relationships among entities can exist on a variety of levels. Relationships can exist between one entity and another or one entity and many entities, or many entities and many other entities. This example illustrates the relationship between entity 1, "Margaret Mitchell" and entity 2, "Gone with the Wind." The relationship here is an "author to title of the work" relationship.

Both the entities and the relationships may have attributes (or data elements) that identify or describe them (Tillett 2004). As illustrated in the example above, one of the attributes for the author is the "birth and death date" and one of the attributes for the title of the work is the "French translation" of the work. Each attribute and relationship is mapped to the four generic user tasks that are performed by users when they are searching and making use of national bibliographies and library catalogs (Joint Steering Committee 2007).

Find materials that correspond to the user's stated search criteria (e.g., in the context of a search for all documents on a given subject, or a search for a recording issued under a particular title). Users access bibliographic records to locate materials that correspond to their search criteria, such as a work by a particular author, family or corporate body. Searching can be limited to a specific title or can include all information sources covering a desired subject.

Identify an entity (e.g., confirming that the document described in a record corresponds to the document sought by the user, or to distinguish between two texts or recordings that have the same title). Users utilize data in bibliographic records to identify an entity and to confirm that this data in the bibliographic record is the information that is required.

Select an entity that is appropriate to the user's needs (e.g., to select a publication in a language the user understands, or to choose a version of a

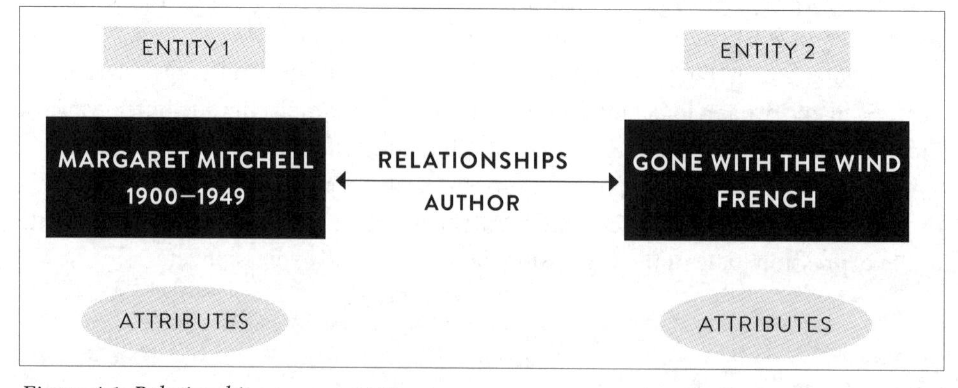

Figure 4.1: Relationships among entities

computer program that is compatible with the hardware and operating system available to the user). Users analyze the retrieved data in bibliographic records to select an entity that is appropriate to their needs. For example, select only materials that are available online, or different form, or text in different language, etc.

Obtain access to the entity described (e.g., to place a purchase order for a publication, to submit a request for the loan of a copy of a book in the library's collection, or to access online an electronic document stored on a remote computer). Users utilize the retrieved data in bibliographic records to acquire the item or obtain access to the entity described. For example, obtain the book from the shelf, ask at the reference desk, request the book from interlibrary loan, etc.

To facilitate the understanding of entities in relationship to the bibliographic record, they were divided into three groups:

GROUP 1 ENTITY

The Group 1 entity is known as the product of intellectual or artistic endeavor that is named *or described* in the bibliographic record (work, expression, manifestation, and item). These are the materials that are held by libraries.

GROUP 2 ENTITY

The Group 2 entity is known as an entity that is *responsible* for intellectual or artistic content, physical production and dissemination, or custodianship of such products (a person or a corporate body). In other words, Group 2 entities represent the people responsible for writing, editing, translating, composing, etc., of the materials in libraries.

GROUP 3 ENTITY

The Group 3 entity includes those entities in groups 1 and 2 that may serve as *subjects* of intellectual or artistic endeavors, in addition to subject entities, such as concept, object, event, and place. In other words, Group 3 entities represent subjects of the materials held by libraries.

GROUP 1

ENTITIES

The Group 1 entity represents the different aspects of user interests in the products of intellectual or artistic endeavor. This group consists of four entities: work, expression, manifestation, and item.

WORK ENTITY

According to the FRBR model, work is defined as a distinct intellectual or artistic creation. The term does not refer to any specific form of expression. Work itself is an abstract idea that does not necessarily signify a book, CD, motion picture, etc. It is rather the intellectual content that can be expressed through a variety of media that we refer to as work. Work is conceived by its author, and the manuscript, the first edition, subsequent translations, etc., are expressions of that work. Work that is defined as an entity in this model enables us to draw relationships among the various expressions of that work. Those would include the various editions of the work, its translations, illustrated edition, abridged edition, arrangements (such as music), variation or version, and simultaneous publication. Tillett looks at what she refers to as the "family of works" (figure 4.2) and draws a line between what constitutes original work, same work, and new work (Tillett 2004).

Original work—According to the family of works model, an original work can be a reproduction of the work in microforms, a copy of the work, an exact reproduction of the work, a facsimile, or reprint of the work.

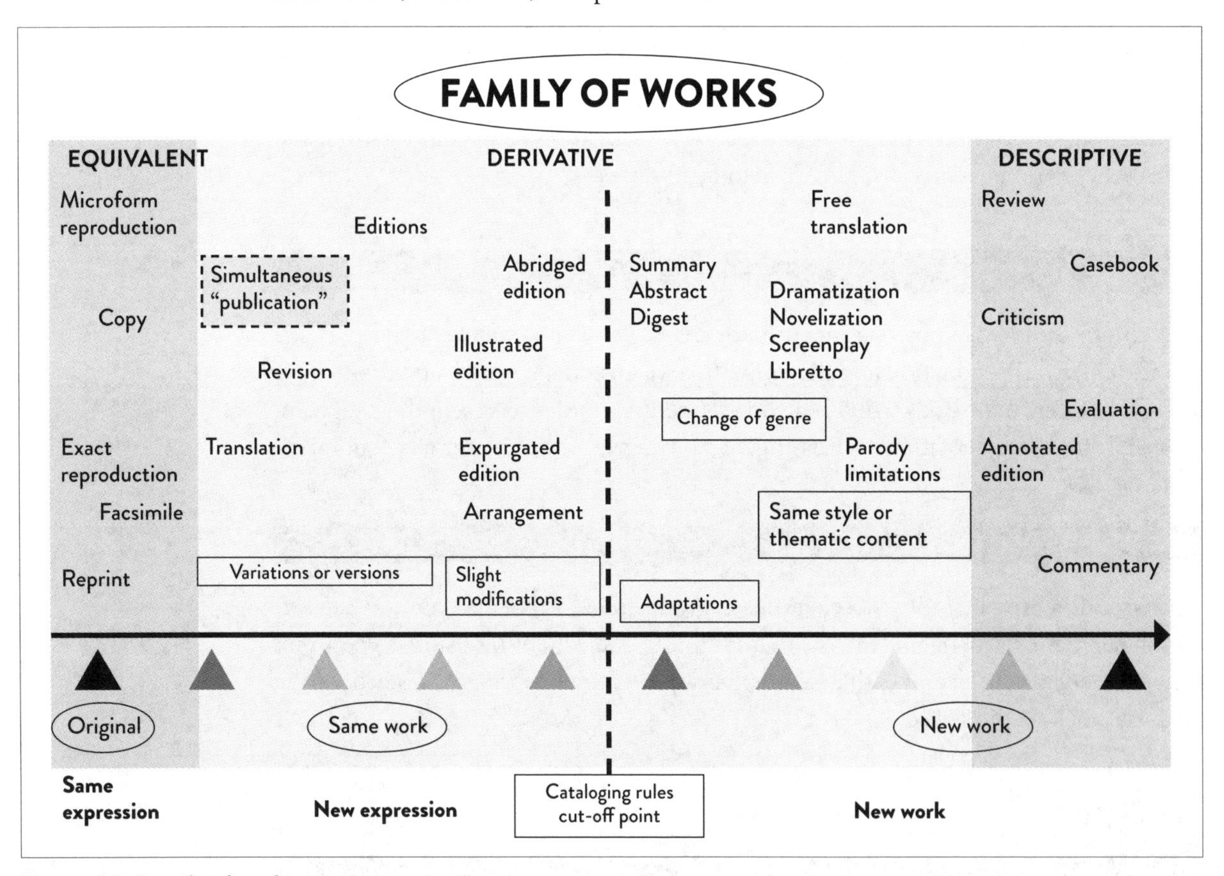

Figure 4.2: Family of works

Figure from Barbara B. Tillett, "Bibliographic Relationships," in *Relationships in the Organization of Knowledge*, edited by Carol A. Bean and Rebecca Green, Boston: Kluwer Academic Publishers, 2001.

w1 Shakespeare, William, 1564-1616. All's well that ends well.

All's well that ends well is a *microfilm reproduction*.

Same work—Same work can be presented as variant texts incorporating revisions or updates of an earlier text, abridgements or enlargements of an existing text, addition of parts or an accompaniment to a musical composition, translations from one language to another, musical transcriptions and arrangements, simultaneous publications, and dubbed or subtitled versions of a film. These are all considered different expressions of the same original work.

w1 Shakespeare, William, 1564-1616. All's well that ends well
e1 All's well that ends well; a new and complete edition
e2 the original and translation into French
e3 Shakespeare's All's well that ends well with alterations by J.P. Kemble

w1 Koyama-Richard, Brigitte. Japanese animation
e1 Animation japonaise (same work published simultaneously published in French)

New work—If the work is significantly revised, reedited, or substantially changed, it becomes a separate work that is distinct from the original work. Examples would be if a work is paraphrased, rewritten, or adapted for children; a parody; musical variations on a theme or free transcriptions of a musical composition; adaptations of a work from one literary or art form to another (e.g., dramatizations, adaptations from one medium of the graphic arts to another, etc.). Abstracts, digests, and summaries are also all considered to represent new works.

w1 Shakespeare, William, 1564-1616. All's well that ends well
w2 Shakespeare's All's well that ends well; as produced in brief at the Globe theatre, by Thomas Wood Stevens
w3 Shakespeare's All's well that ends well comedy adapted to the stage by J.P. Kemble
w4 All's well that ends well a videorecording produced by Jonathan Miller and directed by Elijah Moshinsky
w5 All's well, that ends well a new critical essays edited by Gary Waller
w6 All's well that ends well : with new dramatic criticism and an updated bibliography edited by Sylvan Barnet.
w7 All's well that ends well A Sound recording

w1 Mitchell, Margaret, 1900-1949's Gone with the wind
w2 Gone with the wind, the screenplay by Sidney Howard ; based on the novel by Margaret Mitchell ; edited and with an introduction by Herb Bridges and Terryl C. Boodman.
w3 Rhett Butler's people: an electronic resource by Donald McCaig.

EXPRESSION ENTITY

Expression is defined as the intellectual or artistic realization of a work. It can take the form of written text, such as words and sentences; musical notation; or other forms of notation appropriate to express the intellectual content of the work. A simple definition is that an expression is a version of the work. A change in the intellectual or artistic content constitutes a new expression.

w1 Mitchell, Margaret, 1900-1949's Gone with the wind
 e1 Original English text of Gone with the wind
 e2 Kaze to tomo ni sarinu, translated into Japanese by ¯Okubo Yasuo
 e3 Przeminelo z wiatrem, translated into Polish by Magda Pietrzak-Merta

Work and expression are important to identify, because they are used to collocate materials collected and organized in libraries.

MANIFESTATION ENTITY

Manifestation is defined as the physical embodiment of an expression of a work. Manifestation is the physical carrier of the expression. Manifestations include varieties of materials for the same work or expression, such as books, CD-ROMs, electronic resources, film posters, audiovisual materials, etc. This means that when production involves changes in the physical form (or format), it results in a new manifestation. A manifestation can be a single item, such as a manuscript of a novel or a tape recording of a conversation, or all the items in the entire first edition of a novel. Manifestation describes shared characteristics of a particular edition of the intellectual work, and helps to differentiate it from other manifestations of the same work. A hard cover edition of a novel is thus distinguished from its paperback edition. Descriptions of the manifestation focus attention on the result of the production process of the manifestation. Thus they are concerned more with the physical attributes of the item.

w1 Treasure Island: a novel by Robert Louis Stevenson
 e1 second edition revised
  m1 Published by Ginn and company in 1911

ITEM ENTITY

The final entity under consideration is the item, which is defined as a single exemplar of a manifestation. Item description focuses on the particular example of a manifestation and describes the differences that may exist between the item and other items that are part of the same manifestation. Usually, instances of manifestation are identical and do not require different item descriptions. If an exemplar of a manifestation undergoes changes that distinguish it from other exemplars of a manifestation, the item record serves to illustrate those differences.

In the library catalog, the item record contains sufficient information to describe the individual and unique characteristics of the item. Although we usually think of an item as a single object, there are circumstances when the item can actually consist of two or more objects. Such is the case with a multivolume set that is published together under a single title.

w1 Treasure Island: a novel by Robert Louis Stevenson
e1 second edition revised
m1 Published by Ginn and company in 1911
i1 copy is signed by C.S. Lewis

RELATIONSHIPS OPERATING AMONG GROUP 1 ENTITIES

In the FRBR conceptual model, relationships serve to show and represent the link between one entity and another. The following diagram, which was reproduced from the FRBR final report, shows the entity-relationship in Group 1 and illustrates how these entities are connected with one another (Joint Steering Committee 2007).

In figure 4.3, *work, expression, manifestation,* and *item* are entities. Relationships are indicated by the terms "is realized through," "is embodied in," and "is exemplified by." The entity *work* is realized through one or more than one expression. An expression, on the other hand, is the realization of one and only one work. An *expression* may be embodied in one or more than one manifestation. A manifestation may embody one or more than one expression. A manifestation may be exemplified by one or more than one item, but an item may exemplify one and only one manifestation.

The arrows in the diagram show how the relationship is represented among the Group 1 entities. Work can have a relation with many expressions. However, an expression is a realization of only one work. That is why the line going down from

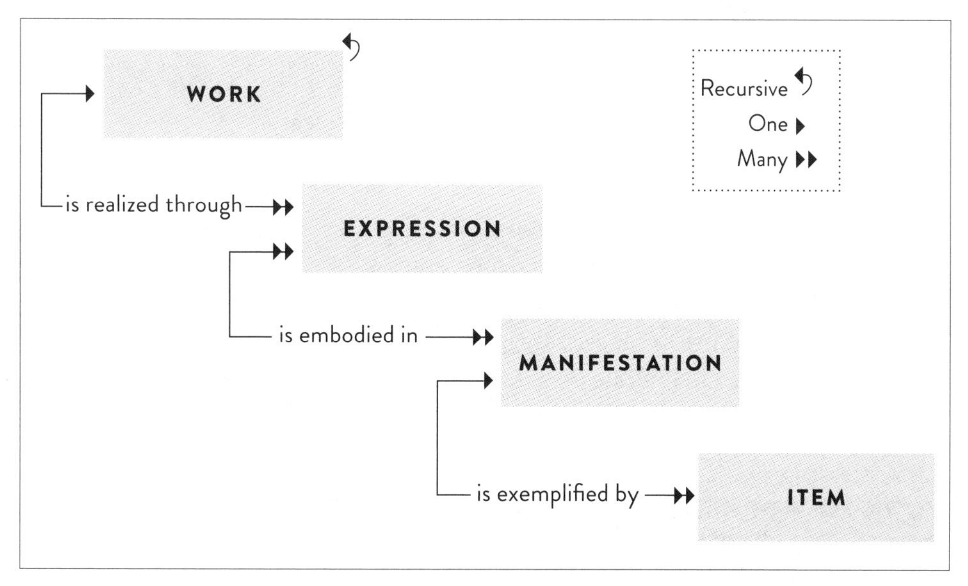

Figure 4.3: Relationships among Group 1 entities

Figure used, with minor modification, from Barbara B. Tillett, "The FRBR Model Bibliographic Relationship," a presentation given at the ALCTS Institute on Metadata and AACR2, San Jose, CA, April 4–5, 2003. http://www.loc.gov/catdir/cpso/frbreng.pdf.

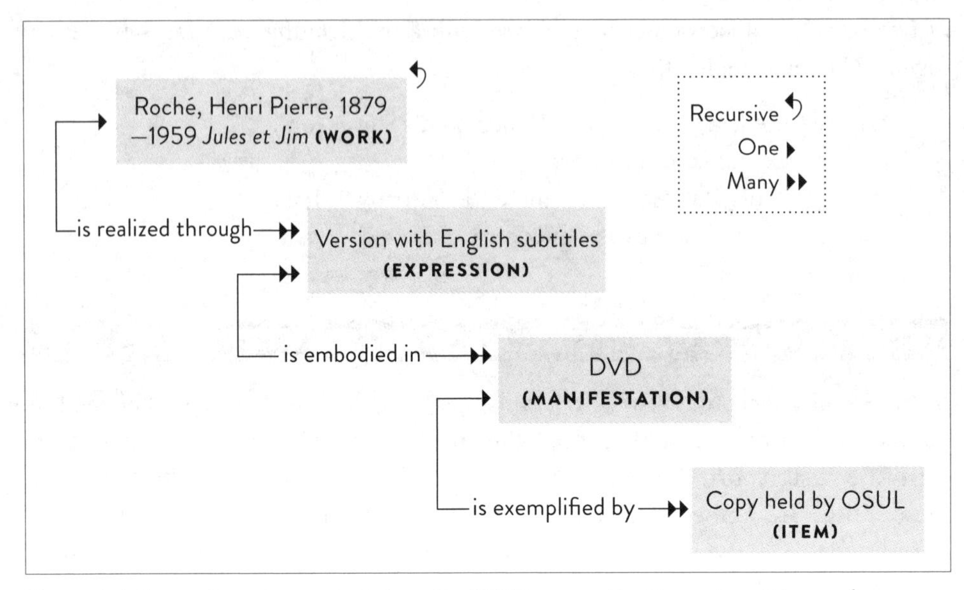

Figure 4.4: Example to demonstrate how the FRBR concept in Group 1 entities works

work to expression has a double arrow and the line going up from expression to work, has only one arrow. The double arrows connecting expression and manifestations represent multiple relationships between them. One expression can have multiple relationships with several manifestations. One manifestation can be embodied in one expression or multiple expressions.

A relationship between manifestation and item works like the relationship between work and expression. One manifestation can have a relationship with multiple items; however, multiple items can have a relationship with only one manifestation. That is why the line going down to relate manifestation to the item has a double arrow and the line going up from item to manifestation, has only one arrow.

Here is a real-life example to demonstrate how the FRBR concept in Group 1 entities works:

In this example (figure 4.4), "Jules et Jim," the original work of Henri Pierre Roche, is realized through another version of expression with English subtitles, which was embodied in a DVD as a manifestation. A copy of the manifestation is held by the OSU Library. The terms "is realized through," "is embodied in," and "is exemplified by" are all terms used to indicate the relationship between the entities in this model. The entity work is the core and the foundation of all the relationships in this model.

WORK-TO-WORK RELATIONSHIP

Many to Many: Book to Movie

w1 Treasure Island by Robert Louis Stevenson
w2 Treasure Island, *adapted* for young readers by Vincent Buranelli ; illustrated by Hieronimus Fromm

w3 Robert Louis Stevenson's Treasure Island, *adapted* by, Jan Fields ; illustrated by, Howard McWilliam
w4 Back to Treasure island, by Harold Augustine Calahan . . . with *illustrations* by L. F. Grant.
w5 Treasure Island, a *dramatization* in five acts, by Beulah Chamberlain, of Robert Louis Stevenson's novel
w6 Treasure Island. *Phonotape*

w1 Jules et Jim by Roché, Henri Pierre,1879-1959.
w2 Jules et Jim : écoupage intégral et dialogues by François Truffaut (*Adaptation and dialogue* by François Truffaut and Jean Gruault after the novel by Henri-Pierre Roche)

In the first example, the work "Treasure Island" by Robert Louis Stevenson has relationships to other works that were created on the basis of that original work. In the example, the second and the third work are adaptation of the original text—these are relationships. The fourth work is a new work from the original text, written by Harold Augustine Calahan. The fifth work is a dramatization, and the sixth work in a phonotape. All of these are related works to the original text, "Treasure Island" by Robert Louis Stevenson.

In the second example, "Jules et Jim" by Roché, Henri-Pierre, is the original work. The dialogue that was written by François Truffaut and Jean Gruault and based on the original work "Jules et Jim" is a new work.

WORK-TO-EXPRESSION RELATIONSHIPS

One to Many: Music to Different Performances, Book in Different Languages

As mentioned earlier, work is the core entity upon which all the relationships in FRBR are built. In a work-to-expression relationship, it is obvious that there is only one work (original text) that can be related to many expressions that are new versions of the original text. The two examples below illustrate the relationships of one work to many expressions.

The work "Treasure Island" by Robert Louis Stevenson is related to many expressions that are new variations of the original text. For example, there are several translations of the original text into many different languages (expressions 1, 2, and 3). There are also two other expressions of the original work that represent other forms of expression. Expression 4 is an illustrated edition and expression 5 is a complete and unabridged edition. In the second example below, there is only one expression of the original text of "Jules et Jim" and that is a translation of the work into English.

w1 Treasure Island by Robert Louis Stevenson
e1 I ha-maṭmon, tirgem me-Anglit Yiśra'el Fishman (Hebrew translation)
e2 Insvla Thesavraria, avctore Roberto Lvdovico Stevenson, latine interpretatvs est Arcadivs Avellanvs (*Latin translation*)

e3 Ṭrejāra Āilyāṇḍa (*Bengali translation*)
e4 Treasure island. *Illustrated* by Lynd Ward. General editor: Grace Hogarth
e5 Treasure Island. *Complete & unabridged*

w1 Jules et Jim by Roché, Henri Pierre,|d1879-1959
e1 Jules and Jim. *Translated* from the French by Nicholas Fry

EXPRESSION-TO-WORK RELATIONSHIP

One to One

The following example illustrates a single instance of a relationship of an expression to a related work.

e1 Treasure Island ; musical score composed and directed by Victor Young ; entire production adapted and directed by George Wells
w1 Treasure Island by Robert Louis Stevenson

EXPRESSION-TO-MANIFESTATION RELATIONSHIP

One to Many: Book to Different Publishers

Expression to manifestation relationships may involve a relationship of one expression to many manifestations. For example, one manifestation can be published by several publishers, as is illustrated in the example below.

e1 Back to Treasure island, by Harold Augustine Calahan . . . with illustrations by L. F. Grant.
m1 New York, Pocket Book, Jrs., 1951
m2 New York, The Vanguard Press , 1935

Many to One: Series, Analytics, and Collected Works

Many expressions may be related to one manifestation. The example below shows that two identical expressions were published twice by the same publisher, but in two different years.

e1 Treasure Island. The original story abridged by Johanna Johnston (1960)
e2 Treasure Island. The original story abridged by Johanna Johnston (1968)
m1 published by Doubleday, Garden City

MANIFESTATION-TO-EXPRESSION RELATIONSHIP

One to Many: Series, Analytics, and Collected Works

In the following example, two identical expressions were published by the same publisher with variation of the date. In this case, the expressions will have only one manifestation.

m1 published by Doubleday, Garden City, N.Y.
e1 Treasure Island. The original story abridged by Johanna Johnston (1960)
e2 Treasure Island. The original story abridged by Johanna Johnston (1968)

Many to One: Different Publishers

In this example, one expression was embodied in three different manifestations that were published by three different publishers.

m1 Boston, Allyn and Bacon
m1 New York, The A. S. Barnes company
m3 Boston, Educational publishing company
e1 Treasure Island. The original story abridged by Johanna Johnston.

MANIFESTATION-TO-ITEM RELATIONSHIP

One to Many: One Book to Multiple Copies

Only one manifestation may be exemplified by many items, as in the following example of one manifestation that is related to three different items.

m1 Treasure Island on 1 CD-ROM
i1 preserved in the rare book room
i2 gift copy
i3 copy 2 is not available

ITEM-TO-MANIFESTATION RELATIONSHIP

One to One

One item may relate to only one manifestation, as is illustrated in the following example.

i1 Autographed
m1 Stevenson, Robert Louis, 1850-1894. Treasure Island

OTHER RELATIONSHIPS—WORK-TO-PART RELATIONSHIP

This relationship helps to establish important connections between the work and its parts, thus establishing important links between a website, for example, and its component parts. Individual articles in a serial or a chapter in a collection of critical essays are other examples of this relationship. We can think of this relationship as that of component parts to the whole. Although the whole-to-part relationship can exist in any media or format, it is an important aspect of describing the web environment. Many websites consist of text, audio, or video materials as well as still images that need to be linked to the whole. At times, it is important to establish those links among component parts within a single resource. Thus, it is necessary to link the video clip that is part of a website with its accompanying text material,

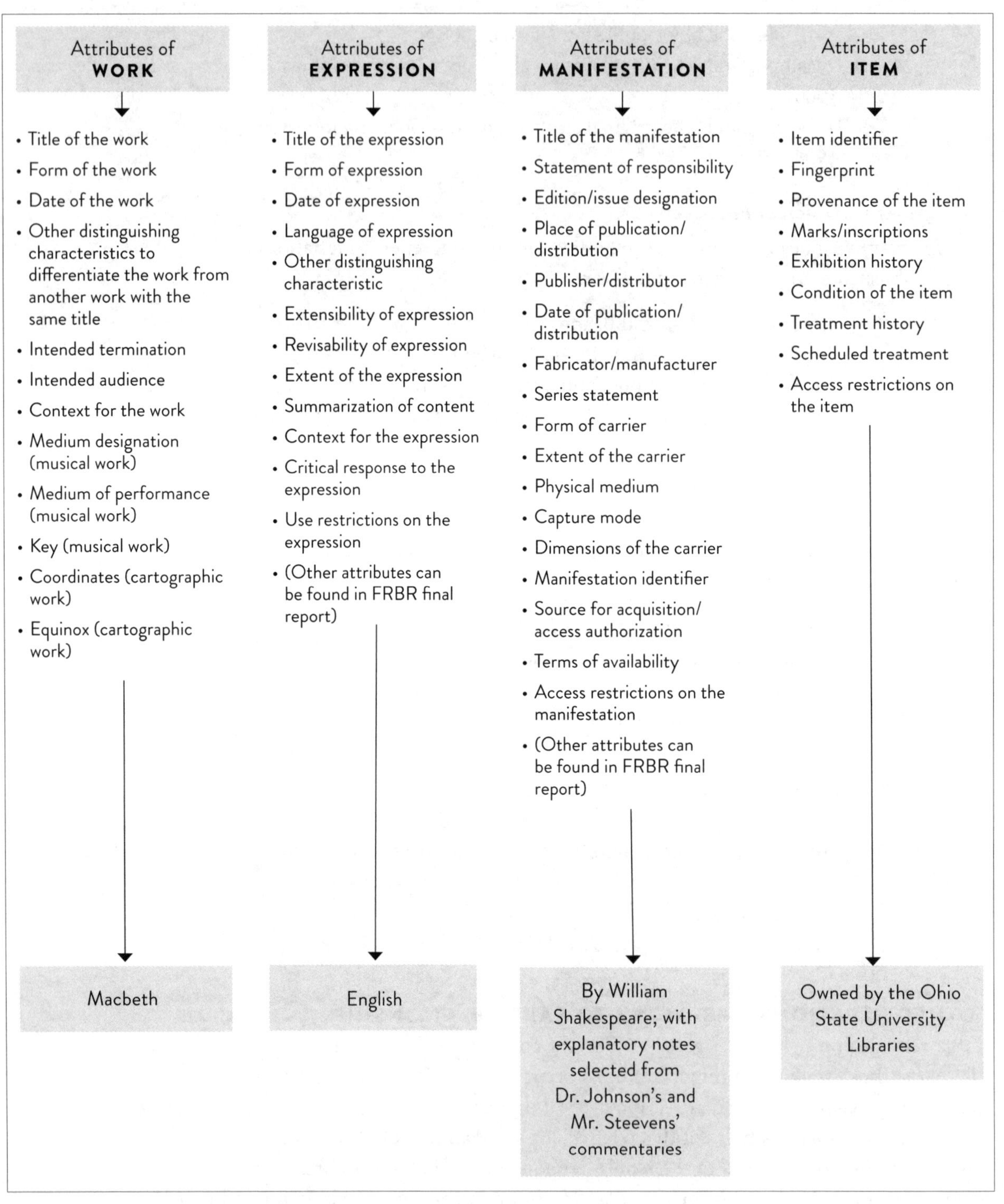

Figure 4.5: Attributes of Group 1 entities

sound recordings, and other related matter. This part-to-part relationship is established to bring together related material that constitutes elements or components of the greater whole.

Relationships among group 1 entities are identified through the examination of the item(s) when they are transcribed. For example, before the cataloging process can begin, the cataloger has to identify the type of material that is being processed. Is the work a book or a serial, is it in a digital format or in print, is it an audio file or a musical score, is it an adaptation or a new work, is it part of a work, a translation, or a new edition of the original work?

Information gathered from examining the item itself will assist in creating and establishing FRBR relationships. The cataloger's judgment will be very important in conducting this type of analysis.

ATTRIBUTES OF GROUP 1 ENTITIES

These attributes are a means of formulating queries and interpreting the responses by the user. FRBR contains detailed lists of attributes for each entity and definitions of each attribute.

The following attributes of Group 1 entities (work, expression, manifestation, and item) appeared in the FRBR report (Joint Steering Committee 2007) (see figure 4.5).

GROUP 2

ENTITIES

Group 2 entities are *responsible* for creating intellectual or artistic content, physical production and dissemination, or custodianship of products that constitute the Group 1 entities. FRBR identifies two entities in group 2; they are a person or a corporate body. FRBR defined "person" as an individual, living or deceased, who is or was involved in the creation or realization of a work. Examples of individuals are authors, composers, artists, editors, translators, directors, performers, etc. Individuals may also be the subject of a work, as is the case with the person who is the subject of a biographical or an autobiographical work.

"Corporate body" is defined as an organization or group of individuals and/or organizations acting as a unit. Examples of a corporate body include "occasional groups and groups that are constituted as meetings, conferences, congresses, expeditions, exhibitions, festivals, fairs, etc. The entity also encompasses organizations that act as territorial authorities, exercising or claiming to exercise government functions over a certain territory, such as a federation, a state, a region, a local municipality, etc. The entity encompasses organizations and groups that are defunct as well as those that continue to operate" (Joint Steering Committee 2007).

A person or a corporate body is an FRBR entity only if it is involved in the creation or realization of a work, or is the subject of a work.

RELATIONSHIPS OPERATING BETWEEN GROUP 2 AND GROUP 1 ENTITIES

There are four relationship types that provide links between Group 1 entities and Group 2 entities. These are:

- "Created by" relationships that link person and corporate body to a work
- "Realized by" relationships that link person and corporate body to expression
- "Produced by" relationships that link person and corporate body to manifestation
- "Owned by" relationships that link person and corporate body to the item

Figure 4.6 illustrates the relationship between Group 1 entities (work, expression, manifestation, and item) with Group 2 entities (person and corporate body). For example, a person creates work, person translates work, person edits work, corporate body creates work, work continues another work that has ceased, etc.

In figure 4.6, the work "The Amber Warning" is created by "Robert Ludlum." This is a relationship between work and a person.

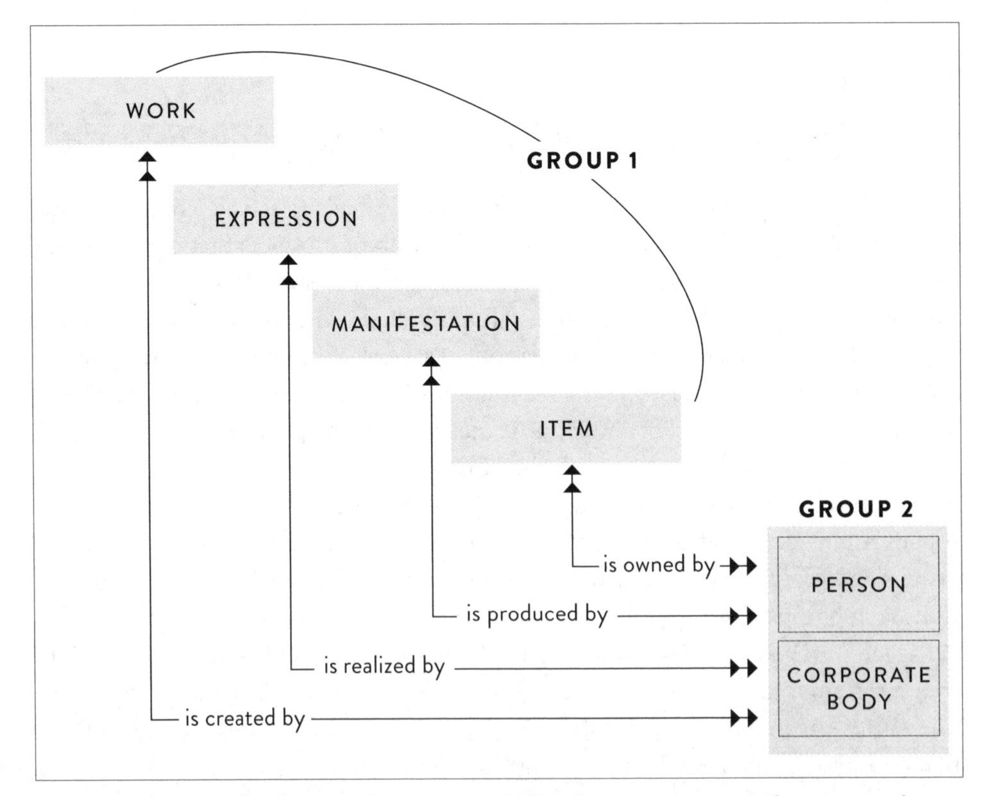

Figure 4.6: Relationship between Group 1 entities (work, expression, manifestation, and item) and Group 2 entities (person and corporate body)

Example of work that is created by person or corporate body:

p1 Ludlum, Robert, 1927-2001
 w1 The Amber warning
 w2 The apocalypses watch
 w3 The Aquitaine progression

cb1 American Library Association
 w1 A.L.A. membership directory
 w2 American Library Association policies
 w3 Annual report

The expression can also be *realized by* linking a person or corporate body to an expression.

cb1 Warsaw Philharmonic
 e1 the 2000 recording of Richard Strauss's Alpine Symphony
 e2 the 2011 recording of Karol Szymanowski's Symphonies
 e3 the 2001 recording of A. Panufnik's Sinfonia Sacra

A relationship can occur when a person or a corporate body are responsible for publishing, distributing, fabricating, or manufacturing the manifestation. The relationship is presented by *produced by*:

cb1 Scholastic Inc.
 m1 the 2008 publication by Scholastic Inc. of Jacqueline B. Glasthal's Five minute daily practice test taking.
 m2 the 2009 publication by Scholastic, Inc. of Pamela Chanko's 25 fun phonics plays for beginning readers
 m3 the 1984 publication by Scholastic Inc. of Patricia Conniffe's Activity book for the Bank Street writer : teacher's guide.

The copy can also be *owned by* a person and a corporate body:

cb1 Case Western Reserve University Library
 i1 a copy of the Louvain lectures (Lectiones Lovanienses) of Bellarmine and the autograph copy of his 1616 declaration to Galileo. Texts in the original Latin (Italian) with English translation, introduction, commentary and notes

ATTRIBUTES OF GROUP 2 ENTITIES

The attributes of a person and a corporate body can be described as follows (figure 4.7): (Joint Steering Committee 2007).

Attributes of **PERSON**	Attributes of **CORPORATE BODY**
• Name of person • Dates of person • Title of person • Other designation associated with the person such as III, Jr., and Professional Engineer, etc.	• Name of the corporate body • Number associated with the corporate body • Place associated with the corporate body • Date associated with the corporate body • Other designation associated with the corporate body such as Inc., Ltd., etc.

Figure 4.7: Attributes of Group 2 entities

GROUP 3

ENTITIES

Group 3 entities include those entities in groups 1 and 2 that may serve as *subjects* of intellectual or artistic endeavor in addition to the subject entities such as concept, object, event, and place.

CONCEPT

Concept is an abstract or general idea inferred or derived from specific instances. The concept of "Arab Spring" (a term that signifies the revolutionary movement sweeping through North Africa and the Middle East) for example, is derived from specific instances, such as the revolts in Tunisia and Egypt in 2011. Concept can be broad in nature or narrowly defined and precise:

- Arab Spring 2011
- Economy
- Biology

OBJECT

FRBR defines "object as a material thing, including animate and inanimate objects occurring in nature; fixed, movable, and moving objects that are products of human creation; objects that no longer exist." Examples of objects include:

- Granite
- The pyramids of Egypt
- Great wall of China

EVENT

Event is an action or occurrence. Historical event, epoch, period of time are examples of an event:

- American Civil War
- Olympic Games
- World War II

PLACE

FRBR defines a place as a location. Terrestrial and extraterrestrial; historical and contemporary; geographic features and geopolitical jurisdictions are examples of place:

- Egypt
- Paris
- Appalachian Mountains

Note that "a concept, an object, an event, or a place" is treated as an FRBR entity only if it is the subject of a work.

RELATIONSHIPS OPERATING BETWEEN GROUP 1, 2, AND 3 ENTITIES

Figure 4.8 shows that Group 3 entities may have relationships with Group 1 and 2 entities. The diagram (which was used with modification from Tillett 2004) illustrates the concept of the relationship among the three groups. The double arrow indicates that the relationship may be one to one, one to many, or many to one.

The subject of the work may be a concept, an object, an event or place, a person or corporate body, an expression, a manifestation, or an item. For example:

c1 Schools—Fiction
  w1 *Harry Potter and the Goblet of Fire*

p1 Harry Potter—Fictional character
  w1 Harry Potter and the Goblet of Fire

In the first example, "School—Fiction" is a subject concept (Group 3) for *Harry Potter and the Goblet of Fire*; however, in the second example, a subject person name (Group 2) expresses the subject content of "Harry Potter—Fictional character."

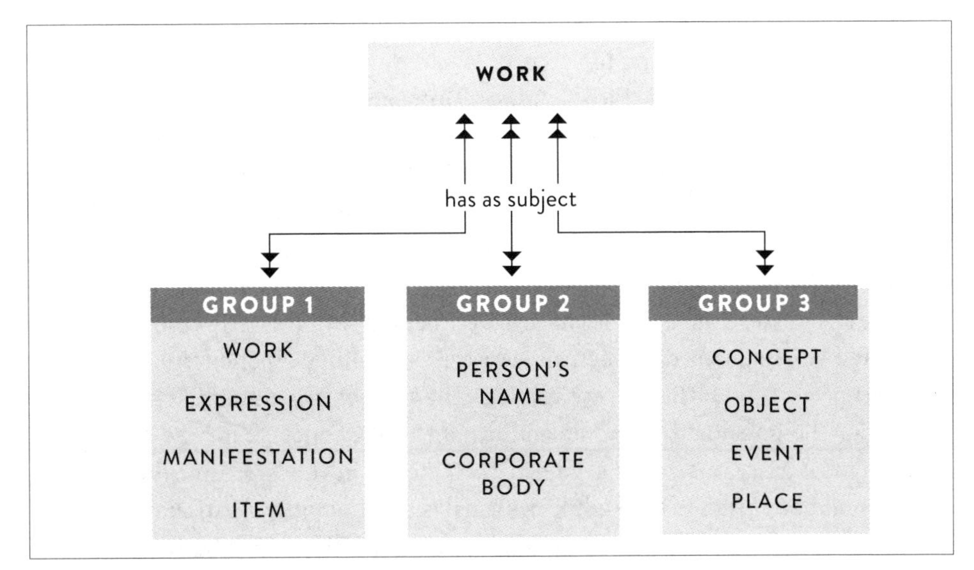

Figure 4.8: Relationships between Group 1, 2, and 3 entities

ATTRIBUTES OF GROUP 3 ENTITIES

Attributes of Group 3 entities are relatively simple. The diagram below (figure 4.9) illustrates the attributes of concept, object, event, and place. For example, the attribute of a concept may be a term, such as "geology," "modernism," and "cubism." Object attributes may be a term such as "vase," "statue," and "building." An attribute of an event could be "Civil War," "Discovery of America," "landing on the moon." Examples of attributes for place are "Egypt," "New York," "Street," "Paris."

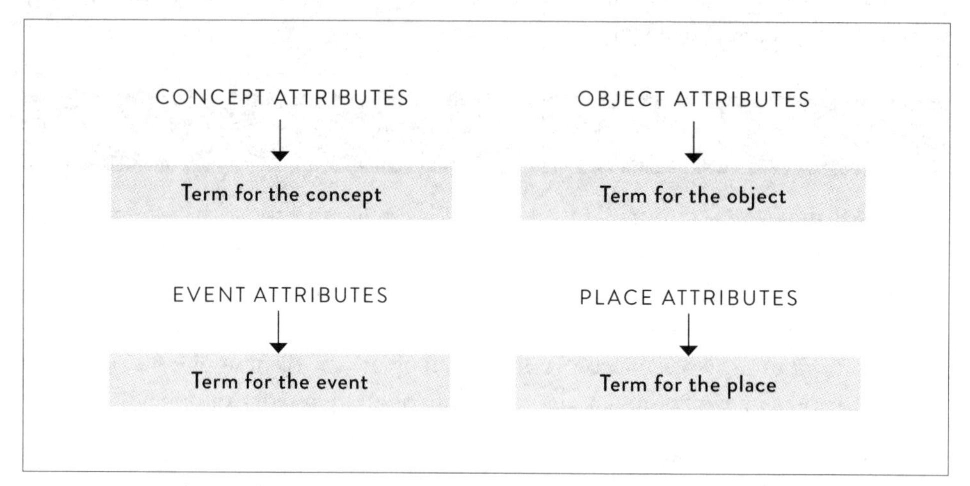

Figure 4.9: Attributes of Group 3 entities

II. HOW THE FRBR MODEL AFFECTS THE CATALOGING DISPLAY

The FRBR concept was developed with the end user in mind. Applying FRBR in the organization of information facilitates a more effective use of data elements that are recorded in the bibliographic record. When designing RDA, the Joint Steering Committee incorporated the FRBR entities. This will have two benefits: (1) the FRBR concept will provide catalogers with better ways of identifying particular entities; (2) a more effective organization of information in the catalog will facilitate the searching experience for the user (Carlyle and Fusco 2007). When looking at RDA Toolkit designs, you will see the alignment of the RDA chapters with FRBR concepts. Figure 4.10 shows this alignment:

Since its release, many libraries have experimented with the FRBR model. Rajapatirana and Missingham described the Australian National Bibliographic Database (ANBD) project to "FRBRize" the catalog. The project was undertaken in 2003 to investigate the potential to support and exploit FRBR concepts for the ANBD. The scope of the inquiry was analysis of records on the ANBD to determine those records which would be clustered through FRBR; analysis of a popular Australian work; and consideration of issues relevant to the application of FRBR to the ANBD. In this proj-

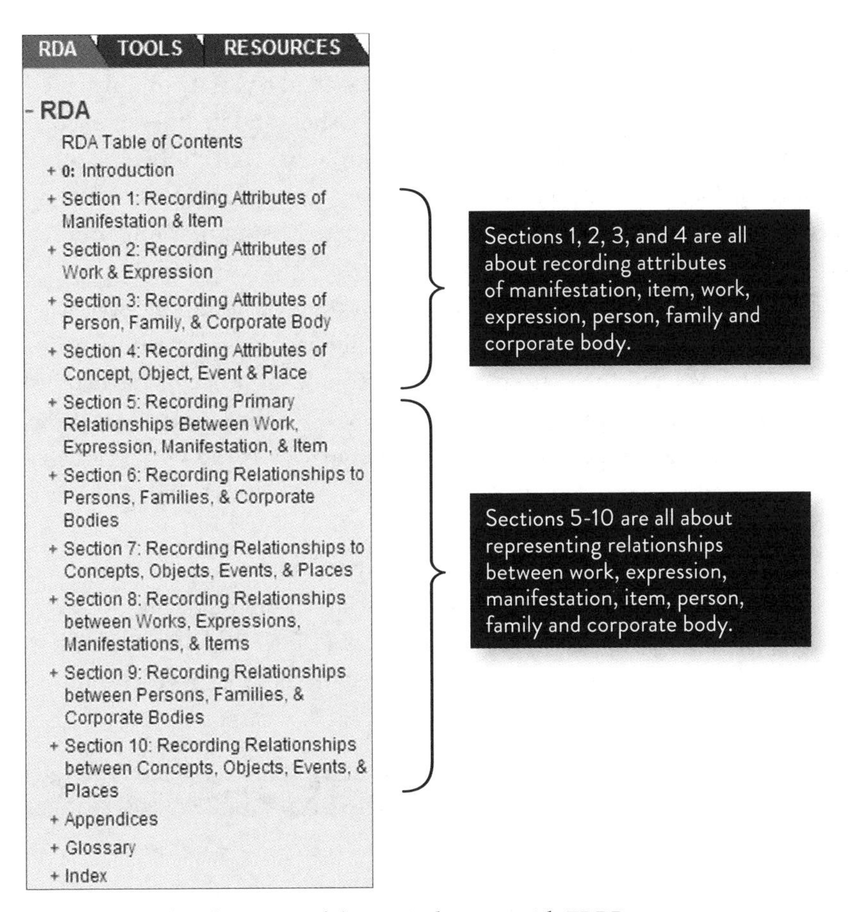

Figure 4.10: The alignment of the RDA chapters with FRBR concepts

ect the Library of Congress (LC) FRBR Display Tool was used in conducting these tests (Rajapatairana and Missingham 2005).

As the understanding of the FRBR model grows, information specialists are encouraged to explore, experiment, and develop prototype applications to FRBRize their catalogs. FRBR has been implemented in libraries, digital libraries, museums, archives, and the Internet. Applications of the FRBR concept developed by the VTLS Virtual system, OCLC's WorldCat, and Denmark's VisualCat have demonstrated how users can benefit from a well-structured system designed around FRBR's entities. OCLC has created a set of algorithms that can be used to "FRBRize" the catalog, and the Library of Congress created a FRBR Display Tool that transforms bibliographic data found in MARC record files into a meaningful display that matches, sorts, and arranges data into work, expression, and manifestation for displays. This tool is free and available from the Library of Congress website (FRBR Display Tool, Version 4.0).

In their article, "From a Conceptual Model to Application and System Development," Salaba and Zhang present a list of FRBR applications that took place prior to 2007 and provide an outline of the current FRBR implementation efforts for various purposes and categories. They also point out that the FRBR model will not benefit all library collections. They categorize the collections that will benefit from the model and identify them as those that consist of works expressed in a variety of ways, such as those published in different editions by different publishers and in different media. This category includes fictional works, music collections, serial collections, and other aggregate works. Salaba and Zhang also provide an overview of applications relating to types of collections and a brief description of predicted issues that might occur when applying the model (Salaba and Zhang 2007).

Until now, traditional cataloging has been done on the manifestation level, with primary focus on describing the "item in hand." Most library catalogs include entries at the manifestation level and the concept of collocation of the work or the expression is not the focus or the structure of either the library online system or of the cataloging rules. As the cataloging paradigm shift takes place and the FRBR model is introduced on a universal level, cataloging will be based on the work entity. This is a significant shift in focus.

The example below shows how the FRBR display represents relationships between work, expression, manifestation, and item (Example: Harry Potter and the Goblet of Fire, FRBR Blog). In this example, we will use the work of J. K. Rowling, the author of the Harry Potter books. Her works may be collocated on the work level as follows:

COLLOCATION BY WORKS

J. K. Rowling (creator of the following works)

Clicking on the icon in front of each work opens the second level of the cluster to show the expression(s) of each of this work:

- The Tales of Beadle the Bard, Standard Edition [Hardcover] (work)
- Fantastic Beasts and Where to Find Them [Paperback] (work)
- Harry Potter and the Philosopher's Stone (work)
- Harry Potter and the Chamber of Secrets (work)
- Harry Potter and Prisoner of Azkaban (work)
- Harry Potter and the Goblet of Fire (work)
- A Parent's Guide to Harry Potter by Gina Burkart (work)
- Fantastic Beasts and Where to Find Them, by Newt Scamander (work)

COLLOCATION BY EXPRESSIONS

This example will use the book *Harry Potter and the Goblet of Fire,* and find other expressions of the original text.

Clicking the icon in front of "Harry Potter and the Goblet of Fire," will display the expression(s) that belong to this work. In the example below, there are five expressions under this work: the original text, translations, videorecordings, audiobooks, and sound recordings.

Harry Potter and the Goblet of Fire (work)
+ Text
+ Translations
+ Videorecording
+ Audiobook
+ Sound recording

COLLOCATION OF MANIFESTATIONS

Clicking the + sign in front of each expression will display the manifestation(s) that are related to individual expression as illustrated below. Clicking on the + in front of each manifestation will display the item(s).

Harry Potter and the Goblet of Fire (work)
+ Text (expression)
+2000—Bloomsbury (UK) hardcover (manifestation)
+2000—Arthur A. Levine Books (US) (manifestation)
+2002—Scholastic (US) paperback (manifestation)
+2000—Thorndike (US)(large print) (manifestation)
+ in the special collection room (item)
+ Translations (expression)
+ Text—Japanese (expression)
+ 2001—Tankobon Hardcover (manifestation)
+ Under maintenance (item)
+ Text—Spanish (expression)
+ 2001—Barcelona, Salamandra (manifestation)
+ autographed by the original author (item)
+ Text—Korean (expression)
+ 2000—Soul, Munhak Such'op (manifestation)
+ Text—Chinese (expression)
+ 2001—Taibei shi,Huang guan wen hua chu ban you xian gong si (manifestation)
+ Videorecording (expression)
+ 2005—Neutral Bay, N.S.W, Distributed by Warner Home Video (manifestation)
+ 2006—Burbank, CA, Warner Home Video (manifestation)
+ Audiobook (expression)
+ 2005—Electronic Arts and Warner Bros. Interactive Entertainment: 2 CD-ROMs (manifestation)
+ 2000—Listening Library: 17 CDs (manifestation)

This example illustrates how the FRBR model enables the user to collocate and cluster the search result. It will be easy for the user to find, identify, select, and obtain what is needed. Displaying clustering data will allow the users to choose and make their own selections. For example, some users will accept alternative formats; others may search for a specific format, language, edition, or even a specific copy. Collocating nonidentical manifestations would bring together, for example, a Video Home System (VHS) and a DVD with the same content, regardless of the carrier of the data. Collocating expressions would bring translations together with the original. Collocating works would bring together related works, such as adaptations of a work into a play, movie, or a musical performance.

CONCLUSION

The FRBR model describes the bibliographic universe that libraries organize and control through the cataloging codes. It is based on a detailed analysis of bibliographic data and maps out relationships between entities and attributes that are relevant to the four user tasks (Joint Steering Committee 2008). It is designed to help users easily navigate the catalog and locate required materials.

Incorporating the FRBR concept into the RDA cataloging instructions will reduce duplication and simplify the cataloging process by allowing the cataloger to make use of existing data. The RDA instructions are based on the FRBR concept and are organized by the elements in the FRBR model. Sections 1 through 4 of RDA cover the elements corresponding to the attributes that were defined in FRBR; sections 5 through10 cover the elements corresponding to the relationships defined in FRBR. For a better understanding of RDA, catalogers should become more familiar with FRBR. This chapter provided a simplified overview of the conceptual model and it is a good starting point for catalogers who are looking for quick information on FRBR.

REFERENCES

Annab, Michael. 2005. “E. F. Codd (Edgar F. ‘Ted’ Codd).” *Search Oracle*. http://searchoracle.techtarget.com/definition/E-F-Codd.

Carlyle, Allyson, and Lisa M. Fusco. 2007. “Understanding FRBR as a Conceptual Model: FRBR and the Bibliographic Universe.” *Bulletin of the American Society for Information Science and Technology*. 33 (6): 264–73. www.asis.org/Bulletin/Aug-07/carlyle_fusco.html.

“Example: Harry Potter and the Goblet of Fire.” *FRBR Blog*. www.frbr.org/eg/hp-goblet-1.html.

Joint Steering Committee for the Development of RDA. (2008). “FRBR to RDA mapping.” www.rda-jsc.org/docs/5rda-frbrrdamapping.pdf.

———. (2007). “Functional Requirements for Bibliographic Records: Final Report.” Last modified December 26, 2007. www.ifla.org/VII/s13/frbr/frbr_current2.htm.

Library of Congress. 2009. "FRBR Display Tool. Version 2.0." Library of Congress Network Development and MARC Standards Office. www.loc.gov/marc/marc-functional-analysis/tool.html.

Rajapatirana, Bemal, and Roxanne Missingham. 2005. "The Australian National Bibliographic Database and the Functional Requirements for the Bibliographic Database (FRBR)." *Australian Library Journal* 54. http://alia.org.au/publishing/alj/54.1/full.text/rajapatirana.missingham.html.

Tillett, Barbara B. 2004. "What Is FRBR? A Conceptual Model for the Bibliographic Universe." Library of Congress Cataloging Distribution Service. www.loc.gov/cds/downloads/FRBR.PDF.

Salaba, Athena, and Yin Zhang. 2007. "From a Conceptual Model to Application and System Development." *Bulletin of the American Society for Information Science and Technology* 33 (6): 17–23. www.asis.org/Bulletin/Aug-07/salaba_zhang.html.

ADDITIONAL RESOURCES

Other reference that were consulted for this chapter include:

Aalberg, Trond. 2006. "A Process and Tool for the Conversion of MARC Records to a Normalized FRBR Implementation." Proceedings of the 9th International Conference on Asian Digital Libraries, 283–92.

Bennett, Rick, Brian F. Lavoie, and Edward T. O'Neill. 2003. "The Concept of a Work in WorldCat: An Application of FRBR." *Library Collections, Acquisitions, and Technical Services* 27.1 (Spring). www.oclc.org/research/publications/archive/2003/lavoie_frbr.pdf.

Denton, William. 2007. "FRBR and the History of Cataloging." In *Understanding FRBR: What It Is and How It Will Affect Our Retrieval?* Edited by Arlene G. Taylor. Westport, CT: Libraries Unlimited.

Dickey, Timothy J. 2008. "FRBRization of a Library Catalog: Better Collocation of Records, Leading to Enhanced Search, Retrieval, and Display." *Information Technology and Libraries* 27 (1).

Hickey, Thomas B., Edward T. O'Neill, and Jenny Toves. 2002. "Experiments with IFLA Functional Requirements for Bibliographic Records (FRBR)." *D-Lib Magazine* 8 (2). www.dlib.org/dlib/september02/hickey/09hickey.html.

McCallum, Sally. 2005. "The FRBR Tool of the Library of Congress." Paper presented at Bibliotheca Universalis: How to Organize Chaos? Satellite Meeting to the 71st World Library and Information Congress, Järvenpää, Finland, August 11–12, 2005. www.fla.fi/frbr05/McCallumHelsinki_frbrtool.pdf.

O'Neill, Edward. 2002. "FRBR: Application of the Entity-Relationship Model to Humphry Clinker." Paper presented at the ALCTS / CCS/ Cataloging and Classification Research Discussion Group, June 15, 2002. Notes taken by Judith Hopkins. www.acsu.buffalo.edu/~ulcjh/FRBRoneill.html.

Riva, Pat. 2007. "Introducing the Functional Requirements for Bibliographic Records and Related IFLA Developments." *Bulletin of the American Society for Information Science and Technology* 33 (6): 7–11. www.asis.org/Bulletin/Aug-07/riva.html.

Schneider, Jodi. 2008. "FRBRizing MARC Records with the FRBR Display Tool." http://jodischneider.com/pubs/2008may_frbr.html.

CHAPTER FIVE

IDENTIFYING MANIFESTATIONS AND ITEMS

ANIFESTATION IS DEFINED IN RDA AS A "PHYSICAL embodiment of an expression" while item is defined as a "single exemplar of a manifestation." RDA provides core elements that are fundamental for identification of resources. The list of elements reflects the attributes of the entities work, expression, and manifestation designated in FRBR as basic requirements for the purposes of identifying those entities.

The following chapters of RDA provide guidelines and instructions for a comprehensive set of elements used to describe all types of library resources:

- Chapter 1 of RDA, "General Guidelines on Recording Attributes of Manifestations and Items," provides guidelines for making the initial determination about what is being cataloged and what changes will be required for a new description, as well as general instructions on transcription.
- Chapter 2 of RDA, "Identifying Manifestations and Items," provides instructions on how to select the source of information and the elements of description.

- Chapter 3, "Describe Carriers," focuses on describing the characteristics of the carrier of the resource.
- Chapter 4, "Providing Acquisition and Access Information," provides instructions on recording the attributes of manifestations and items that are used to support acquisition and access.
- Chapter 27, "Related Manifestations," provides instructions on recording relationships between manifestations.
- Chapter 28 provides instructions for recording relationships between items.

Each of the first four chapters provides guidelines for meeting the user's tasks as they are defined in FRBR. For example, elements that are described in RDA chapter 2, "Identifying Manifestations and Items," meet the FRBR user's task "identify." Elements described in chapter 3, "Describe Carriers," meet the FRBR user's task "select." Elements described in chapter 4, "Providing Acquisition and Access Information," meet the FRBR user's task "obtain."

I. GENERAL PRINCIPLES

LANGUAGE AND SCRIPT (RDA 1.4)

Transcribe the elements in the language and script in which they appear on the source. As an alternative, transcribe the elements in a transliterated form instead, or as an option, transcribe the elements in both forms, vernacular form and transliteration.

TRANSCRIBING THE ELEMENTS (RDA 1.7)

As a general rule, transcribe the element as it appears on the source of information.

Alternatives: RDA provides options for transcribing the elements based on the cataloging agency preferences (RDA 1.7.1–1.7.9 and in the appendixes).

- If the agency creating the description has established in-house guidelines for capitalization, punctuation, numerals, symbols, abbreviations, etc., use those guidelines.
- If the agency creating the description designated a published style manual, etc., (e.g., *The Chicago Manual of Style*) as its preferred guide, use the guidelines of that style manual.
- Take what you see, especially when capturing digital data from scanning or downloading.

The following are the RDA general guidelines for recording capitalization, punctuation, symbols, abbreviations, etc.

CAPITALIZATION (RDA 1.7.2)

When transcribing an element according to RDA guidelines, apply the following:

Capitalize the first word of a title (RDA Appendix A.4.1). This includes:

Title proper (RDA 2.3.1)
Parallel title (RDA 2.3.3)
Variant title (RDA 2.3.6)
Earlier variant title (RDA 2.3.7)
Later variant title (RDA 2.3.8)
Key title (RDA 2.3.9)
Abbreviated title (RDA 2.3.10)
Devised title (RDA 2.3.11)
Title proper of series (RDA 2.12.2)
Parallel title of series (RDA 2.12.3)
Title proper of subseries (RDA 2.12.10)
Parallel title of subseries (RDA 2.12.11)

245 00 $a In search of excellence : $b lessons from America's best-run companies.

(Proper title is in all capital letters on the preferred source of information.—First word of the title is capitalized.)

Do not apply the guideline for capitalization of the first word in the following instances:

Other title information (RDA 2.3.4)
Parallel other title information (RDA 2.3.5)
Other title information of series (RDA 2.12.4)
Parallel other title information of series (RDA 2.12.5)
Other title information of subseries (RDA 2.12.12)
Parallel other title information of subseries (RDA 2.12.13)

Do not capitalize Arabic or a Hebrew article (RDA Appendix 4.1):

ha-Milon he-hadash
al-Watan al-'Arabi

Do not capitalize a title preceded by punctuation indicating that the beginning of the phrase from which the title is derived has been omitted (RDA Appendix 4.2):

. . . if elected
. . . and master of none

Do not capitalize a compound term with unusual capitalization and describe it as it appears in the source (RDA Appendix 4.1):

e-commerce
eBay

http://english.aljazeera.net/watch_now/
eBooks
re:Organize

ABBREVIATIONS (RDA 1.7.8 AND APPENDIX B)

RDA allows for describing what you see on the resource. In this case, you are not required to abbreviate words or substitute the prescribed abbreviation in any title tag or statement of responsibility. If a word appears in an abbreviated form, transcribe it as it appears:

245 $a Fifth edition
(Source of information reads "Fifth edition".)

245 00 $a A.L.A.
(Source of information reads "A.L.A".)

RDA appendix B provides guidance on when to use abbreviations when transcribing a specific element.

INACCURACIES (RDA 1.7.9 AND RDA 2.3.1.4)

In RDA, catalogers are allowed to describe what they see on the resource being described. In this case, they are allowed to transcribe an inaccuracy or a misspelled word in any transcription area as it appears on the resources. For example:

245 04 $a The wolrd of Internet
245 00 $a Law and mariage in medieval and early modern times : $b proceedings of the eighth Carlsberg Academy Conference on Medieval Legal History 2011 / $c edited by Per Andersen.
245 10 $a Love and freindship and other early works / $c Jane Austen.
245 04 $a The poets guide to the birds / $c edited by Judith Kitchen and Ted Kooser.

A note can be made to correct the inaccuracy and create an access point for the corrected title as a variant title (RDA 2.3.6). For example:

245 04 $a The wolrd of Internet
246 1 $i Title should read: $a The world of Internet

245 00 $a Law and mariage in medieval and early modern times: $b proceedings of the eighth Carlsberg Academy Conference on Medieval Legal History 2011 / $c edited by Per Andersen.
246 1 $i Title should read: $a Law and marriage in medieval and early modern times

245 10 $a Love and freindship and other early works / $c Jane Austen.
246 1 $i Title should read: $a Love and friendship and other early works
245 04 $a The poets guide to the birds / $c edited by Judith Kitchen and Ted Kooser.
246 1 $i Title should read: $a Poet's guide to the birds

However, in transcribing the title proper of a serial or integrating resource, correct obvious typographic errors and make a note that gives the title as it appears on the source of information (RDA 2.3.1.4):

245 00 $a Housing starts
246 1 $a Title appears on v. 1, no. 1 as: $a Housing sarts

PUNCTUATION (RDA 1.7.3)

There are two options for using punctuation: (1) transcribe punctuation as it appears on the source (RDA 1.7.3), or (2) use the ISBD prescribed punctuation in RDA Appendix D 1.2:

245 00 $a Why are the Arabs not free?
245 10 $a "Evil" Arabs in American popular film : $b orientalist fear / $cTim Jon Semmerling.

ISBD CONVENTIONS IN RDA

When using the ISBD conventions, cataloger has to follow:

Ending Punctuation

"When punctuation occurring within or at the end of an element is retained, give it with normal spacing. Prescribed punctuation is always added, even though double punctuation may result" (RDA Appendix D 1.2.1):

250 $a 3rd ed..
not
250 $a 3rd ed.

Bracketing

"When adjacent elements within one area are to be enclosed in square brackets, enclose each in its own set of square brackets" (RDA Appendix D 1.2.1):

260 $a [Washington, D.C.] : $b [Government Printing Office], $c [2009?]
not
260 $a [Washington, D.C. : $b Government Printing Office, $c 2009?]

ACCENTS AND OTHER DIACRITICAL MARKS (RDA 1.7.4)

Transcribe accents and other diacritical marks as you find them in the source (RDA 1.7.4):

245 14 $a Les origines républicaines de Vichy / $c Gérard Noiriel.

SYMBOLS (RDA 1.7.5)

Transcribe symbols and other special characters, etc., as they appear on the source of information (RDA 1.7.5). For example:

245 10 $a Barnes & Noble : $b groundbreaking entrepreneurs / $c by Kayla Morgan.
245 10 $a All-in-One : $b CompTIA A+ certification exam guide / $c Mike Meyers.

SPACING OF INITIALS AND LETTERS (RDA 1.7.6)

Transcribe letters appearing in the source as initials or acronyms without any spaces between then, regardless of any spacing that appears in the source and whether or not the letters have full stops between them (RDA 1.7.6). For example:

245 00 $a D.A.R.E. (Drug Abuse Resistance Education)
245 00 $a ABC news.
245 00 $a ALCTS.

SQUARE BRACKETS

Square brackets are used when information is taken from outside the resource:

[1978]
(Date of publication is taken from outside the resource.)

[London]
(Place of publication is taken from outside the resource.)

II. PRE-CATALOGING DECISIONS—IDENTIFICATION OF THE RESOURCE BEING CATALOGED

Before starting the cataloging process, the cataloger needs to decide what is being cataloged. Is it a whole, a part, a part of a part, or the whole and its parts together? (RDA 2.1 and 2.13) [MARC 21 leader Bibl lvl] Most resources fall into the following categories:

- Single part monograph; e.g., a single volume monograph and a PDF file, where the resource is issued as a single physical unit.

- Multipart monograph; e.g., encyclopedias, dictionaries, and multi-volume sets where the resource, issued in two or more parts, is complete or is intended to be completed within a finite number of parts.
- Integrated resource; e.g., loose-leaf, manuals, and websites where adding and changing the content is dynamic but the updates and changes remain integrated into the whole.
- Serial; e.g., periodicals, monographic series, and newspapers where the resource is issued in successive parts, usually bearing numbering, and having no predetermined conclusion.

The second step for the cataloger is to determine if a new description is needed. For example, if the resource is a multipart monograph, an integrating resource, or a serial, and there is already a bibliographic record for it in the database, it is necessary to determine if a new description should be created or if you should add information to the existing record (RDA 1.6).

A new description is not needed when there are minor changes in the title proper; one spelling versus another; abbreviated word or sign or symbol versus spelled-out form; addition and deletion of an article, preposition, or a conjunction; or addition or deletion of punctuation.

RDA provides clear guidelines for when the catalogers need to create a new record for a resource. The decision to create a new record is based on the following criteria:

Mode of issuance (RDA 2.13) to determine whether the resource is issued in one or more parts, how it is updated, and the intended termination

Media type (RDA 3.2) to determine the intermediation device required to view, play, and run the content of resource. For example: if media type changes from audiocassette to MP3

Major change in the title proper for serial (RDA 2.3.2.13) such as addition, deletion, change, and/or reordering of any of the first five words of the title that has an impact on changing the meaning and the subject of the title; change in a corporate body name given anywhere in the title

Change in responsibility for serial (RDA 6.1.3.2) affecting the primary access point

Change in edition statement for serial (RDA 1.6.2.5) indicating a significant change to the scope and the coverage of a resource

Re-basing for integrated resource (RDA 1.6.3.3) when a new set of base volumes is issued for an updating loose-leaf

If the resource contains a change that would require a *new* description, the cataloger will need to decide on the type of description (RDA 2.1).

Comprehensive description (RDA 2.1.2): Single description for a resource described as a whole—resource issued as a single unit (RDA 2.1.2.2); resource issued in more than one part (RDA 2.1.2.3); resource issued as an integrated resource (RDA 2.1.2.4).

Analytical description (RDA 2.1.3): Description of a part of a larger resource, e.g., resource issued as a single unit (RDA 2.1.3.2); resource issued in more than one part (RDA 2.1.3.3); resource issued as an integrated resource (RDA 2.1.3.4).

Hierarchical description (RDA 1.5.4): Multilevel description of the whole and of each part, e.g., create a record for the series and a record for individual titles within the series. This will allow the display of the individual record or a multilevel description in which the description of the whole and the description of its parts are combined in a single hierarchical display.

PREFERRED SOURCE OF INFORMATION (RDA 2.2)

Determine your preferred source of information based on the type of resource. The RDA instruction suggests the use of the whole resource as the preferred source of information (RDA 2.1.2.2).

RDA provides specific instruction for the preferred source of information.

For resources consisting of one or more pages, leaves, sheets, or cards (or images of one or more pages, leaves, sheets, or cards) (RDA2.2.2.2), use the title page, title sheet, or title card as the preferred source of information. If the resources lack a title page, title sheet, or title cards, use the cover title, caption, masthead, or colophon.

For resources consisting of moving images (RDA 2.2.2.3), use the title frame, title screen, label, or embedded metadata in textual form containing a title as the preferred source of information.

OTHER RESOURCES (RDA 2.2.2.4)

If none of the sources listed above indicate which element should be used as the preferred source of information, use the label bearing a title that is permanently printed on or affixed to the resource, excluding accompanying textual material or a container (e.g., a label on an audio CD or a model), or use any embedded metadata in textual form that contains a title.

RESOURCE WITHOUT SOURCE OF INFORMATION

If the resource does not contain a source of information, use (a) accompanying material, (b) a container, such as a box, (c) another published description of the book, (d) any other available source (RDA 2.2.4).

RESOURCE WITH MULTIPLE TITLE PAGES

If there are multiple title pages in more than one language or script, use the following as the preferred source of information, in the following order of preference (RDA 2.2.3.1):

- The source in the language or script that corresponds to the language or script of the content or the predominant language or script of the content of the resource.

- The source in the language or script of translation, if the resource contains the same work in more than one language, script, or translation is known to be the purpose of the resource.
- The source in the original language or script of the content, if the resource contains the same content in more than one language or script and the original language or script can be identified.
- The first occurrence of the sources.

If there are multiple title pages or other sources bearing different dates, use the information from the one with the latest date (RDA 2.2.3.2).

If the resource is a facsimile or a reproduction of an original resource and contains a preferred source of information for the reproduction as well as the original, use the source of information for the reproduction as the preferred source of information (RDA 2.2.3.3).

If information is taken from a source outside the resource itself, indicate that by a note or use a square bracket (RDA 2.2.4 and 2.20.2.3):

490 1 $a [A continuing legal education series]
500 $a Series statement from jacket.

For an integrating resource, (e.g., updating website, updating loose-leaf) choose a source of information identifying the current iteration of the resource as a whole (RDA 2.1.2.4).

III. RECORDING ELEMENTS OF DESCRIPTION OF THE MANIFESTATION

From the RDA general principle just discussed, you have learned about describing the elements for the manifestation in the language and script found in the resources with an alternative for transcribing materials in non-Latin script. You also learned about transcribing the elements as they appear on the source of information in terms of capitalization, punctuation, abbreviations, inaccuracies, etc.

You have made decisions about the resource being cataloged and decided if a new description is needed and determined your source of information. Next you will record the elements for describing manifestation. Each element will be accompanied by the RDA instruction number, MARC 21 tag, and an indication if the element is core.

RECORDING MANIFESTATION ELEMENTS

IDENTIFIER FOR THE MANIFESTATION (RDA 2.15) [MARC 21 TAGS 020, 022, 024, 027, 028, 030, 074, 086] (CORE ELEMENT)

The identifier for the manifestation is a number or number/letter string associated with a manifestation that was designed to differentiate that manifestation from other manifestations. RDA guidelines prefer to record any internationally recognized identifier such as ISSN, ISBN, and LCCN. *Note that the URLs are not considered to be the identifiers* (RDA 4.6).

020 0715629123 (pbk.)
020 0312125550 (International edition)
020 115375990X (large print)
020 3854852177
022 0 1648-6897
022 2042-9738 **$y** 2042-9746

TITLE (RDA 2.3) [MARC 21 TAG 245]

Title is defined as a "word, character, or group of words and/or characters that names a resource or a work contained in it." Title information is categorized by the following:

Title proper
Parallel title
Other title information
Collective title and title of individual contents
Resource lacking collective title
Statement of responsibility relating to the title proper
Variant title

The following section will describe each of these elements.

1. TITLE PROPER (RDA 2.3.2) [MARC 21 TAG 245, SUBFIELD $a] (CORE ELEMENT)

Title proper is defined as the chief name of resources including the alternative title. Title proper is described as it appears on title page or other preferred source of information (RDA 1.3, 2.3.2.2, 2.3.1.4). This includes the same spelling, inaccuracy, punctuation, and capitalization.

245 10 $a Index villaris, or, an alphabetical table of all the cities, market-towns, parishes, villages, and private seats in England and Wales / by Mr. Adams.
245 10 $a Tillie Olosn, a profile
246 1 $i $a Title should read: $a Tillie Olson, a profile

245 10 $a Sports leaders & success : $b 55 top sports leaders & how they achieve greatness
246 3 $a Sport leaders and success

245 00 $a Business library review
245 10 $a Symphony 1 in c minor, op. 68
245 10 $a Arizona : $b Globe : 1:100,000-scale topographic map : 30 x 60 minute series (topographic)

However, there is an exception for recording the title proper: "When transcribing the title proper of a serial or integrating resource, correct obvious typographic errors, and make a note giving the title as it appears on the source of information" (RDA 2.3.1.4; see also 2.20.2.4). This means that when cataloging serials, you should correct obvious typographical errors in the title proper. If it is considered important for access, provide the errant form of the title in a MARC 21 tag 246:

245 00 $a Zoology studies
246 1 $i Misspelled title on number 1: $a Zooology studies

"If a title of a serial includes a date, name, number, etc., that varies from issue to issue, omit this date, name, number, etc. Use a mark of omission (. . .) to indicate such an omission" (RDA 2.3.1.4):

245 00 $a . . .annual report
(Source of information reads: 1995 annual report.)

245 00 $a Summary tables of the . . . annual report on the statistics of railways in the United States for the year . . .
(Source of information reads: Summary tables of the 24th annual report on the statistics of railways in the United States for the year 1911-.)

Omit introductory words such as "Disney presents," if they are not intended to be part of the title (RDA 2.3.1.6):

245 00 $a King Kong
(Source of information reads: Radio Pictures presents King Kong.)

245 00 $a Don Juan
(Source of information reads: Warner Bros. Pictures, Inc. and the Vitaphone Corporation presents Mr. John Barrymore as Don Juan.)

245 00 $a Complete book of wedding music
(Source of information reads: Mel Bay presents complete book of wedding music.)

For a facsimile and a reproduction that has a title different from the original manifestation, choose the title of the facsimile or the reproduction as the title proper (RDA 2.3.2.3):

245 00 $a Colonial era history of Dover, New Hampshire : $b a facsimile of the 1923 edition with a completely new every-name index by Marlene A. Towle
(Original title is History of Dover, New Hampshire.)

If the title of the original manifestation appears on the same source of information as the title of the facsimile or reproduction, record it as a parallel title proper. If it is in a different language from the facsimile or reproduction (RDA 2.3.3), record it as other title information (RDA 2.3.4) or as title of related manifestation (RDA 27.1).

2. PARALLEL TITLE PROPER (RDA 2.3.3) [MARC 21 TAG 245, SUBFIELD $b] (Note that in RDA, parallel titles are not core elements. They may be recorded, but they are not required.)

Parallel title is defined as a title proper in another language and/or script. RDA does not have restrictions on how many parallel titles can be recorded. They can all be recorded in the order they are presented on the source of information (RDA 2.3.3.3). Parallel titles can be taken from any source within the resources (RDA 2.3.3.2):

245 00 $a Reading in 3 languages = $b la lecture en 3 idiomas
245 10 $a Aḥlām fatrat al-naqāhah = $b the dreams of departure / $c Naguib Mahfouz ; translated from the Arabic and with an afterword by Raymond Stock.
245 00 $a Journal de mécanique théorique et appliquée = $b Journal of theoretical and applied mechanics
245 10 $a Dionysos kai he dionysiake tragoidia = $b Dionysus und die dionysische Tragödie = Dionis i dionisiĭskaia tragedii͡a : V͡iacheslav Ivanov : filologicheskie i filosofskie idei o dionisiĭstve = Dionysus and Dionysian tragedy : Vyacheslav Ivanov : philological and philosophical ideas on Dionysiasm / $c Filip Vestbruk.
245 10 $a Environment and development : $b China and India = Paryāvaraṇa evaṃ vikāsa : Cīna aura Bhārata = Huan jing yu fa zhan bi jiao : Zhongguo yu Yindu / $c a joint study by Chinese Academy of Environmental Planning (CAEP) and The Energy and Resources Institute (TERI).

3. OTHER TITLE INFORMATION (RDA 2.3.4) [MARC 21 TAG 245, SUBFIELD $b] (Note that in RDA, other title information is not a core element. Other titles may be recorded, but they are not required.)

Other title information is defined as any title other than proper and parallel title. It is preceded by a space-colon-space following the title proper:

245 10 $a Toms, coons, mulattoes, mammies, and bucks : $b an interpretive history of Blacks in American films / $c Donald Bogle.
245 00 $a Gender, language, and myth : $b essays on popular narrative/ c edited by Glenwood Irons.

245 00 $a Education 14-19 : $b critical perspectives /c edited by Sally Tomlinson.
245 10 $a Life according to Leslie : $b memories and recollections /c Leslie Porter ; edited by Igrid Rockberger.

If the other title information appears in more than one language or script, record the other title information that is in the same language as the title proper.

4. COLLECTIVE TITLE AND TITLE OF INDIVIDUAL CONTENTS (RDA 2.3.2.6)

When the resource bears the collective title and the titles of individual contents within the resource, record the collective title as the title proper (RDA 2.3.2.6):

245 10 $a Five novels
(Source of information also includes the title of individual novels: Adventures of Tom Sawyer; Prince and the pauper; Adventures of Huckleberry Finn; Connecticut Yankee in King Arthur's court; Tragedy of Pudd'nhead Wilson. A 505 contents note can also be added if more clarification is needed. As an optional instruction, the title of the individual contents can be recorded as titles of related works using MARC field 700 12 $i contains (work) $a author. $t title (RDA 25.1). (This will be discussed in detail in the "Identifying Work and Expression" chapter.)

5. RESOURCE LACKING COLLECTIVE TITLE FOR THE COMPILATION (RDA 2.3.2.9)

If there is no collective title for the compilation, record the titles proper of the parts in the order in which they appear on the source of information (RDA 2.3.2.9):

245 00 $a Fall River legend / Morton Gould. Facsimile / Leonard Bernstein.

In addition to (or instead of) constructing access points for each of the works in the compilation, construct an authorized access point representing the compilation using a *devised title* formulated according to the instructions given under RDA 2.3.2.11. Explain in a note that the title was devised (RDA 2.3.2.10).

245 00 $a [Three Norwegian symphonies].
→ 500 $a Title devised by cataloger.
505 0 $a Sinfonia espressiva / Conrad Baden—Symphony no. 3, op. 26 / Hallvard Johnsen—Symphony no. 2 / Bjarne Brustad.
700 12 $a Baden, Conrad. $t Symphonies, $n no. 6.
700 12 $a Johnsen, Hallvard. $t Symphonies, $n no. 3, op. 26.
700 12 $a Brustad, Bjarne. $t Symphonies, $n no. 2.

(Note in this example that access points have been created for each work.)

6. RESOURCE WITH NO TITLE (RDA 2.3.2.10)

If there is no title on the source, and a title cannot be found using an external resource, devise a title based on the nature of the content or subject. Indicate in a note that the title was devised (RDA 2.3.2.10).

Example:

245 05 $a [The Egyptian revolution]
→ 500 $a Title devised by cataloger

7. STATEMENT OF RESPONSIBILITY (RDA 2.4) [MARC 21 TAG 245, SUBFIELD $c] (CORE ELEMENT)

Statement of responsibility is defined as a "statement associated with the title proper of a resource related to the identification of any persons, families, or corporate bodies credited with a major role in creating the intellectual content of the work." The statement of responsibility is transcribed in this order:

(a) the one identifying the creator or creators, or
(b) the first one appearing in the source (RDA 1.3, 2.4.1.4, 2.4.2.2, and 2.4.2.3).

RDA states that the statement of responsibility should be transcribed in the form in which it appears on the source of information (RDA 2.4.1.4).

245 10 $a Being polite to Hitler / $c a novel by ROBB FORMAN DEW
(The author's name appears on the source of information in capital letters. Catalogers can record the statement of responsibility in capital letters, or follow in-house guidelines, style manual, or RDA appendix A instruction for capitalization [RDA 1.7.].)

RDA expanded the source for statement of responsibility relating to a title proper to any source. If the element is taken from outside the source, enclose the element in square brackets.

The statement of responsibility may include a single name or more than one name (2.4.1.5 RDA). If there is more than one name, only the first name recorded is required for all resources:

245 00 $a Education and social inequality in the global culture / $c Joseph Zajda, Karen Biraimah, William Gaudelli, editors.
245 10 $a Lives of girls and women / $c Alice Munro ; abridged by Ruth Fraser.
245 10 $a Decisive inventions versus decisive battles / $c by Dr. C. C. Williams.
245 13 $a Le temps des banquets : $b politique et symbolique d'une génération (1818-1848) / $c Vincent Robert .

245 00 $a Proceedings : $b AIDS Prevention and Services Workshop, February 15-16, 1990, Washington, D.C. / $c edited by Vivian E. Fransen.
245 00 $a Devenir Céline : $b lettres inédites de Louis Destouches et de quelques autres, 1912-1919 / $c édition et postface de Véronique Robert-Chovin.
245 00 $a Architectural engineering and design management : $b embracing complexity in the built environment / $c guest editor, Halim Boussabaine.
245 02 $a A Questionnaire to evaluate your library and library board / $c American Library Trustee Association Publications Committee.

A word or a phrase may be added in square brackets to the statement of responsibility when the responsibility's relationship to the title proper is not clear (RDA 2.4.1.7):

245 00 $a. . . / $c [compiled by] Ted Rueter.

According to RDA, the noun phrase occurring in conjunction with a statement of responsibility is always considered part of the statement of responsibility (RDA 2.4.1.8):

245 10 . . . / $c novel by John Scott.
245 10 . . . / $c research and text by Colin Barham.
245 14 $a The girl who fell from the sky / $c a novel by Heidi W. Durrow.

The Rule of Three

Pre-RDA rules indicated that in cases where more than three authors share responsibility for the creation of a work, the catalog should provide an added entry only under the first author named. This practice discriminates unfairly against the authors whose names are not included and hampers those patrons who only recall the name of one or more of those authors overlooked by the catalog.

RDA instructions consider the statement of responsibility that includes more than one person, etc., as a single statement regardless of whether the person, family, or corporate bodies named in it perform the same function or different function (RDA 2.4.1.5):

245 00 $a Selected papers on international arbitration / $c editors, Daniele Favalli, Xavier Favre-Bulle, Andreas Furrer, Daniel Girsberger, Philipp Habegger, Laurent Killias, Christoph Müller, Paolo Michele Patocchi, Urs Weber-Stecher.
245 00 $a This Is the Flow : $b The Museum as a Space for Ideas / $c edited by Rutger Wolfson; text by Cornel Bierens, Edwin Carels, Guus Beumer, Valentijn Byvanck, Chris Darke.
245 10 $a Criminal Law / $c by Joseph G. Cook, Linda A. Malone, Paul Marcus, Geraldine Szott Moohr.

245 00 $a Rutter's child and adolescent psychology / $c edited by Michael Rutter, Dorothy V. M. Bishop, Daniel S. Pine, Stephen Scott, Jim Stevenson, Eric Taylor, Anita Thapar.
245 00 $a Best practices of online education : $b a guide for Christian higher education / $c edited by Mark A. Maddix, Northwest Nazarene University, James R. Estep, Lincoln Christian University, Mary E. Lowe, Erskine Theological Seminary.
245 00 $a Southern leatherside (Lepidomeda aliciae) monitoring summary, statewide 2006-2008 / $c regional contributions from Michael E. Golden, Callie A.W. Grover, E. Jordanna Black, and Melinda R.M. Bennion, Southern Region ; Julie Stahli, Christopher Crockett, and Michael Mills, Central Region ; compiled by Sarra L. Jones.

RDA provides the option to omit all but the first of each group of such persons, families, or bodies. Indicate the omission by summarizing what has been omitted in the language and script preferred by the agency preparing the description. Indicate that the summary was taken from a source outside the resource itself as instructed under (RDA 2.2.4):

245 00 $a This Is the Flow : $b The Museum as a Space for Ideas / $c edited by Rutger Wolfson; text by Cornel Bierens [and four others].
245 10 $a Criminal Law / $c by Joseph G. Cook [and three others].
245 00 $a Rutter's child and adolescent psychology / $c edited by Michael Rutter [and six others].
245 14 $a The unanimous life : $b Deimantas Narkevičius / $c Philippe Pirotte [and five others].
245 00 $a Trying sex offense cases in Massachusetts / **$c** editor, Stephanie Page ; authors, Janice Bassil [and 24 others].

8. VARIANT TITLE (RDA 2.3.6) [MARC 21 TAG 246, SUBFIELD $a]

(Note that in RDA, variant titles are <u>not</u> core elements. They may be recorded, but they are not required.)

Variant forms of a title are associated with the resource, whether they are or are not on the resource being described. These variant titles can be found on the jacket, spine, title screen, cover, caption title, running title, container, or in accompanying materials. Variant titles are recorded in MARC 21 tag 246 only if they differ substantially from the title statement in MARC 21 tag 245 and if they contribute to further important identification of the item:

245 00 $a Library literature & information science.
246 14 $a Library literature and information science
500 $a Title from cover.

245 00 $a Marcel Marceau, ou, L'art du mime.
246 30 $a Marcel Marceau
246 30 $a Art du mime

245 00 $a Index villaris, or, An alphabetical table of all the cities, market-towns, parishes, villages, and private seats in England and Wales.
246 30 $a Index villaris
246 30 $a An alphabetical table of all the cities, market-towns, parishes, villages, and private seats in England and Wales

245 10 $a Dionysos kai he dionysiake tragoidia = Dionysus und die dionysische Tragödie = Dionis i dionisiĭskaia trage͡diia : V͡iacheslav Ivanov : filologicheskie i filosofskie idei o dionisiĭstve / $c Filip Vestbruk.
246 1 $i Title on page 298: $a Dionysus and Dionysian tragedy : Vyacheslav Ivanov : philological and philosophical ideas on Dionysiasm
246 31 $a Dionysus und die dionysische Tragödie
246 31 $a Dionis i dionisiĭskaia trage͡diia : V͡iacheslav Ivanov : filologicheskie i filosofskie idei o dionisiĭstve

245 04 $a The one hundred new tales = $b Les cent nouvelles nouvelles.
246 31 $a Cent nouvelles nouvelles

245 00 $a Adult education @ 21st century.
246 3 $a Adult education at twenty-first century

245 02 $a L'Africa romana : $b le ricchezze dell'Africa :isorse, produzioni, scambi : atti del XVII Convegno di studio, Sevilla, 14-17 dicembre 2006.
500 $a On spine: Africa romana 17.

(Note that in RDA, variant titles are NOT core elements. They may be recorded, but they are not required.)

EDITION STATEMENT (RDA 2.5) [MARC 21 TAG 250] (CORE ELEMENT)

The edition statement is a statement identifying the edition to which a resource belongs. The statement may include the edition statement, statement of responsibility relating to the edition, statement relating to a named version of an edition, and statement of responsibility relating to a named revision of an edition.

The edition statement is transcribed as it appears on the source of information (RDA 2.5.1.4). No abbreviations are used unless they appear on the source used for the edition statement. For example:

250 $a Second revised edition.
250 $a Second edition 1988 revision.
250 $a New ed..
250 $a 3e..
250 $a Preliminary draft.
250 $a 2 nd ed..
250 $a Draft unedited version.
250 $a 5 th ed. rev. and augm..
250 $a Paper edition.
250 $a Updated edition.
250 $a *** ed..
250 $a Special educational edition.
250 $a War edition.
250 $a Facsimile edition.

Statement of responsibility relating to the edition (RDA 2.5.4). (Note that in RDA, statements of responsibility relating to the edition *are not* core elements. They may be recorded, but they are not required.)

Record the person, family, or corporate body that is associated with the particular edition being described. For example:

250 $a 4th ed. / $b revised by J.G. Le Mesurier.
250 $a Rev. ed. / $b with revisions and an introduction by Paul Watson.
250 $a Second edition/ $b revised and updated by Joseph Allan.
250 $a Fifth edition / $b edited by John Miller.

Designation of a named revision of an edition (RDA 2.5.6) (core element) is a word, character, or a group of words and/or characters identifying a particular edition revision and it is transcribed as found (*do not abbreviate or convert numerals).*

250 $a Second revised edition.
250 $a Second edition 1988 revision.
250 $a Draft unedited version.
250 $a 5th ed. rev. and augm..
250 $a Version X.

PUBLICATION STATEMENT (RDA 2.8) [MARC 21 TAG 260] (CORE ELEMENT)

1. PUBLISHER INFORMATION

The publication statement identifies the place or places of publication, producer or producers, and the date or dates of production of a resource.

Source of information of the production statement is taken from:

- Preferred source of information as the title proper (RDA 2.3.2.2), or
- Another source within the resource itself, such as storage medium, accompanying materials, container (RDA 2.2.2) if they are issued as part of the resource itself; or other source of information, such as accompanying materials and container that are not part of the resource (RDA 2.2.4)

Place of Publication (RDA 2.8.2) [MARC 21 Tag 260, Subfield $a] (Core Element)

The place of publication is transcribed in the same form as it appears on the source of information. Include both the local place name (city, town, etc.) and the name of the larger jurisdiction or jurisdictions (state, province, etc., and/or country) if present on the source of information (RDA 2.8.2.3). Provide a note when the name of the place is known to be fictitious or requires clarification (RDA 2.8.2.3):

260 $a Malden, Massachusetts : $b
260 $a Ostfildern : $b
260 $a St. Paul, MN : $b
260 $a Champaign, Ill : $b
260 $a Rio de Janeiro : $b
260 $a New York : $b
260 $a Chichester, UK : $b
260 $a Amsterdam, Netherlands : $b
260 $a Belfast : $b
500 $a Published in Dublin : $b
260 $a Bs. As : $b
500 $a Actually published in Buenos Aires.
260 $a Peterborough Ont., Canada : $b
260 $a Frankfurt, M : $b
500 $a actually published in Heusenstamm.

When there is more than one place of publication on the source of information, record all in the order indicated by the sequence, layout, or typography of the names on the source of information (RDA 2.8.2.4). For core element, only the first place of publication is recorded and the current place, if it differs, is required.

260 $a Oxford; $a New York; $a London : $b
or
260 $a Oxford : $b

260 $a Lanham, Maryland; $a Toronto ; $a Plymouth, UK : $b
or
260 $a Lanham, Maryland : $b

Record the name of the place of publication in square brackets if it is taken from other sources of information (RDA 2.8.2.6.1).

260 $a [Philadelphia] : $b

If the place of publication is uncertain, indicate the probable place of publication by a question mark (RDA 2.8.2.6.2):

260 $a [Tampa?]
(Probable place of publication)

If the country, state, province, etc., of publication is known, supply that name:

260 $a [Canada]
(Known country, state, province, etc.)

If the country, state, province, etc., of publication is uncertain, supply the name of the probable country, state, province, etc., of publication followed by a question mark.

260 $a [Spain?] : $b

If neither a known nor a probable local place or country, state, province, etc., of publication can be determined, indicate "Place of publication not identified" (RDA 2.8.2.6):

260 $a [Place of publication not identified] : $b

Publisher's Name (RDA 2.8.4) [MARC 21 Tag 260, Subfield $b] (Core Element)

Transcribe the publisher's names in the same form as they appear on the source of information (RDA 2.8.4.3):

260 : $b Ediciones Univeridad de Salamanca, $c
260 : $b Academia del hispanismo, $c
260 : $b Juris Publication, $c
260 : $b Gallimard, $c
260 : $b IOS Press, $c
260 : $b Wiley-Blackwell, $c
260 : $b McGraw Hill Medical, $c
260 : $b Saunders/Elsevier, $c
260 : $b Springer Pub. Co., $c
(On the source of information, the publisher's name is "Springer Pub. Co".)

260 : $b NBM ComicsLit., $c
(On the source of information the publisher's name is "NBM ComicsLit".)

260 : $b The Scarecrow Press, Inc., $c

When there is more than one publisher on the source of information, record all in the order indicated by the sequence, layout, or typography of the names on the source of information (RDA 2.8.2.5). For core element, only the first publisher's name recorded is required.

260 : $b American Broadcasting Co. [production company] :
$b Released by Xerox Films. $c

or

260 : $b American Broadcasting Co. [production company], $c

260 : $b John Wiley & Sons : $b International Institute for Learning, $c

or

260 : $b John Wiley & Sons, $c

260 : $b Iron and Steel Board : $b British Iron and Steel Federation, $c

or

260 : $b Iron and Steel Board, $c

If no publisher's name is identified on the source of information, record "Publisher not identified" (RDA 2.8.4).

260 : $b [Publisher not identified], $c

Date of Publication (RDA 2.8.6) [MARC 21 Tag 260, Subfield $c] (Core Element)

Provide the date of publication as it appears on the source of information:

260 ,$c 2001.
260 ,$c 1928.

If the date of publication is not identified, supply a probable date (RDA 1.9)

260 ,$c [2000].

Either one of two consecutive years

260 ,$c [1981 or 1982].

Probable year

260 ,$c [2011?]

Probable range of years ("between ___ and ___?")

260 ,$c [between 2008 and 2010?]
260 ,$c [between 1400 and 1500?]
260 ,$c [between 1970 and 1979?]

Earliest or latest possible date known ("not before," "not after," or "between ___ and ___")

260 ,$c [not before January 25, 2011]
260 ,$c [between January 25, 2010 and March 2, 2011]

If the first issue, part, or iteration is available and the resource continues to be published (e.g., multi-part monograph, serials, and integrated resources) record the date of the first issue followed by a dash to indicate that this resource continued to be published (RDA 2.8.6.5).

260 ,$c 2010-

If the publication has completed or ceased, provide the beginning and ending dates of publication if you have the first/last issue, part, or iteration.

260 ,$c 1991-1996.

If the date is unknown, record that the date of publication is not identified.

260 ,$c [date of publication not identified]

2. DISTRIBUTING STATEMENT (RDA 2.9) (CORE ELEMENT)

If the elements of the publication statement cannot be identified, then the distribution statement can be used.

Place of Distribution (RDA 2.9.2) (Core Element)

Record the place of distribution when the place of publication is not identified. If there is more than one place of distribution, only the first place of distribution recorded is required.

260 $a [place of publication not identified] : $b Wiley-Blackwell ; $a Manchester, $c

(On the verso of title page "University of Manchester, Department of Medical Biochemistry [distributor], Manchester." "Manchester" was given when a place of publication could not be identified.)

Distributor's Name (RDA 2.9.4) (Core Element)

Record the distributor's name, if available, when the publisher's name is not identified. If there is more than one distributor's name, only the first one is required when the core element is used.

260 $a New York : $b [publisher not identified] : $b Distributed by New York Graphic Society, $c

(In this example, the publisher's name is not identified. The verso of the title page indicated that the resource is published in New York and distributed by the New York Graphic Society.)

260 $a [Place of publication not identified] : $b [publisher not identified] ; $a London : $b Guild Sound and Vision [distributor]

(In this example, the place of publication and publisher information are not identified. On the verso of the title page of the resource: Distributed by Guild Sound and Vision, London.)

260 $a Chicago : $b [publisher not identified] : $b RD Distributors, $c
(In this example, the publisher's name is not identified. On source: Chicago, 2009, on the verso RD Distributors, Evanston.)

Date of Distribution (RDA 2.9.6) (Core Element)

260 $a [Place of publication *not* identified] : $b [publisher not identified], $c [date of publication not identified], 2001.
(On the source: 2001 distribution. There is no subfield in MARC 21tag 260 to show that this is a date of distribution.)

260 $a Omaha, Nebraska : $b Mean Pub. Co., $c [date of publication not identified], 2009.
(On the verso of title page: 2009 distribution.)

3. MANUFACTURE STATEMENT (RDA 2.10) [MARC 21 TAG 260, SUBFIELDS $e, $f, $g] (CORE ELEMENT)

Place of manufacture is a place associated with the printing of the resource in published form.

Place of Manufacture (RDA 2.10.2) [MARC 21 Tag 260, Subfields $e]

When neither the place of publication nor place of distribution are identified and manufacture information is on the resource, record the place of manufacture. *If there is more than one place of manufacture, only the first* place of manufacture *recorded is required.*

260 $a [place of publication not identified] : $b Koenig Books, $c 2010 $e (London)
(On the source: Published 2010 by Koenig Books; 2010 printing, London. The place of manufacture is presented in MARC 21 tag 260 $e.)

260 $a [Place of publication not identified] : $b International Group, $c 2009 $e (New York)
(On the source: Published 2009 by the International Group; 2009 printing, Johnson Graphics, New York and Buenos Aires. No distribution information available.)

Manufacturer's Name (RDA 2.10.4) [MARC 21 Tag 260, Subfield $f] (Core Element)

The name of manufacturer is the name of a person, family, or corporate bodies responsible for printing a resource in published form.

When neither the publisher's name nor the distributor's name is identified and manufacturer information is on the resource, record the name of manufacturer. *If there is more than one* name of manufacturer, *only the first name* of manufacturer *recorded is required:*

260 $a [place of publication not identified] : $b [publisher not identified] , $c 2011 $e (London : $f CTD Printer Limited)
(On the sources: Published 2011; printed in London by CTD Printers Limited.)

260 $a London : $b [publisher not identified]; $c 2010 $f (CTD Printers Limited)
(On the source: Published in London 2010; 2010 printing, London. CTD Printers Limited. The name of manufacture is presented in MARC 21 tag 260 $f.)

260 $a Boston : $b [publisher not identified], $c 2010 $f (Kinsey Printing Company)
(On the source: Published in Boston, 2010; Cambridge, Kinsey Printing Company, No distribution information is available.)

260 $a [Place of publication not identified] : $b [publisher not identified], $c 2009 $e (Arlington, VA : $f B. Ross Printing).
(On the source: Published 2009; printed by B. Ross Printing (Arlington, VA), May 2009, No distribution information.)

Date of Manufacture (RDA 2.10.6) [MARC 21 tag 260, Subfield $g] (Core Element)

The date of manufacture is the date of production of the resource.

When neither the date of publication nor the date of distribution *nor copyright date* are identified and manufacture information is on the resource, record the date of manufacture:

260 $a Tampa : $b Garrison Publishers, $c [date of publication not identified] $g (2010).
(On source: Garrison Publishers, Tampa; 2010 Printing, no distribution or copyright date is recorded on the item.)

260 $a [Place of publication not identified] : $b [publisher not identified], $c [date of publication not identified] $e (London : $f ZZZ Printers, $g 2009).
(On source: Printed for distribution in Western Europe by ZZZ Printers [London, Zurich, and Vienna] in 2009.)

COPYRIGHT DATE (RDA 2.11) (CORE ELEMENT)

The copyright date is defined as a legal date associated with the claim of protection under copyright or similar regime. If neither the date of publication nor the date of distribution is identified, and the copyright date is on the source, record the copyright date. The copyright date is usually given on the verso of the title page. Precede all copyright dates by the symbol ©. For sound recordings use the phonogram symbol ℗. If the symbols cannot be entered in the system then use the words copyright or phonogram:

260 $a [place of publication not identified] : $b Wiley-Blackwell , $c [date of publication not identified], ©2009.
260 $a London : $b Library Unlimited, $c [date of publication not identified], ℗2010.

EXTENT STATEMENT (RDA 3.4) [MARC 21 TAG 300, SUBFIELD $a, $b, $c, $e]

Extent is the number and type of units and/or subunits that makes up the resource. A unit is a physical or logical constituent of a resource (e.g., a volume, audiocassette, film reel, map, or digital file). A subunit is a physical or logical subdivision of a unit (e.g., a page of a volume, a frame of a microfiche, a record in a digital file). In addition to the resource unit and subunit, extent includes:

- Illustrative content (RDA 7.15)
- Dimensions (RDA 3.5)
- Accompanied materials (RDA 3.4.5)

Extent is a core element if the resource is complete or if the total extent is known:

300 $a 309 pages
300 $a 1 online resource (xxvi, 140 pages)
300 $a approximately 500 pages
300 $a xv, 408 pages, 30 unnumbered pages of plates
300 $a 1 computer disc

An incomplete serial will have extent. The term designating the type of unit will be recorded without a number (RDA 3.4.1.10):

- Volumes
- Boxes
- Microscopic slides

The source of information for extent is the resource itself (RDA 3.4.1.2) and is described by giving the number of units and an appropriate term from the *type of carrier list* (MARC 21 tag 338) in the singular or plural as applicable (RDA 3.3.1.3) or using other terms. For example:

300 $a 1 computer disc : $b digital, stereo ; $c 4 3/4 in.
(Computer disc is selected from the carrier type list.)
or
300 $a 2 CD-ROMs : $b digital, stereo ; $c 4 3/4 in.
(CD-ROM is selected from another extent list of terms.)

(Note that the carrier type is not the same as the attribute for extent. The elements that are used in the carrier type are based on controlled vocabulary. The extent element uses terms from the carrier type element when it is appropriate in the singular or plural as applicable, and also uses other terms.) In addition to using the carrier type terms for extent, there are additional terms that can be used:

- Other
- Approximately
- Unspecified

"Other" is used only when none of the terms listed above apply to the carrier or carriers of the resource being described. "Approximately" is used when the number of units used is not readily ascertained. "Unspecified" is used if the carrier type or types applicable to the resource being described cannot be readily ascertained.

Note that in recording extent, abbreviations are not to be used. Spell out words such as "pages, volume." The term "i.e." is replaced by "that is" and "ca." is replaced by "approximately."

RDA provides guidelines for describing not only the number of units, but also the subunits (RDA 3.4.1.7). It also calls for specifying the number of subunits in each unit followed by "each," if the resource consists of more than one unit, each unit having the same number of subunits. (RDA 3.4.1.9). When the total number of units is not complete or unknown, the term designating the type of unit without the number should be recorded.

1. BASIC INSTRUCTIONS ON RECORDING EXTENT (RDA 3.4.1)

Microfiche (RDA 3.4.1.7.4)

300 $a 1 microfiche (20 frames)

Electronic Resources (RDA 3.4.1.7.5)

300 $a computer discs

Online PDF

300 $a 1 online resource (59 pages)

DVD

300 $a 1 DVD

Videodiscs (RDA 3.4.1.7.8)

300 $a 1 videodisc (30,487 frames)

PDF File Accessed Online

300 $a 1 PDF file (38 pages)

Audio Recording—Book

300 $a 3 audio discs (approximately 3 hr.)

Audio Recording—Music

300 $a 1 CD

Sound Recording

300 $a 1 audio disc

Extent of Cartographic Resources (RDA 3.4.2)

RDA specifies the following list of terms to use in recording the extent for cartographic resources:

Atlas	*Map*	*Remote-sensing image*
Diagram	*Model*	*Section*
Globe	*Profile*	*View*

Atlas

300 $a 1 atlas (2 volumes)

Map

300 $a 1 map

Globe

300 $a 1 globe

Recording Extent for Notated Music (RDA 3.4.3)

300 $a 1 vocal score (xii, 324 pages)

300 $a 1 choir book

Recording Extent for Still Image (RDA 3.4.4)

RDA specifies the following list of terms to use in recording the extent for Still Image:

Activity card	*Chart*	*Collage*	*Drawing*
Flash card	*Icon*	*Painting*	*Photograph*
Picture	*Postcard*	*Poster*	*Print*
Radiograph	*Study print*	*Technical drawing*	*Wall chart*

300 $a 1 picture

300 $a approximately 200 photographs

Extent of Text (RDA 3.4.5)

RDA provides detailed instruction and examples of various cases of recording extent. The following examples illustrate some cases.

The extent for a single volume (RDA 3.4.5.2) is recorded in terms of pages, leaves, or columns.

300 $a 123 pages, 28 unnumbered pages
300 $a xxi, 300 pages
300 $a 356 leaves
300 $a 203 columns

When the page numbers are given in words and not in numbers, translate the words into numbers:

300 $a 50 pages
(Page number is in words [fifty].)

When the resource's pages, leaves, or columns are not numbered, either count the pages or estimate the number of pages (RDA 3.4.5.3):

300 $a 50 unnumbered pages
(Notice that the word "unnumbered" is used here rather than square brackets enclosing the numeral.)

300 $a Approximately 500 leaves
(Notice that the word "approximately" is spelled out.)

300 $a 1 volume (unpaged)

When the numbering on the last page, leaf, or column does not represent the total number of pages, leaves, or columns, record the incorrect number followed by "that is" and the correct number (RDA 3.4.5.5):

300 $a 394, that is, 349 pages
300 $a 209, that is, 210 leaves
(Notice here that "i.e." is replaced by "that is".)

If the last part of a volume is missing, record the number of the last numbered page, leaf, or column followed by "incomplete" (RDA 3.4.5.6):

300 $a xxx, 239 pages (incomplete)

If pages, leaves, or columns are missing from the first and the last part of a volume, record the first and the last pages, leaves, or columns, preceded by the appropriate term (RDA 3.4.5.7):

300 $a pages 34-100
300 $a leaves 22-234

RDA provides guidelines for complicated or irregular pages, leaves, or columns (RDA 3.4.5.8). For example:

300 $a 789 pages in various paging
300 $a 589 leaves in various foliations
300 $a 456 columns in various numbering
300 $a 5897 pages, 3495 pages, 6798 variously numbered pages
300 $a 1 volume (various paging)

If the resource contains leaves or pages of plates that are not part of the resource, record the number of pages or leaves of plates at the end of the pagination number (RDA 3.4.5.9):

300 $a 345 pages, 34 leaves of plates
300 $a 234 pages, 19 unnumbered pages of plates
300 $a 203 pages, 10 unnumbered pages of plates

Folded leaves or pages are described as "folded" (RDA 3.4.5.10):

300 $a 34 folded leaves
300 $a 456 pages, 34 leaves of plates (some folded)

If the resource consists of more than one part or volume, record the number of part or volume:

300 $a 3 volume

If the resource is an updating loose-leaf (RDA 3.4.5.19), record "1 volume" followed by "loose-leaf" in parentheses:

300 $a 1 volume (loose-leaf)

Extent of a Three-Dimensional Form (RDA 3.4.6)

RDA specifies the following list of terms to use to record the extent of a three-dimensional form:

coin	*diorama*	*exhibit*	*game*
jigsaw puzzle	*medal*	*mock-up*	*model*
sculpture	*specimen*	*toy*	

300 $a approximately 200 specimens
300 $a 1 Jigsaw puzzle (500 pieces)
300 $a 3 game

2. ILLUSTRATIVE CONTENT (RDA 7.15) [MARC 21 TAG 300, SUBFIELD $b]

Record other illustrative content as appropriate. The list below provides terms to be used as appropriate:

Charts	*Coats of arms*	*Facsimiles*	*Forms*
Genealogical tables	*Graphs*	*Illuminations*	*Maps*
Music	*Photographs*	*Plans*	*Portraits*
Samples			

300 $a . . . $b 1 form, 5 maps, 4 facsimiles
300 $a . . . $b illustrations (some color), maps (some color)
300 $a . . . $b blue and white
300 $a . . . $b 30 phonographs (some color)

3. DIMENSION (RDA 3.5) [MARC 21 TAG 300, SUBFIELD $c]

Dimension is the measurement of the carrier and/or the container of the resource. Dimension follows the extent of the resource. The way of measuring the dimension of a resource is based on the type of resource itself. In most cases, dimension includes the measurements of height, width, depth, length, gauge, and diameter of the carrier or the container of the resource.

In RDA, metric symbols are not considered to be abbreviations and should be used in MARC 21 tag 300 subfield $c (RDA Appendix B.5.1). For example, use cm (for centimeters) [no period]. Abbreviations for measurements of duration (RDA B.5.3) should be used. For example, min (for minutes) and sec (for seconds) (see RDA B.7 for a list of usable abbreviations).

In accordance with ISBD punctuation instructions, the MARC 21 tag 300 should not end with a full stop, unless the MARC 21 tag 300 is followed by a series statement (in a MARC 21 tag 490). If the MARC 21 tag 300 ends in a dimensional indicator such as "sec.," "min.," or "in.," then the line may appear to have a full stop. However, this full stop is part of the abbreviation. In this case a full stop should be added for the ISBD punctuation, for example, 300 $c 45 min.

4. ACCOMPANIED MATERIALS: (RDA 27.1) [MARC 21 TAG 300 SUBFIELD $e]

RDA provides three options:

Describe accompanying materials in MARC 21 tag 300 subfield $e

or

Describe accompanying materials in a second MARC 21 tag 300, whichever seems most appropriate

or

Give the accompanying materials in a note

Examples:

300 $a 1 computer disc (2 text files. 27 image files) : $b CD-ROM, PDF, JPEG, color illustrations; $c 4 ¾ in., in pocket enclosure (22 cm) + $e 1 press release (1 page; $c 30 cm)

or

300 $a 1 computer disc (2text files. 27 image files) : $b CD-ROM, PDF, JPEG, color illustrations; $c 4 ¾ in., in pocket enclosure (22 cm)

300 $a 1 press release (1 page; $c 30 cm)

or

500 $a Accompanied by 1 press release (1 page; $c 30 cm)

Use the name of a carrier type from RDA 3.3.1.3, unless it is a booklet or some other material not on that list:

336 $a text $2 rdacontent

336 $a still image $2 rdacontent

337 $a computer $2 rdamedia
337 $a unmediated $2 rdamedia
338 $a computer $2 rdacarrier
338 $a sheet $2 rdacarrier

DESCRIBING CARRIERS

CONTENT, MEDIA, AND CARRIER TYPES (RDA 3.2, 3.3, 6.9) [MARC 21 TAGS 336, 337, 338] (CORE ELEMENT)

These three new MARC 21 tags were created to replace the former AACR2 General Material Designation (GMD) that was placed in 245 $h. These tags use closed vocabularies that RDA developed with the ONIX publishing community. The following is an explanation of the use and the vocabulary of these tags.

1. CONTENT TYPE (RDA 6.9) [MARC 21 TAG 336, SUBFIELD $2]

Includes terms to inform the user how the content of the work is expressed and what form of communication and which human sense is used. For example: performed music, text, or two-dimensional moving image. RDA chapter 7 provides guidelines for describing content.

Content type is based on the following controlled terms:

Cartographic dataset
Cartographic image
Cartographic moving image
Cartographic tactile image
Cartographic tactile three-dimensional form
Cartographic three-dimensional form
Computer dataset
Computer program
Notated movement
Notated music
Performed music
Sounds
Spoken word
Still image
Tactile image
Tactile notated music
Tactile notated movement
Tactile text
Tactile three-dimensional form
Text
Three-dimensional form
Three-dimensional moving image
Two-dimensional moving image
Other
Unspecified

336 $a two-dimensional moving image $2 rdacontent
336 $a text $2 rdacontent

2. MEDIA TYPE (RDA 3.2) [MARC 21 TAG 337]

"Categorization reflecting the general type of intermediation device required to view, play, run, etc., the content of a resource." Media type is not a core element. RDA devised terms based on controlled vocabulary to be used in this tag:

Audio	*Computer*	*Microform*	*Microscopic*
Projected	*Stereograph*	*Unmediated*	*Video*

337 $a video $2 rdamedia
337 $a computer $2 rdamedia

3. CARRIER TYPE (RDA 3.3) [MARC 21 TAG 338]

"A categorization reflecting the format of the storage medium and housing of a carrier in combination with the type of intermediation device required to view, play, run, etc., the content of a resource."

RDA devised terms for the carrier type based on controlled vocabulary to be used in this tag:

Audio carriers

Audio cartridge
Audio cylinder
Audio disc
Audio roll
Audiocassette
Audiotape reel
Sound track reel

Computer carriers

Computer card
Computer chip cartridge
Computer disc
Computer disc cartridge
Computer tape cartridge
Computer tape cassette
Computer tape reel
Online resource

Microform carriers

Aperture card
Microfiche
Microfiche cassette
Microfilm cartridge
Microfilm cassette
Microfilm reel
Microfilm roll
Microfilm slip
Microopaque

Projected image carriers

Film cartridge
Film cassette
Film reel
Film roll
Filmslip
Filmstrip
Filmstrip cartridge
Overhead transparency
Slide

Unmediated carriers

Card
Flipchart
Object
Roll
Sheet
Volume

Video carriers

Video cartridge
Videocassette
Videodisc
Videotape reel

Stereographic carriers

Stereograph card
Stereograph disc

338 $a Videodisc $2 rdacarrier
338 $a microfiche $2 rdacarrier
(Notice that Carrier and Media type are in RDA Section 1, Part 3. They are related to the manifestation. Content type is in RDA Section 2, 6. It is related to the expression.)

4. SPECIFIC EXAMPLES OF 336, 337, AND 338 TAGS IN RELATION TO THE 300 TAG

Microfiche (RDA 3.4.1.7.4)

300 $a 1 microfiche (20 frames)
336 $a text $2 rdacontent
337 $a unmediated $2 rdamedia
338 $a microfiche $2 rdacarrier

Electronic Resources (RDA 3.4.1.7.5)

300 $a computer discs ; $c 12 cm
336 $a text $2 rdacontent
337 $a computer $2 rdamedia
338 $a computer disc $2 rdacarrier

Online PDF

300 $a 1 online resource (59 pages) : $b text file, PDF
336 $a text $2 rdacontent
337 $a computer $2 rdamedia
338 $a online resource $2 rdacarrier

DVD

300 $a 1 DVD
336 $a two-dimensional moving object $2 rdacontent
337 $a video $2 rdamedia
338 $a video disc $2 rdacarrier

Videodiscs (RDA 3.4.1.7.8)

300 $a 1 videodisc (30,487 frames) : $b digital, sound, color ; $c 12 cm
336 $a two-dimensional moving image $2 rdacontent
337 $a video $2 rdamedia
338 $a videodisc $2 rdacarrier

PDF File Accessed Online

300 $a 1 PDF file (38 pages)
336 $a text $2 rdacontent
337 $a computer $2 rdamedia
338 $a online resource $2 rdacarrier

Audio Recording—Book

300 $a 3 audio discs (approximately 3 hr.) : $b CD audio, digital ; $c 12 cm
336 $a spoken word $2 rdacontent
337 $a audio $2 rdamedia
338 $a audio discs $2 rdacarrier

Audio Recording—Music

300 $a 1 CD-ROM : $b digital, Real audio, Windows media ; $c 12 cm
336 $a performed music $2 rdacontent
337 $a audio $2 rdamedia
337 $a computer $2 rdamedia
338 $a audio disc $2 rdacarrier
338 $a computer disc $2 rdacarrier

(In this example, the 337 and 338 are repeatable to reflect the content.)

Sound Recording

300 $a 1 audio disc : $b digital, stereo ; $c 12 cm
336 $a performed music $2 rdacontent
337 $a audio $2 rdamedia
338 $a audio disc $2 rdacarrier

Atlas

300 $a 1 atlas (2 volumes)
336 $a cartographic image $2 rdacontent
337 $a unmediated $2 rdamedia
338 $a volume $2 marcrdacarrier

Map

300 $a 1 map
336 $a cartographic image $2 rdacontent
337 $a unmediated $2 rdamedia
338 $a sheet $2 rdacarrier

Globe

300 $a 1 globe
336 $a cartographic image $2 rdacontent
337 $a unmediated $2 rdamedia
338 $a object $2 rdacarrier

Notated Music

300 $a 1 vocal score (xii, 324 pages)
336 $a notated music $2 rdacontent
337 $a unmediated $2 rdamedia
338 $a volume $2 marccarrier

300 $a 1 choir book
336 $a text $2 rdacontent

337 $a unmediated $2 rdamedia
338 $a volume $2 marccarrier

Still Image (RDA 3.4.4)

300 $a 1 picture
336 $a Still image $2 rdacontent
338 $a volume $a rdacarrier

300 $a approximately 200 photographs
336 $a still image $2 rdacontent
338 $a volume $2 rdacarrier

Single Volume

300 $a 123 pages, 28 unnumbered pages
336 $a text $2 rdacontent
337 $a unmediated $2 rdamedia
338 $a volume $2 rdacarrier

300 $a xxi, 300 pages
336 $a text $2 rdacontent
337 $a unmediated $2 rdamedia
338 $a volume $2 rdacarrier

300 $a 356 leaves
336 $a text $2 rdacontent
337 $a unmediated $2 rdamedia
338 $a volume $2 rdacarrier

300 $a 203 columns
336 $a text $2 rdacontent
337 $a unmediated $2 rdamedia
338 $a volume $2 rdacarrier

Multivolume

300 $a volumes
336 $a text
337 $a unmediated $2 rdamedia
338 $a volume $2 rdacarrier

300 $a 6 volumes
336 $a text
337 $a unmediated $2 rdamedia
338 $a volume $2 rdacarrier

SERIES STATEMENT (RDA 2.12) [MARC 21 TAG 490] (CORE ELEMENT)

The series statement is transcribed in the same way as the title and statement of responsibility. This element includes:

- Title proper of series (RDA 2.12.2) (core element)
- Parallel title proper of series (RDA 2.12.3)
- Other title information of series (RDA 2.12.4)
- Parallel other title information of series (RDA 2.12.5)
- Statement of responsibility (RDA 2.12. 6)
- ISSN (International Standard Serial Number) (RDA 2.12.8)
- Numbering within series (RDA 2.12.9) (core element)
- Subseries (RDA 2.12.10) (core element)

1. PROPER TITLE IS TRANSCRIBED AS IT APPEARS ON THE SOURCE OF INFORMATION

490 1 $a Methods in molecular biology ; $v 146
490 1 $a Vassar Miller prize in poetry series ; $v number 12
490 1 $a Monografie della Scuola archeologica di Atene e delle missioni italiane in Oriente ; $v volume 18
490 1 $a ABC series
490 1 $a MSHA handbook series ; $v handbook no. PH 06-V-1

2. STATEMENT OF RESPONSIBILITY RELATING TO SERIES (RDA 2.12.6)

The statement of responsibility that is related to series is recorded only if it is important for the identification of the series:

490 1 $a Technical memorandum / $c Bureau of Reclamation ; $v number 233.

3. TAKE THE ISSN OF A SERIES (RDA 2.12.8) FROM ANY SOURCE WITHIN THE SOURCE

490 1 $a Religion in philosophy and theology, $x 1616-346X ; $v 34
490 1 $a FAO fisheries and aquaculture technical paper, $x 2070-7010
490 0 $a NATO science for peace and security series. D, Information and communication security, $x 1874-6268 ; $v volume 18

4. NUMERIC AND/OR ALPHABETIC DESIGNATION OF THE FIRST ISSUE OR PART OF A SEQUENCE (RDA 2.6.2) [MARC 21 TAG 490, SUBFIELD $v] (CORE ELEMENT)

Record the numeric and/or alphabetic designation of the first issue or part of a sequence of numbering of a serial:

490 1 $a . . .. $v Number 1
490 1 $a . . .. $v Issue 1
490 1 $a . . .. $v Vol. 1, no. 4
490 1 $a . . .. $v New series, v.1, no. 1
490 1 $a . . .. $v Volume 1, issue 3

PROVIDING ACQUISITION AND ACCESS INFORMATION (RDA 4.6) [MARC 21 TAG 856 SUBFIELD $u]

RDA provides guidelines and instructions on recording the attributes of manifestations and items that are most often used to support acquisition and access. The elements covered include:

- Terms of availability (RDA 4.2)
- Contact information (RDA 4.3)
- Restrictions on access (RDA 4.4)
- Restrictions on use (RDA 4.5)
- Uniform resource locator (RDA 4.6)

Although all elements listed above are important, the uniform resource locator (URL) is the only element that will be covered in this section. The URL is the address of a remote access resource. The URL provides access to the resource using a standard Internet browser. Record the URL in MARC 21 tag 856. If there is more than one URL, record one or more (depending on the local cataloging policy). Record the URL for related resources as part of the description of the related manifestation:

856 42 $3 Cover image $u http://catalogimages.wiley.com/images/db/jimages/9780470289525.jpg
856 42 $3 Contributor biographical information $u www.loc.gov/catdir/enhancements/fy1106/2010048264-b.html

LANGUAGE OF THE CONTENT (RDA 7.12) [MARC 21 TAGS 041 AND 546]

Record details of the language or languages used to express the content of the resource if they are considered to be important for identification or selection:

041 0$ $a eng $a ger
546 $a Text in English and German.

SCRIPT OF THE CONTENT (RDA 7.13.2) [MARC 21 TAG 546]

Record the script or scripts used to express the language content of the resource using one or more of the terms listed in ISO 15924 (www.unicode.org/iso15924/codelists.html).

NOTES: (RDA 2.20) [MARC 21 TAGS 5XX]

The notes element is used for additional descriptive information that cannot be presented in the descriptive elements. They are added for the purpose of clarification or adding useful information for the user. Notes can be taken from the resource itself or from outside the resource. The following examples illustrate various types of notes:

1. SOURCE OF TITLE (RDA 2.20.2.3)

500 $a Title from journal home page (viewed July 25, 2002)
500 $a Cover title.
500 $a Caption title.

2. TITLE VARIATIONS, INACCURACIES, AND DELETION (RDA 2.20.2.4)

245 4 $a The wolrd of Internet.
500 $a Title should read: World of Internet

3. GENERAL NOTE

500 $a Publisher's licensing agreement prohibits multiple on-line access.
500 $a Includes index.
500 $a Rev. ed. of: Biochemistry. 2nd ed. 2007.
500 $a Translation of the 4th German edition [of Pflanzenbiochemie]
500 $a Title from OhioLINK ETD abstract web page (viewed Apr. 28, 2010)
500 $a Advisor: Nicola E. Brasch.
500 $a Keywords: Vitamin B12; Cobalamin Metabolism; Oxidative Stress; Reactive Oxygen Species; Cobalamin Synthesis.
500 $a "Russian State Naval Archives (RGAVMF); Institute of History and Area Studies, Aarhus University."
500 $a Description based on: Vol. 132, no. 6 (Dec. 1975); title from cover.
500 $a Latest issue consulted: Vol. 189, no. 5 (1 Mar. 2004)
500 $a Description based on: Vol. 1, no. 1 (spring 2009); title from cover.
500 $a Latest issue consulted: Vol. 1, no. 1 (spring 2009)

4. NUMBERING PECULIARITIES NOTE

515 $a Vol. 1, no. 1 (spring 2009) also called Inaugural issue.

5. ADDITIONAL PHYSICAL FORM AVAILABLE NOTE

530 $a Issued also online.

6. RESTRICTION ON ACCESS

506 $a Full text release delayed.

7. ISSUED WITH (MARC 21 TAG 501)

501 $a On reel with: They're in the Army now.

8. THESIS NOTE (MARC 21 TAG 502)

502 $a Ph.D. $c Kent State University $d 2010.

9. BIBLIOGRAPHY AND/OR INDEX (MARC 21 TAG 504)

504 $a Includes bibliographical references (pages 1-100) and index.
500 $a Includes index.
504 $a Bibliography: pages 100-109.

10. CONTENTS (MARC 21 TAG 505)

505 1 $a How these records were discovered—A short sketch of the Talmuds—Constantine's letter.

11. SUMMARY (MARC 21 TAG 520)

520 $a Is there a "crisis" in the disciplines of education? In this text, leading scholars consider the changing fortunes of the disciplines as education moved away from the dominance of psychology as a result of the growing importance of the other disciplines.

12. SYSTEM REQUIREMENTS (21 TAG 538)

538 $a Mode of access: World Wide Web.

13. NOTE ON ISSUE, PART, OR ITERATION USED AS THE BASIS FOR IDENTIFICATION OF THE RESOURCE (RDA 2.20.13) (MARC 21 TAG 588)

588 $a Description based on: 1, published in 2009; title from title page.

588 $a Description based on: Tom 3, vypusk 4 (okti͡abr′/dekabr′ 2009); title from cover.
588 $a Latest issue consulted: Tom 3, vypusk 4 (okti͡abr′/dekabr′ 2009).
588 $a Description based on: Január 2008; title from image of cover (viewed Nov. 1, 2010).
588 $a Latest issue consulted: September 2010 (viewed Nov. 1, 2010).
588 $a Description based on: Vol. 32, No. 25 (June 24, 2011).

IV. SPECIFIC INSTRUCTIONS FOR SPECIAL MATERIALS

RDA contains specific instructions for special materials. These instruction are found in various chapters and places in RDA. This section discusses selected materials that require specific cataloging instructions.

INSTRUCTIONS FOR CATALOGING ELECTRONIC RESOURCES

When describing electronic resources, add the following elements if they are available and are considered important for identification or selection of the resource (Stanford University Libraries Technical Services. 2012).

FILE TYPE (RDA 3.19.2) [MARC 21 TAGS 256 AND 516]

Record the file type (audio files, video files, and data files), using one or more appropriate terms from the list below.

Audio file	*Data file*	*Image file*
Program file	*Text file*	*Video file*

300 $a 1 online resource (8 audio files)
300 $a 1 online resource (1 audio file, 3 video files)

If there are many files, or files of different types, do not include this information in MARC 21 tag 300. Instead, add this information in MARC 21 tag 516 note, if considered important.

ENCODING FORMAT (RDA 3.19.3) [MARC 21 TAGS 300 $b, 538]

Record the encoding format using one or more appropriate terms from the list provided in RDA instruction 3.19.3.3. Some formats (e.g., XML) apply to more than one category. In MARC 21 tag 300 $b, state whether there are illustrations (if the content is primarily textual (RDA 7.15)), and give color if present (RDA 7.17.3). Add "sound," if present (RDA 7.18).

If encoding format is too complicated to be explained in the MARC 21 tag 300 and is considered important, explain it in a MARC 21 tag 538 (RDA 3.19.3.4)

300 $a 1 online resource (15 video files) : $b color, sound, MPEG4
300 $a 1 online resource (ix, 120 pages) : $b illustrations (chiefly color), PDF

FILE SIZE (RDA 3.19.4) [MARC 21 TAGS 256, 300 $a]

Record the file size if it is available and is important for identification or selection. Give file size in bytes, kilobytes (*KB*), megabytes (*MB*), or gigabytes (*GB*), as appropriate:

300 $a 1 online resource (1 video file, 6.8 KB, 36 min.)

DIGITAL FILE CHARACTERISTICS (RDA 3.19.5 AND 3.19.7) [MARC 21 TAG 538]

Resolution and transmission can be added in MARC 21 tag 538 if it is too complicated to be explained and it is important for identification or selection (RDA 3.19.3.4).

Resolution (RDA 3.19.5) [MARC 21 Tag 538]

Record the resolution by giving the measurements of the image in pixels, if it is available and is considered important for identification or selection:

538 $a 3.1 megapixels

Transmission Speed (RDA 3.19.7) [MARC 21 Tag 538]

Record the transmission speed of the file, in kilobytes per second (*kbps*), if it is available and is considered important for identification or selection (e.g., for streaming audio or video).

538 $a 2048x1536 pixels.

Regional Encoding (RDA 3.19.6) [MARC 21 Tag 538]

Record the regional encoding if it is available and is considered to be important for identification or selection.

538 $a all regions

Date Viewed (RDA 2.20.13.5) [MARC 21 Tag 588]

588 $a viewed Feb. 7, 2011.

For online resources, make a note identifying the date on which the resource was viewed for description.

Equipment or System Requirement (RDA 3.20) [MARC 21 Tag 538]

Record any equipment or system requirements beyond what is normal and obvious for the type of carrier or type of file (e.g., the make and model of equipment or hardware, the operating system, the amount of memory, or any plug-ins or peripherals required to play, view, or run the resource).

538 $a Links require Internet access and Adobe Acrobat Reader
538 $a Special software or hardware requirements.

INSTRUCTIONS FOR CATALOGING SERIALS

A serial is a resource issued in successive parts, usually bearing numbering, that has no predetermined conclusion (e.g., periodical, newspaper).

Mode of issuance for serials is recorded in "BLvl" in the fixed field area (figure 5.1):

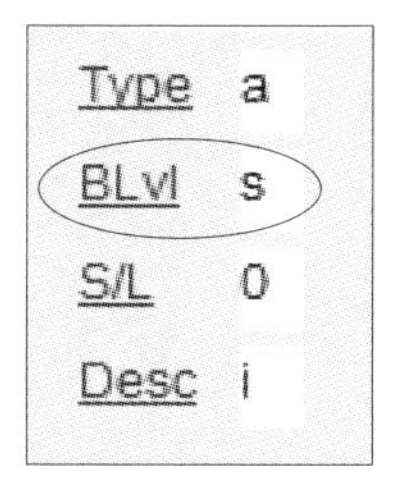

Figure 5.1

TITLE PROPER

Transcribe title as found on resource (RDA 1.7.9). However, "when transcribing the title proper of a serial or integrating resource, correct obvious typographic errors, and make a note giving the title as it appears on the source of information " (RDA 2.3.1.4). This means that when cataloging serials, correct obvious typographical errors in title proper. Give errant form in the MARC 21 tag 246 if it is considered to be important for access.

Example:

245 00 $a Housing starts
246 3 $a Sources of information on v.1, no. 1 reads: Housing sarts

"If a title of a serial includes a date, name, number, etc., that varies from issue to issue, omit this date, name, number, etc. Use a mark of omission (. . .) to indicate such an omission."

Example:

Report on the . . . Conference on Development Objective and Strategy
Source of information reads: Report on the 4th Conference on Development Objective and Strategy

KEY TITLE (RDA 2.3.9) [MARC 21 TAG 222]

Key title is defined as a unique name assigned to a resource by the International Standard Serial Number (ISSN) registry agency for a unique title assigned to a continuing resource (serial or integrating resource). The key title is recorded as it appears on the source.

222 0 $a Journal of polymer science. Part B. Polymer letters
222 0 $a Volunteer (Washington)
(Add qualifiers to make it unique when necessary.)

ABBREVIATED TITLE (RDA 2.3.10) [MARC 21 TAG 210]

Abbreviated title is defined as a title that has been abbreviated for the purpose of indexing or identification. It is recorded as it appears on the source of information. The abbreviated title is based on the title contained in MARC 21 tag 222. It is recorded as it appears on the source.

210 0 $a Manage. improve. cost reduct. Goals
222 0 $a Management improvement and cost reduction goals

Numbering (RDA 2.6.2) [MARC 21 tag 362 First Indicator 0 or 1)] (Core Element)

Transcribe the numbering of serials as it appears on the resources or according to the cataloging policy of agency. The numbering can be given in MARC 21 tag 362 first indicator "0" as formatted tag or 362 first indicator "1" as unformatted tag.

362 0 $a April 2010-
362 0 $a Volume 1, issue 1
362 1 $a Began in 1990s.

CHRONOLOGICAL DESIGNATION OF THE FIRST ISSUE OR PART OF SEQUENCE (RDA 2.6.3 AND 2.6.4) [MARC 21 TAG 362] (CORE ELEMENT)

This element contains the chronological designation relating to the first and last issue of a serial (if the serial is completed). The designation is presented in the form of date (year; year and month; month, day, and year):

362 0 $a Volume.16, issue 7 (February 16, 2010)-
(Formatted tag)

362 0 $a Volume 1, issue 1 (2010)-
362 0 $a 2010-
362 1 $a Began with: Volume 40, number1 (February 2010)
(Unformatted tag)

362 0 $a Volume 1, number 1 (18 June 2002)-volume 9, issue 3 (8 April 2010)

FREQUENCY (RDA 2.14) [MARC 21 LEADERS 008/18–19; 310/321] (NOT A CORE ELEMENT)

Record the frequency of released issues or part of a serial or the frequency of updates to integrated resources.

MARC 21 characters position 18 is used for frequency and 19 for regularity.

MARC 21 tag 310 is used to record the current publication frequency (this tag is not repeatable) and MARC 21 tag 321 is used to record the former publication frequency (this tag is repeatable).

Example:

008	position 18	Freq	m
008	position 19	Regl	r
310	Monthly 1968-		
321	Five issues yearly, $b 1950-1967		

If the identification of serials is not based on the first released issue or part, make a note identifying the issue or part used as the basis of the identification. (2.20.13 RDA) [MARC 21 tag 588]:

588 $a Identification of the resource based on: Volume 1, number 3 (August 1999).

If more than one issue or part has been consulted, make a separate note identifying the latest issue or part consulted in preparing the description. Do not make a note of earliest and/or latest issues or parts recorded in the numbering of serials element (RDA 2.6):

588 $a Identification of the resource based on: no. 7 (June/December 2007)
588 $a Latest issue consulted: no. 12 (June/December 2009)
362 0 $a Number 8 (Jan./June 1997)-
588 $a Latest issue consulted: no. 12 (Jan./June 1999).

Make a note identifying the earliest issue or part consulted and its date of publication. If other issues or parts have also been consulted, make a separate note identifying the latest issue or part consulted and its date.

588 $a Identification of the resource based on: Labor and economic reforms in Latin America and the Caribbean, 1995

NOTE ON CHANGE IN CARRIER CHARACTERISTIC (RDA 3.22.6) [MARC 21 TAG 500]

If the carrier type or other carrier characteristics are changed in a subsequent issue or part, make a note if the change is considered important for identification or selection:

500 $a Some issues have audiocassette supplements, 1984-1997; compact disc supplements, 1998-

LATER TITLE PROPER (RDA 2.3.8) [MARC 21 TAG 246]

Later title proper is defined as a title proper appearing on a later issue or part of multipart monograph or serial that differs from the title of the first or earlier issue or part. This element applies to serials and multipart monographs. The later titles proper can be recorded if the change in the title proper is minor and if it is considered to be important. Make a note on the numbering or publication dates to which the change of the title proper applies. Make a general note if the changes have been numerous:

Annual report on pipeline safety
(Later title proper appearing in issues from 1999. The title proper recorded as: Annual report of pipeline safety.)

246 10 $a Annual report of pipeline safety.
500 $a Some issues have title: Annual report on pipeline safety.

INSTRUCTIONS FOR CATALOGING INTEGRATING RESOURCES (UPDATED LOOSE-LEAF OR WEBSITE)

EARLIER TITLE PROPER (RDA 2.3.7) [MARC 21 TAG 247]

Earlier title proper is defined as a title proper appearing on the earlier iteration of an integrating resource that is different from the current one. This element applies to integrating resources according to RDA and is given in MARC 21 tag 247; it is also given for serials in MARC 21 tag 246 when description is not "backed up." The earlier titles proper can be recorded if they are considered to be important. Make a note on the publication date to which the earlier title proper applies. For the online resource, make a note of the earlier title proper as it was viewed. Make a general note if the changes have been numerous.

Business library for businessmen.
(Earlier title proper issued 1925. Current title proper: The cumulative loose-leaf business encyclopedia.)

245 04 $a The cumulative loose-leaf business encyclopedia.
500 $a Published 1925 under title: Business library for businessmen.

NOTE ON ITERATION USED AS THE BASIS FOR IDENTIFICATION OF THE RESOURCES (2.20.13 RDA) [MARC 21 TAG 588)

It is a note on issue, part, or iteration used as the basis for identification of the resource. This note may also include the date on which an online resource was viewed for description.

588 $a Identification of resources based on version consulted: Jan. 12, 2012.

INSTRUCTIONS FOR SOUND RECORDING (GLENNAN 2011)

TYPE OF RECORDING (RDA 3.16.2.3) [MARC 21 TAG 300 SUBFIELD $b]

Record the type of recording using an appropriate term from the list below:

Analog *Digital*

300 $a 1 CD (45 min.) : $b digital ; $c 12 cm
300 $a 1 audiocassette : $b analog, 4.75 cm/s, 4 track ; $c 10 × 7 cm, 4 mm tape

RECORDING MEDIUM (RDA 3.16.3.3) [MARC 21 TAG 300 SUBFIELD $b]

Record the recording medium using an appropriate term from the list below:

Magnetic *Magneto-optical* *Optical*

300 $a 1 compact disc : $b digital, optical, 1.4 m/s ; $c 4 3/4 in.

PLAYING SPEED (RDA 3.16.4.3) [MARC 21 TAG 300 SUBFIELD $b]

Record the playing speed of an audio recording if it is considered important for identification or selection, using an appropriate measure of speed as instructed below:

Record the playing speed of an analog disc in revolutions per minute (*rpm*).

300 $a 1 audio disc : $b analog, stereo, 33 1/3 rpm ; $c 12 in.

GROOVE CHARACTERISTICS (RDA 3.16.5.3) [MARC 21 TAG 300 SUBFIELD $B]

Record the groove width of an analog disc if it is considered important for identification or selection, using an appropriate term from the list below:

Coarse groove *Microgroove*

300 $a 1 audio disc : $b analog, 33 1/3 rpm, microgroove ; $c 30 cm

TRACK CONFIGURATION (RDA 3.16.6.3) [MARC 21 TAG 300 $b]

For soundtrack films, record the track configuration using an appropriate term from the list below:

Center track *Edge track*

TAPE CONFIGURATION (RDA 3.16.7.3) [MARC 21 TAG 300 SUBFIELD $B]

For tape cartridges, cassettes, and reels, record the tape configuration (i.e., the number of tracks on the tape) if it is considered important for identification or selection.

RECORDING CONFIGURATION OF PLAYBACK CHANNELS (RDA 3.16.8.3) [MARC 21 TAG 300 SUBFIELD $b]

Record the configuration of playback channels if the information is readily ascertainable, using one or more appropriate terms from the list below:

Mono *Stereo* *Quadraphonic* *Surround*

300 $a 1 audio disc : $b digital, 1.4 m/s, stereo, surround ; $c 12 cm

SPECIAL PLAYBACK CHARACTERISTICS (RDA 3.16.9.3) [MARC 21 TAGS 300 SUBFIELD $B AND 538]

Record special playback characteristics if they are considered important for identification or selection, using one or more appropriate terms from the list below:

CCIR standard	*CX encoded*	*dbx encoded*
Dolby	*Dolby-A encoded*	*Dolby-B encoded*
Dolby-C encoded	*LPCM*	*NAB standard*

INSTRUCTIONS FOR CATALOGING CARTOGRAPHIC RESOURCES

LAYOUT (RDA 3.11.2) [MARC 21 TAG 300]

If the layout of a cartographic image other than an atlas is continued at the same scale on the other side of the sheet or sheets, record "*both sides.*"

300 $a 1 map : $b both sides, color ; $c 103 x 57 cm,
on sheet 54 x 67 cm

If the same image is represented in more than one language on each side of the sheet, record "*back to back.*" If it is needed for identification or selection, record details of the layout of cartographic images in a note:

300 $a 2 maps : $b back to back, color ; $c 103 x 57 cm,
on sheet 54 x 67 cm

DIGITAL FILE CHARACTERISTICS (RDA 3.19.8.3) [MARC 21 TAG 352]

For digitally encoded cartographic content, record the following information if it is important for identification or selection:

a. data type (e.g., raster, vector, or point)
b. object type (e.g., point, line, polygon, pixel)
c. number of objects used to represent spatial information

Record details of the digital representation of cartographic content (e.g., topology level, compression) if they are considered important for identification or selection (RDA 3.19.8.4):

352 $a Raster : $b pixel $d (5,000 x $e 5,000) ; $q Tiff.

LONGITUDE AND LATITUDE (RDA 7.4.2) [MARC 21 TAG 255]

For terrestrial cartographic content, record the coordinates in the following order:

- Westernmost extent of area covered (longitude)
- Easternmost extent of area covered (longitude)
- Northernmost extent of area covered (latitude)
- Southernmost extent of area covered (latitude).

Express the coordinates in degrees (°), minutes ('), and seconds (") of the sexagesimal system (360° circle) taken from the Greenwich prime meridian. Precede each coordinate by W, E, N, or S, as appropriate. Separate the two sets of longitude and latitude by a diagonal slash without a space. Separate each longitude or latitude from its counterpart by a hyphen without a space:

255 $a Scale 1:250,000 $c W 85°20'00"-W 81°04'00"/N 34°42'00"-N 30°52'00".

HORIZONTAL SCALE OF CARTOGRAPHIC CONTENT (RDA 7.25.3) [MARC 21 TAG 255]

Record the horizontal scale of the resource as a representative fraction expressed as a ratio:

255 $a Scale approximately 1:610,000.
255 $a Scale 1:3,500,000.

VERTICAL SCALE OF CARTOGRAPHIC CONTENT (RDA 7.25.4) [MARC 21 TAG 255]

When describing a relief model, other three-dimensional cartographic resource, or a two-dimensional cartographic representation of a three-dimensional entity (e.g., block diagram or profile), record the vertical scale in addition to the horizontal scale:

255 $a Scale 1:15,000
255 $a Scale 1:8,000

PROJECTION OF CARTOGRAPHIC CONTENT (RDA 7.26) [MARC 21 TAG 255]

Transcribe the statement of projection if it appears on the resource, its container or case, or ancillary material:

255 $a Scale 1:10,000 : $b transverse Mercator projection $c (E 43°57'00"—E 44°03'30"/N 13°38'00"—N 13°33'30").

TITLE PROPER FOR CARTOGRAPHIC MATERIALS (RDA 2.3.2.8.2) [MARC 21 TAG 245]

When the title proper of cartographic materials includes a statement of scale, include the statement of scale as part of the title proper:

245 00 $a Topographic 1:500,000 low flying chart.

V. RELATED MANIFESTATIONS (RDA 27) [MARC 21 TAGS 5XX AND 76X–787] AND RELATED ITEMS (RDA 28.1) [MARC 21 TAGS 5XX AND 76X–787]

As was discussed in the FRBR chapter, relationships are the links we make between one entity and another. They assist users in navigating the bibliographic universe represented in our catalogs. In RDA, you record a relationship whenever you:

- Add access points for creators (authors, editors, annotators, illustrators, etc.).
- Add an access point for a related work (e.g., succeeding or preceding title of a serial, adaptation, supplement, sequel, part of a larger work) or *expression* (revised version, translation, etc.).
- Add the succeeding name of a corporate body in a 510 field in an authority record, or a 500 for the pseudonym of a personal name in an authority record (if you do authority work).
- Add subject headings to records.

Relationships are mostly recorded in the bibliographic record through access points associated with work, expression, manifestation, and items and/or through access points or structured and unstructured descriptions for related works, expressions, manifestations, and items. Sometimes relationships are recorded in authority records (related persons and corporate bodies). This section will address related manifestations and related items.

RELATED MANIFESTATIONS (RDA 27) [MARC 21 TAGS 5XX AND 76X–787]

The related manifestation is a manifestation issued or published in a different format that is related to the resource being described. Examples for related manifestation are reproduction, different formats of the same expression (e.g., book is also published as a PDF file), reprints, reissues, and facsimiles:

There are two methods to express related manifestation:

- Identifier
- Description
    - Structure description of the related manifestation
    - Unstructured description of the manifestation

THE USE OF IDENTIFIER FOR RELATED MANIFESTATION

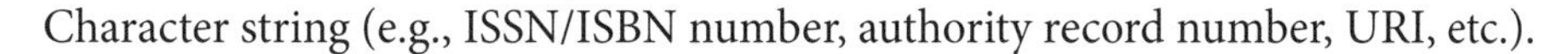

Character string (e.g., ISSN/ISBN number, authority record number, URI, etc.).

534 $p Originally published in English : $c Garden City, N.Y. : Anchor Books, 1974-1978, $n under title : $t Anchor atlas of world history. $z 0385061781 (v. 1) $z 0385133553 (v. 2).

534 $cp 1987 $o Finlandia Records FACD357

STRUCTURED DESCRIPTION FOR RELATED MANIFESTATION

1. A NOTE THAT USES ISBD PUNCTUATION TO IDENTIFY THE ELEMENTS

534 $p Electronic reproduction of (manifestation): $a Olarte Martínez, Matilde. $t Miguel de Irizar y Domenzain (1635-1684?) : biografia, epistolario y estudio de sus lamentaciones. $c 1992. $e 1045 pages : music. $n Doctoral thesis.

2. LINKING MARC 21 TAGS 76X–787

(Notice that when the reproduction is in a different carrier than the original, use MARC 21 tag 776 to record the original manifestation. When the carrier of reproduction is the same as the carrier of the original, use MARC 21 tag 775. Use relationship designator from RDA Appendix J, "Reproduction of manifestation" in subfield $i. You may also include the call number and the LCCN.)

245 00 $a IET electrical systems in transportation.
246 30 $a Institute of Engineering and Technology electrical systems in transportation
246 1 $i At head of title: $a IET Journals
260 $a [U.K.] : $b Institute of Engineering and Technology, $c 2011-
530 $a Also issued online.
776 08 $i Online version: $t IET electrical systems in transportation $x 2042-9746 $w (DLC) 2011261048$w (OCoLC)723082276.

(In this example, the MARC 21 tag 776 first and second indictors are "08" and the subfield "$i" show that this serial is also issued in electronic version.)

245 10 $a OneFiveFour / $c Lebbeus Woods.
246 3 $a One Five Four
260 $a New York, New York : $b Princeton Architectural Press, $c 2011.

→ 775 0 $i Reproduction of (manifestation): $a Woods, Lebbeus. $t OneFiveFour $d New York : Princeton Architectural Press, 1989.

(Carrier of reproduction same as original: use MARC 775.)

100 1 $a Woods, Rebecca, $e author.
245 10 $a Hannah of Silver Falls / $c Rebecca Woods.
260 $a Springville, Utah : $b Sweetwater Books, $c [2011], ©2011.
→ 775 08 $i Reproduction of (manifestation): $a Woods, Rebecca $t Hannah of Silver Falls $d Springville, UT : CFI, c1997 $h vii, 254 p. ; 23 cm.

100 1 $a Gairdner, James, $d 1828-1912.
245 14 $a The English Church in the sixteenth century : $b from the accession of Henry VIII to the death of Mary / $c by James Gairdner.
260 $a London : $b Macmillan and Co., $c 1902.
300 $a xv, 430 pages (some folded) : map ; 20 cm.
→ 776 0 $i Reproduction of (manifestation) $a Gairdner, James, $d 1828-1912 $t English Church in the sixteenth century $d London : Macmillan and co., limited; 1902 $h xv, 430 pages : folded map. 20 cm $n Call number of original: BX5052 .H6 vol. 4 $w 02021454.

(Use relationship designator from RDA appendix J, "Reproduction of Manifestation in subfield $i". The call number and the LCCN are included.)

100 1 Lightner, Adna H., $e author.
245 12 A wayside violet / $c by Adna H. Lightner.
260 Woodbridge, Conn. : $b Research Publications, $c 1978.
300 1 microfilm reel (125 pages) ; $c 35 mm.
08 $i Reproduction of (manifestation): $a Lightner, Adna H. $t Wayside violet $d Cincinnati : Wrightson, 1885 $h 125 pages; 18 cm. $w (DLC) 28863665.

(Carrier of reproduction is not the same as carrier of original: use MARC 776.)

UNSTRUCTURED DESCRIPTION FOR RELATED MANIFESTATION

Unstructured description for related manifestation is a full or partial description of related resource written as a sentence or a paragraph in MARC 21 tags 5xx.

Example:

→ 580 $a Continued in 1982 by: U.S. exports. Schedule E commodity groupings by world area and country

→ 580 $a Also issued electronically via World Wide Web in PDF format

→ 580 $a Issued also in French under title: Revue économique de l'OCDE.

Note: Catalogers may use their own judgment about including other manifestation relationships in bibliographic records and using relationship designators that are found in Appendix J.4 of RDA (see Relationships in Bibliographic References and in Authority Records: Module 5).

VI. RELATED ITEMS (RDA 28.1) [MARC 21 TAGS 5XX AND 76X–787]

A related item is an item that is related to the resource being described. For example, an item used as the basis for a microform reproduction is a related item. Bound with facsimiles, and items added to an individual copy of a manifestation in a special collection are other types of related items.

There are two methods to express related item:

- Identifier:

  500 $a "With a facsimile reproduction of Faraday's manuscript lecture notes from Royal Institution MS F4 J21" ←

  (Accession number provided for related item.)

- Description:
  - Structure description of the related item
  - Unstructured description of the item

EXAMPLES OF STRUCTURED DESCRIPTION OF RELATED ITEM USING BOUND WITH NOTE

110 2 $a Committee of the Corporation of Washington.
245 10 $a Memorial of the Committee of the Corporation of Washington, relating to the pecuniary claims of said corporation on the general government &c. December 16, 1835, referred to the Committee on the District of Columbia.
→ 501 $i Bound with: Report of the Committee on the District of Columbia in relation to the city of Washington. Washington: Printed at the Globe Office, 1835.

EXAMPLE OF STRUCTURE DESCRIPTION OF RELATED ITEM USING MARC 21 TAGS 775 AND 776

(Notice that when the reproduction is in a different carrier than the original, use MARC 21 tag 776 to record the original manifestation. When the carrier of reproduction is the same as the carrier of the original, use MARC 21 tag 775. Use relationship designator from RDA appendix J, "Reproduction of Manifestation " in subfield $i. You may also include the call number and the LCCN.)

100 1 $a Donizetti, Gaetano, $d 1797-1848, $e composer.
245 14 $a Der Liebestrank = $b L'elisire d'amore : komische Oper in zwei Akten / $c Musik von G. Donizetti.
246 31 $s Elisire d'amore
300 $a 1 computer disc (1 vocal score (256 pages) : $b DVD-ROM, PDF, JPEG ; $c 4 3/4 in.
→ 500 $a Electronic reproduction of printed vocal score held by the Österreichische Nationalbibliothek, call number OA.1550.Mus. Includes PDF file of entire volume and JPEG files for each individual page.
→ 776 08 $i Electronic reproduction of (item): $a Donizetti, Gaetano, 1797-1848. $t Liebestrank. $d Wien : Pietro Mechetti qm. Carlo, [1844].

Note: Catalogers can use their judgment to use relationship designators in RDA appendix J.5 in subfield $i if MARC 21 content designation does not give relationship.

UNSTRUCTURED DESCRIPTION FOR RELATED ITEM

Unstructured description for related item is a full or partial description of related item written as a sentence or a paragraph in MARC 21 tag 5xx.

245 04 $a The North American Chekhov Society bulletin.
→ 500 $a Print version of the North American Chekhov Society bulletin.

REFERENCES

Glennan, Kathy. 2011. "RDA: An Overview of Descriptive Elements: Extent, Content/Media/Carrier, Series." Paper presented at the RDA Preconference, Music Library Association Annual Meeting, February 9, 2011. http://bcc.musiclibraryassoc.org/BCC-Historical/BCC2011/05-RDA-descr.pdf.

International Standards Organization. ISO 15924 (www.unicode.org/iso15924/codelists.html).

"Relationships in Bibliographic References and in Authority Records: Module 5." Paper presented at RDA for Georgia Conference, August 9–10, 2011. http://tinyurl.com/GaConference2011.

Stanford University Libraries Technical Services. 2012. "Online Monographs—Cataloging (RDA)." http://lib.stanford.edu/rda-online-monograph-cataloging-guidelines.

ADDITIONAL RESOURCES

Attig, John. 2009. "RDA: Ready for Takeoff?" Paper presented at the New England Library Association Annual Conference, October 18–20, 2009.

Baxmeyer, Jennifer W. 2010. "RDA: What Happens Now?" Presentation, Princeton University Library, July 8, 2010. www.slideshare.net/cellobax/rda-update.

Case, Christopher. 2010. "AACR2 and RDA Examples." https://wiki.library.jhu.edu/display/MSELTS/AACR2-RDA+Examples.

Davis, Renette. 2010. "RDA Serials Cataloging: Changes from AACR2 to RDA." www.renettedavis.com/presentations.html.

Delsey, Tom. 2009. "AACR2 versus RDA." Paper presented at the Canadian Library Association Preconference, May 29, 2009. http://tsig.wikispaces.com/file/view/AACR2_versus_RDA.pdf.

Elrod, J. McRee. 2010a. "RDA/AACR2 Changes." Last modified August 15, 2010. http://special-cataloguing.com/node/1397.

———. 2010b. "Electronic Recourse Cataloging Cheat Sheet." Last modified July 15, 2010. www.slc.bc.ca/cheats/er.htm.

Joint Steering Committee for Development of RDA. 2008. "List of Changes to AACR2 Instructions." 5JSC/RDA/Full draft/Workflows/Book; November 17, 2008. www.rda-jsc.org/docs/5sec7rev.pdf.

Knowlton, Steven A. "Resource Description and Access (RDA) in Australia." www.nla.gov.au/acoc/resource-description-and-access-rda-in-australia. Accessed May 30, 2013.

———. 2008. "How the Current Draft of RDA Addresses Cataloging of Reproductions, Facsimiles and Microforms." Paper presented at the ALCTS Continuing Resources Section Meeting, Anaheim, CA, June 28, 2008. http://stevenknowlton.webs.com/RDA.pdf.

Library of Congress. 2009. "Examples for RDA—Compared to AACR2 (Work in Progress)." Paper presented at the Special Libraries Association Conference, June 16, 2009. www.sla.org/PDFs/SLA2009/2009_rdaexamples.pdf.

Library of Congress, Network Development and MARC Standards Office. 2012. "Term and Code List for RDA Carrier Types." www.loc.gov/standards/valuelist/rdacarrier.html.

———. 2011. "Term and Code List for RDA Content Types." www.loc.gov/standards/valuelist/rdacontent.html.

———. 2011. "Term and Code List for RDA Media Types." www.loc.gov/standards/valuelist/rdamedia.html.

MARC 21 Format for Bibliographic Data. 2010a. "Leader." Last modified May 31, 2011. www.loc.gov/marc/bibliographic/bdleader.html.

MARC 21 Format for Bibliographic Data. 2010b. "008 Fixed Length Data Elements." Last modified March 25, 2010. www.loc.gov/marc/bibliographic/bd008.html.

Mason, James. 2010. "RDA: Approaching Implementation." Paper presented at the Bibliographic Control Committee, Music Library Association. http://bcc.musiclibrary assoc.org/Presentations/RDA-implementation-MLA-2010.pdf.

"NCSU RDA Training FAQ." 2011. North Carolina State University Library, Raleigh, NC. https://staff.lib.ncsu.edu/confluence/display/MNC/NCSU+RDA+Training+FAQ. Last modified October 31, 2011.

Nimsakont, Emily Dust. 2010. "Cataloging with RDA: An Overview." Paper presented at NCompass Live, May 19, 2010. www.slideshare.net/enimsakont/cataloging-with-rda-an-overview.

"OCLC-MARC Format Update 2010 including RDA Changes." *OCLC Technical Bulletin*. 258, May 2010. www.oclc.org/support/documentation/worldcat/tb/258/default.htm.

Oliver, Chris. 2009. "Looking at RDA through Examples and a Workflow." Paper presented at the Music Library Association, May 6, 2009. http://tinyurl.com/Oliver2009.

Prager, George. 2010. "MARC 21 Changes for RDA." Paper presented at MARC and RDA: An Overview, July 12, 2010. www.aallnet.org/sis/tssis/annualmeeting/2010/handouts/g5-marcandrda-prager-handout.pdf.

"RDA Alternatives and Options." 2010. Proposed Practice for the RDA Test. Last modified April 26, 2010. www.loc.gov/catdir/cpso/RDAtest/RDA_alternatives.doc.

"RDA Cataloging Examples." 2010. *The Bib Blog*. June 2, 2010. www.yorku.ca/yul/bibserv/blog/?p=346.

"RDA Practice Bibliographic Record: Audio Recording." 2010. North Carolina State University Library. Raleigh, NC. https://staff.lib.ncsu.edu/confluence/download/attachments/17600159/audiobook-1-marc21-rda-example.pdf?version=3&modificationDate=1287169087000.

"RDA Practice Bibliographic Record: Multipart Monograph RDA Test Workflow." North Carolina State University Library. Raleigh, NC. https://staff.lib.ncsu.edu/confluence/display/MNC/Multipart+Monograph+RDA+Test+Workflow.

RDA Toolkit. 2010– . Chicago: American Library Association; Ottawa: Canadian Library Association; London: Chartered Institute of Library and Information Professionals (CILIP). www.rdatoolkit.org.

Sanchez, Elaine. "AACR2, RDA and You: Your Thoughts." Paper presented at the Amigos RDA@Your Online Library Conference, Feb. 4, 2011. www.slideshare.net/es02/sanchez-presentationfinalrev5.

Schiff, Adam. "Changing AACR2 Records to RDA Records." www.lib.uchicago.edu/staffweb/depts/cat/rda/rdaexamples.pdf.

Tillett, Barbara, and Judith Kuhagen. 2010. "RDA Test: Train-the-Trainer." *Training Modules*. Northeastern University, Boston, MA. Library of Congress webcasts are available from www.loc.gov/bibliographic-future/rda/trainthetrainer.html. The accompanying PowerPoint slides available on www.loc.gov/catdir/cpso/RDAtest/rdatraining.html.

Woodcock, Linda, Susan Andrews, and Adam Schiff. 2010. "RDA? Game On." Paper presented at the BCLA/BCATS Preconference, April 22, 2010. http://eprints.rclis.org/bitstream/10760/15047/1/RDA_BCLA-preconference-full_e_lis.pdf.

CHAPTER SIX

IDENTIFYING WORKS AND EXPRESSIONS AND THE ENTITY RESPONSIBLE FOR CREATING THEM

N THE PRECEDING CHAPTER, THE FOCUS WAS ON DE-scription. We learned how to describe manifestation and item, which are FRBR Group 1 entities 3 and 4.

This chapter will be devoted to identifying works and expressions, which are the other two FRBR/FRAD Group 1 entities.

This chapter will also introduce the concepts of *person* and *corporate body* which are entities that are responsible for creating work and expression. These entities belong to FRBR and FRAD Group 2.

We will also discuss the relationships between Group 1 entities (work, expression, manifestation, and item) and Group 2 entities (person, family, and corporate body).

Instructions for identifying work, expression, and entities responsible for creating them are scattered throughout various chapters of RDA.

RDA Chapter 6 provides instructions on how to choose and record preferred and variant titles for works, and how to record other identifying attributes of the work or expression. More important in this chapter are the following instructions:

- Constructing Access Points to Represent Works and Expressions. (RDA 6.27.1-6.27.1.8)
- Identify the Preferred Title. (RDA 6.2.2)
- Preferred Title for a Part or Parts of a Work. (RDA 6.2.2.9)
- Preferred Title for a Compilation of Works of One Person, Family, or Corporate Body. (RDA 6.2.2.10)
- Preferred Title of Musical Works. (RDA 6.14.2)
- Preferred Title of Legal Works. (RDA 6.19.2)
- Preferred Title of Religious Works. (RDA 6.23.2)
- Additions to Access Points Representing Works. (RDA 6.27.1.9)

RDA Chapter 19 provides instructions on recording relationships of persons, families, and corporate bodies associated with a work—creators and others. (RDA 19.2)

RDA Chapters 9, 10, and 11 provide instructions on constructing authorized and variant access points representing persons, families, and corporate bodies.

RDA Chapter 20 provides instructions on recording relationships to persons, families, and corporate bodies associated with an expression, e.g., editors, translators, illustrators, performers, etc. More importantly, this chapter provides guidelines on recording contributions as described in RDA instruction 20.2.

RDA Chapter 17 provides instructions on recording primary relationships between a work, expression, manifestation, and item. Two important instructions are:

- Work manifested (RDA17.8)
- Expression manifested (RDA17.10)

The following table provides some terms that catalogers will need to help them in identifying and recording attributes of work and expression.

TERM	DEFINITION
Work and expression	**Work** refers to a distinct intellectual or artistic creation (also called "naming the work"). In AACR2, this process is called "determining the main entry." **Expression** refers to the intellectual or artistic realization of a work in the form of alpha-numeric, musical or choreographic notation, sound, image, object, etc. (also called "naming the expression").
Title	**Title of the work** is a "word, character, or group of words and/or characters by which a work is known." **Preferred title of the work** is "the title or form of title chosen as the basis for the *authorized access point* representing the work." This title is the form used when constructing the authorized access point to name the work. **Variant title of the work** "refers to a title or a form of the title by which the title is known that differs from the title or the form of title chosen as the preferred title of the work."
Access point	**Access point** refers to a name and/or title, term, code, etc. under which the work will be found. **Preferred access point** refers to a standardized access point representing the entity. The preferred access point is constructed using the preferred title for the work preceded by a preferred access point representing a person, family, or corporate body responsible for the work. **Variant access point** refers to an alternative to the preferred access point representing an entity. A variant access point representing the work or expression is constructed using a variant title for the work preceded by the corporate body responsible for the work.

I. IDENTIFYING THE WORK

GENERAL PRINCIPLES

Constructing an authorized access point that represents works/expressions is the process of determining what combination of author/title/uniform title will be used to construct the preferred access point.

The following elements are used to construct the authorized access point to identify the work:

A. Preferred title of the work (RDA 6.2.2) (core element)
B. Additions to the preferred title (RDA 6.27.1.9)
C. Creator (RDA 19.2) [MARC 21 tags 100–111]
    Person
    Family
    Corporate body
D. Variant title for the work (not a core element; will not be addressed in this chapter)

Four tags in MARC 21 are used for naming the work:

Author + title proper *or* 1xx + 245
Author + uniform title + title proper *or* 1xx + 240 + 245
Uniform title + title proper *or* 130 + 245
Title proper alone *or* 245

RDA elements for identifying work or expression can be given in the context of either bibliographic data or authority data.

There are three important instructions to follow when constructing the preferred title:

1. Do not omit introductory phrases and statement of responsibility from the preferred title until there is evidence of more than one form of title and the most common form can be determined. Preferred title based on the first manifestation received.
2. When the work is published simultaneously in the same languages under different titles, choose the preferred title based on the first resource received.
3. Do not use "Selection" by itself as the preferred title. Use "Works. Selections," instead.

RDA provides general instructions on transcribing titles of the work (RDA 6.2.1). For example:

Appendix A3 provides instructions for capitalization of title.
Appendix B3 provides instruction for recording abbreviations in title.

When a title contains numbers or diacritics, record them as they appear on the source of information. Omit initial article, unless the title is accessed by that article. Do not insert a space between a period and an initial article.

PREFERRED TITLE OF THE WORK (RDA 6.2) (CORE ELEMENT)

Preferred title (RDA 6.2.2.1) is a "title or form of title chosen as basis for the authorized access point representing that work."

Most of what we catalog are materials that have been published once or several times with no change in the title. This means that the proper title in MARC 21 tag 245 will be identical to the preferred title and will not have MARC 21 tag 240. Therefore, the authorized access point representing that person, family, or corporate body, formulated according to the guidelines and instructions given under RDA 9.19.1 for persons, RDA 10.10.1 for families, or RDA 11.13.1 for corporate bodies + the preferred title of the work, formulated according to the instructions given under RDA 6.2.2 will be translated into MARC 21 tags as follows:

100/110/111 = creator +
245 = preferred title (title proper)
or
245 alone = preferred title (title proper)

110 2 $a World Bank
245 10 $a Atlas of global development : $b International Bank for Reconstruction and Development / $c The World Bank.
or
245 04 $a The Inquisitions : $b manuscripts of the Spanish, Portuguese and French Inquisitions in the British Library, London / $c Dr. John Edwards, editor.

For other works including translation, adaptation, commentaries, musical works, biblical, legal works, compilations, serials with same title proper as other serials, etc., the preferred title or name of the work is often different from the titles proper of original work. To bring all the various titles of a work together, you will need to determine the preferred title of the work. Preferred title of the work is recorded in MARC 21 tags 1xx +240 +245 or 130 + 245. For example:

100/110/111, 7xx = creator +
240 = preferred title +
245 = title proper +
or
130 = preferred title +
245 = title proper

100 1 $a Arriaga Jordán, Guillermo, $d 1958- $e author.
240 10 $a Dulce olor a muerte. $l English
245 10 $a Sweet scent of death / $c Guillermo Arriaga ; translated from the Spanish by John Page

or

130 0 $a Bible. $p Gospels. $l English. $f 2012.
245 10 $a Common English Bible Gospel Parallels / $c edited by Joel B. Green, W. Gil Shin.

Sources of information for a preferred title of the work are based on the following (RDA 6.2.2.2–6.2.2.5):

RDA distinguishes between the source of the preferred title for works created before 1501 and after 1500 (RDA 6.2.2.2).

For a work created after 1500 (RDA 6.2.2.4), use as the preferred title the title in the original language by which the work has become known through use in resources embodying the work (usually the first manifestation received) or reference sources. For example:

On the source of information "The Salinas: upside-down river" by Anne B. Fisher ; illustrated by Walter K. Fisher. This work has not been published before. The preferred title will be recorded as follows:

245 14 $a The Salinas : $b upside-down river / $c by Anne B. Fisher ; illustrated by Walter K. Fisher.

On the source of information "The tragedy of Romeo and Juliet" the preferred title of the work will be recorded under Shakespeare's first published "Romeo and Juliet."

240 10 Romeo and Juliet
245 14 The tragedy of Romeo and Juliet / $c by William Shakespeare ; edited by Barbara A. Mowat and Paul Werstine.

For simultaneous publications with different titles proper in the same language in different countries, choose the preferred title based on the title of the resource first received (RDA 6.2.2.4).

Example:

The American edition of "Harry Potter and the philosopher's stone" is received first. The preferred title will be based on the title proper of the manifestation first received.

→ 245 10 $a Harry Potter and the philosopher's stone / $c by J.K. Rowling ; illustrations by Mary GrandPré.

Another edition was published in Canada under a different title in the same language, "Harry Potter and the sorcerer's stone." The preferred title will be:

→ 240 10 $a Harry Potter and the philosopher's stone
245 10 $a Harry Potter and the sorcerer's stone / $c by J.K. Rowling ; illustrations by Mary GrandPré.

This figure illustrates the concept of simultaneous publication

American edition received first	Canadian edition received first
245 10 $a Harry Potter and the philosopher's stone / $c by J.K. Rowling ; illustrations by Mary GrandPré .	245 10 $a Harry Potter and the sorcerer's stone / $c by J.K. Rowling ; illustrations by Mary GrandPré.
The Canadian edition is received later. Create a new record as follows:	The American edition is received later. Create a new record as follows:
240 10 $a Harry Potter and the philosopher's stone 245 10 $a Harry Potter and the sorcerer's stone / $c by J.K. Rowling ; illustrations by Mary GrandPré.	240 10 $a Harry Potter and the sorcerer's stone 245 10 $a Harry Potter and the philosopher's stone / $c by J.K. Rowling ; illustrations by Mary GrandPré.

For simultaneous publication with different titles proper in different languages, choose the preferred title based on the title of the resource received first. For example:

A serial published simultaneously in German and English versions. If the German-language version was received first and the English-language version was received later, the preferred title will be the title from the German-language version.

For a work created before 1501, use the preferred title from modern reference sources (RDA 6.2.2.5). If modern reference sources have inconclusive evidence for a work created before 1501, use modern editions, early edition, and manuscript copies, in this order.

LANGUAGE AND SCRIPT OF THE WORK (RDA 5.6)

RDA provides choices for recording the language and script of the title of the work (RDA 5.4). The first choice is to record the title of the work as it appears on the resource. The second choice is to transliterate the title as a substitute for, or in addition to, the form found on the resource, if the title is given in a non-Latin script.

In American libraries, the romanized form of the title will be used in the bibliographic and authority records. Use the authority record MARC 21 4xx tag to record variant access points in the original language and script of the work.

CORE ELEMENTS FOR WORK

- Preferred title for the work (RDA 6.2).
- Additions to the preferred title for differentiation (RDA 6.27.1.9).

HOW TO CONSTRUCT AN AUTHORIZED ACCESS POINT FOR WORK

Instructions in RDA 6.27.1–RDA 6.27.1.8 describe how to construct an authorized point:

- Preferred title is the basis.
- Additions to the preferred title as instructed under RDA 6.27.1.9.
- Precede the preferred title for the work by the authorized access point for the person, family, or corporate body responsible for the intellectual or artistic content of the work (RDA 0.6.3 and RDA 6.27.1).

The following section will be devoted to identifying and recording work, expression, and entities responsible for the creating of works and expressions and the relationships.

A. PREFERRED TITLE IS THE BASIS

RECORDING THE PREFERRED TITLE FOR A PART OR PARTS OF A WORK (RDA 6.2.2.9)

One Part (RDA 6.2.2.9.1)

Record the preferred title for one part according to RDA 6.2.2.9.1) instructions:

130 0 $a Sinbad the sailor.
(Preferred title for a part of The Arabian nights.)

130 0 $a King of the hill (Television program)
(Preferred title for a part of television program The Simpsons.)

Compilation of Works (RDA 6.2.2.10)

As a general guideline for preferred title for compilations of one person, family, or corporate body, use one of the following conventional collective titles:

- Complete works (RDA 6.2.2.10.1). Use "works" as the preferred title for a compilation of works that consists of the complete works of a person, family, or corporate body.

Example:

If the works are completed by one person, family, or corporate body, the preferred title is under the conventional collective title "works," followed by the date completing the work in subfield "f" in MARC 21 tag 240.

100 1 $a Molière, $d 1622-1673, $e author.
→ 240 10 $a Works. $f 1684
245 14 $a Les oeuvres de Monsieur Moliere.

- Complete works in a single form (RDA 6.2.2.10.2) . Use one of the following conventional collective titles as the preferred title for a compilation of works (other than music, see RDA 6.14.2.8):

Correspondence	*Essays*	*Novels*	*Plays*
Poems	*Prose works*	*Short stories*	*Speeches*

Example:

100 1 $a Shaw, Bernard, $d 1856-1950; $e author.
→ 240 10 $a Plays. $f 1951
245 10 $a Seven plays / $c Bernard Shaw.

If none of the above is appropriate, use a term chosen by the cataloger.

- For other compilations of two or more works in the same form or different form (RDA 6.2.2.10.3) give preferred title for each work or provide conventional collective title + selection.

Authorized access points for each work/expression can be given in MARC 21 tag 7xx.

Examples:

If there are two or more works of one person, family, or corporate body in a particular form or various forms, give analytical authorized access points for all the works, or give a conventional collective title + "Selections." Catalogers can decide to provide each work separately in MARC 21 tag 700 or to record a conventional collective title in MARC 21 tag 240, or both. The first example below shows the use of the conventional collective title, while the second and third examples show both, the conventional collective title and the title of each work in MARC 21 tag 700.

100 1 $a Chesnutt, Charles W. $q (Charles Waddell), $d 1858-1932, $e author.
→ 240 10 $a Works. $k Selections $f 2002
245 10 $a Stories, novels & essays / $c Charles W. Chesnutt.

100 1 $a Austen, Jane $d 1775-1817, $e author.
→ 240 10 $a Works. $k Selections
245 10 $a Pride and prejudice and sense and sensibility / $c Jane Austen.
500 0 $a Pride and prejudice -- Sense and sensibility.
→ 700 12 $a Austen, Jane $d 1775-1817. $t Pride and prejudice.
→ 700 12 $a Austen, Jane $d 1775-1817. $t Sense and sensibility.

100 1 $a Faulkner, William, $d 1897-1962, $e author.
→ 240 10 $a Short stories. $k Selections
245 10 $a Hunting stories / $c William Faulkner; introduction by Cleanth Brooks.
505 0 $a The old people—The bear.

→ 700 12 $a Faulkner, William, $d 1897-1962. $t Old people.
→ 700 12 $a Faulkner, William, $d 1897-1962. $t Bear.

In the compilation of some of the works in a single form by the same person, the conventional collective title is used as the preferred title:

100 1 $a Auden, W. H. $q (Wystan Hugh), $d 1907-1973, $e author.
→ 240 10 $a Poems. $k Selections
245 10 $a Selections from poems by Auden / $c lithographs by Henry Moore.

100 1 $a Dick, Philip K, $e author.
→ 240 10 $a Novels. $k Selections
245 10 $a Four novels of the 1960s / $c Philip K. Dick.

In the compilation of works by different persons, families, or corporate bodies, construct the authorized access point representing the work using the preferred title for the compilation.

245 00 $a Poetics : $b essays on the art of poetry / $c compiled by Paul Mariani and George Murphy.

245 00 $a Classic sea stories / $c compiled by Glen and Karen Bledsoe.
505 0 $a Grain ship / Morgan Robertson -- Roll call of the reef / Sir Arthur Quiller-Couch -- Derelict / William Hope Hodgson -- Descent into the maelström / Edgar Allan Poe -- Raid on the oyster pirates / Jack London.
(Authorized access points for individual work can be created for each title.)

In a compilation of works by different creators with no collective title, the preferred access point is under the title. Construct access points for each of the works in the compilation (RDA 6.27.1.4):

245 00 $a Lost horizon / $c by James Hilton. The Red pony / by John Steinbeck. The Third man / by Graham Greene. A Single pebble / by John Hersey. The Light in the Piazza / by Elizabeth Spencer. Seize the day / by Saul Bellow.
700 12 $a Steinbeck, John, $d 1902-1968. $t Red Pony.
700 12 $a Greene, Graham, $d 1904-1991. $t Third man.
700 12 $a Hersey, John, $d 1914-1993. $t Single pebble.
700 12 $a Spencer, Elizabeth. $t Light in the piazza.
700 12 $a Bellow, Saul. $t Seize the day.

Catalogers can also devise a title proper if they choose to do this. In the example below, the preferred title is the devised title in the MARC 21 tag 245. The cataloger will create a MARC 21 tag 505, with the first indicator 0 that will list the works in the compilation. A separate MARC 21 tag 700 will be created for each work.

→ 245 00 $a [five American classic novels].
→ 500 $a Title devised by cataloger.
505 0 $a Lost horizon / $c by James Hilton -- The Red pony/ by John Steinbeck --The Third man / by Graham Greene -- A Single pebble / by John Hersey --The Light in the Piazza / by Elizabeth Spencer --Seize the day / by Saul Bellow.
700 12 $a Steinbeck, John, $d 1902-1968. $t Red Pony.
700 12 $a Greene, Graham, $d 1904-1991. $t Third man.
700 12 $a Hersey, John, $d 1914-1993. $t Single pebble.
700 12 $a Spencer, Elizabeth. $t Light in the piazza.
700 12 $a Bellow, Saul. $t Seize the day.

PREFERRED TITLE OF A MUSICAL WORK (RDA 6.14) (CORE ELEMENT)

Choose as the preferred title for a musical work the composer's original title in the language in which it was presented (RDA 6.14.2.3).

100 1 $a Rimsky-Korsakov, Nikolay, $d 1844-1908.
→ 240 10 $a Zolotoĭ petushok
245 14 $a The golden cockerel / $c Rimsky-Korsakov.
(The preferred title in MARC 21 tag 240 is in composer's original title in the language in which it was presented.)

Omit from the chosen title the following (RDA 6.14.2.4):

- Statement of medium of performance.
- Key.
- Serial, opus, and thematic index numbers.
- Numbers (unless they are an integral part of the title).
- Date of composition.
- Adjectives and epithets not part of the original title of the work.

PREFERRED TITLE FOR A MUSICAL WORK (RDA 6.14.2 .5) [MARC 21 TAGS 130, 245, 100-111 SUBFIELD $t]

When a preferred title consists solely of the name of one type of composition (symphony, etc.), record the accepted form of name in the language preferred by the agency creating the cataloging.

100 1 $a Boccherini, Luigi, $d 1743-1805.
→ 240 10 $a Quintets, $m guitar, violins, viola, violoncello, $n G. 450, $r G major
245 10 $a Quintetto VI in sol maggiore (G. 450) / $c Luigi Boccherini ; revisione di Ruggero Chiesa.
(The English form was used as the preferred title in MARC 21 tag 240 in the bibliographic record.)

100 12 $a Barber, Samuel, $d 1910-1981. $t *Songs*, $n op. 13.
not
100 12 $a Barber, Samuel, $d 1910-1981. $t *Gesange*, $n op. 13.
(The English form was used as the preferred title access point in MARC 21 tag 100 in the authority record.)

100 1 $a Mozart, Wolfgang Amadeus, $d 1756-1791. $t *Pieces*, $m musical clock, $n K. 608, $r F minor.
not
100 1 $a Mozart, Wolfgang Amadeus, $d 1756-1791. $t *Stücke*, $m musical clock, $n K. 608, $r F minor.
(The English form was used as the preferred title access point in MARC 21 tag 100 in the authority record.)

Compilations of Musical Works (RDA 6.14.2.8.1–6.14.2.8.6)

There are two choices to assign preferred title for compilations of musical works:

1. Use "Works" if the compilation represents the complete work of the creator (RDA 6.14.2.8.2)

or

2. Use a term chosen by the cataloger if the compilation contains the complete works in a single form.

100 1 $a Beethoven, Ludwig van, $d 1770-1827, $e composer.
→ 240 10 $a Symphonies. $k Selections
245 10 $a Symphony no. 1 in C major, op. 21; $b Symphony no. 2 in D major, op. 36 / $c Beethoven.
700 10 $a Beethoven, Ludwig van, $d 1770-1827. $t Symphonies, $n no. 1, op. 21, $r C major.
700 10 $a Beethoven, Ludwig van, $d 1770-1827. $t Symphonies, $n no. 2, op. 36, $r D major.

100 1 $a Schubert , Franz, $d 1797-1828, $e composer.
→ 240 10 $a Symphonies. $k Selections
245 10 $a Two symphonies / $s Franz Schubert.
700 12 $a Schubert, Franz, $d 1797-1828. $t symphonies, $n D. 200, $r D major.
700 12 $a Schubert, Franz, $d 1797-1828. $t symphonies, $n D. 485, $r Bb major.

When the compilation is not complete, identify each of the works in the compilation separately (RDA 6.14.2.8.6):

245 00 $a Piano concerto no. 25 / $c Mozart. Piano concerto no. 1 / Beethoven.

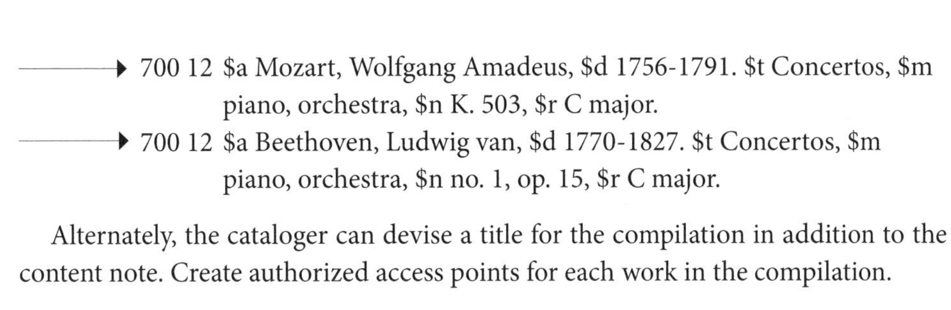

700 12 $a Mozart, Wolfgang Amadeus, $d 1756-1791. $t Concertos, $m piano, orchestra, $n K. 503, $r C major.
700 12 $a Beethoven, Ludwig van, $d 1770-1827. $t Concertos, $m piano, orchestra, $n no. 1, op. 15, $r C major.

Alternately, the cataloger can devise a title for the compilation in addition to the content note. Create authorized access points for each work in the compilation.

245 00 $a [Two Symphonies]
500 $a Title devised by cataloger.
505 0 $a Piano concerto no. 25 / $c Mozart. Piano concerto no. 1 / Beethoven.
700 12 $a Mozart, Wolfgang Amadeus, $d 1756-1791. $t Concertos, $m piano, orchestra, $n K. 503, $r C major.
700 12 $a Beethoven, Ludwig van, $d 1770-1827. $t Concertos, $m piano, orchestra, $n no. 1, op. 15, $r C major.

Medium of performance (RDA 6.15) [MARC 21 tag 382], numeric designation (RDA 6.16) [MARC 21 tag 383], and key (RDA 6.17) [MARC 21 tag 384] are core elements for musical works that may be recorded as separate elements, as additions to access points, or as both, to differentiate a musical work from another work with the same name.

There is no limitation on the number of recording media of performance that can be listed. For example: Quartets, flute, violin, harp, piano, etc.

100 1 $a Beethoven, Ludwig van, $d 1770-1827.
240 10 $a Sonatas, $m piano, $n no. 14, op. 27, no. 2, $r C# minor
382 $a piano
383 $a no. 14, $b op. 27, no. 2
384 $a C# minor
(In this example, the medium of performance was added in the bibliographic record as a separate element in MARC 21 tag 382 and as addition to access point in MARC 21 tag 240 $m.)

100 1 $a Mahler, Gustav, $d 1860-1911. $t Symphonies, $n no. 2, $r C minor
382 $a soprano $a alto $a mixed voices $a orchestra
383 $a no. 2
384 $a C minor
(In this example, the medium of performance was added in the authority record as a separate element in MARC 21 tag 382.)

100 1 $a Hovhaness, Alan, $d 1911-2000. $t Island of Mysterious Bells
382 $a harps (4)
383 $b op. 244
(In this example, the medium of performance was added in the authority record as a separate element in MARC 21 tag 382.)

Numeric designation of a musical work includes three types of designations:

- Serial numbers : $a
- Opus numbers : $b
- Thematic index numbers : $c

Provide as many numeric designations as available. Provide the designator in abbreviated form according to appendix B 5.4.

100 1 $a Vivaldi, Antonio, $d 1678-1741. $t Cimento dell'armonia e dell'inventione. $n N. 1-4

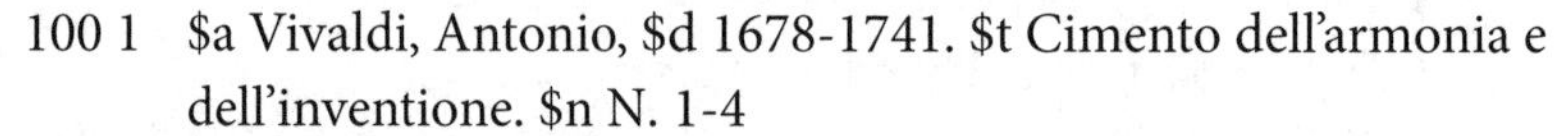

→ 383 $b op. 8, no. 1-4

→ 383 $c F. I, 22-25 $d Fanna $2 mlati

(In this example, the numeric designation was added in the authority record as a separate element in MARC 21 tag 383.)

100 1 $a Krommer, Franz, $d 1759-1831, $e composer.

240 10 $a Concertos. $k Selections

382 $b clarinet $n 2 $a chamber orchestra

→ 383 $b op. 36 $b op. 86 $b op. 35

(In this example, the numeric designation was added in the bibliographic record as a separate element in MARC 21 tag 383.)

Keys are used as a core element to differentiate a musical work from another work with the same title. They may be applicable when creating the authorized access point:

100 1 $a Beethoven, Ludwig van, $d 1770-1827. $t Symphonies, $n no. 7, op. 92, $r A major.

100 1 $a Schubert, Franz, $d 1797-1828, $t Symphonies, $n D. 200, $r D major.

(In the two examples above, the key was added to the access point in the authority record in MARC 21 tag 100 $r.)

100 1 $a Godowsky, Leopold, $d 1870-1938.

240 10 $a Etude macabre

282 $a piano

→ 284 $a D minor

(In this example, the key was added in the bibliographic record as a separate element in MARC 21 tag 384.)

Adaptations of Musical Works (RDA 6.28.1.5)

When the musical work has been substantially changed by the performer or the adapter, it should be considered as a new work. In this case, the performer or the adapter will be considered the creator of the work:

100 1 $a Manoukian, Catherine.
245 10 $a Chopin on violin / $c Catherine Manoukian.
(Chopin's music originally composed for the piano; arranged here for violin.)

Librettos (RDA 6.28.1.2)

Librettos are not considered musical works with the composer as the creator. RDA views a libretto as a textual work and a separately created work. In RDA, the librettist is recorded as the creator, rather than the composer of the related musical work.

In this case, the creator will be the authorized access point. In order to provide an access point for the libretto, use appendix J.2.5 to add the phrase Libretto for (work) in MARC 21 tag 700, subfield $i. If the composer of the musical work is mentioned in the libretto, an access point may be made for the composer:

100 1 $a Ghislanzoni, Antonio, $d 1824-1893.
245 10 $a Aida : $b opera in quattro atti / $c libretto di Antonio Ghislanzoni ; musica di Giuseppe Verdi.
700 1 $i Libretto for (work) $a Verdi, Giuseppe, $d 1813-1901. $t Aida.

To assist users in finding resources, catalogers can give a variant access point (MARC 21 tag 400 in the authority record) using the access point for the related musical work (RDA 6.27.4.2):

RDA heading and reference in authority record:

100 1 $a Ghislanzoni, Antonio, $d 1924-1893. $t Aida.
400 1 $a Verdi, Giuseppe, $d 1813-1901. $t Aida. $s Libretto

PREFERRED TITLE OF A LEGAL WORK (RDA 6.19–6.22) (CORE ELEMENT) [MARC 21 TAGS 130, 245, 100–111 SUBFIELD $t]

Signatory to a Treaty, etc. (RDA 6.22)

Signatory to a treaty, etc., is a "government or other party that has formally signed a treaty, etc., as an adherent to its terms and conditions." RDA 6.22.1.1 defines "Signatory to a treaty, etc. as a core element when needed to differentiate a work from another work with the same title or from the name of a person, family, or corporate body." It is also a "core element when identifying a bilateral treaty, etc."

Treaties are recorded under the first country mentioned, regardless of the number of signatories or alphabetical order. In the case of a treaty between one country and a group of countries, the authorized access point will be under the one country (see RDA 11.13.1 for corporate body).

For a treaty or any other formal agreement between two or more national governments, give the first-named signatory with preferred title "Treaties, etc." as the authorized access point for the work (RDA 6.29.1.15).

110 1 $a France.
→ 240 10 $a Treaties, etc.
245 10 $a Agreement between France, Russia, Great Britain and Italy, signed at London April 26, 1915.
→ 710 1 $a Russia.
→ 710 1 $a Great Britain.
→ 710 1 $a Italy.
(How many signatories other than the first-named signatory are given in the MARC 21 tag 710 is cataloger's judgment.)

If the work is a bilateral treaty, both signatories will be recorded; however, the second signatory will be given in subfield $g as part of the authorized access point for the treaty (MARC 21 tag 240).

110 1 $a Canada.
→ 240 10 $a Treaties, etc. $g United States, $d 1930 May 26.
245 10 $a Convention between Canada and the United States for the protection, preservation and extension of the sockeye salmon fisheries in the Fraser River system, signed at Washington on the 26th day of May, 1930.
710 1 $a United States.
("The first signatory in 110 tag is recoded as "creator" (RDA 19.2), the second signatory in the preferred title (240) is based on RDA 6.22 instruction. It is the cataloger's judgment to provide an access point for the second signatory "United States" in the 710 tag, subfield 1.")

PREFERRED TITLE OF A RELIGIOUS WORK (RDA 6.23) (CORE ELEMENT)

Sacred scriptures, such as the Bible, Quran, Talmud, and Vedas are recorded under the preferred title that is commonly identified in the reference source in the preferred language of the creator of the data that deal with the religious group or groups to which the scripture belongs. If no such source is available, use general reference sources (RDA 6.23.2.5):

130 0 $a Qur'an.
not
130 0 $a Koran

Parts of the Bible (RDA 6.23.2.9)

Record "Old Testament" and "New Testament" as subdivisions of the preferred title for the Bible:

130 0 $a Bible. $p Old Testament.
not
130 0 $a Bible. $p O. T.

130 0 $a Bible. $p New Testament.
not
130 0 $a Bible. $p N. T.

Omit the name of the Testament in the preferred title for individual books or groups of books:

130 0 $a Bible. $p Gospels.
not
130 0 $a Bible. $p N.T. $p Gospels.

For books of the Catholic or Protestant canon, record the brief citation form of the Authorized Version as a subdivision of the preferred title of the Bible (RDA 6.23.2.9.2).

130 0 $a Bible. $p Revelation.

B. ADDITION TO THE PREFERRED TITLE (RDA 6.27.1.9)

There are four additions to the preferred title that can be used to differentiate a work from another with the same title or with the same creator. RDA 6.4 states that these elements can be given as additions to the authorized access point, as separate elements, or as both. Apply cataloger's judgment about how to add these elements to the preferred title:

- Form of work (RDA 6.3) (core element) refers to the class of genre to which the work belongs, such as plays, short stories, poems, computer files, etc. RDA 6.3 doesn't have a controlled vocabulary, so the cataloger will need to choose a term. LC has created genre/form terms that can be used to select the form of the work.

  Example:

  130 0 $a Ocean's eleven (Motion picture)

- Date of the work (RDA 6.4) (core element) is the earliest date associated with a work. If the date of creation is not available, the date of first publication or release can be used.

  Examples:

  130 0 $a Ocean's eleven (Motion picture : 2001)
  110 2 $a Connecticut Commission on Children. $t Annual report (2005)

- Place of origin of the work RDA (6.5) (core element) refers to the country or other territorial jurisdiction from which a work originated (includes local place). It is a core element if needed to differentiate a work from another.

Example:

130 0 $a Advocate (Boise, Idaho)

- Other distinguishing characteristics of the work (RDA 6.6) (core element) refers to characteristic other than the form of work, date of work, or place of origin of the work that serves to differentiate a work from another work with the same title or from the name of a person, family, or corporate body.

  Example:

  130 0 $a Research paper (JJ Society)

The cataloger can provide more than one addition to the preferred title, if needed.

Examples:

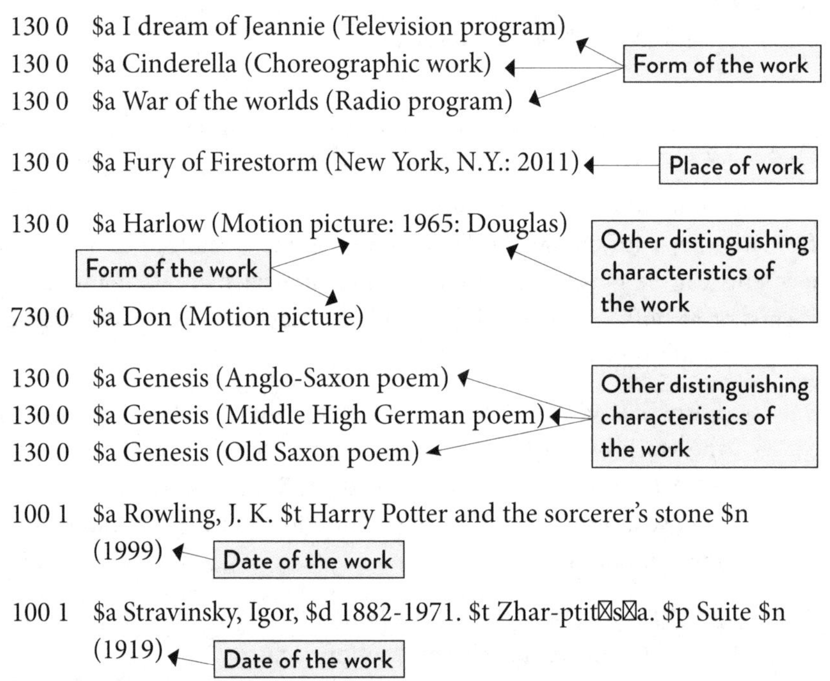

C. THE PREFERRED TITLE FOLLOWS THE AUTHORIZED ACCESS POINT FOR THE CREATOR (RDA 19) [MARC 21 TAGS 100–111, 700–711]

Once the preferred title is identified and established, the next step is to identify and construct the authorized access point for the creator of the work or expression who is responsible for the intellectual or artistic content of the work. RDA instructions 0.6.3 and 6.27.1 state that when creating the authorized access point for the work, precede the preferred title for the work, if appropriate, by the authorized access point representing the person, family, or corporate body responsible for the work.

CREATOR OF THE WORK (RDA 19.2) (MARC 21 TAG 1XX) (CORE ELEMENT)

RDA defines creator as a "person, family, or corporate body responsible for the creation of a work" (RDA 19.2) (core element).

Work can be created by only one creator or the responsibility for the creation of the work can be shared between two or more creators performing the same functions and jointly collaborating in the creation of the work (RDA 6.27.1.2–6.27.1.3). In this case, only the creator having principal responsibility named first in the resource is required.

If the principal responsibility cannot be determined, only the first-named creator is required.

Corporate bodies are considered as creators when works that are issued by or have been caused to be issued by or have originated with a corporate body and fall into one or more of the following categories (RDA 19.2.1.1.1):

a. Works of an administrative nature dealing with the corporate body itself or its internal policies, procedures, finance, and/or operation; or its officers, staff, and/or membership (e.g., directories); or its resources (e.g., catalog, inventories).

   110 2 $a National Certified Pipe Welding Bureau.
   (Authorized access point representing the creator for: Membership directory / $c National Certified Pipe Welding Bureau.)

   110 2 $a Victoria & Albert Museum, $e author.
   700 1 $a Parry, Linda, $e author.
   (Authorized access point representing the creator for: The Victoria & Albert Museum's textile collection : $b British textiles from 1850 to 1900 / $c by Linda Parry.)

   110 1 $a Canadian Botanical Association, $e issuing body.
   (Authorized access point representing the creator for: Directory of the Canadian Botanical Association & Canadian Society of Plant Physiologists.)

b. Works that record the collective thought of the body (e.g., reports of commissions, committees, official statements of position on external policies).

   110 2 $a New Zealand. $b Great Barrier Island Committee of Inquiry, $e issuing body.
   (Authorized access point representing the creator for: Great Barrier Island: $b report of the Great Barrier Island Committee of Inquiry.)

c. Works that report the collective activity of a conference, an expedition, an event.

   111 2 $a International Conference on Advances in Steel Structures $d (1996: $c Hong Kong)

(Authorized access point representing the creator for: Advances in steel structures : $b Proceeding of International Conference on Advances in Steel Structures, 11-14 December 1996, Hong Kong / $c edited by S.L. Chan and J.G. Teng.)

d. Works that result from the collective activity of a performing group as a whole.

110 2 $a Fabulous Thunderbirds (Musical group), $e producer.
(Authorized access point representing the creator for: Hot number / $c The Fabulous Thunderbirds.)

e. Cartographic works originating with a corporate body other than a body that is merely responsible for their publication or distribution.

110 2 $a World Bank, $e issuing body.
(Authorized access point representing the creator for: World atlas of the child / $c prepared by the World Bank in recognition of the International Year of the Child.)

f. Legal, government, and religious works such as laws, decrees of the chief executive that have the force of law, administrative regulations, constitutions, bills and drafts of legislation, etc.

110 2 $a Ohio. $b Department of Education.
(Authorized access point representing the creator for: The Ohio Law for State Support of Public Schools.)

RECORDING CREATORS (RDA 19.2.1.3)

According to general instruction, the creator is recorded under first author, regardless of how many authors are jointly contributing to the work. For a work created by only one person, family, or corporate body, the authorized access point will be under this creator:

100 1 $a Nahavandi, Afsaneh, $e author.
(Authorized access point representing the creator for: The art and science of leadership / $c Afsaneh Nahavandi.)

100 1 $a Glazunov, Aleksandra Konstantinovich, 1865-1936, $e composer.
(Authorized access point representing the creator for: Quartet no. 3 in G. Major, opus 26: "Quartet Slav" for 2 violins, viola & violoncello / $c by Alexander Glazunov.)

100 1 $a Professor, $e author.
(Authorized access point representing the creator for: Angela : $b a revealing close-up of the woman and the trial / $c by the Professor, real name of the person is not known.)

110 2 $a Seafarers' Education Service.
(Authorized access point representing the creator for: Libraries at sea : $b four years' experience / $c A record of work done by the Seafarers' Education Service from December, 1919 to May, 1924.)

For a work by two or more persons, families, or corporate bodies having the same responsibility for creating the work, the authorized access point will be under the first creator having principal responsibility, if indicated. If the principal responsibility cannot be determined, record the first name of the creator that appears on the source of information. Use appendix I to choose one or more appropriate terms representing the person, family, or corporate body to indicate the nature of the relationship (RDA 18.5.1.3):

100 1 $a Stokstad, Marilyn, 1929- $e author.
700 1 $a Cothren, Michael W., $e author.
(Authorized access points representing the creator for: Art history : $b portable edition / $c Marilyn Stokstad, Michael W. Cothren.)

100 1 $a Hyslop, Stephen G. $q (Stephen Garrison), $d 1950- $e author.
700 1 $a Somerville, Bob, $e author.
700 1 $a Thompson, John M. $q (John Milliken), $d 1959- $e author.
(Authorized access points representing the creator for: Eyewitness to history : $b from ancient times to the modern era / $c Stephen G. Hyslop, Bob Somerville and John Thompson.)

Or under first named creator if no principal responsibly is indicated

100 1 $a Allmark, Peter, $e author.
700 1 $a Salway, Sarah, $e author.
700 1 $a Crisp, Richard, $e author.
700 1 $a Barley, Ruth, $e author.
(Authorized access point representing the creator for: DWP Research Report 684—Ethnic Minority Customers of the Pension, Disability and Careers Service: An Evidence Synthesis / $c by Peter Allmark, Sarah Salway, Richard Crisp and Ruth Barley. Number of access points for other creators is the cataloger's judgment.)

100 1 $a Brookshear, J. Glenn, $e author.
700 1 $a Smith, David T. $q (David Timothy), $d 1958- $e author.
700 1 $a Brylow, Dennis, $e author.
(Authorized access point representing the creator for: Computer science: $b an overview / $c J. Glenn Brookshear; with contributions from David T. Smith, Dennis Brylow.)

111 2 $a Midwest Labor Law Conference, $c Columbus, Ohio, $d 1964, $e issuing body.
710 2 $a Ohio State Bar Association, $e issuing body.

710 2 $a Ohio Legal Center Institute, $e issuing body.
(Authorized access point representing the creator for: Reference manual for continuing legal education program / $c A cooperative effort of the organized Bar of Ohio, law schools, and local bar associations.)

If the work has more than one person, family, or corporate body having different responsibility for creating the work, the authorized access point will be under first-named creator.

100 1 $a Lutgens, Frederick K, $e author.
700 1 $a Tarbuck, Edward J, $e author.
700 1 $a Tasa, Dennis, $e illustrator.
(Authorized access point representing the creator for: Foundations of earth science / $c Frederick K. Lutgens, Edward J. Tarbuck ; illustrated by Dennis Tasa.)

100 1 $a Lewellen, Judie, $e author.
700 1 $a Bryson, Mary, $e illustrator.
700 1 $a Wahman, Wendy, $e illustrator.
(Authorized access point representing the creator for: The teen body book : $b a guide to your changing body / $c by Judie Lewellen ; illustrated by Mary Bryson and Wendy Wahman.)

110 2 $a Frederick S. Wight Art Gallery.
700 1 $a Shapira, Nathan H., $e curator.
700 1 $a Klier, Hans von, $d 1934- $e designer.
700 1 $a King, Perry A., $d 1938- $e designer.
(Authorized access point representing the creator for: Design process : $b Olivetti, 1908-1978, Frederick S. Wight Art Gallery, University of California, Los Angeles, California, March 27 to May 6, 1979 / $c curator, Nathan H. Shapira ; exhibition design, Hans von Klier ; catalog design, Perry A. King.)

If the person, family, or corporate body is responsible for creating a new work based on a previously existing work, the new author will be selected as the authorized access point.

100 1 $a Carr, Jan, $e author.
700 1 $a Martin, Ann M., $d 1955- $e author.
(Authorized access point representing the creator for: The Baby-sitters Club (BSC) / $c adapted by M.J. Carr from The Baby-sitters Club movie; based on the best-selling series by Ann M. Martin.)

100 1 $a Reilly, Claudia, $e author.
700 1 $a Henley, Beth. $t Crimes of the heart.
(Authorized access point representing the creator for: Crimes of the heart: $b a novel / $c by Claudia Reilly; based on the screenplay by Beth Henley.)

CONSTRUCTING THE AUTHORIZED ACCESS POINT FOR PERSON, FAMILY, AND CORPORATE BODY (RDA CHAPTERS 8 TO 11)

Elements in chapters 8 to 11 are used to construct authorized access points. These access points are created in the authority record to be used in the bibliographic record tags 1xx, 6xx, and 7xx.

NAME OF A PERSON (RDA CHAPTER 9)

RDA defines the name of a person as a "word, character, or group of words and/or characters by which a person is known." This includes fictitious characters. To construct the authorized access point for a person's name you will use the following (RDA 9.19.1.1):

Preferred name is the basis (preferred name of the person [core element]) of the name to be used when constructing the authorized access point in the bibliographic records and in 1xx tags of the name authority records.

Variant name of the person (optional element but will be discussed here) is a form of the name that is varied from the name in 1xx. The variant form of the name is recorded in 4xx tag in name authority records.

Additions to the preferred name (RDA 9.19.1.2–9.19.1.7).

1. PREFERRED NAME OF THE PERSON (RDA 9.2.2–9.2.2.23) (MARC 21 TAG 100)

The sources of information for the preferred name of a person are listed below in RDA instructions in this order:

- Preferred sources of information (RDA 2.2.2) in resources associated with the person
- Other formal statements appearing in resources associated with the person
- Other sources including reference sources

As a general guideline, take what you see from the source, except for a few cases when you will need to use:

- Appendix A.2 for capitalizations (RDA 8.5.2).
- Appendix B.3 for abbreviations used in name (RDA 8.5.7).
- Retain hyphens between forename and surname (RDA 8.5.4).

    100 0 $a Mary-Ann.

- Insert space after full stop following initials (RDA 8.5.6.1).

    100 0 $a Dr. X.
    100 0 $a A. H. John.

RDA provides detailed instructions on choosing and recording the preferred name of the person. RDA instruction 9.2.2 includes specific cases that pertain to preferred name for persons, with examples. The following section will provide specific cases that are commonly used by catalogers. For other cases consult the RDA 9.2.2 instruction.

CHOOSING THE PREFERRED NAME OF A PERSON (RDA 9.2.2.3) (MARC 21 TAG 100)

Choose the name by which the person is commonly known as the preferred name for that person. This will include real name, pseudonym, title of nobility, nickname, initial, phrase, etc.:

100 0 $a H. L. B. $q (Henry L. Brianceau)
not
100 0 $a Henry L. Brianceau.

100 0 $a Louis $b XVI, *$c* King of France, $d 1754-1793.
not
100 0 $a Lewis XVI.

100 1 $a Seuss, $c Dr.
not
100 1 $a Geisel, Theodor Seuss, $d 1904-

DIFFERENT FORMS OF THE SAME NAME OF A PERSON (RDA 9.2.2.5)

Fullness (RDA 9.2.2.5.1)

Some names may appear in different forms. If the form of a person's name varies in fullness, in this case choose the most commonly used form of name;

100 1 $a West, Morris, $d 1916-1999.
(Most common form - West Morris; occasional form - Morris L. West; Michael East; Julian Morris.)

100 1 a Kenny Carolyn.
(Most common form Kenny Carolyn. Occasional form Carolyn Bereznak Kenny; Carolyn B. Kenny.)

Language (RDA 9.2.2.5.2)

In some cases, the person's name appears in different language forms. In this situation, choose the form that corresponds to the language of most of the resources as a preferred name;

100 1 $a Mikes, George.
not
100 1 $a Mikes, György.

Name Written in a Non-Preferred Script (RDA)

For names written in a non-preferred script that differs from the preferred scripts of the agency creating the data, transliterate the name according to the scheme adopted by the agency creating the data. As an alternative, choose the form of the name that is well established in reference sources of the agency creating the data:

100 0 $a Avicenna, $d 980-1037.
Name appears in original script as ابن سينا

100 0 $a Aristotle.
Name appears in original script as أرسطو
(In these two examples, the name is well established in reference sources.)

100 1 $a Bao, Yan.
Name appears in original script as 包艳.
(In this example, the name was transliterated according to the scheme adopted by the agency creating the data.)

Spelling (RDA 9.2.2.5.4)

For variant spellings, choose the form found in the first resource received, not the predominant spelling:

Sarah Smith.
Sara Smith.

Change of Name of a Person (RDA 9.2.2.7)

If a person changed his or her name, use the latest name as the preferred name:

100 1 $a Conrad, Joseph.
not
Teodor Józef Konrad Korzeniowski.

Individuals with More than One Identity (RDA 9.2.2.8)

When a person has more than one identity, for example, in the case of an author who uses a pseudonym, the real name and the pseudonym are separate identities and each should be chosen for the preferred name, as appropriate:

100 1 $a Lewis, C. S. $q (Clive Staples), $d 1898-1963.
100 1 $a Hamilton, Clive, $d 1898-1963.
(Pseudonym used to publish "Spirits in Bondage.")

Surname (RDA 9.2.2.9.1–9.2.2.9.6)

When the name contains a surname, record the surname as the first element (RDA 9.2.2.9):

100 1 $a Smith, Alan A.
100 1 $a Hinton, Ernest.

Record the initial that represents a surname as the first name when at least one part of the name is given in full (RDA 9.2.2.9.1):

100 1 $a G., Warren.
100 1 $a W., Bambang.

If the name by which a person is known consists of a surname only, treat the word or phrase associated with the name in resources associated with the person or in reference sources as an integral part of the name.

There are three cases when the term of address may be part of a preferred name:

When the name consists only of the surname (RDA 9.2.2.9.3):

100 1 $a Seuss, $c Dr.

1. If a married person is identified only by a partner's name and a term of address (RDA 9.2.2.9.4):

100 1 $a Davis, Mrs.

2. When the preferred name includes words or numerals indicating relationships, such as Sr., Jr., fils, III, II, etc., include the numeral or words with the preferred name (RDA 9.2.2.9.5). Notice that terms such as Filho, Junior, Netto, or Sobrinho that follow the Portuguese surname are part of the surname. Terms such as Jr., Sr., fils, pere, and numbers such as III occurring in languages other than Portuguese following the person's forename or forename preceded by a comma are also part of the name:

100 1 $a Smith, Joseph, $c Sr., $d 1771-1840.
100 1 $a Smith, Joseph, $c Jr., $d 1805-1844.
100 1 $a Smith, Joseph, $c III, $d 1832-1914.

Compound Surname (RDA 9.2.2.10)

A compound surname consists of two or more proper names. When recoding compound names, separate them either by a space or a hyphen:

Fitzgerald-Jones, Sandra.

Surname with Separately Written Prefixes (RDA 9.2.2.11)

If the surname includes an article or a preposition, or both; choose the part most commonly used as the first element:

De Villiers, Anna Johanna Dorothea.
(Enter under the prefix.)

De Morgan, Augustus.
(Enter under the prefix.)

Von Wielligh.
(Enter under the prefix.)

Abu Zahrah, Muhammad.
(The prefix here is neither an article, a preposition, nor a combination of the two. These kinds of names are always entered under the prefix.)

De la Mare, Walter, $d 1873-1956.
(Enter under the prefix.)

Names Consisting of a Phrase (RDA 9.2.2.22)

Names consisting of phrases are names that do not include a forename and names that consist of a forename or forenames preceded by words other than the term of address or title of position or office. These kinds of names are recorded directly:

100 0 $a Dr. X.
100 0 $a Miss Piggy.
100 0 $a Poor Richard.
100 0 $a Mother Hen.

Phrase Preceded by a Term of Address, Consisting of a Forename or Forenames Preceded by a Term of Address, etc. (RDA 9.2.2.23)

If part of a phrase consisting of a forename(s) is preceded by a term of address (e.g., a word indicating relationships such as aunt, uncle, chef, cousin), include them in the preferred name:

100 1 $a Emeril, Chef.

2. VARIANT NAMES FOR THE PERSON (RDA 9.2.3) (MARC 21 TAG 400) IN THE NAME AUTHORITY RECORD

RDA defines a variant name of a person as a "name or form of name by which the person is known that differs from the name or form of name chosen as the preferred name" (RDA 9.2.3.1). Variant name can be used when the name, form of name used by a person, found in reference sources, or resulting from differences in transliteration is different from the preferred name.

RDA provides instructions for a variety of cases when recording a variant form of name is necessary. The following examples illustrate specific cases for recording variant names for the person:

Mahfuz, Nagib, $d 1911-2006.
(Form recorded as preferred name: Maḥfūẓ, Najīb, $d *1911-2006.)*

Joseph, Jaime.
(Form recorded as preferred name: Joseph A., Jaime.)

Hen, Mother.
(Form recorded as preferred name: Mother Hen.)

X, $c Mr.
(Form recorded as preferred name: Mr. $c X.)

Louis $b VI, **$c** le Gros, King of France, $d 1078-1137.
(Form recorded as preferred name: Louis $b *VI,* $c *King of France,* $d *1078-1137.)*

Arthur, George, $c Sir, Bart., $d 1784-1854.
(Form recorded as preferred name: Arthur, George, $c *Sir,* $d *1784-1854.)*

Morgan, Augustus de, $d 1806-1871.
  Ti-mo-kan, $d 1806-1871.
(Form recorded as preferred name: De Morgan, Augustus, $d *1806-1871.)*

Smith, James Fitzgerald-
(Form recorded as preferred name: Fitzgerald-Smith, James.)

John, G. R. $q (Geryk R.)
(Form recorded as preferred name: John, Geryk.)

3. ADDITIONS TO THE PREFERRED NAME

There are some RDA elements that can be used to differentiate between two persons that have the same name. These are:

Title or other designation associated with the person (RDA 9.4 and 9.6)
Date associated with the person and period of activity (RDA 9.3.2–9.3.4)
Fuller form of the name (RDA 9.5)
Period of activity of person (RDA 9.3.4)
Field of activity (RDA 9.15)
Profession or occupation (RDA 9.16)

TITLE OR OTHER DESIGNATION ASSOCIATED WITH THE PERSON (RDA 9.4) (MARC 21 100 TAG, SUBFIELD $c)

Title of the person is a "word or phrase indicative of royalty, nobility, or ecclesiastical rank or office, or a term of address for a person or religious vocation" (RDA 9.4.1). This information can be taken from any source. Adding titles or other designations added to names is limited to:

a) A title of royalty (see RDA 9.4.1.4) or nobility (see RDA 9.4.1.5)

b) The term Saint (see RDA 9.6.1.4)

c) Title of religious rank (see RDA 9.4.1.6–9.4.1.8)

d) The term Spirit (see RDA 9.6.1.5)

e) A term indicating profession or occupation (see RDA 9.16) or field of activity of the person (see RDA 9.15), in that order of preference, for a person whose name consists of a phrase or appellation not conveying the idea of a person.

100 0 $a Adrian $b IV, $c Pope, $d died 1159.
100 1 $a Holden, David, $c soldier.
100 0 $a Fahd ibn ʻAbd al-ʻAzīz, $c King of Saudi Arabia, $d 1923-2005.
100 0 $a Louis $b VI, $c Landgrave of Hesse-Darmstadt, $d 1630-1678.
100 0 $a Cleopatra, $c Queen of Egypt, $d died 30 B.C.
100 0 $a Tawfiq Pasha, $c Khedive of Egypt, $d 1852-1892.
100 0 $a Abbās $b II, $c Shah of Iran, $d 1633-1668.
100 0 $a Albert, $c Duke of York, $d 1895-1952.
100 1 $a Belloni, Girolamo, $c marchese, $d 1688-1760.
100 1 $a Muhammad Omar, $c Mullah, $d 1960-
100 1 $a Abecassis, David, $c Rabbi.

Other designations that are associated with the person can be used. For Christian saints, use saint; for Spirits, used spirit. Record "Saint" preceded by comma and "Spirit" enclosed in parentheses at end of access point:

100 1 $a Abbott, $c Mrs., $d approximately 1614-1640.
100 1 $a Thouret, Jeanne Antide, $c Saint, $d 1765-1826.
100 1 $a Achorn, Kendall Lincoln, $d 1882-1916, $c (Spirit)
100 1 $a Brandon, Wilfred, $d died 1781, $c (Spirit)

DATE ASSOCIATED WITH THE PERSON AND PERIOD OF ACTIVITY (RDA 9.3.2–9.3.4) (MARC 21 TAG 100, SUBFIELD $d)

Dates associated with the person are core elements and they include the date of birth (RDA 9.3.2), date of death (RDA 9.3.3), if available, and period of activity of the person (RDA 9.3.4) if needed to differentiate persons with the same name. The period of activity of the person is defined as a "date range of dates indicative of the period in which a person was active in his or her primary field of endeavour." The date of birth and death are RDA core elements. Information about the date of birth and death can be obtained from any source (RDA 9.3.1.3). In recording the birth and death dates, use the following terms. Notice that these abbreviations are not in appendix B of RDA:

- Use "century" instead of "cent."
- Use "Approximately" instead of "ca."
- Use the term "born" and "died." Library of Congress's practice is to use a hyphen after date of birth or the date of death when recording the date in an authorized access point.
- Use "active" or "flourished" instead of "fl."

Birth date:

100 1 $a Arıt, Fikret, $d 1918-
100 1 $a Ẓarghāmī, Farīdūn, $d 1932 or 3-
100 1 $a Smith, John, $d born 1825.

Death date:

100 1 $a James, Abraham, $d died 1827.
100 1 $a Bourbon, Louis, bâtard de, $d died 1487.
100 0 $a Evaristus, $c Pope, $d died approximately 107.

Period of activity:

100 1 $a Miller, J. Edgar, $d 1899-1993
100 0 $a Pantaleão $c de Aveiro, $d 16th century.
100 1 $a Zāri'ān, Naṣr Allāh, $d 1901?-1987.

FULLER FORM OF NAME (RDA 9.5) (MARC 21 TAG 100, SUBFIELD $q)

RDA defines fuller form of a name as a "full form of a part of a name represented only by an initial or abbreviation in the form chosen as the preferred name, or a part of the name not included in the form chosen as the preferred name." The fuller form may consist of spelled out forenames and surnames for the initials. This information is added in the chosen preferred name in $q and is added in parentheses and can be obtained from any sources:

100 1 $a Michaels, William J. $q (William Jordan), $d 1911-2000.
100 1 $a George, A. $q (Arthur), $d 1946-
100 1 $a Allan, A. D. H. $q (Alexander Dean Hugh)

FIELD OF ACTIVITY OF A PERSON (RDA 9.3.4) (MARC 21 100 TAG, SUBFIELD $c)

RDA defined the tag of activity of a person as "tag of endeavour, area of expertise, etc., in which a person is or was engaged." Adding this information to the name of person will further provide a distinction between one person from another with the same name. This addition will be recorded in subfield $c and enclosed in parentheses:

100 1 $a Gillespie, Helen, $c (owner of Dance news)
100 1 $a Edwards, J. P., $c (Horror fiction writer)
100 1 $a Wilson, Conrad, $c (music critic)
100 1 $a Lang, Peter, $c stamp collector

PROFESSION OR OCCUPATION (RDA 9.16) (MARC 21 100 TAG, SUBFIELD $c)

Adding this information to the name of a person will further provide a distinction between one person from another with the same name. This addition will be recorded in subfield $c and enclosed in parentheses:

100 1 $a Andrés, David, $c (notary)
100 1 $a Abbott, L. W., $c (composer)
100 1 $a Adams, Fred, $c (musician)
100 1 $a Abbott, Chris, $c (singer)
100 1 $a Audley, John, $c (preacher of the Gospel)
100 1 $a Ahmad, Farid, $c (consultant)

Notice that in RDA profession/occupation and tag of activity are always added in parentheses, even for names in which the entry element is a surname.

NEW MARC 21 TAGS FOR AUTHORITY FORMAT FOR PERSON

To accommodate RDA, some new elements were created for the authority records. These elements are:

Special coded dates (RDA 9.3) (MARC 21 tag 046)
Associated place (RDA 9.8–9.11) (MARC 21 tag 370)
Address (RDA 9.12) (MARC 21 tag 371)
Field of activity (RDA 9.15) (MARC 21 tag 372)
Affiliation (RDA 9.13) (MARC 21 tag 373)
Occupation (RDA 9.16) (MARC 21 tag 374)
Gender RDA (9.7) (MARC 21 tag 375)
Associated language (RDA 9.14) (MARC 21 tag 377)

The MARC 21 tags 370, 371, 373, 375, and 377 are not used in the authorized access points, but are used only in the authority record for differentiating between authors with the same name.

If there is no tag for the information that you want to add, you can use a note tag. The following example illustrates how the authority record shows the new elements for identifying persons in the authority file:

046 $f 19650731 (*born July 31, 1965*)
100 1 $a Rowling, J. K.
370 $a Gloucestershire, England (*country associated with the person and place of birth)*
372 young adult fantasy (*field of activity)*
373 University of Exeter (*associated group)*
374 $a writer (*occupation*)
375 $a female (*gender*)
377 $a eng (*associated language*)
400 $a Rowling, Joanne K. $q (Joanne Kathleen)
400 $a Rowling, Dz͡h. K.
670 $a Harry Potter, 1998 : $b CIP t.p. (J.K. Rowling) (RDA 8.12)

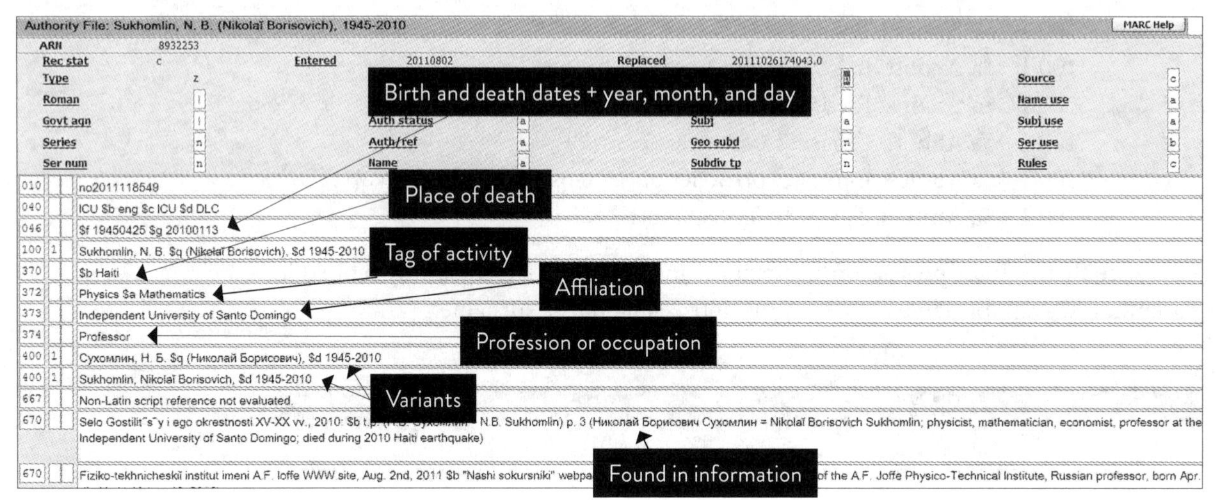

Figure 6.1: Example illustrates how the authority record shows the new elements for identifying a corporate body in the authority file

Note the 670 in the record. This is one of the tags used to help the user understand why the preferred form of name was chosen. RDA finally gives us instructions on how to create source found notes and other cataloger notes for the authority record.

Example of a person from the LC authority file (figure 6.1):

NAME OF FAMILY (RDA CHAPTER 10)

RDA defines a name of the family as a "word, character, or group of words and/or characters by which a family is known." This includes fictitious characters as well. Family name is created only if the family is presented as the creator, contributor, etc., of a resource. Family name will be established in the name authority file. If a family is the subject of a work, the name of the family must be established in the LSCH.

Chapter 10 of RDA provides a definition of the term Family as "two or more persons related by birth, marriage, adoption, civil union, or similar legal status, or who otherwise present themselves as a family" (RDA 8.1.2).

Chapter 10 of RDA provides instructions for choosing and recording preferred names for families. As a general guideline, information can be taken from any source. To construct the authorized access point of a family name, you will use the following (RDA 10.10.1.1).

- Preferred name is the basis
- Additions to the name of family (RDA 10.19.1.2–10.10.1.5)

1. PREFERRED NAME OF FAMILY (RDA CHAPTER 10.2.2) (MARC 21 TAG 100, FIRST INDICATOR 3)

Preferred name of the family is defined as the "name or form of name chosen as the basis for authorized access point representing that family." RDA instruction is to choose the source of information from the following:

- Preferred sources of information (RDA 2.2.2) in resources associated with the family
- Other formal statements appearing in resources associated with the family
- Other sources including reference sources

Choose as the preferred name for the family that name by which the family is commonly known. In some cases, a surname or its equivalent, the name of a royal house, dynasty, or a name of a clan can be used as preferred family name:

100 3 $a Bach.
100 3 $a Kennedy family.
100 3 $a Windsor family.
100 3 $a Cameron family.

In those cases when the family's name is represented by different language forms, choose the form that corresponds to the language of most of the resources as a preferred name (RDA 9.2.2.5.2).

When the family name is written in a non-preferred script (Chinese) that is different from the preferred script of the data creator (English), transliterate the name according to the scheme adopted by the agency creating the data (RDA 9.2.2.5.3).

For variant spellings, choose the form found in the first resource received and not the predominant spelling (RDA 9.2.2.5.4).

DIFFERENT NAME FOR THE SAME FAMILY (RDA 10.2.2.6) (MARC 21 TAG 100 FIRST INDICATOR 3)

RDA instruction is to choose the commonly known name of the family. If this is not available, choose the name of the family that appears most frequently in resources associated with the family or the name that appears most frequently in reference sources, in that order.

CHANGE OF NAME OF THE FAMILY (RDA 10.2.2.7) (MARC 21 TAG 100 FIRST INDICATOR 3)

When the name of the family changes, choose the new name as the preferred name of the family:

100 3 $a Yan family.
(Family Name changed its surname from De La Resureccion to Yan family in 1849.)

SURNAMES (RDA 10.2.2.8) AND NAMES OF ROYAL HOUSES, DYNASTIES, CLANS, ETC. (RDA 10.2.2.9)

If the preferred name of the family consists of surnames, names of royal houses, dynasties, clans, etc., choose it as the preferred name of the family:

100 3 $a'Adil Shahi dynasty.
100 3 $a Aisin Gioro family.
100 3 $a Aisin Gioro dynasty.
100 3 $a Cameron family.

2. ADDITIONS TO THE PREFERRED NAME OF FAMILY

- Type of family (RDA 10.3) (core element)
- Date associated with the family (RDA 10.4) (core element)
- Place associated with the family (RDA 10.5) (core element)
- Prominent member of the family (RDA 10.6) (core element)

Type of family (RDA 10.3) (core element) is a "categorization or generic description for the type of family." Use the appropriate term to indicate the type of family, such as "family, clan, royal house, dynasty, etc.":

100 3 $a Arey family.
100 3 $a Normandy, Dukes of.
100 3 $a Nayak (Dynasty : $d 1529-1739 : $c Madurai, India)
100 3 $a Chichibu no Miya (Royal house)

DATE ASSOCIATED WITH THE FAMILY (RDA 10.4) (MARC 21 TAG 100 FIRST INDICATOR 3 AND SUBFIELD $d) (CORE ELEMENT)

The date associated with the family is taken from any source and the source should be indicated. The date is recorded in $d of the authorized access point as shown in the example:

100 3 $a Achaemenid (Dynasty : $d 559-330 B.C.)
100 3 $a Āravīḍu (Dynasty : $d approximately 1570-approximately 1646)
100 3 $a Pahlavi (Dynasty : $d 1925-1979)

PLACE ASSOCIATED WITH THE FAMILY (RDA 10.5) (CORE ELEMENT)

This refers to the place where a "family resides or has resided or has some connection." Place associated with the family can be used in the authorized access points to differentiate between two families that have the same name. Record the place name in the form prescribed in chapter 16:

100 3 $a Fuessenich (Family : $d 1918-1992 : $c Connecticut)
100 3 $a Yan (Family : $c China)

Prominent member of the family (RDA 10.6) (core element) is used to distinguish a family from another family with the same name. The information is given in $g in the authorized access point:

100 3 $a Gubler (Family: $g Gubler, Kasper, 1835-1917)
100 3 $a Peale (Family : $g Peale, Charles Willson, 1741-1827)

NEW MARC 21 TAGS FOR AUTHORITY FORMAT FOR FAMILY NAME

- Special coded date (RDA 10.4) (MARC 21 tag 046)
- Associated place (RDA 10.5) (MARC 21 tag 370)
- Family information: Type of family (RDA 10.3); prominent member (RDA 10.6); Hereditary title (RDA 10.7)

Example:

046 $a 1918 $t 1992
100 3 $a Fuessenich (Family : $d 1918-1992 : $c Connecticut)
370 $c U. S. $e Litchtag, Connecticut
376 $a Family $b Fuessenich, Cleveland B., 1918-1992

Example of a family authority record from the LC authority file (figure 6.2):

NAME OF CORPORATE BODY (RDA CHAPTER 11) [MARC 21 TAGS 110,111]

RDA defines corporate body as "an organization or group of persons and/or organizations that is identified by a particular name and that acts, or may act, as a unit." Corporate bodies include associations, organizations, business firms, nonprofit enterprises, radio and television stations, government agencies, religious bodies, conferences, local churches, ad hoc events (such as athletic contests, exhibitions, expeditions, fairs, and festivals), vessels (e.g., ships and spacecraft), etc. (RDA 11.0)

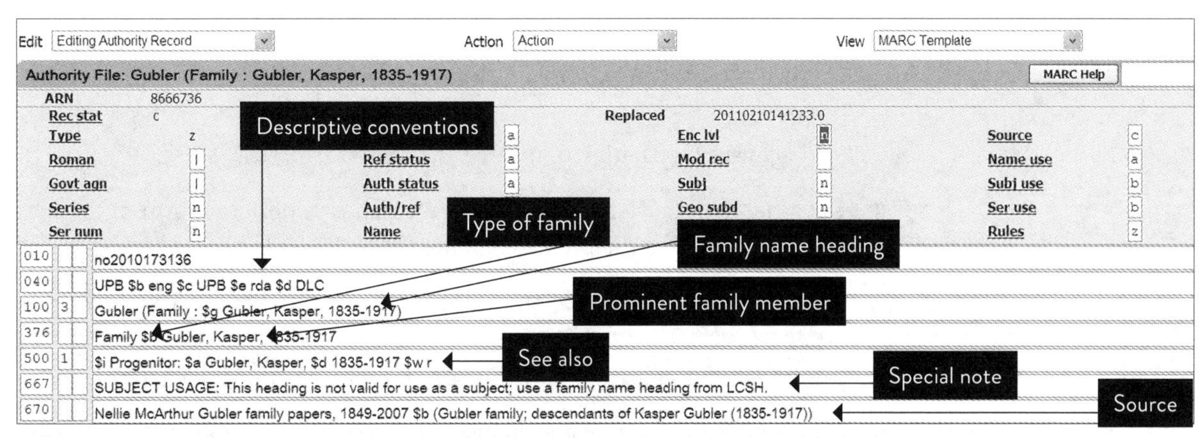

Figure 6.2: Example of a family name from the LC authority file

Sources of information for the preferred name of a person are listed below in RDA instructions in this order:

- Preferred sources of information (RDA 2.2.2) in resources associated with the person
- Other formal statements appearing in resources associated with the person
- Other sources including reference sources

To construct authorized access point for a corporate body, you will need to use the following (RDA 11.13.1.1):

- Preferred name is the basis
- Additions to the preferred name of corporate body for breaking conflict between two or more corporate bodies or meetings that have the same name (RDA 11.13.1.2–11.13.1.8)

1. PREFERRED NAME FOR CORPORATE BODY (RDA 11.2.2)

Choosing the preferred name of the corporate body (RDA 11.2.2.3)—Choose the form by which the corporate name is most commonly known:

110 1 $a Victoria. $b Body Corporate Regulations Review Committee.
110 2 $a Optical Society of America.
110 2 $a African Mountains Association.
111 2 $a African Mountains Workshop.
110 2 $a 924 Gilman Street Project.
110 2 $a Mountain Trail Association.
110 2 $a Bombardment Group (H) Association.
110 2 $a Atlanta Committee on Latin America.

DIFFERENT FORMS OF THE SAME NAME (RDA 11.2.2.5)

When a variant spelling of the same name appears on the resources associated with the body, choose the form found in the first resource received (RDA 11.2.2.5.1):

110 2 $a WICOCA (Organization)
not
Wisconsin Interfaith Committee on Central America

If there is more than one language form of the name, choose the form in the official language of the body as the preferred name (RDA 11.2.2.5.2):

110 2 $a Inter-church Committee on Human Rights in Latin America.
not
Comité inter-église sur les droits de l'homme en Amérique latine

If the name of the corporate body changes, choose the new name as the preferred name (RDA 11.2.2.6):

110 2 $a Pennsylvania State University.
(Earlier name—Pennsylvania State College.)

Omit the initial article, unless the name is to be tagged under the article (RDA 11.2.2.8)

110 2 $a Danske Præsteforening.
not
Den Danske Præsteforening

Omit from the name of a conference, congress, meeting, exhibition, fair, festival, etc., indications of its number or year of convocation, etc. (RDA 11.2.2.11):

110 1 $a World Energy Conference Congress and Its Implications for New Zealand.
not
13th World Energy Conference Congress and Its Implications for New Zealand.

111 2 $a Presidential Campaign Decision Making Conference.
not
1984 Presidential Campaign Decision Making Conference.

110 2 $a San Francisco Art Association. $b Annual Drawing and Print Exhibition.
not
San Francisco Art Association. Twenty-second Annual Drawing and Print Exhibition

The year appears in the authorized access point (in subfield $d, not in subfield $a):

111 2 $a Presidential Campaign Decision Making Conference $d (1984: $c Cambridge, Mass.)

2. ADDITIONS TO THE PREFERRED NAME OF A CORPORATE BODY FOR BREAKING CONFLICT BETWEEN TWO OR MORE CORPORATE BODIES OR MEETINGS THAT HAVE THE SAME NAME

If the corporate body is not a conference, add information from the list below as needed to break a conflict between two or more corporate bodies that have the same name:

- Place associated with the corporate body (RDA 11.3)
- Location of headquarters (RDA 11.3.3)
- Date associated with the corporate body (RDA 11.4)
- Associate institution (RDA 11.5)
- Type of jurisdiction (RDA 11.7.1.5)
- Other designation associated with the corporate body (RDA 11.7)

PLACE ASSOCIATED WITH THE CORPORATE BODY (RDA 11.3) [MARC 21 TAGS 110 OR 710 SUBFIELD $c]

Location of the corporate body is the local place where the meeting, festival, conference, etc., was held. Information about the location of the conference can be taken from any source:

110 2 $a Catholic Church. $b Concilium Plenarium Americae Latinae $d (1899 $c Rome, Italy)

LOCATION OF HEADQUARTERS (RDA 11.3.3)

Location of headquarters refers to the country, state, province, etc., or local place of headquarters, or geographic area where the organization has its headquarters:

110 2 $a Trinity University (San Antonio, Texas)
110 2 $a National Association of Insurance Commissioners (U.S.). $b Meeting (1982: $c Dallas, Texas)

DATE ASSOCIATED WITH THE CORPORATE BODY (RDA 11.4) [MARC 21 TAGS 110 OR 710 SUBFIELD $d]

Date of establishment (RDA 11.4.3) and date of termination (RDA 11.4.4). Record the date in which a corporate body was established or terminated or resolved:

110 1 $a Minnesota. $b Constitutional Convention $d (1857: $g Republican)

ASSOCIATED INSTITUTION (RDA 11.5)

Record the name of the institution if it provides better identification than the local place name or if the local place name is unknown or cannot be determined:

110 2 $a Academy of International Business. $b UK Chapter. $b Conference $d (1997: $c Leeds University Business School)

OTHER DESIGNATION ASSOCIATED WITH THE CORPORATE BODY (RDA 11.7)

Other designation might be needed to differentiate the corporate body from another with the same name. The designator is a word, phrase, or abbreviation indicating incorporation or legal status. Add the designator in parentheses to the preferred name of the corporate body:

110 2 $a Apollo 11 (Spacecraft)
110 2 $a ANAP (Organization)
110 2 $a CMQ-TV (Television station: Havana, Cuba)

If the corporate body is a conference, exhibition, etc., add information from the list below as needed to break a conflict between two or more meetings that have the same name:

- Number of a conference, etc. (RDA 11.6)
- Location of a conference, etc. (RDA 11.3.2 and 11.5)
- Date of a conference, etc. (RDA 11.4.2)
- Other designation associated with the corporate body (RDA 11.7)

NUMBER OF A CONFERENCE, ETC. (RDA 11.6) [MARC 21 TAGS 111 $n OR 711 SUBFIELD $n]

The number of a conference is a designation of the sequencing of a conference, etc., within a series of conferences, etc. It records in English ordinal numerals such as 1st, 2nd, 3rd, etc.

111 2 $a Topical Meeting on Optical Fiber Communication $n (6th: $d 1983: $c New Orleans, Louisiana)
111 2 $a African Literature Association. $b Meeting $n (27th: $d 2001: $c Richmond, Virginia)

LOCATION OF CONFERENCE, ETC. (RDA 11.3.2 AND 11.5) [MARC 21 TAGS 111 $c OR 711 SUBFIELD $c]

If conference, meeting, festival, etc., was held in more than one location, record each of the places separated by semicolons in the access point (appendix E.2.2.4). The location for online conference, meeting, etc., is online. Location of the conference is given in "$c":

111 2 $a International Conference on Southern Song Official Ware of Laohudong Kiln Site in Hangzhou, China $d (2002: $c Hangzhou Shi, China)
111 2 $a Presidential Campaign Decision Making Conference $d (1984: $c Cambridge, Massachusetts)

DATE OF CONFERENCE, ETC. (RDA 11.4.2) [MARC 21 TAGS 111 711 SUBFIELD $d]

Date of conference is the date or range of dates, given as year or years, in which a conference, etc., was held:

111 2 $a Topical Meeting on Optical Fiber Communication $n (6th: $d 1983: $c New Orleans, Louisiana)
111 2 $a African Literature Association. $b Meeting $n (27th: $d 2001: $c Richmond, Virginia)
111 2 $a "20th Century Fantasy: From Beatrix to Harry" International Literary Conference $d (2002: $c Kent State University, Ashtabula, Ohio)
111 2 $a A&WMA/EPA International Specialty Conference $d (1996: $c Research Triangle Park, North Carolina)

To code elements for identifying a corporate body in the authority file, new MARC tags were created:

- Special coded dates (MARC 21 tag 046) (RDA 11.4)
- Associated place (MARC 21 tag 370) (RDA 11.3)
- Address (MARC 21 tag 371) (RDA 11.9)
- Tag of activity (MARC 21 tag 372) (RDA 11.10)
- Associated language (MARC 21 tag 377) (RDA 11.48)

Note that MARC 21 tags 371, 372, and 377 are not used in the authorized access points:

If there is no tag for the information that you want to add, you can use a note tag. The following example illustrates how the authority record shows the new elements for identifying a corporate body in the authority file:

046 $s 2007 (start date)
110 $a Canada. $b Public Safety Canada
410 $a Canada. $b Sécurité publique Canada (2007)
370 $e Ottawa, Ontario (headquarters)
371 $a 269 Laurier Ave. W. $b Ottawa $d Canada $e K1A 0P8 (address)
372 $a Public Safety Canada was created to ensure coordination across all federal departments and agencies responsible for national security and the safety of Canadians (tag of activity)
377 $a eng $a fre (associated languages)

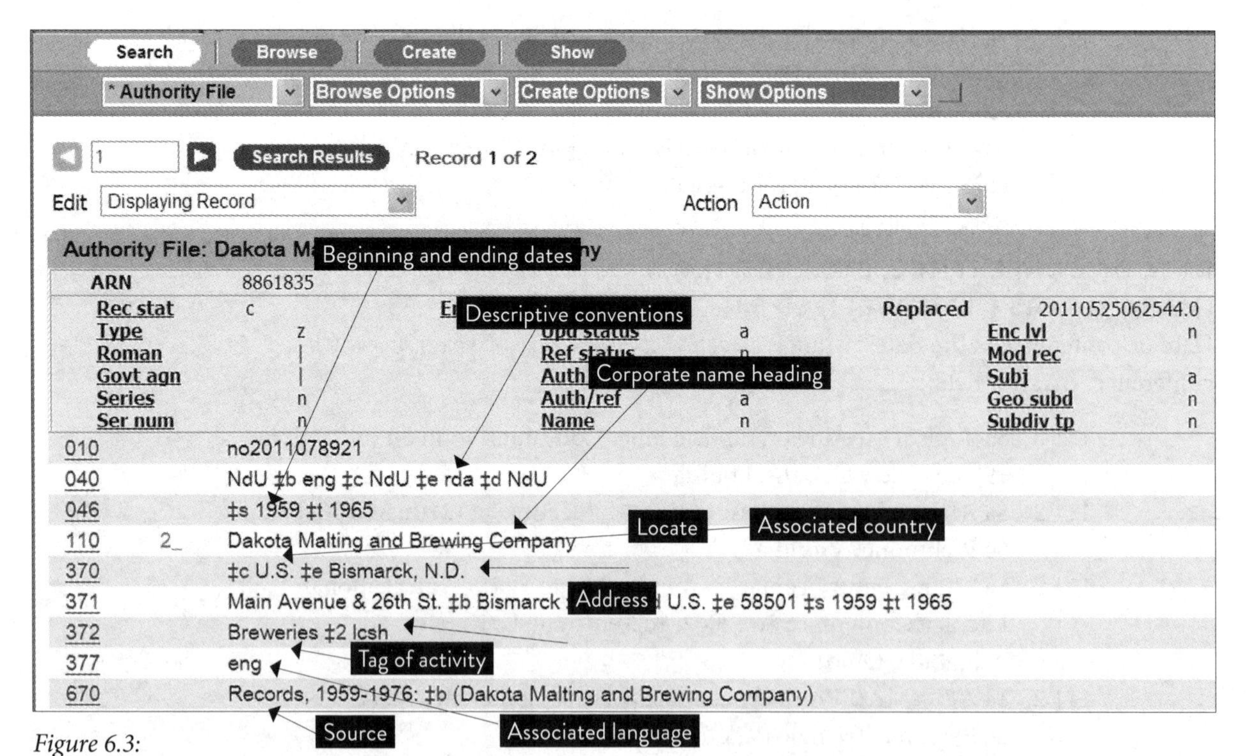

Figure 6.3:
Example illustrates how the authority record shows the new elements for identifying a corporate body in the authority file

Include statement of frequency as on item, e.g., "Annual. . . ," "Biennial . . ." Do not abbreviate the word "Department" in a preferred name:

Example of authority record for corporate name from LC authority file (see figure 6.3).

II. IDENTIFYING EXPRESSIONS

Expression refers to the intellectual or artistic realization of a work in the form of alphanumeric, musical or choreographic notation, sound, image, object, etc. Expression refers to the way the work is expressed through language, sound, movement, etc. Remember, a separate form of title does not exist in the Functional Requirements for Authority Data (FRAD) model. To construct the authorized access point for an expression, use the work or the part of the work as a base and then add one or more of the following expression attributes (RDA 5.5/5.6 and 6.27.3):

- Content type (RDA 6.9)
- Date of expression (RDA 6.10)
- Language of expression (RDA 6.11)
- Other distinguishing characteristic of expression (RDA 6.12)
- Identifier of expression (RDA 6.13)

CONTENT TYPE (RDA 6.9)

Content type is a categorization reflecting the fundamental form of communication in which the content is expressed and the human sense through which it is intended to be perceived. Use controlled vocabulary of terms in RDA 6.9.1.3. Content type can be used as part of the authorized access point and is recorded in MARC 21 authority record tag 130 or 240, subfield $h:

130 0 $a Gone with the wind (Motion picture). $h Sound recording.
240 10 $a Nachtin Venedig (Korngold and Marischka). $h Performed music. $f 1967

DATE OF EXPRESSION (RDA 6.10)

Date of expression is the earliest date associated with the expression and it is used to distinguish between one expression of a work from another expression of the same work. The date is recorded in MARC 21 bibliographic record, tag 130 or 240, subfield $f:

130 0 $a Bible. $l Latin. $s Vulgate. $f 1454

Language of expression (RDA 6.11) refers to the language in which the work is expressed. The language term is used from MARC 21 bibliographic record, tag 130 or 240, in subfield $l:

041 1 $a ger $h lat
100 1 $a Luther, Martin, $d 1483-1546.
240 10 $a Decem praecepta Wittenbergensi praedicata populo. $l German
245 10 $a Martin Luthers Dekalogredigten in der Übersetzung von Sebastian Münster / $c herausgegeben von Michael Basse.
546 $a German translation of the author's original Latin work.

If a single expression of the work involves more than one language, record all of the languages:

245 10 $a Antigo Testamento Poliglota : $b Hebraico, Grego, Português, Inglês.
546 $a Text in Greek, Hebrew, Portuguese, and English in columns on facing pages.
730 02 $a Bible. $p Old Testament. $l Hebrew. $f 2003.
730 02 $a Bible. $p Old Testament. $l Greek. $f 2003.
730 02 $a Bible. $p Old Testament. $l Portuguese. $f 2003.
730 02 $a Bible. $p Old Testament. $l English. $f 2003.

For different expressions of the same work, record each expression in the 700 tag and use subfield $l to indicate the language of the expression:

041 0 $a lat $a eng
100 1 $a Buchanan, George, $d 1506-1582, $e author.
245 10 $a Poetic paraphrase of the Psalms of David = $b Psalmorum Davidis paraphrasis poetica / $c George Buchanan ; edited, translated, and provided with introduction and commentary by Roger P. H. Green.
246 3 $a Psalmorum Davidis paraphrasis poetica
546 $a Text in Latin with parallel English translation; preface, introduction and commentary in English.
700 12 $a Buchanan, George, $d 1506-1582. $t Psalmorum Davidis paraphrasis poetica. $l English. $s (Green)
700 12 $a Buchanan, George, $d 1506-1582. $t Psalmorum Davidis paraphrasis poetica. $l Latin. $s (Green)

OTHER DISTINGUISHING CHARACTERISTICS OF THE EXPRESSION (RDA 6.12)

Provide other distinguishing characteristics of the expression to differentiate between one expression of a work from another expression of the same work. Some of these characteristics are:

$k for Selections
240 10 $a Correspondence. $k Selections

$o for musical work
240 10 $a Songs, $K selection; $o arranged

$s for version of religious work such as Bible
130 0 $a Bible. $l Latin. $s Vulgate. $f 1454.
130 0 $a Bible. $p New Testament. $l English. $s New Living Translation. $f 1999.

III. RELATIONSHIPS

In cataloging, access point is a name, term, code, etc., under which a bibliographic record may be searched and identified in a computer system. To provide consistency and accuracy in retrieval, RDA provides instruction on how to record access points. The objective of the data recorded is to reflect the attributes of a work or expression that should allow the user to find, identify, select, and obtain a work or expression that meet the criteria of the search. To ensure these objectives will be met, the data recorded should enable the user to differentiate the work and expression from other works and expressions.

Relationships among entities are a very important part of the FRBR model. The objective of recording relationships between person, family, or corporate bodies and the resource is to help the user find all the resources that embody the particular work and expression and all items exemplified by the manifestation. Relationships are links that catalogers make between one entity and another. These links assist the users in navigating the bibliographic universe represented in our catalogs. In RDA, you record a relationship whenever you:

- Add access points for creators (authors), editors, annotators, illustrators, etc.
- Add an access point for a related work (e.g., succeeding or preceding title of a serial, adaptation, supplement, sequel, part of a larger work), expression (revised version, translation), etc.
- Add the succeeding name of a corporate body in the MARC 21 tag 510 in the authority record, or a MARC 21 tag 500 for the pseudonym of a personal name in an authority record (if you do authority work).

Where do we record relationships?

Relationships are recorded mostly in the bibliographic record (access points for persons associated with work, expression, manifestation, item; access points or structured/unstructured descriptions for related works, expressions, manifestations, items). Sometimes, relationships are recorded in authority records (related persons and corporate bodies).

Chapters 8 to11 show how to identify the person, family, or corporate body and create the authorized access points. As mentioned before, these access points are recorded in authority records to be used in bibliographic records or as related authorized access points in other authority records. There are relationships within the resource itself; relationships for persons, families, and corporate bodies related to a work, expression, manifestation, or item; there are related works, expressions, manifestations, and items that are related to a resource; and relationships between the group 2 entities, persons, families, and corporate bodies. For example, the relationship between someone's real identity and a pseudonym. The following RDA chapters cover relationships among entities. Not all of them will be represented here; only the most important will be highlighted. It is also important to mention that in developing this section, the author relied on the "Train the Trainer Module 8: Relationships" by Tillett (2010). (www.loc.gov/catdir/cpso/RDAtest/rdatraining.html).

A. RELATIONSHIPS BETWEEN A WORK, EXPRESSION, MANIFESTATION, AND ITEM (RDA CHAPTER 17)

There are two core elements that are important here when you catalog compilations of works or expressions:

- Work manifested (RDA 17.8)—Work embodied in a manifestation
- Expression manifested (RDA 17.10)—Expression embodied in a manifestation (this element is core if there's more than one expression of the work manifested).

There are two methods to record primary relationships between a work, expression, manifestation, and item:

- Using an identifier for the work, expression, manifestation, and item (will not explain in this chapter)
- Using an authorized access point representing work or expression

IDENTIFIER

Identifier is a character string (usually numeric) that identifies an item, (e.g., ISSN/ISBN number, authority record number, URI, etc.). Per LC policy, the identifier cannot be used alone to establish a relationship.

Examples:

ISBN: 9781741461633
ISSN: 0366-7405
LCCN: 2008252287
(URLs are not considered to be identifiers and cannot be used as such in developing relationships.)

AUTHORIZED ACCESS POINTS FOR RELATED WORKS USING MARC 21 TAG 700 AS AUTHOR/TITLE ACCESS POINT

100 1 $a Twain, Mark, $d 1835-1910, $e author.
245 10 $a Mark Twain's Adventures of Tom Sawyer and Huckleberry Finn / $c edited by Alan Gribben.
505 0 $a Adventures of Tom Sawyer—Adventures of Huckleberry Finn.
→ 700 12 $a Twain, Mark, $d 1835-1910. $t Adventures of Tom Sawyer.
→ 700 12 $a Twain, Mark, $d 1835-1910. $t Adventures of Huckleberry Finn.

(MARC 21 tag 700 2nd indicator "2" indicates relationship; otherwise, use "contains (work)" relationship designator. Adding the 505 tag is cataloger's judgment. If more than one work is embodied in the manifestation, only the predominant or first named work is required ("Work Manifested" RDA 17.8). LC's policy is to give analytical authorized point for predominant or first work in compilation when it represents a substantial part of the resource. Other access points are cataloger's judgment.)

AUTHORIZED ACCESS POINTS FOR THE EXPRESSIONS USING MARC 21 TAG 700 AS AUTHOR/TITLE ACCESS POINT

100 1 $a Petterson, Per, $d 1952-, $e author.
240 10 $a Novels. $l English. $k Selections
245 10 $a Two Norwegian novels / $c Per Petterson.
505 0 $a Out stealing horses—To Siberia.
→ 700 12 $a Petterson, Per, $d 1952- $t Ut og stjæle hester. $l English.
→ 700 12 $a Petterson, Per, $d 1952- $t Til Sibir. $l English.

(Notice that the second indicator in MARC 21 tag 700 indicates a relationship of the parts to the whole. There is no need to add the content note 505 to justify the 7xx.)

100 1 $a Kafka, Franz, $d 1883-1924, $e author.
→ 240 10 $a Short stories. $l English. $k Selections
24 14 $a The metamorphosis and other stories / $c Franz Kafka; translated by Joyce Crick; with an introduction and notes by Ritchie Robertson.
505 0 $a Meditation—The judgment—The metamorphosis—In the penal colony—Letter to his father.
→ 700 12 $a Kafka, Franz, $d 1883-1924. $t Urteil. $l English.
→ 700 12 $a Kafka, Franz, $d 1883-1924. $t Verwandlung. $l English.
→ 700 12 $a Kafka, Franz, $d 1883-1924. $t der Strafkolonie. $l English.
→ 700 12 $a Kafka, Franz, $d 1883-1924. $t Brief an den vater. $l English
→ 700 1 $a Crick, Joyce.

(MARC 700 tag 2nd indicator "2" indicates relationship; otherwise, use "contains (work)" relationship designator. If more than one expression is

embodied in the manifestation only the predominant or first named expression manifested is required (expression manifested (RDA 17.10). LC's policy is to give analytical authorized access point for predominant or first expression in the compilation when it represents a substantial part of the resource. Other access points are cataloger's judgment.)

B. RECORDING RELATIONSHIPS TO PERSON, FAMILY, AND CORPORATE BODIES ASSOCIATED WITH THE RESOURCE (RDA CHAPTERS 18 TO 22) [MARC 21 TAGS 1XX AND 7XX SUBFIELD $e]

Types of relationships:

- Relationship associated with work

  Examples:

  authors, film directors, producers, issuing body, sponsoring bodies, compilers, composers, etc.

- Relationship associated with expression

  Examples:

  editors, translators, illustrators, performers, art directors, interviewees

- Relationship associated with manifestation

  Examples:

  publishers, distributors, manufacturers, book designers, engravers, printers

- Relationship associated with item

  Examples:

  current owners, former owner binders, inscribers, curators, annotators

There are two methods to record relationship to person, family, and corporate bodies associated with the work, expression, manifestation, and item:

- The use of identifier for the work, expression, manifestation, and item (will not explain in this chapter).
- The use of authorized access point representing work, expression, manifestation, and item.

AUTHORIZED ACCESS POINT REPRESENTING WORK, EXPRESSION, MANIFESTATION, AND ITEM

"Record one or more appropriate terms from the list in appendix I with an identifier and/or authorized access point representing the person, family, or corporate body to indicate the nature of the relationship more specifically than is indicated by the defined scope of the relationship element itself."

700 1 $a Austin, Fay Angela, $e author.
(Relationship designator for the person associated with the Work in MARC 21 tag 700 $e.)

700 1 $a Feldhaus, Anne, $e translator.
(Relationship designator for person associated with the expression in MARC 21 tag 700 $e.)

710 2 $a Geological Society of America, $e publisher.
(Relationship designator for corporate body associated with the Manifestation in MARC 21 tag 700 $e.)

110 2 $a Columbus Globes GmbH, $e current owner.
(Relationship designator for corporate body associated with the item in MARC 21 tag 110 $e.)

CONTRIBUTOR (RDA CHAPTER 20)

LC considers contributors as a core element. Contributors are those persons, families, or corporate bodies that are associated with expressions in roles such as editors, translators, illustrators, performers, arrangers of music, compilers, writers of added commentary, composers, etc. Contributors are given as authorized access points in MARC 21 tags 7XXs in the bibliographic record. Relationship designators are used from RDA appendix I in subfield $e of MAC 21 tags 7XXs:

100 1 $a Heaton, John M., $d 1925- $e author.
700 1 $a Groves, Judy, $e author.
700 1 $a Appignanesi, Richard, $e editor.
(Authorized access points representing the contributor and editor for: Introducing Wittgenstein / $c John Heaton and Judy Groves ; edited by Richard Appignanesi.)

700 1 $a Dew, John M, $e compiler.
(Authorized access points representing the compiler for: Mining people—a century : $b highlights of the first hundred years of the AusIMM 1893-1993 / $c compiled by John M. Dew.)

700 1 $a Cronin, Mike, $e editor.
700 1 $a Regan, John $q (John M.), $e editor.
(Authorized access points representing the editor for: Ireland : $b the politics of Independence, 1922-49 / $c edited by Mike Cronin and John M. Regan.)

100 1 $a Riḍā, Ḥasan, $e author.
240 10 $a Dāstān-i Karbālā. $l Divehi

700 1 $a Dīdī, Muḥammad Aḥmad, $e translator.
(Authorized access points representing the translator for Shahidunge sāhibā / $c [tarjamah] Muḥammad Aḥmad Dīdī.)

Other relationships:

700 1 $a Zell, F., ‡d 1829-1895, $e librettist.
700 1 $a Korngold, Erich Wolfgang, $d 1897-1957, $e arranger of music.
700 1 $a Schwarzkopf, Elisabeth, $e singer.
700 1 $a Ackermann, Otto, $d 1909-1960, $e conductor.

C. RELATIONSHIPS BETWEEN A WORK, EXPRESSION, MANIFESTATION, AND ITEM (CHAPTERS RDA 24 AND 26)

Before exploring these methods, there are some terms that need to be explained first (RDA 24.1.3):.

The term *related work* refers to a work that is related to the work represented by an identifier, an authorized access point, or a description. Examples of related works are adaptation, commentary, supplement, part of a large work, etc.

The term *related expression* refers to an expression related to the expression represented by an identifier, an authorized access point, or a description. Examples include translation and a revised version.

Related manifestation and item are explained in chapter 6 under section "recording relationships for manifestations and item."

Relationship designator is a designator that indicates the nature of relationships between works, expressions, manifestations, and the item. Examples are continued by, motion picture adaptation of, augmented by, based on, etc. The relationship designator can be found in RDA appendix J2.

Recording relationships between works, expression, manifestation, and the item can be indicated by using one or more of the following methods (RDA 24.4):

- Identifiers (RDA 24.4.1)
- Authorized access points (RDA 24.4.2)
- Structured or unstructured descriptions (RDA 24.4.3)

The cataloger can decide to use an authorized access point or a description or both. Catalogers also have the option of using relationship designators from RDA appendix J2, if needed.

RELATIONSHIP: RELATED WORK (RDA 24.4)

RDA instruction 24.4 covers the relationship between a work and other works. Examples of a work to work relationship are: adaptations, commentary, parodies, supplements, earlier/later serials, paraphrases, remakes of, contained in, preceded by, relationship between the parts to the whole, etc. There are three methods to indicate relationships for related works:

- Identifiers such as ISBN

  020 $a 9781741461633

- Authorized access points (MARC 21 tags 1xx and 7xx)

  100 1 $a Winik, Jay, $d 1957-, $e author.
  245 10 $a April 1865 : $b the Month That Saved America / $c Jay Winik
  (Relationship designator in MARC 21 tag 100 $e indicates the nature of the relationship between the entities represented by authorized access points. Relationship designators are available in RDA appendixes I-L.)

  100 1 $a Faulkner, William, $d 1897-1962, $e author.
  240 10 $a Poems. $k Selections. $f 1981
  245 10 $a Helen, a courtship ; and, Mississippi poems / $c by William Faulkner introductory essays by Carvel Collins and Joseph Blotner.
  700 12 $a Faulkner, William, $d 1897-1962. $t Helen, a courtship.
  700 12 $a Faulkner, William, $d 1897-1962. $t Mississippi poems.
  (Authorized access points are used to represent the relationship between the parts to the whole. The 2nd indicator in MARC 21 tag 700 indicates the relationship. Using a relationship designator from appendix J is not needed in this case.)

- *Description (either unstructured or structured).* Used with related works, expressions, manifestations, or items, *not* for personal names, families, or corporate bodies.

  a. *Structured description.* A note that uses ISBD punctuation to identify the elements:

  500 $a Reprint of: The Stones of Florence / Mary McCarthy—New York : Harcourt Brace, 1959.

  Linking tags for a related work of a serial using MARC 21 780 and 785 tags.

  245 04 $a Journal of bioethics.
  785 00 $a $t Journal of medical humanities $x 1041-3545 $w (DLC) 90642583 $w (OCoLC) 18731853.
  (Note that if MARC coding describes relationship, then relationship designators aren't necessary. In this example, the second indicator in the MARC 21 tag 785 shows a relationship between the target item and the succeeding

entry, and indicates that the title in tag 245 is continued by the title in MARC 21 tag785. The title will be indexed as "continued by".)

245 04 $a The Journal of medical humanities and bioethics.
780 00 $t Journal of bioethics $x 0278-9523 $w (DLC) 85642232 $w (OCoLC) 7938841.
(Note that if MARC coding describes relationship, then relationship designators aren't necessary. In this example the second indicator in the MARC 21 tag 785 shows a relationship between the target item and the succeeding entry, and indicates that the title in MARC 21 tag 245 is continued by the title in the MARC 21 tag 785.)

b. *Unstructured description.* Full or partial description of related resource written as a sentence or a paragraph.

580 $a Merger of: Inside energy/with federal lands and: Energy report.

STRUCTURED DESCRIPTIONS FOR A RELATED WORK OF A SERIAL USING MARC 21 780 AND 785 TAGS

245 04 $a Journal of bioethics.
785 00 $a $t Journal of medical humanities $x 1041-3545 $w (DLC) 90642583 $w (OCoLC)18731853.
(The second indicator in the 785 tag shows a relationship between the target item and the succeeding entry, and indicates that the title in tag 245 is continued by the title in the 785 tag. The title will be indexed as "continued by".)

245 04 $a The Journal of medical humanities and bioethics.
780 00 $t Journal of bioethics $x 0278-9523 $w (DLC) 85642232 $w (OCoLC) 7938841.
(The second indicator in MARC 21 tag 785 shows a relationship between the target item and the succeeding entry, and indicates that the title in tag 245 is continued by the title in the MARC 21 tag 785.)

RELATED EXPRESSION (RDA 26.1)

The relationship between expression and other expressions can be in a form of translations, revisions, editions, abridgements, etc. The following are examples that illustrate related expressions in a variety of methods.

AUTHORIZED ACCESS POINT FOR THE EXPRESSION (TRANSLATION) USING THE MARC 21 700 TAG AND THE SUBFIELD "I"

100 0 $a Simenon, Georges, $d 1903-1989, $e author.
240 10 $a Long course. $l English

245 14 $a The long exile / $c Georges Simenon ; translated from the French by Eileen Ellenbogen.
700 1 $i Translation of: $a Simenon, Georges, $d 1903-1989 $t Long course.
(Notice here the relationship between the translation and the original as expressed by 700 $i, which is taken from appendix J.)

UNSTRUCTURED DESCRIPTION OF A SERIAL IN A DIFFERENT EXPRESSION USING THE MARC 21 780 TAG

245 04 $a The woman citizen : $b official organ of the National American Woman Suffrage Association.
580 $a Formed by the union of: Woman voter, and: National suffrage news, and: The woman's journal (Boston, Mass.: 1917).
780 14 $a Woman's journal (Boston, Mass.: 1917) $w (DLC) 94094330 $w (OCoLC)7699241.
(Notice that MARC 21 tag 580 was used as an unstructured description to represent the relationship.)

580 $a Also issued in Arabic, French, and Spanish editions.
(Language editions are related expressions. In this example of a serial, an unstructured description in tag 580 is used to give the relationship.)

STRUCTURED DESCRIPTION FOR RELATED EXPRESSIONS (TRANSLATION) USING MARC 21 500 TAG

100 1 $a Rahner, Karl, $d 1904-1984, e author.
240 10 $a Hörer des Wortes. $l English
245 10 $a Hearer of the word : $b laying the foundation for a philosophy of religion / $c Karl Rahner ; translation of the first edition by Joseph Donceel ; edited, and with an introduction by Andrew Tallon.
500 $a Translation of : Hörer des Wortes / Rahner, Karl, $d 1904-1984.—1st ed.—München : Kösel, (1969).—220 pages; 23 cm.
(Notice the use of the relationship designator from appendix J; "translation of," followed by elements of description in an ISBD display.)

Or use an unstructured description for the related expression using MARC 21 500 tag as a note:

500 $a Translation of the author's work Hörer des Wortes.

STRUCTURED DESCRIPTION FOR RELATED EXPRESSIONS (TRANSLATION) USING MARC 21 765 TAG

100 1 $a Pasternak, Boris Leonidovich, $d 1890-1960, $e author.
240 10 $a Doktor Zhivago. $l English

245 10 $a Doctor Zhivago / $c Boris Pasternak ; translated from the Russian by Richard Pevear and Larissa Volokhonsky ; with an introduction by Richard Pevear.
765 0 $a Pasternak, Boris Leonidovich, $d 1890-1960. $t Doktor Zhivago $b Pantheon pbk. Ed. $d New York : Pantheon Books, 1991 $h xxiii, 558 pages ; $c 20 cm $w (DLC) 90053445.

(Notice that the 765 tag was used to indicate the original language. The second indicator is blank to indicate that this expression is a translation. This will eliminate the need to use the relationship designator from appendix J2.)

ADDITIONAL RESOURCES

RDA Toolkit is the main source of the information for this chapter. In addition, the following sources were consulted:

Curran, Mary. 2009. "Serials in RDA: A Starter's Tour and Kit." *The Serials Librarian* 57 (4): 306–23.

Davis, Renette. 2010. "RDA Serials Cataloging: Changes from AACR2 to RDA." www.renettedavis.com/presentations.html.

Hillmann, Diane, Karen Coyle, John Philipps, and Gorden Dunsire. 2010. "RDA Vocabularies: Process, Outcome, Use." *D-Lib Magazine* 16 (1/2). http://dlib.org/dlib/january10/hillmann/01hillmann.html.

Hitchens, Alison. 2011. "Identifying Persons, Corporate Bodies; Relationships. Resource Description and Access (RDA): What You Need to Know." www.rda-jsc.org/docs/BCLAPresentation.ppt.

Hitchens, Alison, and Ellen Symons. 2009. "Preparing Catalogers for RDA Training." *Cataloging and Classification Quarterly* 47: 691–707.

Joint Steering Committee for Development of RDA. 2013. "RDA: Resource Description and Access: Background." www.rda-jsc.org/rda.html.

———. 2013. "RDA: Resource Description and Access: Frequently Asked Questions." www.rda-jsc.org/rdafaq.html#faq.

Library of Congress. 2010. "Documentation for the RDA Test: Training Materials for RDA Test Participants." www.loc.gov/catdir/cpso/RDAtest/rdatraining.html.

———. "Examples for RDA – Compared to AACR2 (Work in Progress)." www.sla.org/PDFs/SLA2009/2009_rdaexamples.pdf.

———. "MARC 21 Format Changes to Accommodate RDA (Draft)." www.loc.gov/marc/formatchanges-RDA.html.

Nicholson, Joseph. "RDA Relationships and RDA for Serials." https://sites01.lsu.edu/wp/louis/files/2012/04/2011RDARelPresFinal.pdf. Accessed May 30, 2013.

Oliver, Chris. 2009. "RDA and AACR2." Paper presented at the Music Library Association, May 4th, 2009.

Paradis, Daniel. 2010. "Significant Changes for Cataloging Music: AACR2 versus RDA." Paper presented at the Music Library Association Annual Conference, San Diego, CA, March 2010. www.rda-jsc.org/docs/10_3_24_MLAannmtg_SignificantchangesforcataloguingmusicAACR2vsRDA.pdf.

"RDA: Approaching Implementation Program Sponsored by the Bibliographic Control Committee (BCC)." 2010. http://bcc.musiclibraryassoc.org/Presentations/RDA-implementation-MLA-2010.pdf.

Schiff, Adam L. 2010. "Changes from AACR2 to RDA: A Comparison of Examples." www.rda-jsc.org/docs/BCLAPresentation.ppt.

Trelton, Charlotte S. 2010. "RDA for Music Cataloguers." New Zealand IAML Conference, November 2010. www.slideshare.net/petesime/rda-for-music-cataloguers.

Yust, Laura. 2011. "RDA: A Hands-On Interaction: Identifying Works." MLA Preconference, February 9, 2011. http://bcc.musiclibraryassoc.org/BCC-Historical/BCC2011/MLA_RDA_Music_Edit.pdf.

CHAPTER SEVEN

RDA TOOLKIT

EFORE EXPLAINING HOW TO SEARCH RDA TOOLKIT, IT IS important to distinguish between this product and RDA itself. RDA is a set of guidelines that provide instruction for descriptive cataloging. RDA Toolkit is an online product that allows users to interact with a collection of documents and resources related to cataloging.

The online interface of RDA Toolkit (www.rdatoolkit .org) allows for efficient and effective browsing through the RDA instructions. RDA contents can be viewed in two ways: through the RDA table of contents or the RDA element set view. The user can navigate back and forth between the RDA instructions, the RDA element set view, AACR2, and other documentation. Users of RDA Toolkit can create a customized version of web-based RDA where they can determine which instructions they need or want to view.

Serials catalogers, for example, can view instructions related specifically to serials. Users can create their own workflows and can share them with other librarians, or can restrict access to them. Because RDA Toolkit is a digital product, it offers flexibility to add and update the instructions without having to insert pages into a print copy. More importantly, RDA Toolkit provides consistency in keeping all the user communities informed about updates and changes in the instructions, at the same time.

RDA Toolkit is published by the Co-Publishers of RDA, consisting of the American Library Association, the Canadian Library Association, and the publishing arm of the Chartered Institute of Library and Information Professionals (CILIP). RDA instructions are available as part of the online package of RDA Toolkit. It was released on June 23, 2010. The Co-Publishers have appointed ALA Publishing to process and manage all the online subscriptions to RDA Toolkit from anywhere in the world. ALA will process payments in the major currencies and will ensure access to, and support of, the electronic product.

Users can subscribe to RDA Toolkit and can also purchase the print version of RDA through the RDA Toolkit website. The website offers information about options for subscription and pricing. The site includes full details for consortial and group subscriptions and special extensions for training and classroom access.

The Co-Publishers have been working with the Library of Congress, OCLC, and others to make linking from their software, such as Cataloger's Desktop, OCLC Connexion, and LIS vendor systems, to RDA Toolkit as seamless and user-friendly as possible. RDA Toolkit is now available via Cataloger's Desktop if you subscribe to both Cataloger's Desktop and RDA Toolkit.

Although the preferred method to access RDA is online via RDA Toolkit, the Co-Publishers offer full-text loose-leaf print versions of both *RDA: Resource Description and Access* and the *RDA: Element Set View*. The print version provides a "snapshot that serves as an offline access point to help solo and part-time catalogers evaluate RDA, as well as to support training and classroom use in any size institution." RDA print products are available directly from each of the Co-Publishers as well as through various approved retailers, wholesalers, and distributors.

I. HOW TO BROWSE AND SEARCH RDA TOOLKIT

The Co-Publishers of RDA have educated the library community about RDA Toolkit's functionality and application through webinars, meetings, conferences, and other means of information sharing. Webinars conducted by the Co-Publishers of RDA are the best way to learn about using RDA Toolkit. All the webinars are available from the RDA Toolkit website or by searching the Internet for "RDA Toolkit Webinars."

The online interface of RDA Toolkit provides users with the option to use either the browse functionality or the search option. The following section describes how to browse and search RDA Toolkit. It discusses how to create and share workflows, and offers a step-by-step explanation of each function, with a screenshot of each function from RDA Toolkit.

II. ACCESSING RDA TOOLKIT

A. SUBSCRIPTION

In order to access RDA Toolkit, it is necessary for you or your institution to subscribe first. This can be done through the RDA Toolkit website (www.rdatoolkit.org).To begin, click on *RDA Toolkit* (figure 7.1) to open the RDA website (figure 7.2).

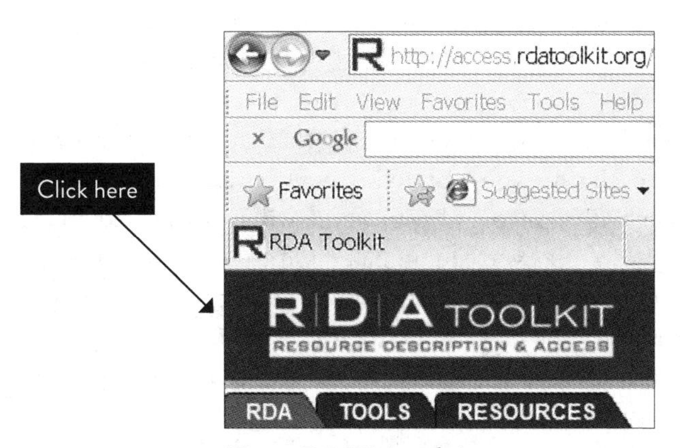

Figure 7.1: RDA website

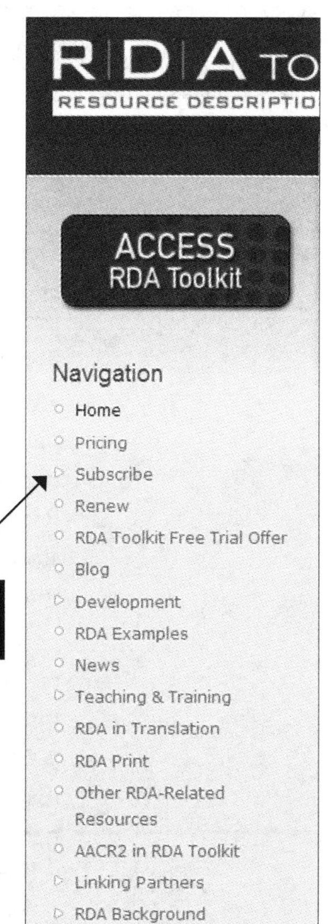

Figure 7.2: Subscription

B. LOG-IN INSTRUCTIONS

You will be able to access RDA Toolkit after your subscription application has been completed. At this point, you will be able to sign in. There are two levels of authentication for each user. The first is designed to identify the subscribing institution, and the second is to identify the individual user.

The first level of authentication is designed to log you into RDA Toolkit using your institution's subscription log-in identification and password (figure 7.3a). Once you log into the system, your institution's name will appear in the upper right hand corner of the RDA Toolkit screen. This confirms that the first level of authentication has been completed and that you are in the system. Enter your log-in and your password, as shown in figure 7.3b.

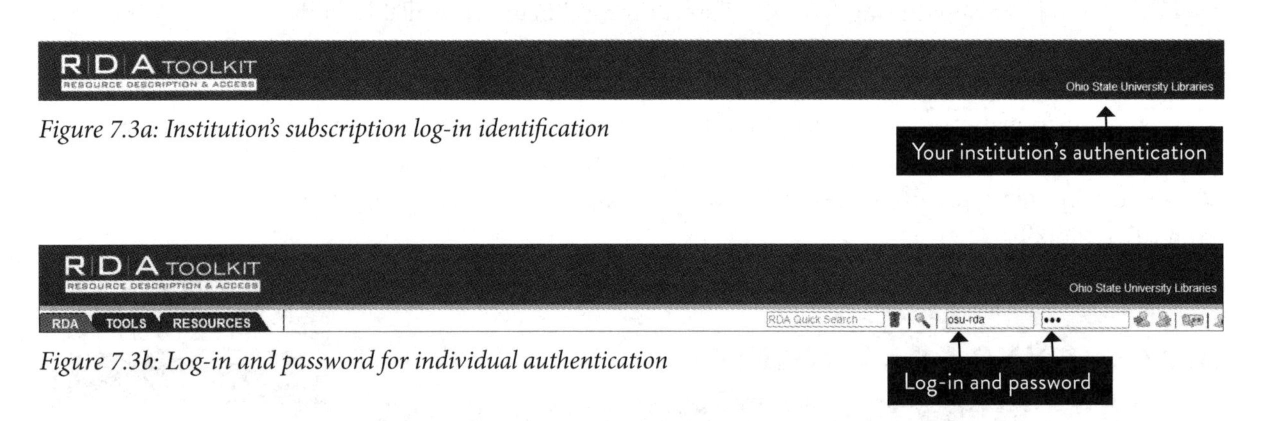

Figure 7.3a: Institution's subscription log-in identification

Figure 7.3b: Log-in and password for individual authentication

The second level of authentication requires you to either log into the previously created individual profile, or to create a new personal profile. If you already have a profile, you will enter your profile name and password and click *Log-in*. If you have not created a profile in the past, you will click on *Create*. You will be prompted to another screen where you will be asked to create your own personal profile. To complete the profile, you will need to provide the following information: full user name, profile name, e-mail address, and password. At the end, you will need to check the RDA Toolkit Terms and Conditions box to indicate that you have read and understood the terms of use. After completing the information in this box, you will click the *Create* button (figure 7.4).

The individual user profile will be created only once. After that, you will need to enter your name and password each time you wish to log in. After creating your profile and signing in, the interface will change and your name will be displayed above your institution's name. This shows that you are affiliated with the organization or institution (figure 7.5). Solo users who have personal subscriptions to RDA Toolkit need only one authentication and will be logged into their user profile directly.

Once you have been authenticated, you will be directed to the *Get Started with RDA Toolkit* screen where you can search, browse, and access all the RDA information and documentation.

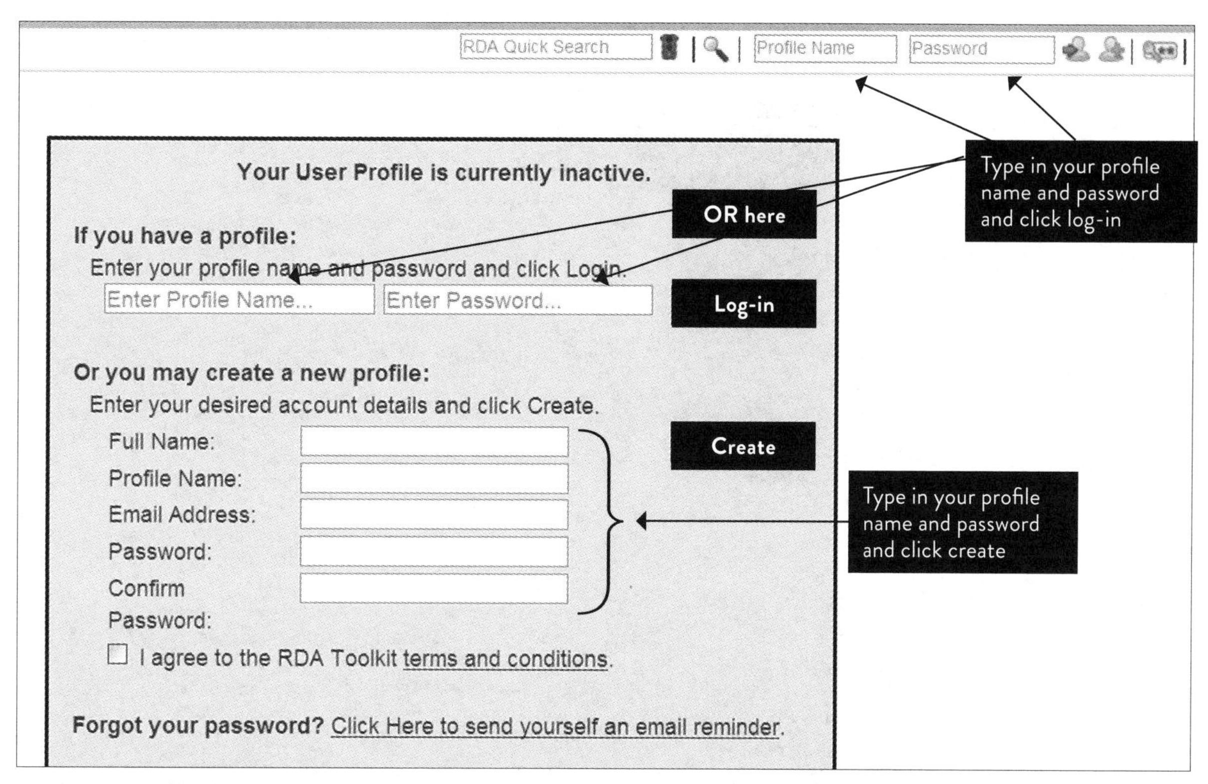

Figure 7.4: Profile creation

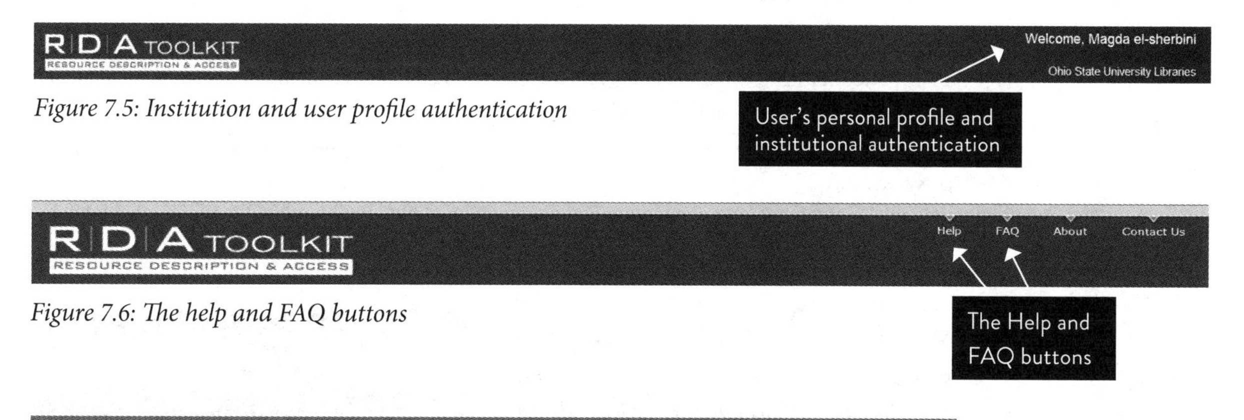

Figure 7.5: Institution and user profile authentication

Figure 7.6: The help and FAQ buttons

C. HELP AND FAQ BUTTONS

The most important buttons for you to consult are the *Help* and *FAQ* buttons that appear in the upper right hand corner of the screen (figure 7.6). This information is accessible from the main RDA website. The *Help* button provides information about the technical support through RDA Toolkit support service.

The *Frequently Asked Questions* (FAQ) button includes various categories of documents that provide specific answers to your queries. The FAQs are grouped under topics to facilitate access and consultation (figure 7.7). The following topics are included under the FAQ section: FAQs about RDA and RDA Toolkit; information

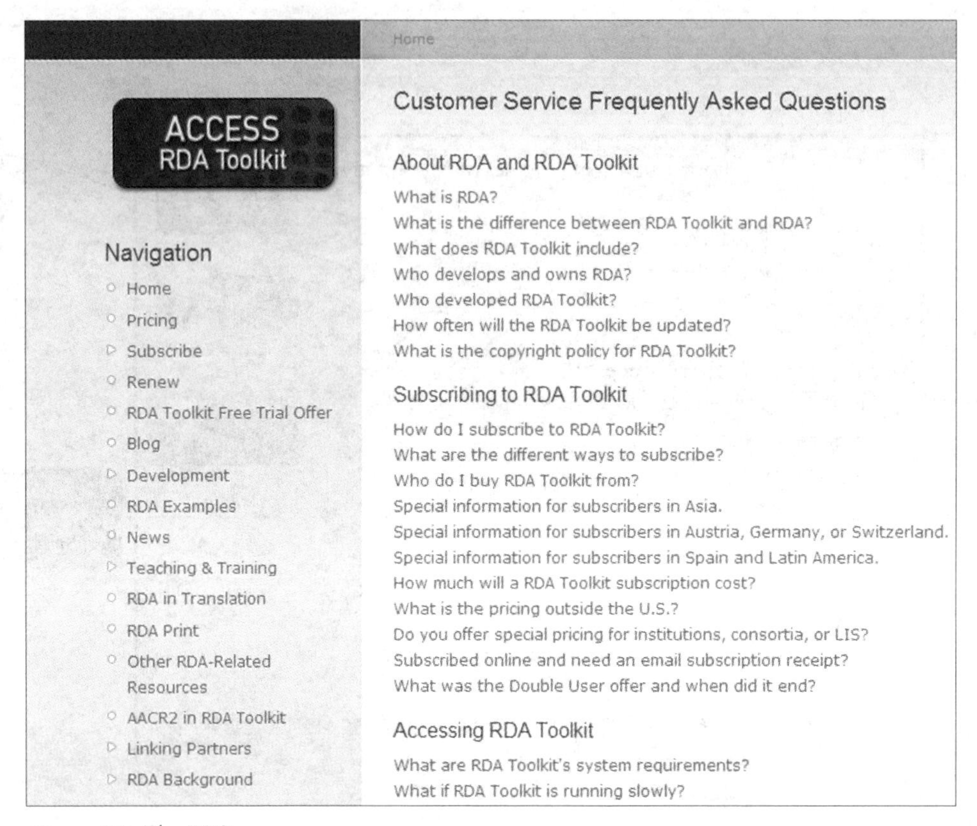

Figure 7.7: The FAQ

about subscribing; accessing RDA Toolkit; trying RDA Toolkit; training and support; implementing RDA; RDA print, etc. It is important for the first time user of RDA Toolkit to consult the FAQs to gain more information and to learn how to navigate RDA Toolkit.

More helpful information can be found at the bottom left hand corner of the RDA Toolkit website (figure 7.8). This is where you will find the RDA Toolkit *Help* tab which provides access to a variety of documents to help you access and search RDA Toolkit (figure 7.9). These documents include information about logging in, creating profiles, navigating RDA Toolkit, search tips, workflows, and other information.

Figure 7.8: RDA Toolkit help

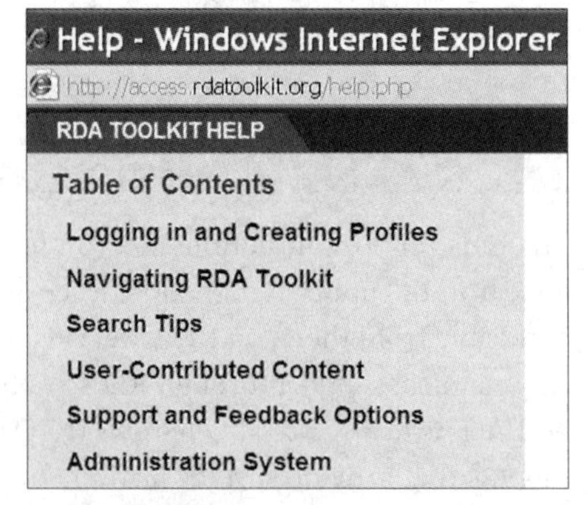

Figure 7.9: Help content

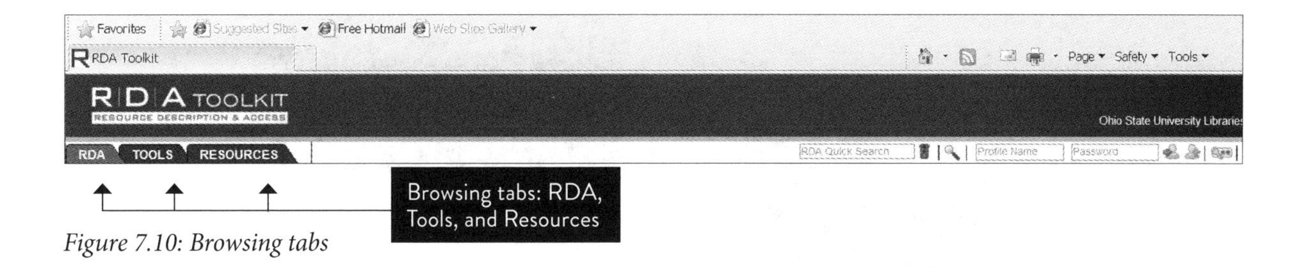

Figure 7.10: Browsing tabs

III. BROWSING RDA TOOLKIT

There are three browsing tabs on the left hand side of the RDA Toolkit screen. They are the *RDA* tab, the *Tools* tab, and the *Resources* tab (figure 7.10). Each tab provides access to different parts of RDA Toolkit.

A. THE RDA TAB

I. BROWSING THE RDA INSTRUCTIONS

The *RDA* tab is the first tab on the left hand side of the RDA Toolkit website. It allows the user to access the full text of RDA. The browse function allows you to access the RDA table of contents that has a very extensive hierarchy (figure 7.11).

RDA TOOLS RESOURCES

- RDA
  RDA Table of Contents
  + 0: Introduction
  - Section 1: Recording Attributes of Manifestation & Item
    + 1: General Guidelines on Recording Attributes of Manifestations and Items
    + 2: Identifying Manifestations and Items
    + 3: Describing Carriers
    + 4: Providing Acquisition and Access Information
  - Section 2: Recording Attributes of Work & Expression
    + 5: General Guidelines on Recording Attributes of Works and Expressions
    + 6: Identifying Works and Expressions
    + 7: Describing Content
  - Section 3: Recording Attributes of Person, Family, & Corporate Body
    + 8: General Guidelines on Recording Attributes of Persons, Families, and Corporate Bodies

Figure 7.11: RDA tab

The plus sign to the left of each topic allows you to select that topic and expand the RDA content as you browse the table of contents. Clicking on an item in the table of contents gives users access to the text of the RDA instruction (figure 7.12). To collapse the table of contents, click on the minus sign that now appears to the left of the item you have selected.

II. FUNCTION BUTTONS

Once you start to browse the RDA table of contents, you will notice that a set of function buttons will appear near the top, on the right side of the screen. These are labeled *Hit, Next Hit, Synch TOC, Return to Search, RDA Elements, Bookmark,* and *Print Text* (figure 7.13).

The function buttons will help you navigate and bookmark RDA Toolkit, limit your search to a specific RDA element, and print an RDA chapter. The use of these function buttons is not restricted to browsing alone. They are used

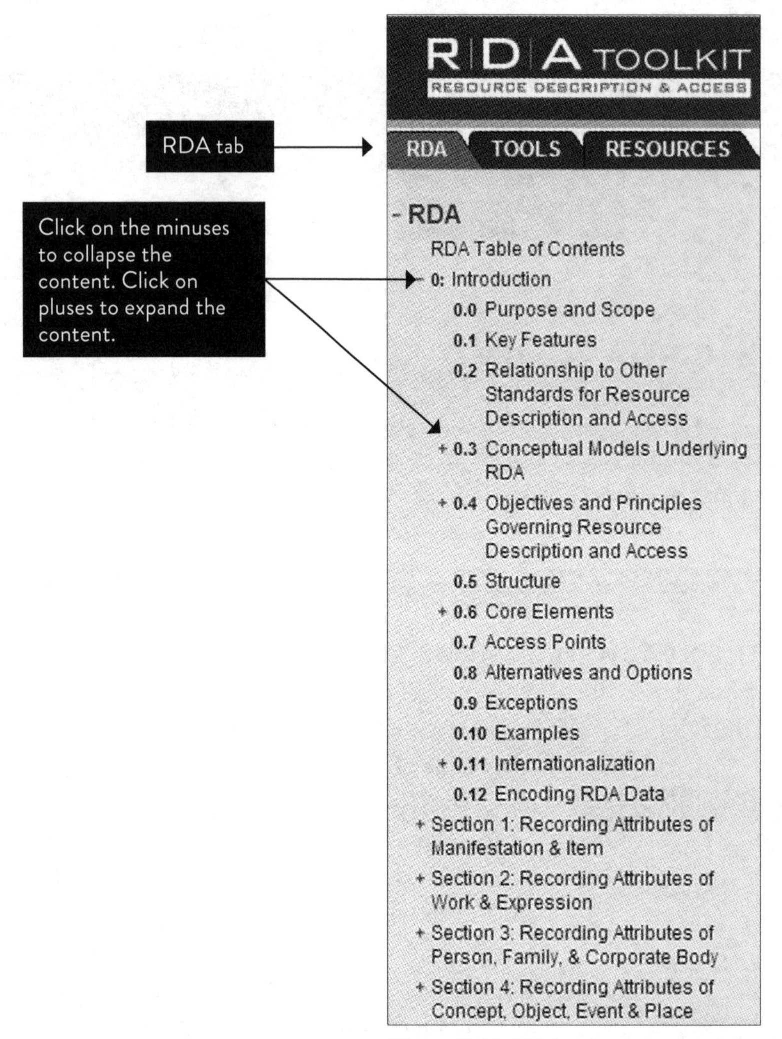

Figure 7.12: RDA tab contents

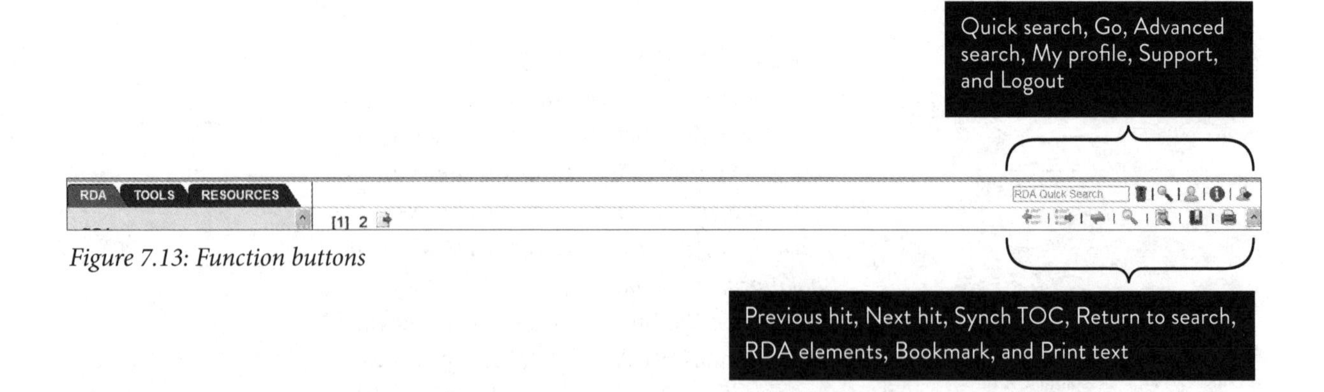

Figure 7.13: Function buttons

with the other two tabs (*Tools* and *Resources*) and with the search function as well. Because these function buttons will be used in browsing and searching RDA Toolkit, it is import to explain in more detail their function and use.

1. *Previous Hit* and *Next Hit*

These two icons help in navigating back and forth in the hierarchy of headings and subheadings. You can use them to move from *Previous* to *Next* screens by clicking on the icon.

For example, a quick search for *Content* retrieved many hits (figure 7.14). Once you click on the first hit, the navigator's icon will appear and will be activated. The red color icon directs you to the *Previous Hit,* and the green color icon directs you to the *Next Hit* (figure 7.15).

In addition to the *Previous Hit* and *Next Hit* icons, you will notice another two new arrows appearing on the left hand side of the page. Between the two arrows you will find the number of pages of the chapter you are viewing. The red arrow directs you to the *Previous Page* and the green arrow directs you to the *Next Page* in the text. These arrows allow for quick navigation within the chapter. More importantly, you will find square brackets [ ] around the number of the page you are viewing (figure 7.16).

Figure 7.14: Quick search of "content"

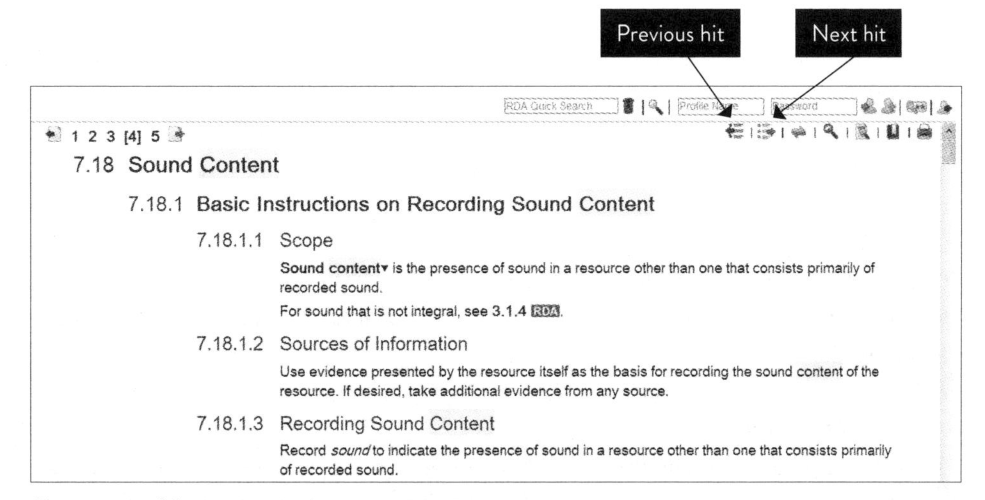

Figure 7.15: Navigation icons

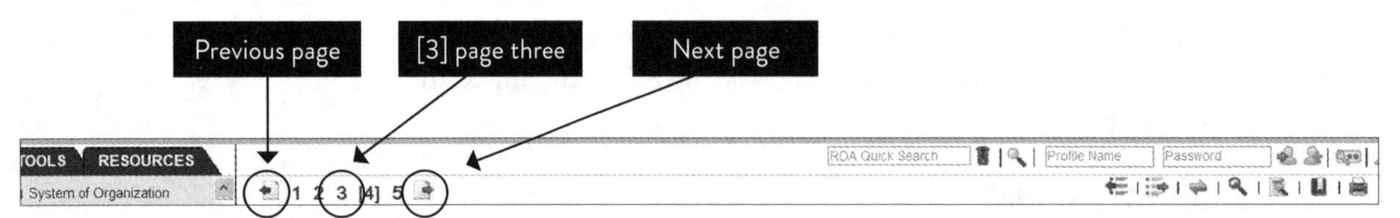

Figure 7.16: Arrows for previous hits and next hit

Figure 7.17: Back and forward navigation

The arrows in the upper left hand corner of the page can be used to move backward and forward in your search (figure 7.17).

2. *Synch TOC* Button

The *Synch TOC* button helps you to synchronize the text on the RDA instruction interface with the *RDA Table of Contents* tab. For example, if you wish to learn about the "General Guidelines on Recording Attributes of Manifestations and Items" of RDA, you would select the topic "General Guidelines on Recording Attributes of Manifestations and Items" under the *RDA* tab and click on the *Synch TOC* button to align the RDA table of contents with the RDA instruction interface screen.

As you synch the two parts of the website, the "General Guidelines on Recording Attributes of Manifestations and Items" in the RDA table of contents will be highlighted to inform you where you are. In this case, the RDA instruction interface will take you to the requested information and will also display the chapter, including the information above and below the requested information. Figure 7.18 shows that the RDA instruction screen is aligned with the RDA table of contents and is highlighted.

3. *Return to Results* Button

If you wish to view the results of your search, click on the *Return to Results* button, located to the right of the *Synch TOC* button. This will take you back to the original search results.

4. *View Text* Button

The View Text function allows you to view the text you have selected. Normally, the RDA instructions will be displayed with full RDA elements and will include exam-

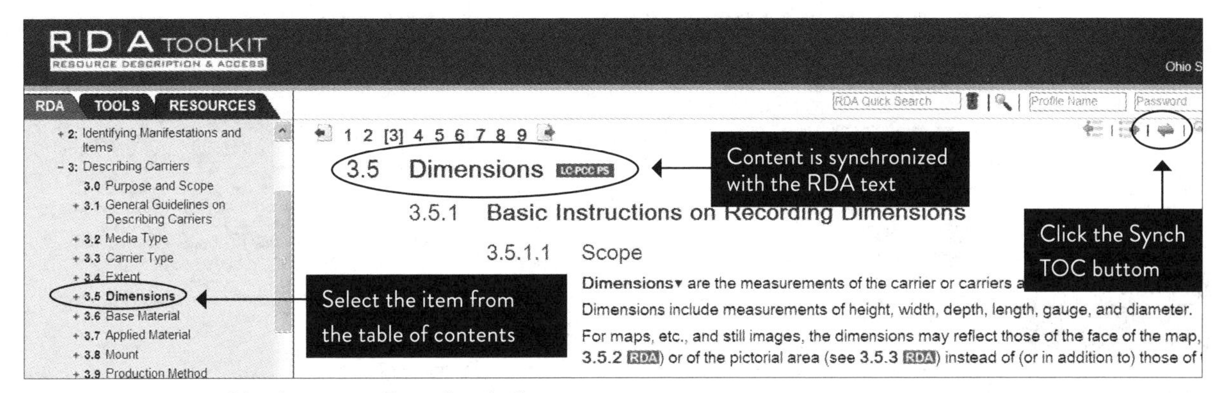

Figure 7.18: RDA table of contents aligned with the RDA text

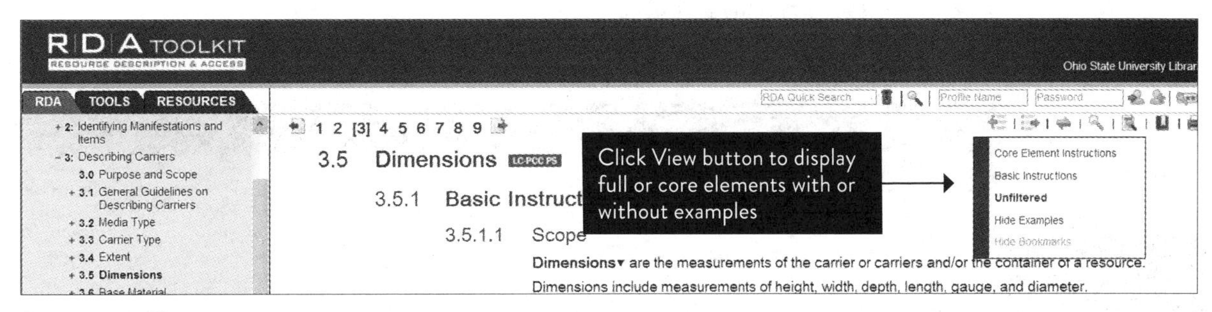

Figure 7.19: View text

Figure 7.20: Filtered and core buttons

ples. The drop-down menu (figure 7.19) lets you choose between the Core and Full versions. The other two items in the drop down menu let you hide examples or bookmarks if you do not want them to be displayed.

If you wish to restrict your search to the instructions for the RDA Core Element, you can choose the *Core* button from the drop down menu. After you make your selection, two new buttons will appear at the top of the screen. The *Filtered* and *Core* buttons indicate that you have limited your search to the core element. Figure 7.20 illustrates this function.

Examples that illustrate the RDA instruction will normally display along with the instruction (figure 7.21). However, if you wish to hide these examples, you can do this from the *View Text* button by clicking on the *Hide Examples* icon. When you make this selection, the *Filtered* button will appear at the top of the page to indicate

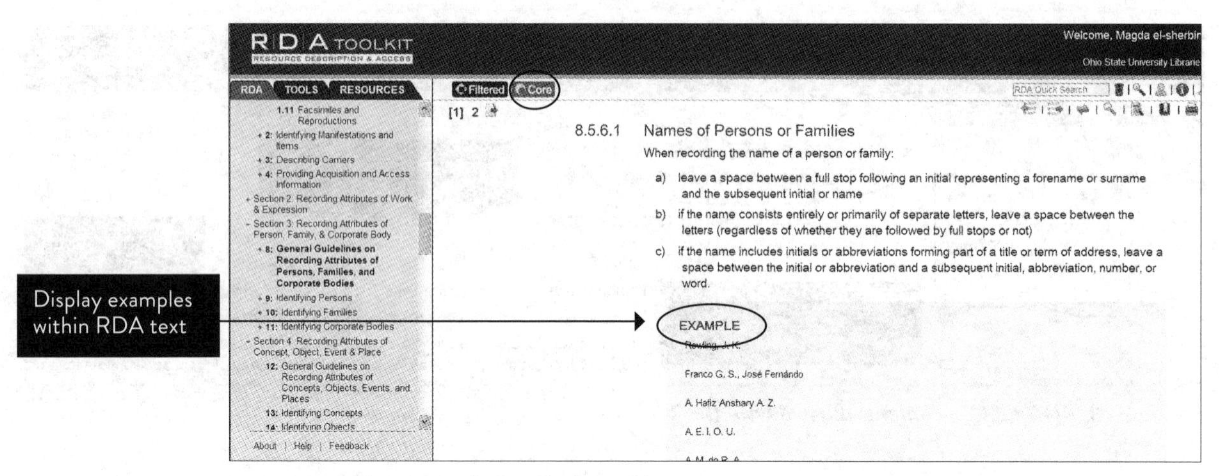

Figure 7.21: View RDA text with examples

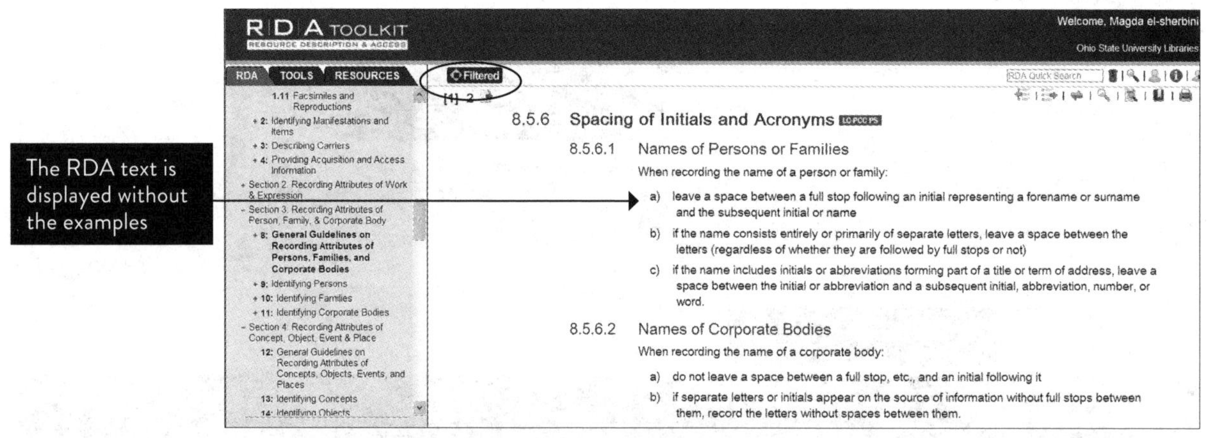

Figure 7.22: View RDA text without examples

that the examples are not displayed in the RDA instruction. Figure 7.22 shows that the examples from the search results in figure 7.21 are now hidden.

5. *Bookmark* Button

This function helps you personalize RDA Toolkit with bookmarks. A bookmark provides a virtual sticky note for a specific set of instructions that are used repeatedly or frequently consulted. You can create a bookmark, name the bookmark, and provide a description of this bookmark. In addition to creating your own bookmarks, you will have access to other users' bookmarks and you may edit them as you wish (figure 7.23a). Bookmarks help those users who work with specific materials and frequently need to consult the same instructions.

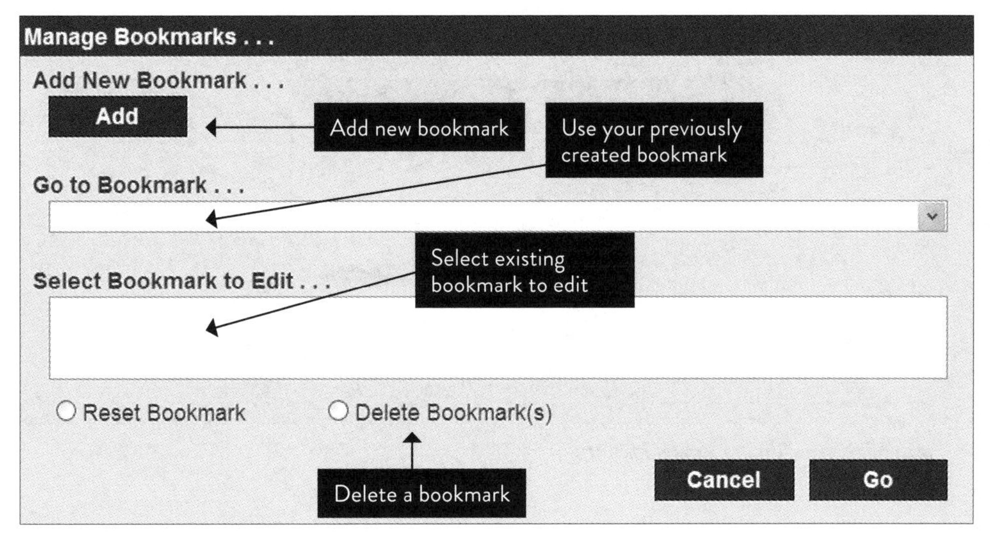

Figure 7.23a: View RDA text without examples

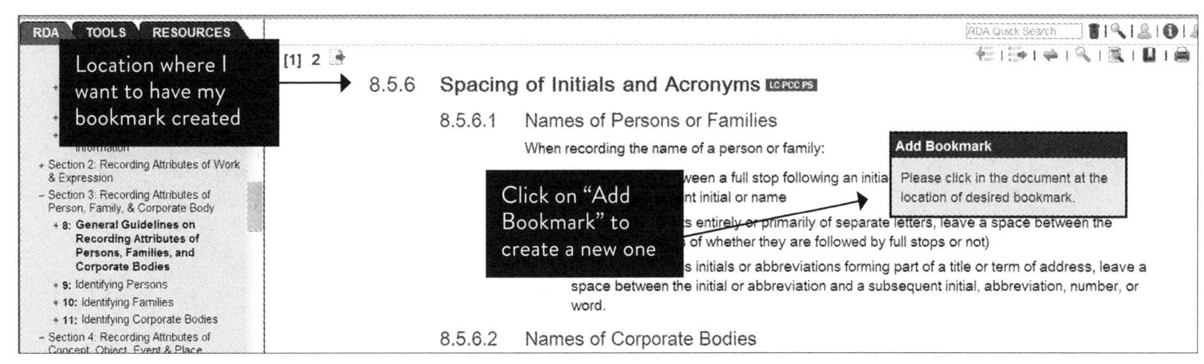

Figure 7.23b: Bookmark box

Should you decide to add a new bookmark, click on the *Add* button and you will be prompted with a box asking you to "*click in the document at the location of desired bookmark*" (figure 7.23b). Move this box to the desired location in the document and click "Add." At this point you will be prompted by another box located next to the selected text to name your bookmark and write an annotation, if one is needed (figure 7.23c). After creating your bookmark, a small sign will appear in front of the selected text (figure 7.23d).

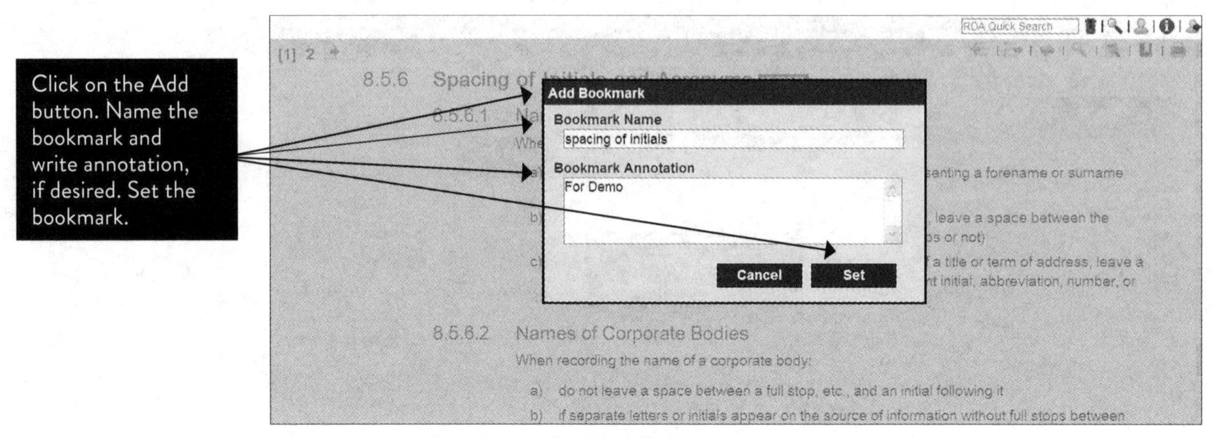

Figure 7.23c: Adding a new bookmark

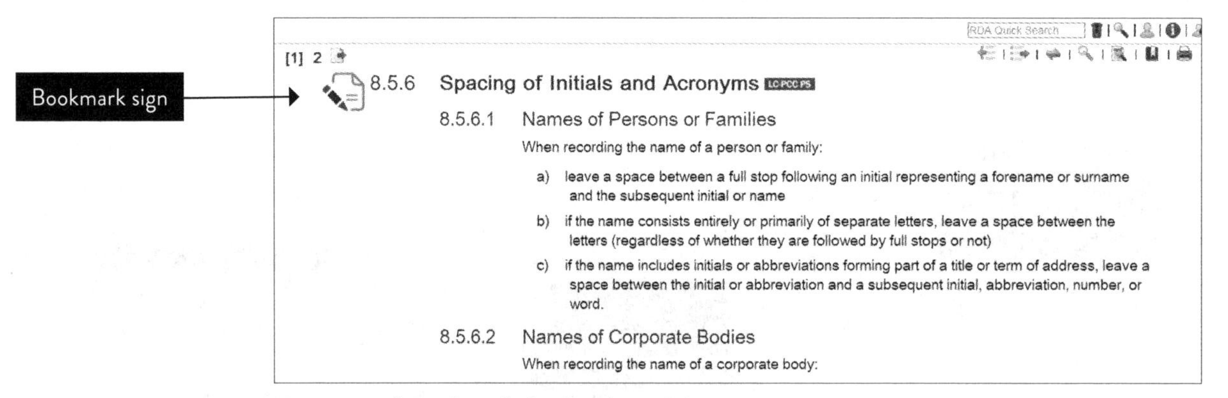

Figure 7.23d: Bookmark displayed in RDA text

6. *Print Text* Button

This function allows you to print a whole chapter of RDA or save it as a PDF file. Although printing RDA instructions is discouraged, it allows some users to practice and become familiar with RDA Toolkit in the print format.

B. THE TOOLS TAB

The *Tools* tab allows you to access a set of tools that are designed to assist you in making your work more effective. After you select the *Tools* tab, you have the option of choosing from a list of documents that include: RDA, Element Set View, RDA Mappings, Workflows, Mappings, Entity Relationship Diagram (ERD), and Schemas (figure 7.24). Pluses and minuses under each item in the table of contents can be used to expand the view to access sub-topics or to collapse the table of contents. Each document in the *Tools* tab will be described in detail.

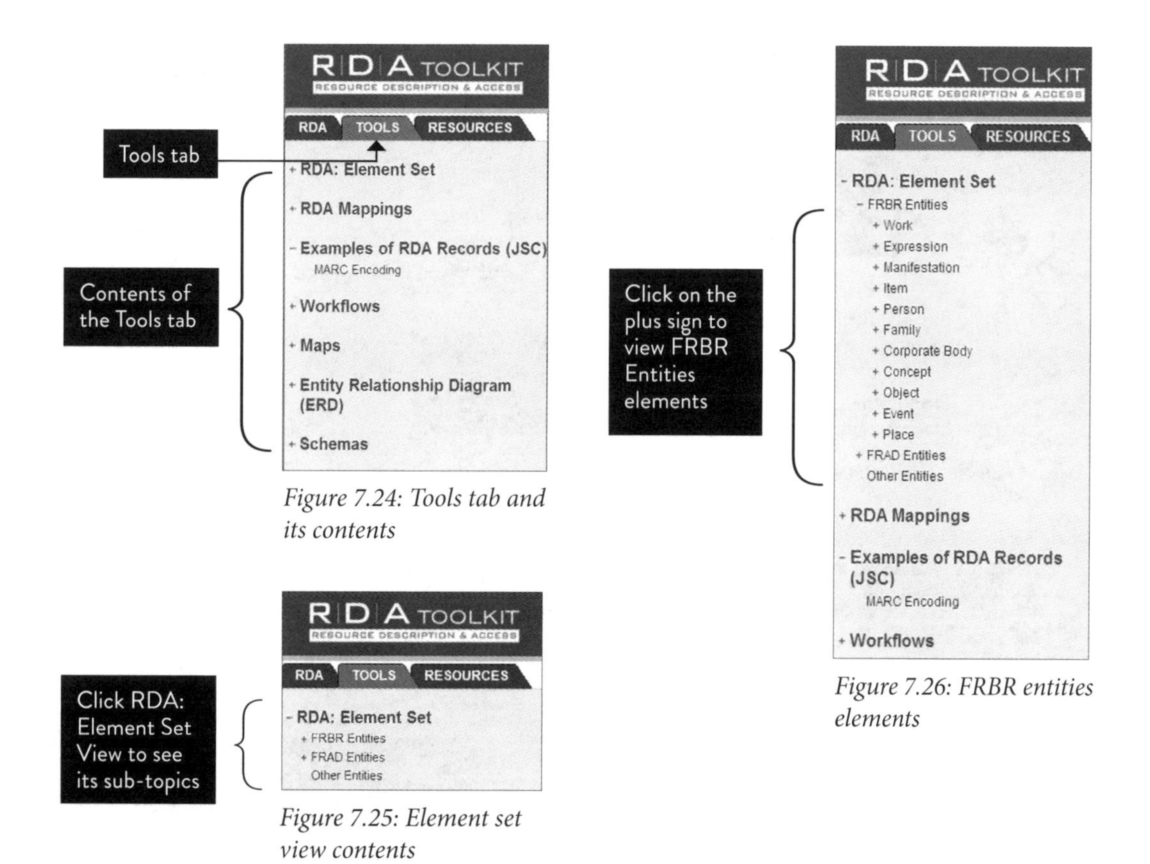

Figure 7.24: Tools tab and its contents

Figure 7.25: Element set view contents

Figure 7.26: FRBR entities elements

I. RDA: ELEMENT SET VIEW

The *RDA: Element Set* view groups elements in the *RDA* tab *by FRBR, FRAD,* and *Other Entities* (figure 7.25).

By clicking *FRBR Entities,* for example, you will be able to display all the entities, listed by the name of the RDA element or sub-element (figure 7.26).

Within each entity, information is displayed alphabetically by the name of the RDA element or sub-element. For example, all the RDA elements that deal with *Work* are listed under the FRBR *Work* section in alphabetical order, as shown in figure 7.27.

RDA content includes the RDA element definition, any RDA-defined vocabularies used in recording the element, and the relevant RDA instructions for recording the element. The RDA: Element Set View is available both on the *Tools* tab in RDA Toolkit and in print. RDA Toolkit offers links from the RDA: Element Set View to the full text of the instructions in RDA, as well as links to current and evolving encoding standards documentation.

To see the RDA Element under the FRBR entity *Work* that is related to recording a dissertation or a thesis, you will first click on the plus sign in front of the FRBR Entity *RDA Element Dissertation or Thesis Information* to expand the search. This will dis-

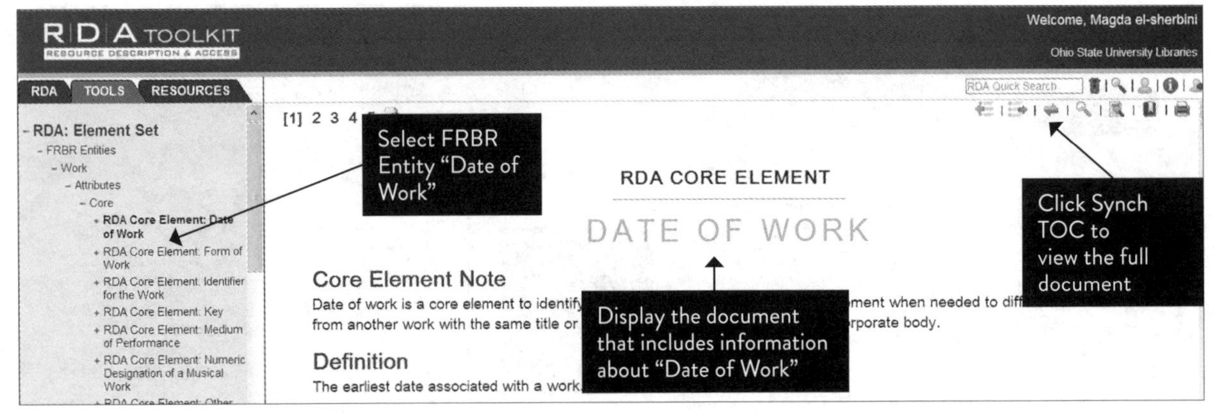

Figure 7.27: Links between the RDA element set view and the RDA text

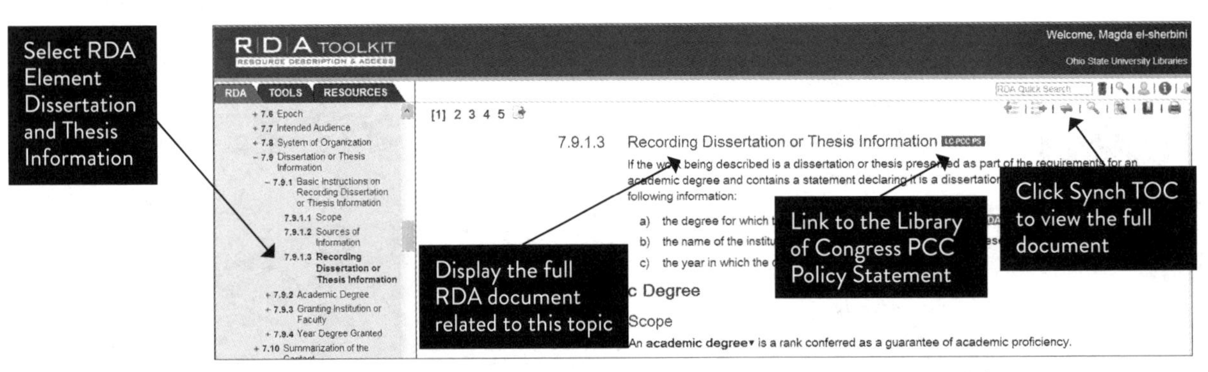

Figure 7.28: Link between RDA element dissertation/thesis information and the RDA instruction related to this element

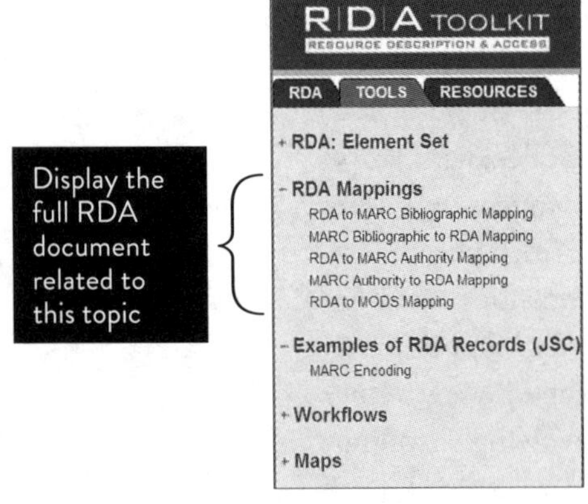

Figure 7.29: RDA mappings

play all the topics that are related to the "RDA Element Dissertation or Thesis Information." Now, it will be possible to select the instructions that are related only to Dissertation or Thesis Information. All instructions in the RDA text are linked to the RDA instruction number to facilitate navigation to the instruction directly. Figure 7.28 shows that when those instructions are selected, the plus sign in front of the "RDA Element Dissertation or Theses Information" changes to a minus as all the elements that are related to the topic are displayed in one place.

II. RDA MAPPING

The second document under the *Tools* tab is *RDA Mapping.* Starting with the *Tools* tab, you will find mapping from RDA to MARC 21 Bibliographic, MARC 21 Bibliographic to RDA, RDA to MARC 21 Authority, MARC 21 Authority to RDA, and RDA to MODS (figure 7.29).

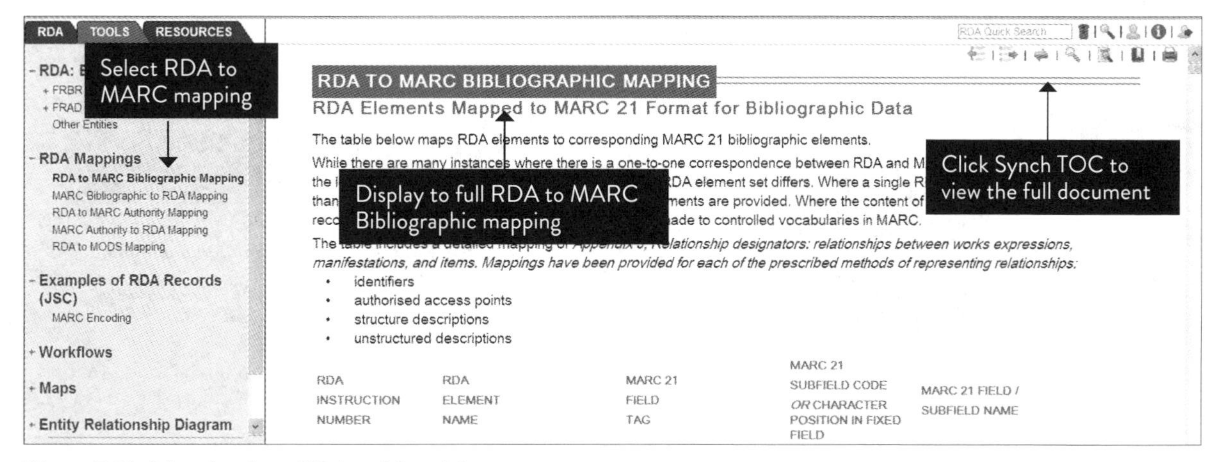

Figure 7.30: Mapping from RDA to Marc 21

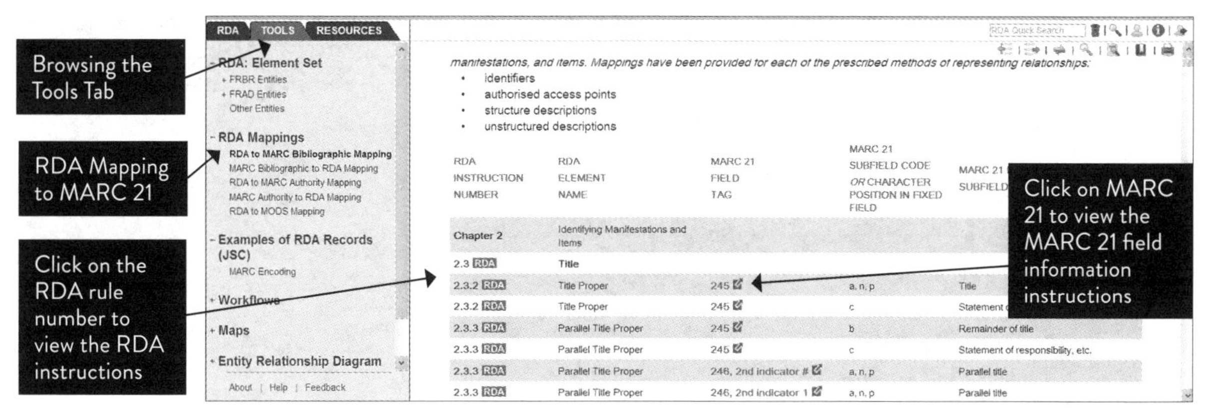

Figure 7.31: Mapping RDA to MARC 21 contents

1. RDA to MARC 21 Bibliographic Mapping

This mapping provides you with a link from the RDA Element to the corresponding MARC 21 Format for Bibliographic Data (figure 7.30).

The mapping table includes the following information: RDA Instruction Number, RDA Element Name, MARC 21 Field and Tag, MARC 21 Subfield Code or Character Position in Fixed Field, MARC 21 Fields/Subfield Name. It also includes the RDA chapter number in its label to show users where the information can be found (figure 7.31).

If you wish to learn about the RDA instruction number 2.3.2 that is related to Title Proper (see 2.3.2 highlight in figure 7.31), you will click on the RDA instruction number link to take you to the RDA instructions (figure 7.32).

Notice that in figure 7.31, browsing began from the *Tools* tab. Once you click on the instruction number from the RDA link, you are taken back to the *RDA* tab which is highlighted to indicate where you are in the search (figure 7.32).

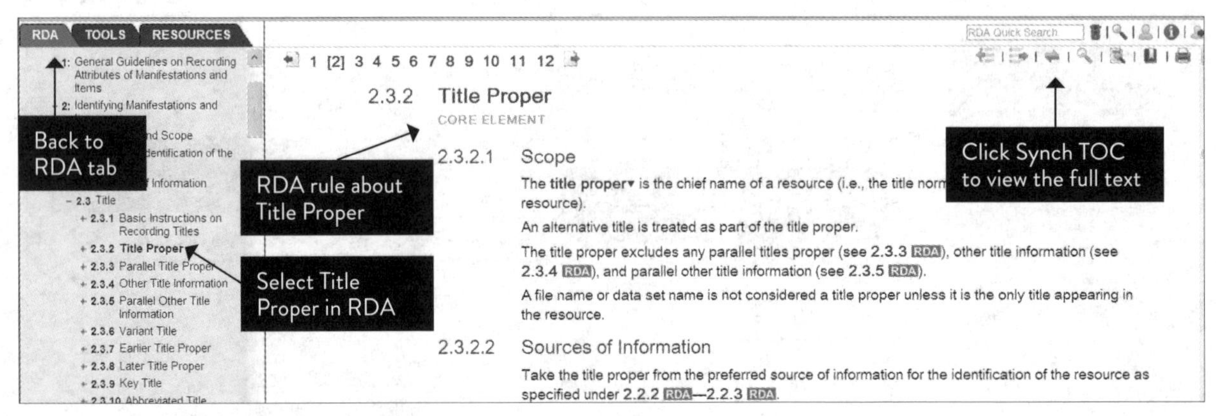

Figure 7.32: Result of clicking on RDA rule number 2.3.2 in figure 7.31

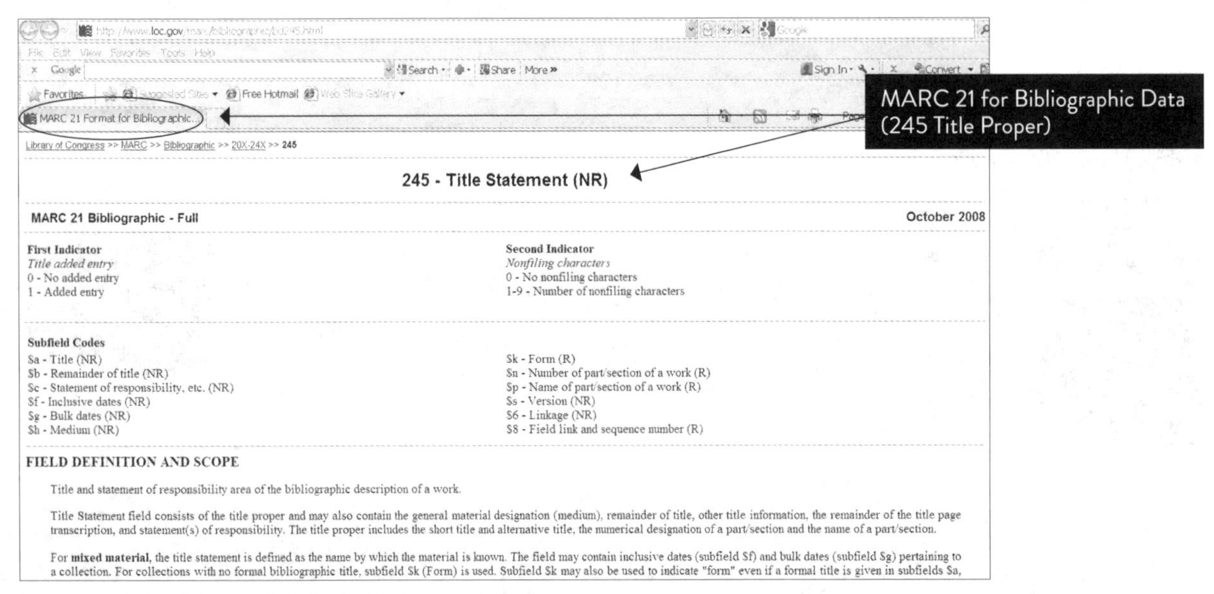

Figure 7.33: Link to MARC 21 for bibliographic data

When you click on MARC 21 field 245 for Title Proper (figure 7.31) the link will take you to the MARC 21 for Bibliographic Data document which provides additional information that is related to field 245 (figure 7.33). Scrolling up and down will allow you to view all the information about the 245 field.

If there is no corresponding information in the MARC field for RDA Instruction number, the MARC 21 field indicates this with "N/A."

2. Mapping from MARC 21 Bibliographic to RDA

This document provides mapping from MARC 21 to RDA. The mapping table includes: MARC 21 Field and Tag, MARC 21 Subfield Code, MARC 21 Field/Subfield Name, RDA Instruction Number, and RDA Element Name (figure 7.34). The table maps MARC 21 bibliographic elements to the corresponding RDA elements.

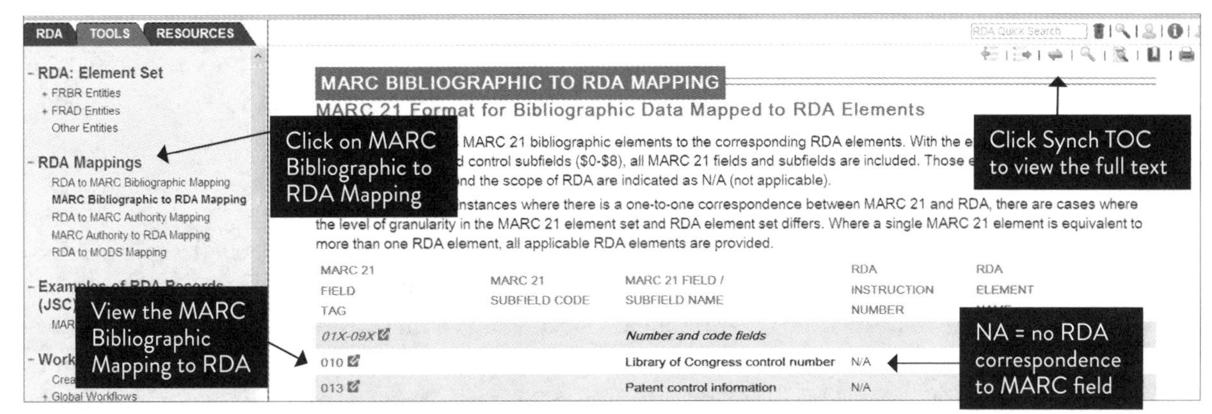

Figure 7.34: Mapping from Marc 21 bibliographic to RDA

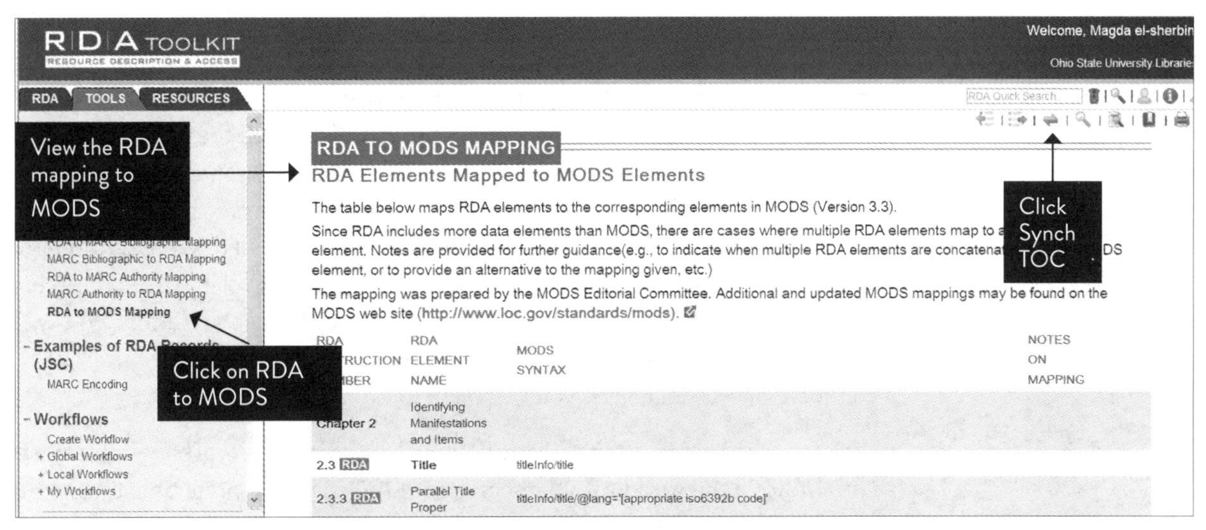

Figure 7.35: Mapping RDA to MODS

With the exception of the leader, control fields (00X) and control subfields ($0-$8), all MARC 21 fields and subfields are included.

N/A under the RDA Instruction number means that there is no corresponding instruction to this field. Clicking on the RDA Instruction number will take you back to the *RDA* tab and will display the RDA instruction.

Mapping RDA to MARC 21 Authority Data and Mapping MARC 21 Authority Data to RDA elements:

These two documents work the same way as mapping RDA Instruction Number to MARC 21.

3. *Mapping from RDA to MODS*

This document provides mapping from RDA elements to the corresponding elements in MODS. Because RDA includes more data elements than MODS, there are cases where multiple RDA elements map to a single MODS element (figure 7.35).

The mapping table includes the RDA Instruction Number, RDA Element Name, MODS Syntax, and Notes on Mapping. In addition, it provides information about the RDA instruction chapter and its label. The links to the RDA Instruction Number take you back to the *RDA* tab.

III. WORKFLOWS

Workflow is a user-centric function that plays an important role in designing a document. It enables you to create documents and interlink them to other RDA Toolkit documents and other resources. Documents in this set are searchable and customizable. Workflows can be created by individuals and groups at all types of institutions, including libraries, consortia, and cooperative programs to suit local needs and share best practices.

Through the workflow function, users will be able to select and sequence instructions as well as add new contents or external links. This function will actually help replace the current cataloger practice of using hand-written sticky notes of instructions or making a paper copy of examples and maintaining files in their desk drawers. The RDA *Workflows* function will help you not only to access all the examples, rules, and procedures created to handle situations that require special handling, and best practices online, but will also help to reuse and share workflows with others so that catalogers can benefit from the best practices and the expertise of other practitioners.

The RDA workflows function is the third document that is available from the *Tools* tab. To create your own workflow, you will click on the *Workflows* button. You will then be prompted to a page titled *Create workflow* with boxes to fill in (figure 7.36).

To complete the screen above, you will need to do the following:

- Indicate the name of your workflow. When creating a workflow, you need to indicate the workflow's name in a mindful way (it is preferable to use the institution's name).
- Decide to either create a new workflow or copy an already existing workflow that is being shared by another cataloger, organization, or institution.

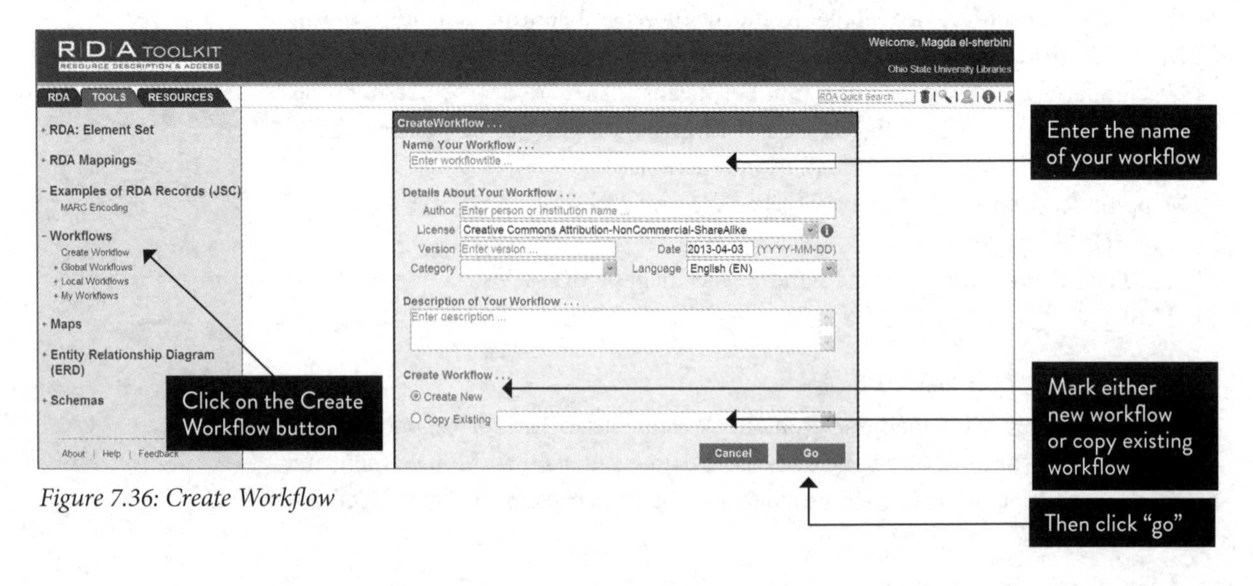

Figure 7.36: Create Workflow

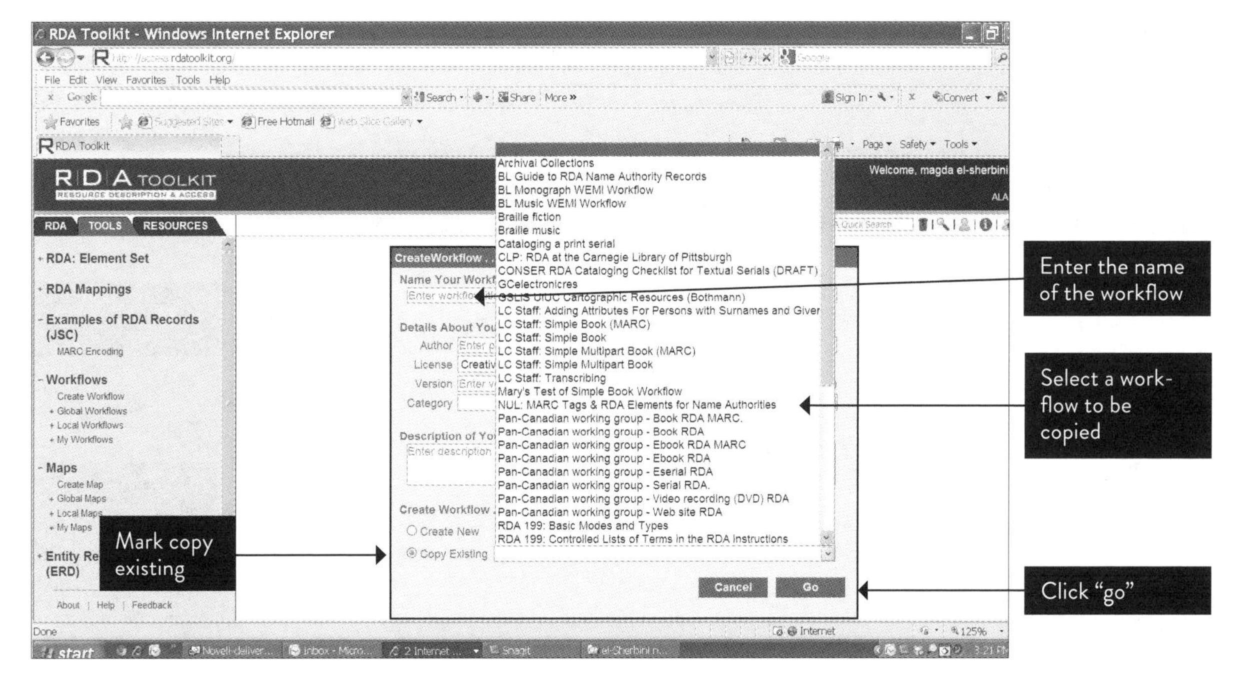

Figure 7.37: Copy existing workflow

- When copying an existing workflow, first you have to access the workflow list by clicking on "copy existing."
- You will be prompted to a list of current workflows.
- You can select the appropriate workflow from the list.
- The name of the copied workflow will be shown in the box labeled *Copy Existing* (figure 7.37).
- After completing the information of the workflow, you will click *Go* to create your own workflow (figure 7.38). You will be prompted to select your new workflow, which will be ready for editing. An *Edit Workflow* tab will appear at the top of the workflow. The *Function* icon for saving, editing, deleting, and sharing mode (private versus public) will also appear and you will see the name of your workflow.

When copying a workflow from another institution or cataloger, or any other source, you have the option to edit, modify, and change the workflow to meet your own needs.

When editing workflows, you can add or delete links, change the font size and color and highlight each section. The editing function works like a word processor and uses the same functionality as MS Word.

After editing the document, you have the option to save the document, delete it, and keep it private or public. There are several workflows that have already been created and are available for use, including the Library of Congress series of workflows and best practices (figure 7.39).

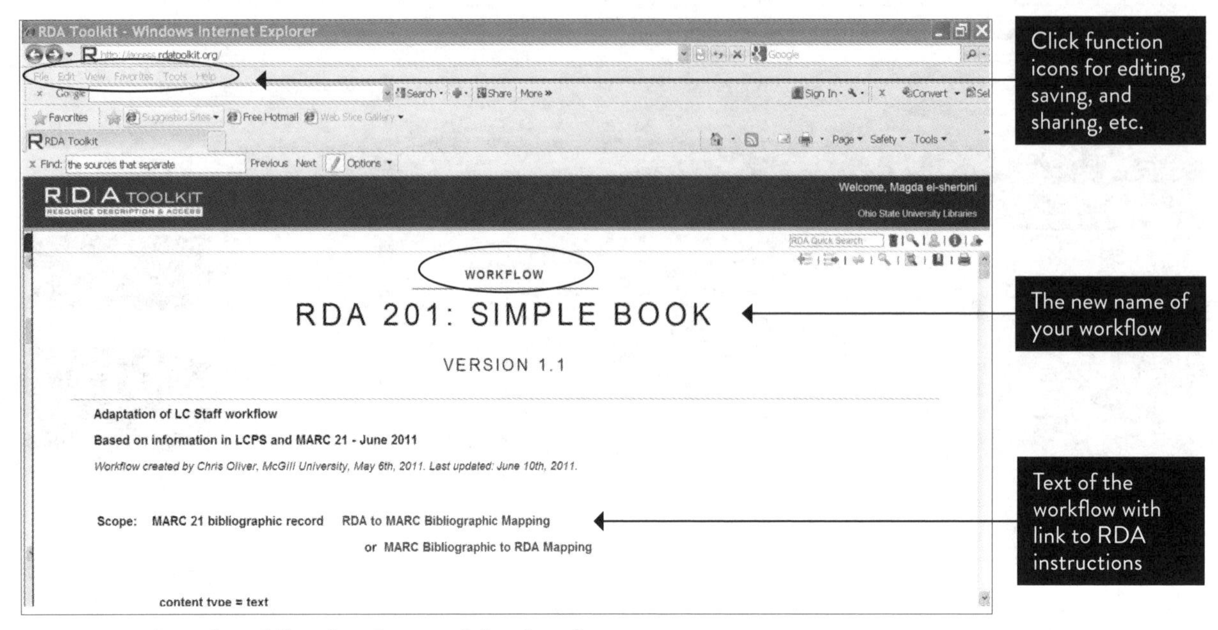

Figure 7.38: Copied workflow for editing to fit local needs

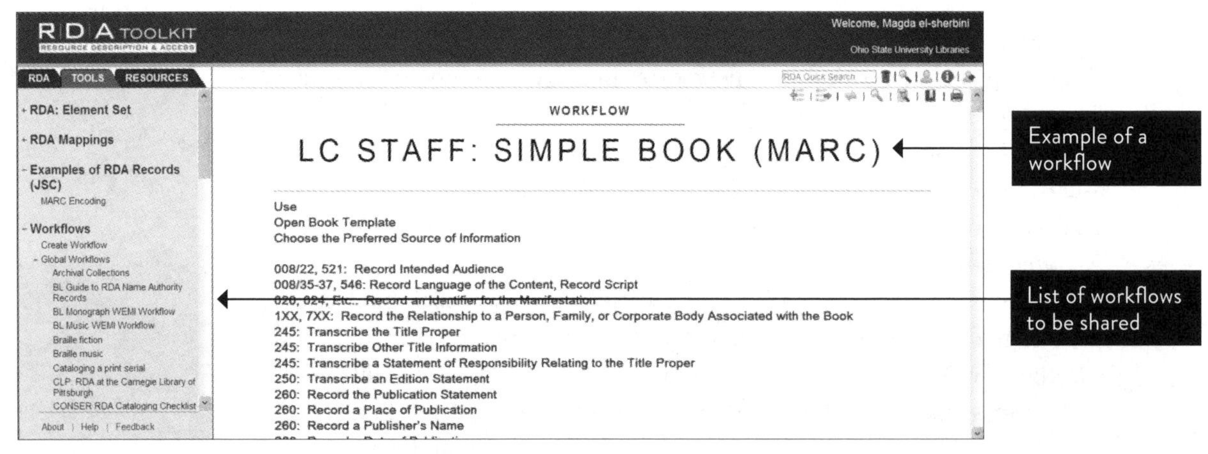

Figure 7.39: Example of a workflow by LC staff for a simple book

When the workflow is created or copied, it will contain different types of links to direct you to the appropriate documents and to point to different sources of information. For example, in the orange circle, links to the RDA element sets view, it takes you to the RDA element set view that will include all the relevant information about the element "Publication Statement." The red triangle will link the term to the RDA glossary. The gray link will take you to the MARC 21 document. The highlighted blue link will link to RDA Toolkit and appendixes, while the green link directs you to the Library of Congress Policy Statements (figure 7.40).

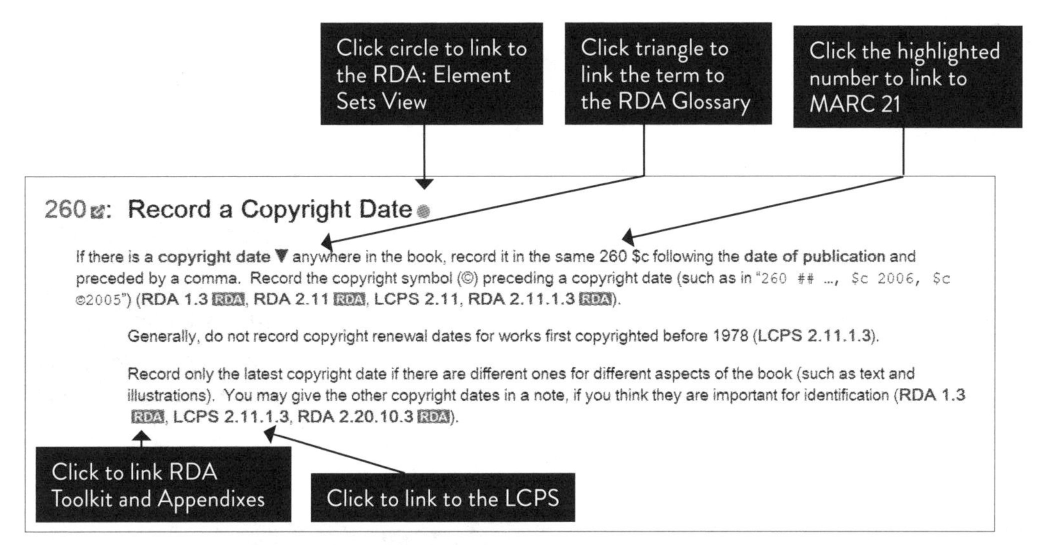

Figure 7.40: Example of a workflow with various types of links

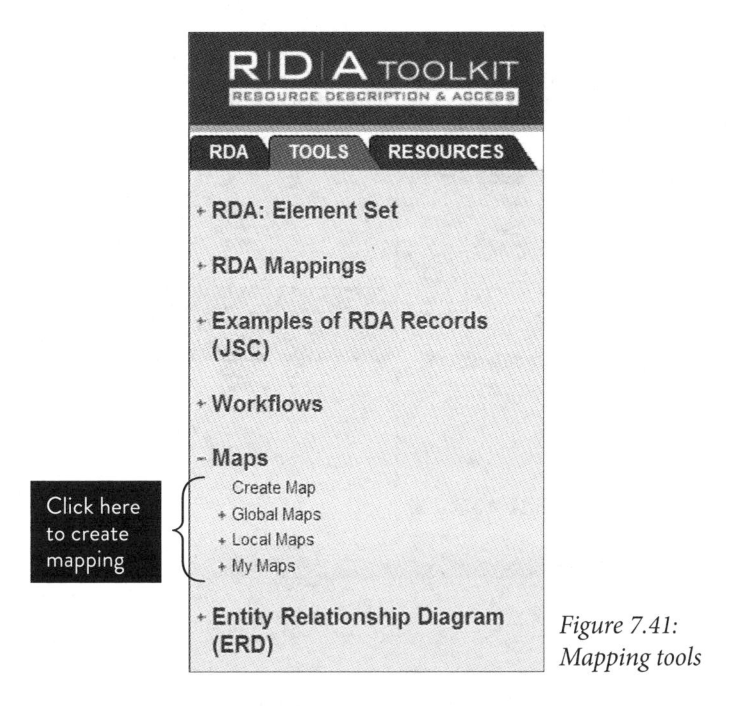

Figure 7.41: Mapping tools

IV. MAPPING TOOLS

The *Mappings* tool helps you create your own mapping and to share your mapping with others (figure 7.41). Creating mapping is very similar to creating a workflow. You will click on the *Create Mapping* icon and you will be prompted to create mapping (figure 7.42).

Create mapping works like creating the workflow.

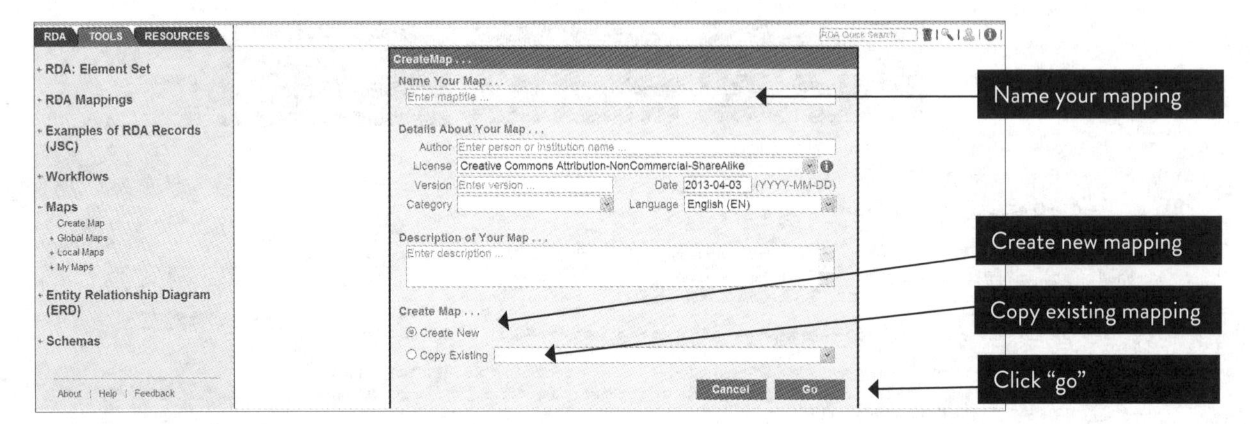

Figure 7.42: Create mapping

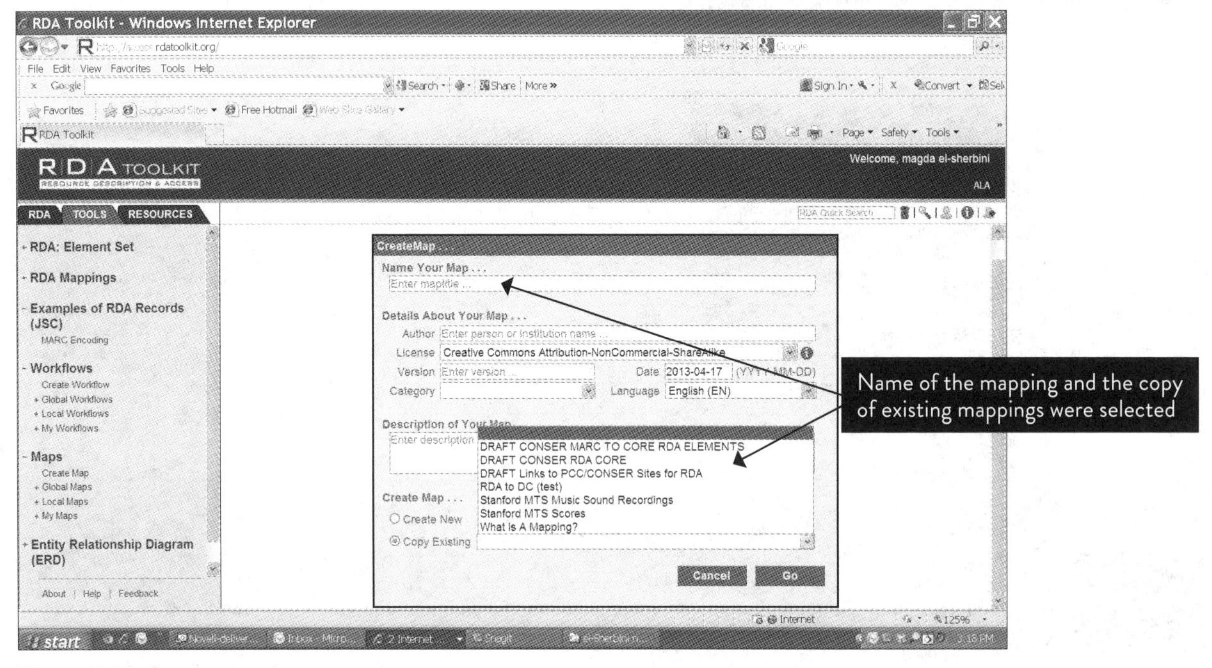

Figure 7.43: Create mapping

- When creating mapping, you will need to indicate the mapping's name in a mindful way (it is preferable to use the institution's name).
- You decide to either create new mapping or copy other existing mappings that are shared by other catalogers, organizations, or institutions (figure 7.42).
- Copy an existing mapping by clicking on "copy existing" (figure 7.42).
- A list of current mappings will be displayed.
- Select the appropriate mapping and click *GO* to create your own mapping (figure 7.43).
- You will be prompted to your new mapping which will be ready for editing. At the top of the mapping screen, you will see the *Edit Mapping* button and

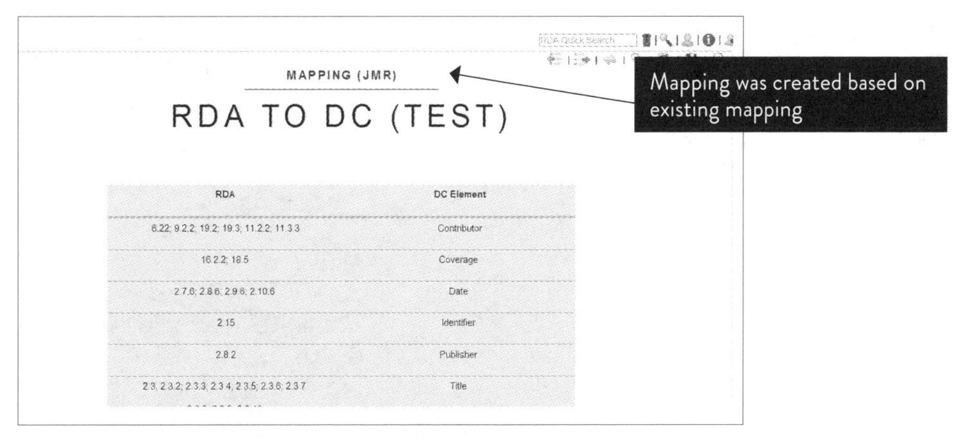

RDA	DC Element
6.2.2; 9.2.2; 19.2; 19.3; 11.2.2; 11.3.3	Contributor
16.2.2; 16.5	Coverage
2.7.6; 2.8.6; 2.9.6; 2.10.6	Date
2.15	Identifier
2.8.2	Publisher
2.3; 2.3.2; 2.3.3; 2.3.4; 2.3.5; 2.3.6; 2.3.7	Title

Figure 7.44: Example of created mapping

the *Function* icons for saving, editing, deleting, and sharing mode (private versus public). You will also see the name of your mapping to indicate who created the mapping (figure 7.44).

V. ENTITY RELATIONSHIP DIAGRAM

Entity Relationship Diagram (ERD) is a collaborative effort between Nannette Naught of IMT, who serves as documents manager and ALA Publishing's technical lead on the project, and Tom Delsey, editor of RDA. The ERDs are visual representations of RDA elements defined or inferred by RDA instructions. Although the ERD might not be used by some catalogers, they are useful for identifying all elements used in RDA so their relationships can be easily seen. They are important for software and database developers, IT staff, and others. As an educator, the author found the diagram helpful in explaining the FRBR concepts and their relationships to RDA. Each diagram is linked back to the text of RDA: Element Set View. The best source of information about the ERD can be found under "Background" on the RDA website. The overview provides relationships between all FRBR and FRAD entities.

1. FRBR Entities

The *FRBR Entities* tab provides a diagram of all FRBR and FRAD entities. FRBR entities include work, expression, manifestation, item, person, family, corporate body, concepts, object, event, and place. Names are listed under FRAD entities (figure 7.45).

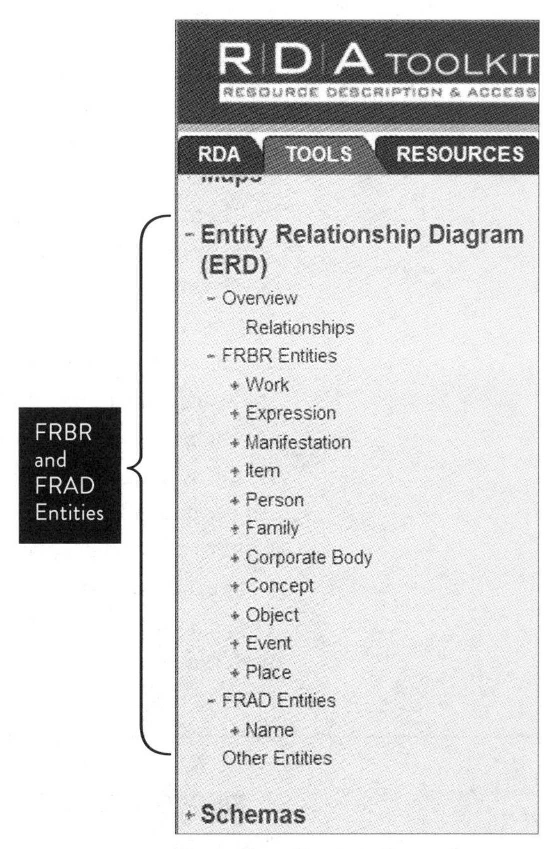

Figure 7.45: Entity relationships

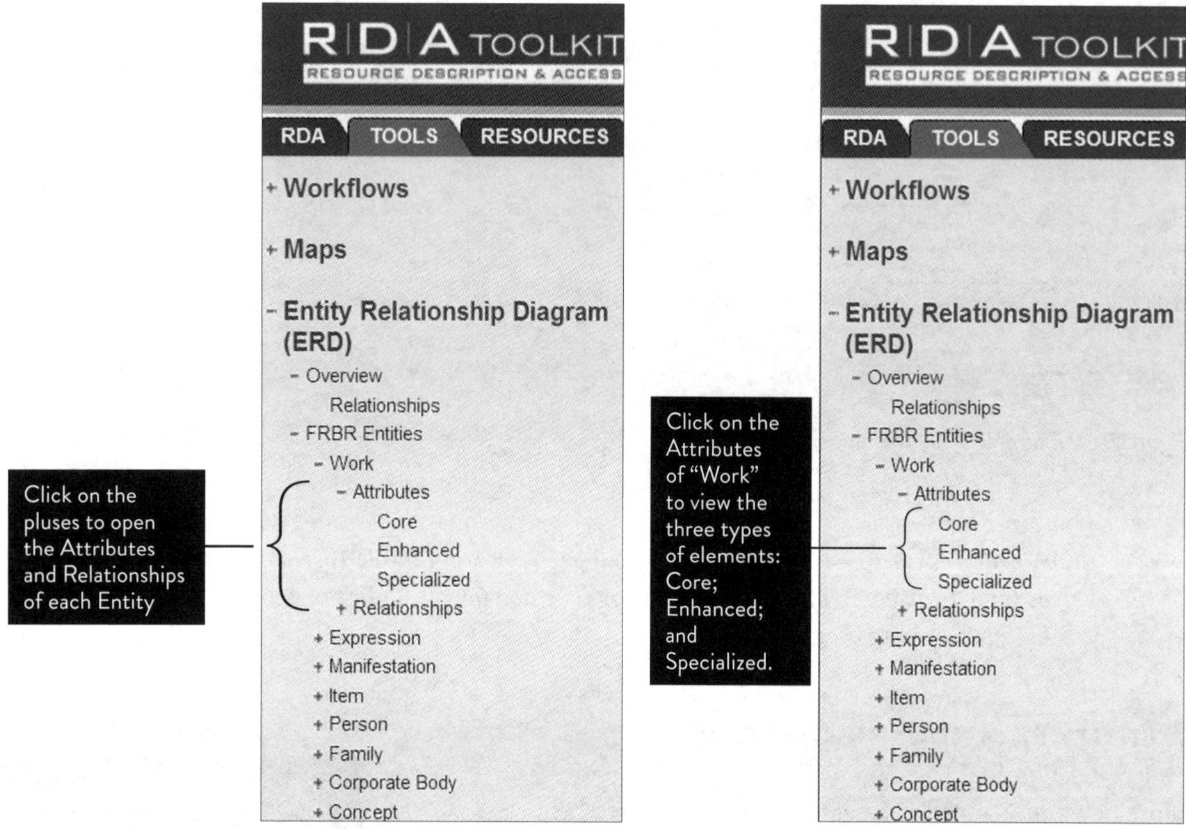

Figure 7.46: Attributes and relationships of each entity

Figure 7.47: Attributes of work

There are two diagrams under each entity; one to show the attributes of the entity and the other to show the relationships beween entities (figure 7.46).

The attribute of a work includes three types of elements: core, enhanced, and specialized (figure 7.47).

The core elements provide the only needed elements for the work, such as title of the work, date of the work, form of the work, etc.

The enhanced attributes provide all the core elements and additional elements of the work that would enhance its accessibility or provide later information for catalogers. Additional information for catalogers might consist of cataloger notes, sources consulted, coverage of the content, intended audience, etc.

Specialized attributes provide core elements and enhanced elements in addition to specialized elements that pertain to specialized materials, such as cartographic materials and dissertations. For example, in recording elements for the work "Dissertation," specialized elements could include the granting institution, or faculty academic degree, or year the degree was granted.

2. FRBR Relationships

The *Relationships* link provides a diagram of FRBR Relationships. The diagrams illustrate three levels of relationships: primary, core, and enhanced (figure 7.48). The

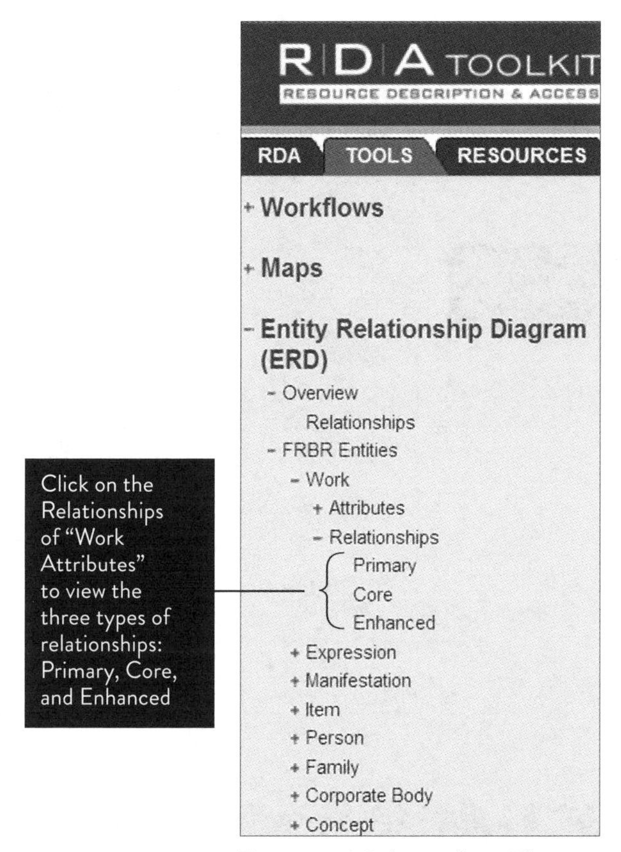

Figure 7.48: Relationships: Elements of a work to other entities

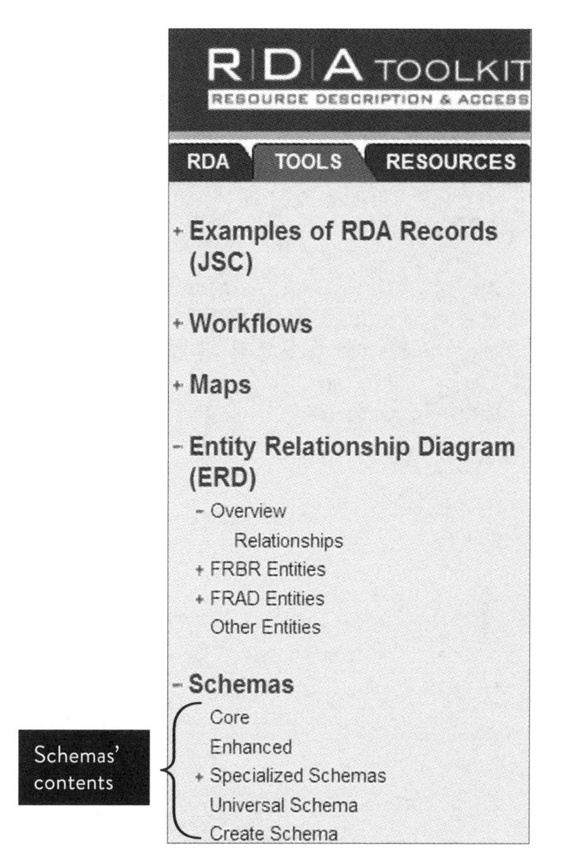

Figure 7.49: Schema—core elements

diagram in FRBR relationships shows primary relationships between work, expression, and manifestation. The core relationships link presents a diagram that illustrates the relationships between the work and its creator, and the work and the other person, family, or corporate body associated with the work. Each relationship is represented by designators such as composer, compiler, editor, addressee, degree-granting institution, director, etc. The enhanced relationships are very complex and represent the relationship between the work and all other works that relate to the original. The relationships are represented by designators.

VI. SCHEMAS

This is the sixth and final tab under the Tools bar. Schemas are defined as machine-readable representations of RDA elements. They are presented on three levels: core, enhanced, and specialized. Thus far, only the core element is live and available for use. The two other elements are still under construction (figure 7.49). The core element set is a subset of the RDA present minimum set of data.

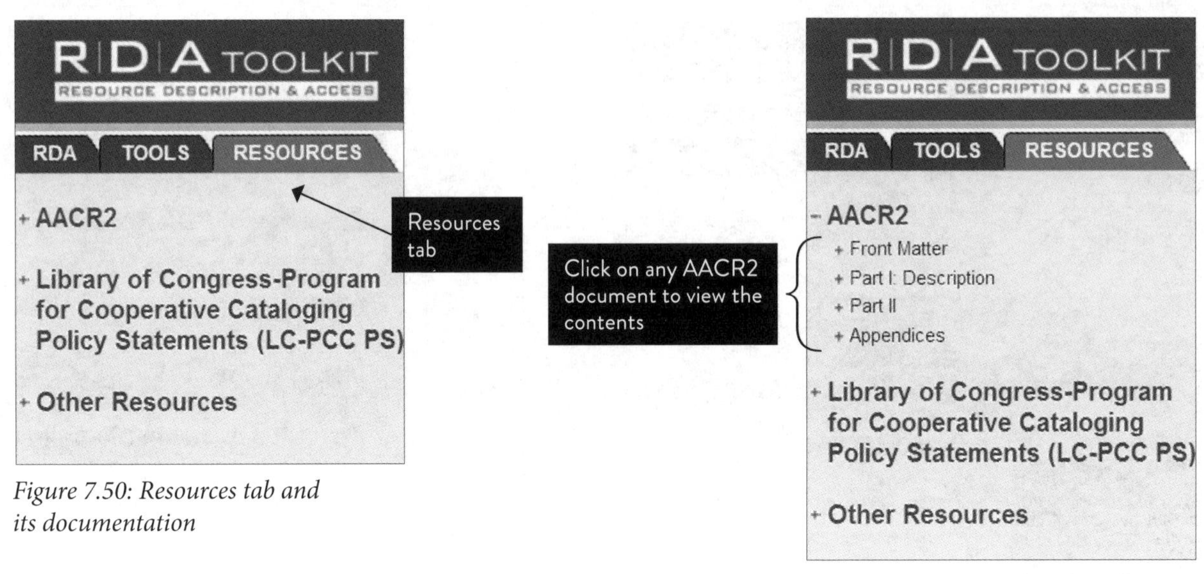

Figure 7.50: Resources tab and its documentation

Figure 7.51: AACR2 documents

C. THE RESOURCES TAB

The RDA *Resources* tab provides access to two significant documents that are helpful to catalogers: AACR2 and the Library of Congress Policy Statements (figure 7.50).

I. AACR2

The AACR2 document consists of four parts: Front Matter, Part I: Description, Part II, and appendixes. These contents will be explained below (figure 7.51).

The *Front Matter* tab provides information about the AACR2 Rules and Committees, a Preface to the 2002 revision, Summary of Rule Revisions since the Second Edition 1998 revision, and a General Introduction. These documents can be expanded by clicking on the plus sign to obtain more information. You can also use the *Synch* button to see where you are within the AACR2 tab content (figure 7.52).

Part I: Description shows the thirteen chapters of the Descriptive part of AACR2. The pluses that accompany each item expand the content for more detailed information and instructions (figure 7.53).

The AACR2 text provides links to other AACR2 rules and, in some cases, to RDA elements. There is mapping between AACR2 and RDA, but not a complete mapping (figure 7.54).

Part II. Introduction: Headings, Uniform Titles, and References works the same way as Part I and includes links to certain AACR2 rules and to RDA elements (figure 7.55).

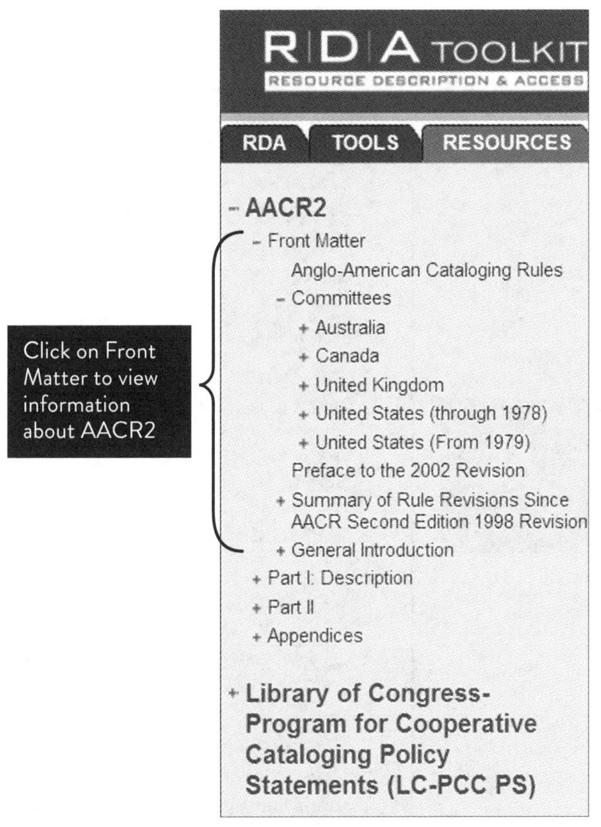

Figure 7.52: Demonstrate the content of front matter

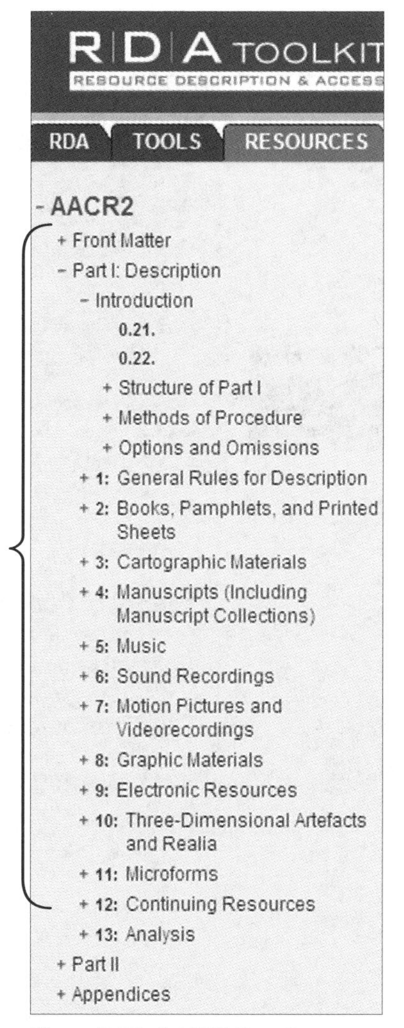

Figure 7.53: AACR2 Part I: Description

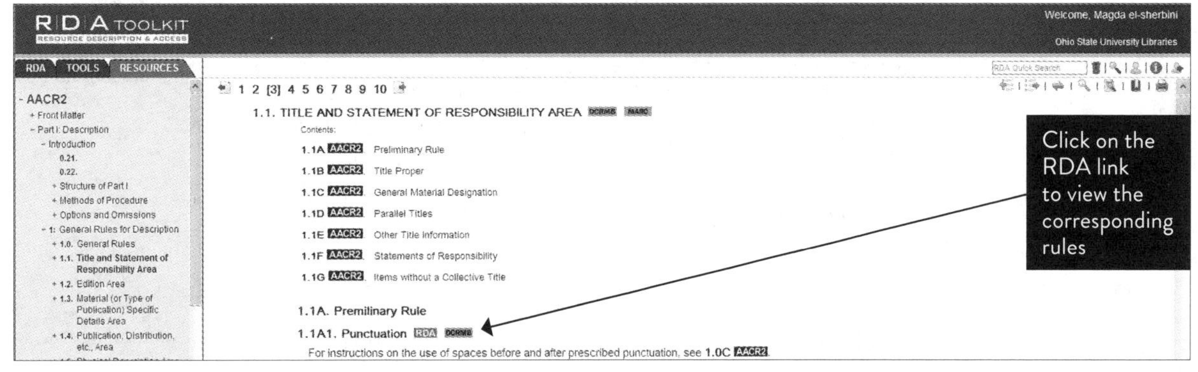

Figure 7.54: Link from AACR2 to RDA

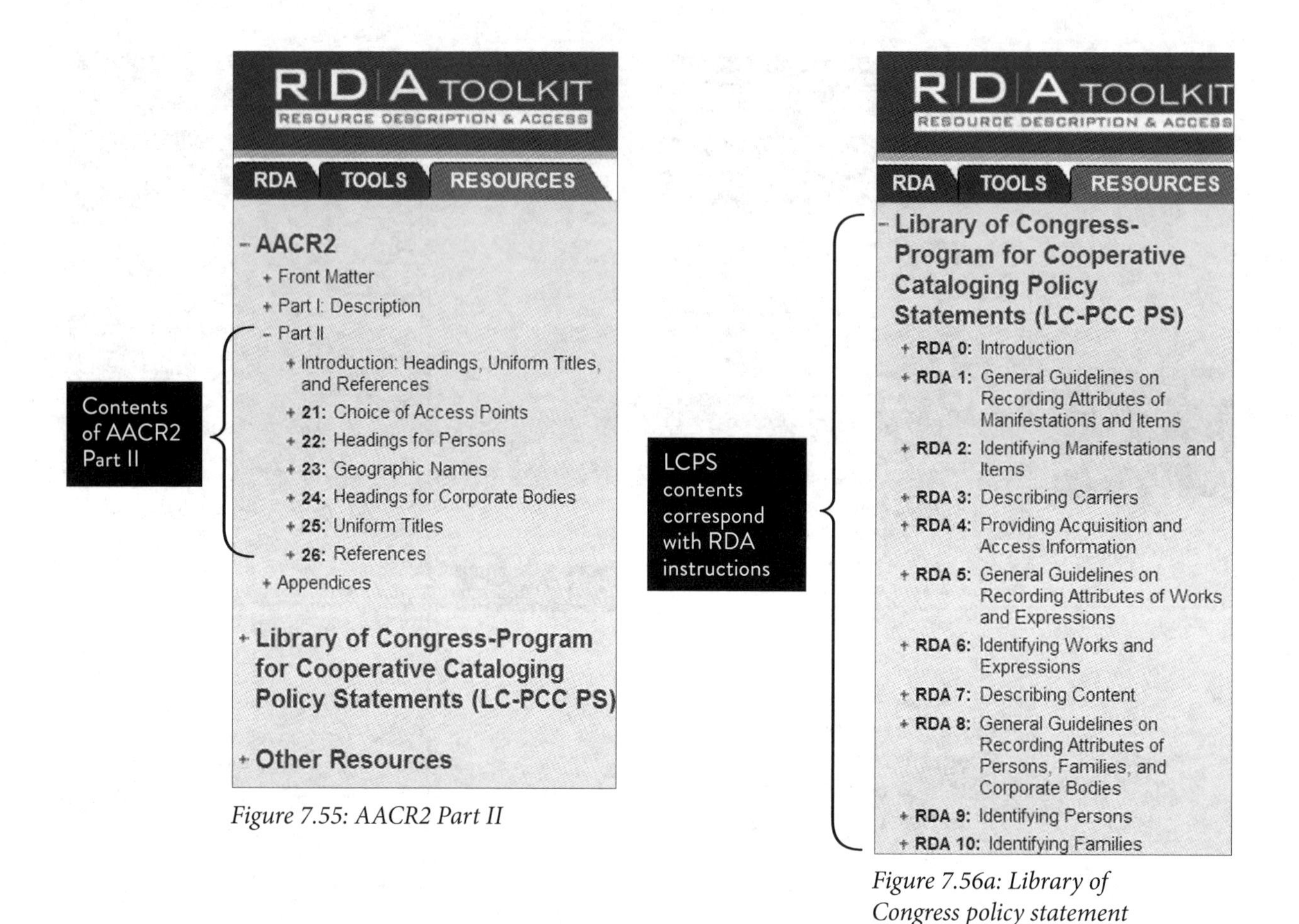

Figure 7.55: AACR2 Part II

Figure 7.56a: Library of Congress policy statement

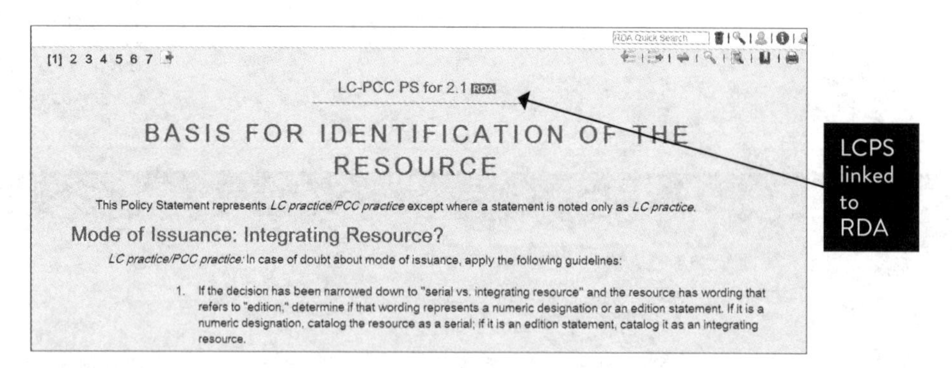

Figure 7.56b: Library of Congress policy statement

II. LIBRARY OF CONGRESS POLICY STATEMENTS (LCPS)

The LCPS contains the Library of Congress Policy Statements that are shared with the library community. It is organized in the same manner as RDA to align the LCPS with RDA elements (figure 7.56a). The Policy Statements are highlighted in green and have the "LC" symbol at the top of each page. The Policy Statements are linked to RDA and to other sections in the Policy Statements (figure 7.56b).

III. THE RESOURCES TAB INCLUDES OTHER USEFUL LINKS TO ADDITIONAL DOCUMENTATION, SUCH AS THE ELEMENT SETS AND ENCODING STANDARD, OPEN ARCHIVES INITIATIVES, CATALOGER'S DESKTOP AND THE XC EXTENSIBLE CATALOG

These will be found under the Resources tab in Other Resources (Figure 7.57).

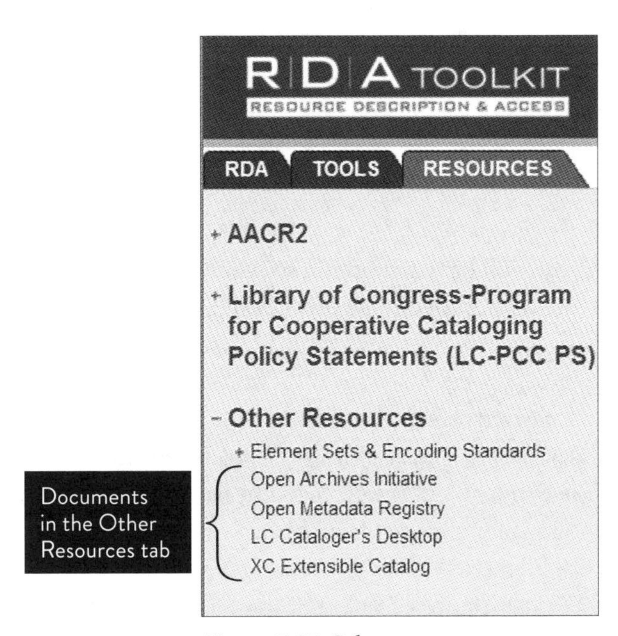

Figure 7.57: Other resources

IV. RDA QUICK AND ADVANCED SEARCH

A. QUICK SEARCH

In addition to browsing RDA Toolkit (as shown in the previous section) you can search RDA Toolkit and the other documents in two ways: *RDA Quick Search* or *Advanced Search*. The search key can be found in the User Menu in the upper right hand corner of RDA Toolkit. These two methods of searching are used for requesting a specific RDA instruction number and search phrase found in RDA chapters, appendixes, glossary, and any RDA documentation (figure 7.58).

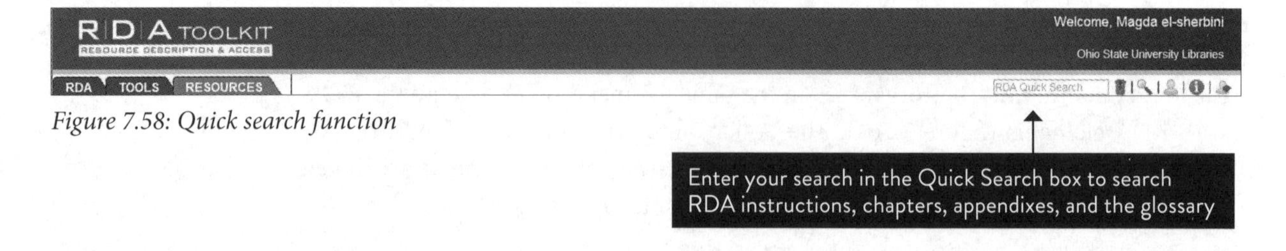

Figure 7.58: Quick search function

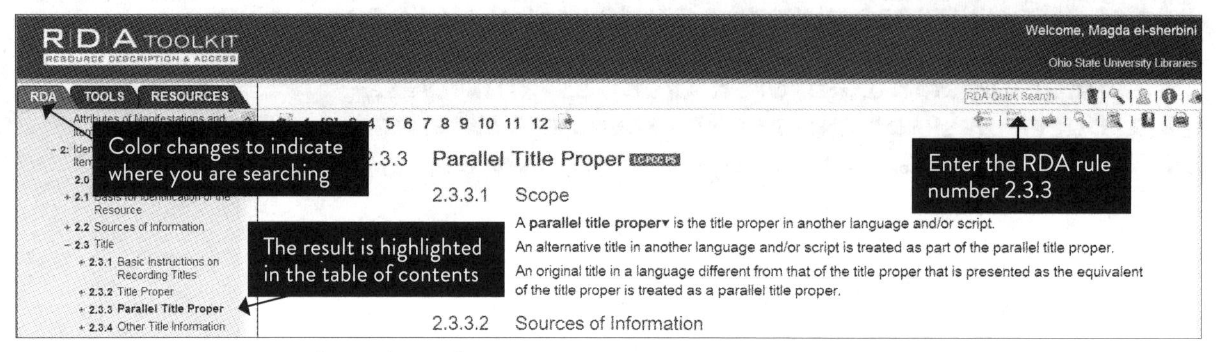

Figure 7.59: Demonstration of a quick search

When using the Quick Search, you will have the option to search either the RDA instruction by typing the full instruction number in the text box or by searching RDA chapters, appendixes, and the glossary using a search phrase. Users also have the option to save their searches.

To demonstrate how the Quick Search works, the instruction number of RDA 2.3.3 was entered in the Quick Search box. The search result produced documents related to RDA 2.3.3 (Parallel Title Proper) and the instruction was retrieved from the *RDA* tab (notice that the RDA tab color changed from brown to light red to indicate that you are searching the RDA Elements). The *Synch* button was also pressed to highlight the instruction in the RDA tab (figure 7.59).

B. ADVANCED SEARCH

The *Advanced Search* works differently than the *Quick Search.* In Advanced Search, you will have the option of searching the RDA instructions by AACR2 rule numbers. You can also search RDA by the RDA instruction types. For example, you can search by all instruction numbers, description types, content types, or media types, etc. (figure 7.60). You can search any document in RDA Toolkit by a phrase or a section. The following section will contain some tips for using the advanced search strategy.

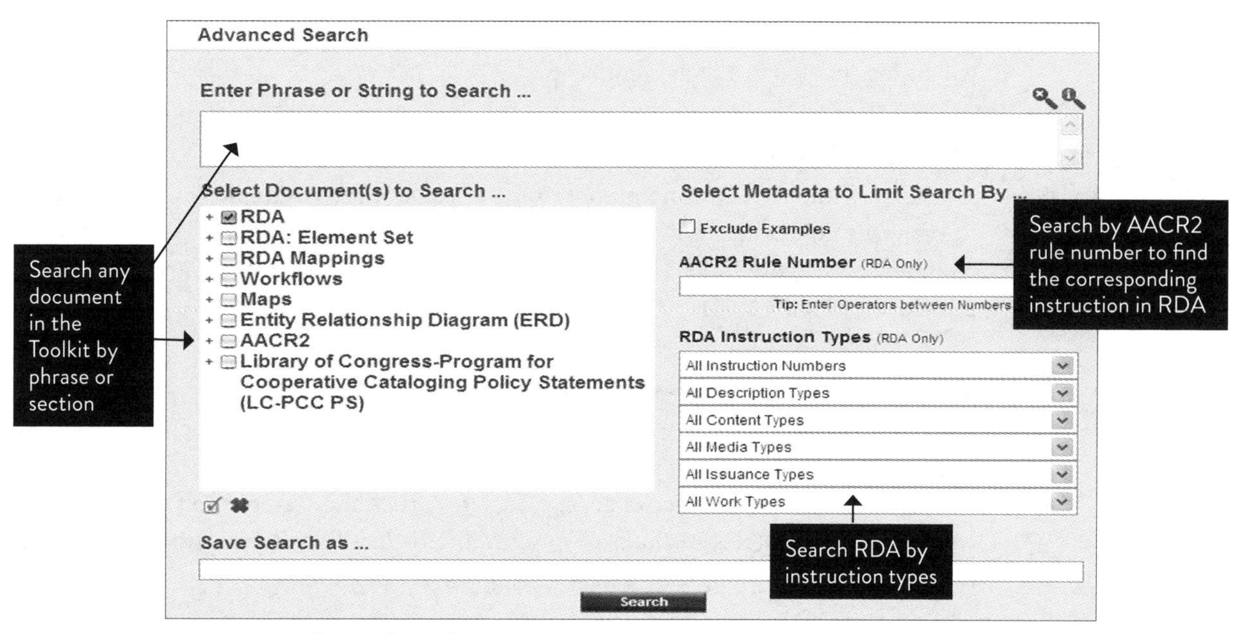

Figure 7.60: Advanced search

SEARCH BY A PHRASE OR WORD STRING

You can enter a phrase or a string search in the Advanced Search and limit this search to a specific document or documents, such as the RDA Element Set View, RDA Mappings, Workflows, and Entity Relationships. These documents can be expanded by clicking on the plus sign to search the specific section. Figure 7.61 shows the search by a phrase or string. You can limit this search by viewing the RDA instructions in RDA, mapping from RDA to MARC 21, workflow, and the LCPS. The result of the search will be displayed at the top of the RDA screen. It will show the number of hits and will display the results based on

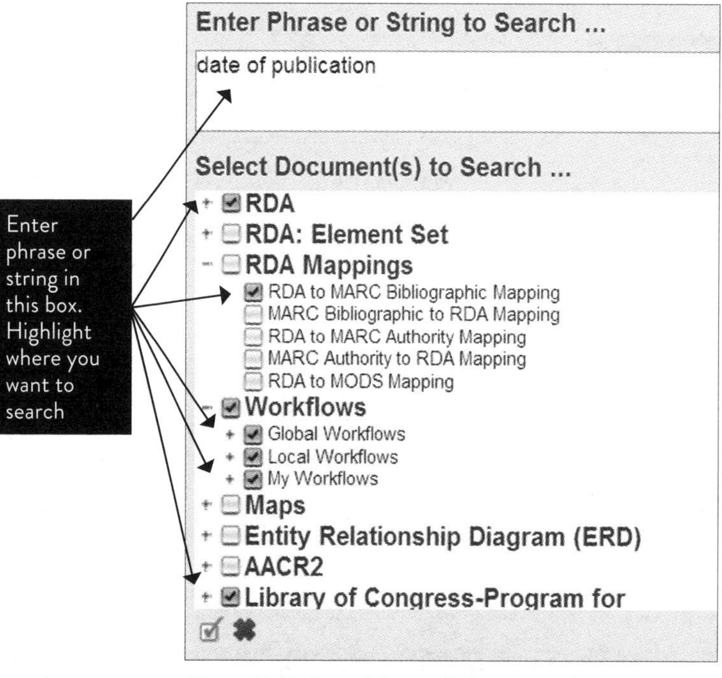

Figure 7.61: Search by a phrase or a string

how many hits you want to display per screen. The terms that you used for searching will be highlighted in yellow (figure 7.62).

SEARCH BY AACR2 RULE NUMBER

If you know the AACR2 rule number for punctuation, for example, and you want to know the equivalent in RDA, type the AACR2 rule number in the "AACR2 Rule Number" box (figure 7.63). This will retrieve the RDA instructions that are related to punctuation (figure 7.64).

SEARCH BY RDA INSTRUCTION TYPE

Some instructions in RDA apply to all resources, but there are some special instructions for specific formats. In the *Search by RDA Instruction Type* menu, the cataloger can display all the instructions that are related to serials, for example. In this case, the cataloger will click on *All Issuance Types* and then select *Serials Only* from the drop down menu (figure 7.65). The results will appear as in Figure 7.66.

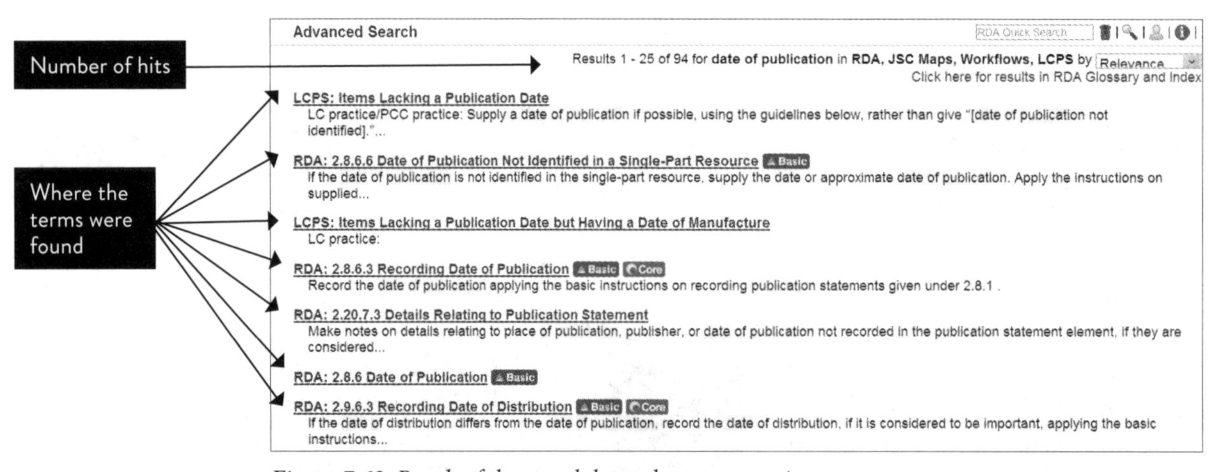

Figure 7.62: Result of the search by a phrase or a string

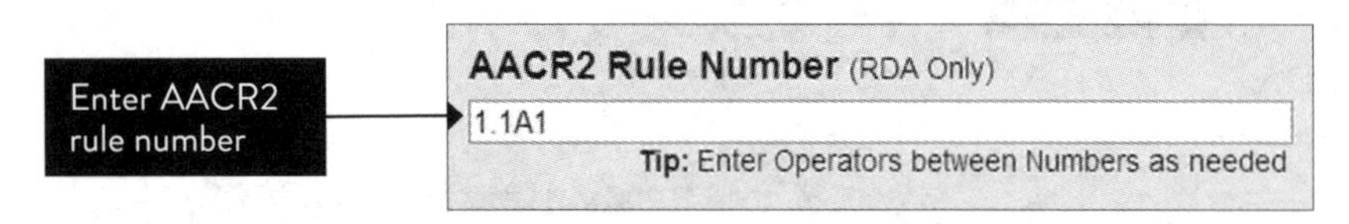

Figure 7.63: RDA search via AACR2 rule number

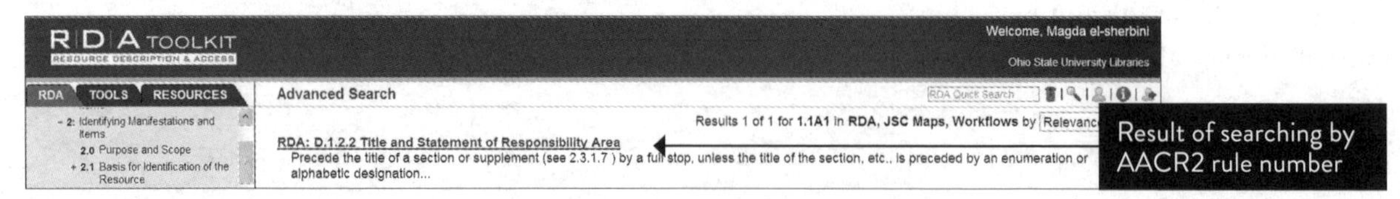

Figure 7.64: The result of searching RDA by AACR2 rule number

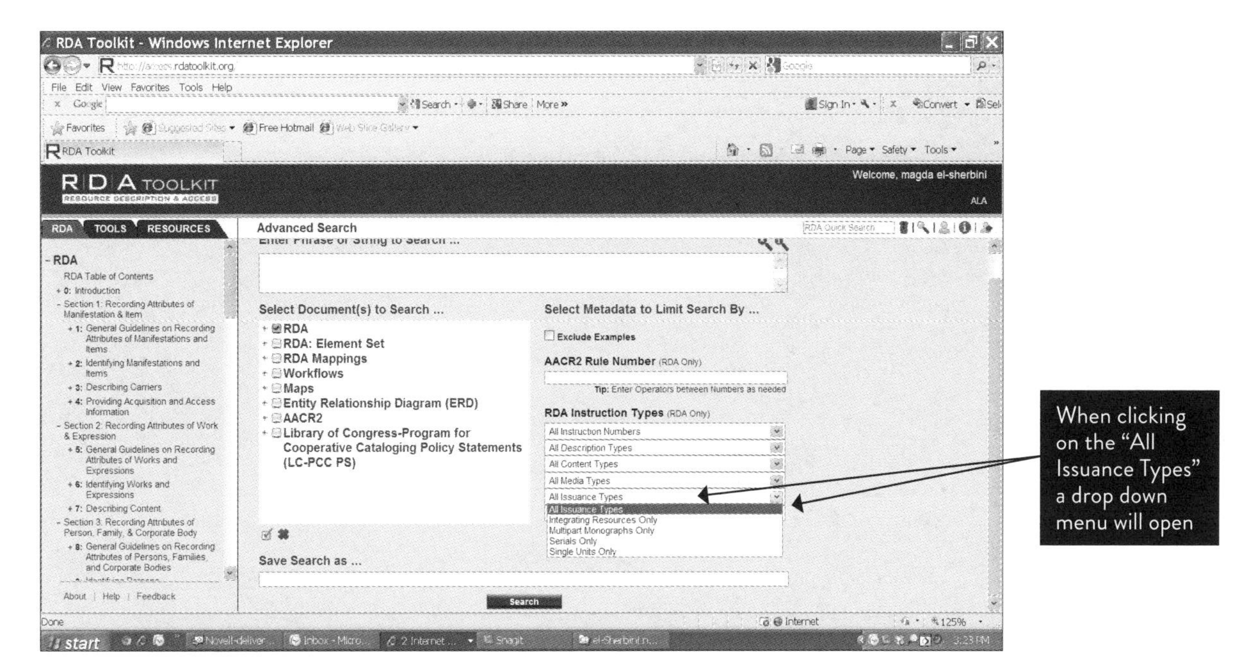

Figure 7.65: Search RDA instruction type

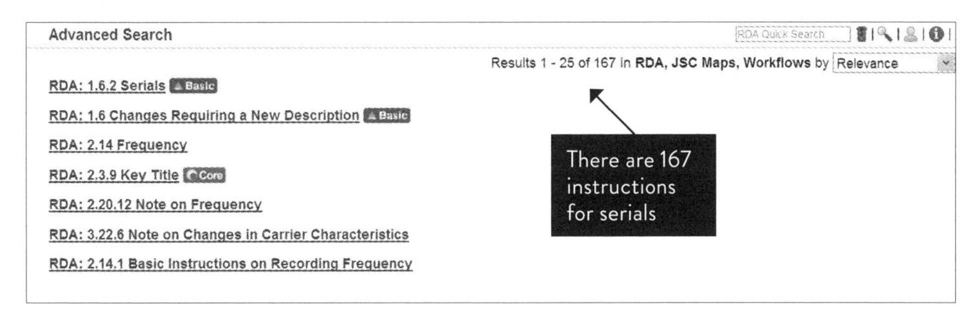

Figure 7.66: Search RDA instruction type

REFERENCES

RDA Toolkit. 2010– . Chicago: American Library Association; Ottawa: Canadian Library Association; London: Chartered Institute of Library and Information Professionals (CILIP). www.rdatoolkit.org.

Tillett, Barbara. 2010. "Train the Trainer Module 8: Relationships." www.loc.gov/catdir/cpso/RDAtest/rdatraining.html.

CHAPTER EIGHT

EXAMPLES OF RDA RECORDS

I. BIBLIOGRAPHIC RECORDS

This chapter includes examples of RDA records. Some of these examples come from AACR2, modified using RDA guidelines. These examples represent various formats, such as monographs, serials, online resources, maps, music, A/V materials, etc. Some of the records used in the examples were taken from The Ohio State University Libraries, OhioLink, Library of Congress and OCLC catalogs, as well as the RDA Test Documentation, and other sources. Each example includes comments to illustrate specific cases. Keep in mind that these examples do not represent all the changes from AACR2 to RDA. Some fields such as subject access points, call numbers, MARC 21 fields 504s , and ISBNs, were removed from the records.

Additional examples can be found at these websites:

- Joint Steering Committee for the Development of RDA, "Complete Examples—Bibliographic Records," www.rda-jsc.org/docs/6JSC_RDA_Complete_Examples_(Bibliographic)_revised.pdf
- Special Libraries Association, "Examples for RDA Compared to AACR2," www.sla.org/PDFs/SLA2009/2009_rdaexamples.pdf
- RDA Toolkit, "Complete Examples," www.rdatoolkit.org/constituencyreview/Phase1AppM_11_10_08.pdf
- City University of New York Cataloging, "Sample RDA Records in OCLC," http://cunycataloging.pbworks.com/w/page/32018740/Sample-RDA-records-in-OCLC
- Library of Congress, "Documentation for the RDA (Resource Description and Access) Test: Examples for RDA—Compared to AACR2," www.loc.gov/catdir/cpso/RDAtest/rdaexamples.html

PRINT MONOGRAPHS

EXAMPLE 1

LEADER 00000cam 2200493 i 4500
001 645702532
005 20110128165224.0
008 101210s2010 enka b 001 0 eng
010 $a 2010530455
040 $a UKM$cUKM$dDLC$dBTCTA$dYDXCP$dBWK$dYHM$dCGU$dXII$dIXA$erda
043 $a e-uk-en
100 1 $a Bennett, N. H., $e author.

245 10 $a WONDERFUL TO BEHOLD : $b A CENTURY HISTORY OF THE LINCOLN RECORD SOCIETY, 1910-2010 / $c NICHOLAS BENNETT.
246 30 $a CENTURY HISTORY OF THE LINCOLN RECORD SOCIETY, 1910-2010
260 $a [Lincoln, England] : $b Lincoln Record Society, $c 2010.
300 $a 255 pages : $b illustrations ; $c 24 cm.
336 $a text $2 rdacontent
337 $a unmediated $2 rdamedia
338 $a volume $2 rdacarrier
490 1 $a Publications of the Lincoln Record Society, $x 0267-2634 ; $v volume 100
505 0 $a The origins of the society -- Charles Wilmer Foster and the foundation of the society--The early years of the society --The Stentons, Domesday book and the registrum antiquissimum --The death of the founder --The impact of the Second World War -- Continuity and change : The society from 1960-2010 --Appendix 1: The members of the society --Appendix 2: The publications of the society.
830 0 $a Publications of the Lincoln Record Society ; $v v. 100.

Note on the record:

Leader 000 i	ISBD punctuations.
040 $e	Description conventions. (rda)
100 $e	Designators to indicate relationships between a resource and persons, families, and corporate bodies associated with a resource. 18.5.1.3 + appendix I
245	The title on the source is in capital letters. Creator of the catalog had to decide to either follow RDA appendix A for capitalization, symbols punctuation, numerals, abbreviations, etc., or to follow established in-house guidelines. In this case, the creator of the record followed the in-house guidelines, which instructed to transcribe data as it. (RDA 2.3.1.4)
260 $c	Place of publication is taken from outside the resource. (RDA 2.8.2.6.1)
300	Pages and illustrations are spelled out. "cm." is not an abbreviation, but is a metric symbol. (RDA 3.5.1.3)
336	Content type.
337	Media type.
338	Carrier type.
490 1 $v	On the source: volume 100. (Volume was spelled out on the source). (RDA 2.12.9.3)

EXAMPLE 2

LEADER 00000cam 100181 i 4500
001 646114422
008 100630s2010 nyu b 001 0 eng d
020 $a 9781441970916
020 $a 1441970916
040 $a BTCTA$beng$cTCTA$dYDXCP$dOHX$dKRS$dOSU$d UtOrBLW$erda
111 2 $a Nebraska Symposium on Motivation $n (57th : $d 2009: $c Lincoln, Nebraska), $e issuing body.
245 10 $a Health Disparities in Youth and Families : $b Research and Applications / $c Gustavo Carlo, Lisa J. Crockett, Miguel A. Carranza, editors.
260 $a New York : $b Springer Verlag, $c [2011], ©2011.
300 $a x, 173 pages : $b illustration ; $c 25 cm.
336 $a text $2 rdacontent
337 $a unmediated $2 rdamedia
338 $a volume $2 rdacarrier
490 1 $a Nebraska symposium on motivation, $x 0146-7875 ; $v 57
500 $a Also available online.
700 1 $a Carlo, Gustavo, $e editor.
700 1 $a Crockett, Lisa J $e editor.
700 1 $a Carranza, Miguel A. $e editor.
811 2 $a Nebraska Symposium on Motivation. $t Nebraska Symposium on Motivation ; $v 57.

Note on the record:

111 2 111 2 $n	Authorized access point for the Symposium (preferred name of the Symposium RDA 11.2.2)
111 2 $d	Date associated with the corporate body (RDA 11.4)
111 2 $c	Location of the Symposium (RDA 11.3.2.3)
111 2 $e	Issuing body is relationship designator from RDA appendix I.
245	Title in capital letters—agency creating the data decided to use their in-house guidelines for capitalizations-all editors are listed in the statement of responsibility.
260 $c	Date of publication is taken from outside the resource. Copyright date is also used.
700 1	Authorized access point for the editors.

EXAMPLE 3

LEADER 00000cam 2200517 i 4500
001 527702647
008 100219s2010 couabf b 000 0 eng
010 $a 2010003691
020 $a 9780813712062 (cloth)
020 $a 0813712068 (cloth)
040 $a DLC$cDLC$dYDXCP$dVVC$dCRU$dUPP$d CGU$dWEA$dIQU$erda
043 $a n-usa—
245 00 $a From rodinia to pangea : $b the lithotectonic record of the Appalachian Region / $c edited by Richard P. Tollo, Mervin J. Bartholomew, James P. Hibbard, and Paul M. Karabinos.
246 30 $a Lithotectonic record of the Appalachian Region.
260 $a Boulder, Colorado : $b Geological Society of America, $c 2010.
300 $a xi, 956 pages, folded leaves of plates : $b illustrations, maps (some color) ; $c 29 cm.
336 $a text $2 rdacontent
337 $a unmediated $2 rdamedia
338 $a volume $2 rdacarrier
490 1 $a Memoir / Geological Society of America ; $v 206
500 $a "This project began at the technical sessions entitled: "From Rodinia to Pangea : the lithotectonic record of plate convergence in eastern North America," held at the annual meeting of the Northeastern Section of the Geological Society of America in Durham, New Hampshire, in March 2007"—Page x.
700 1 $a Tollo, Richard P., $e editor.
700 1 $a Bartholomew, Mervin J., $e editor.
700 1 $a Hibbard, James P., $e editor.
700 1 $a Karabinos, Paul M., $e editor.
710 2 $a Geological Society of America, $e publisher.
710 2 $a Geological Society of America, $b Northeastern Section, $e publisher.
830 0 $a Memoir (Geological Society of America) ; $v 206.

Note on the record:

245	Title was in capital letters on the resource, but agency creating the data decided to follow RDA appendix A for capitalization—All editors are listed in the statement of responsibility.
300	Spell-out pages; illustration; folded; color.
700 1	Authorized access points for all the editors.
710 2	Authorized access points for corporate bodies.
700 $e and 710 $e	Relationships designations.

EXAMPLE 4

LEADER 00000nam 2200000 i 4500
001 46685454
008 010306s2001 nyu b 000 0 eng
010 $a 2001336531
020 $a 0060194650
040 $a DLC$cDLC$erda
043 $a n-us—$an-us-va
100 1 $a Winik, Jay, $d 1957-, $e author.
245 10 $a APRIL 1865 : $b the Month That Saved America / $c Jay Winik.
246 30 $a Month that saved America
250 $a FIRST EDITION.
260 $a [New York] : $b Harper Collins Publishers, $c [2001], ©2001.
300 $a xxiv, 449 pages ; $c 24 cm
336 $a text $2 rdacontent
337 $a unmediated $2 rdamedia
338 $a volume $2 rdacarrier
504 $a Includes bibliographical references (pages [389]-448).

Note on the record:

245	Agency creating the data decided to record the title as is on the source of information including capitalization.
250	On the source of information "FIRST EDITION."
260 $c	Date of publication is taken from other source. Copyright date is on the verso of the title page. Both dates will be recorded. The copyright date is recorded preceded with the appropriate symbol.

STATEMENT OF RESPONSIBILITY

EXAMPLE 5

LEADER 00000cam 2200325 i 4500
001 441142405
008 100708s2011 flua b 001 0 eng
010 $a 2010029122
020 $a 9781439828588 (hardcover : alk. paper)
020 $a 143982858X (hardcover : alk. paper)
040 $a DLC$cDLC$dYDX$dUKM$dBTCTA$dYDXCP$dCDX$erda
245 00 $a Semi-field methods for the environmental risk assessment of pesticides in soil : $b SETAC Workshop PERAS, Coimbra, Portugal / $c [editors] Andreas Schaeffer, Paul J. van den Brink, Fred Heimbach, Simon P. Hoy, Frank M.W. de Jong, Jorg Rombke, Martina Roß-Nickoll, Jose P. Sousa.
260 $a Boca Raton, FL : $b CRC Press, $c [2011], ©2011.
300 $a xxxviii, 105 pages : $b illustration ; $c 25 cm
336 $a text $2 rdacontent
337 $a unmediated $2 rdamedia
338 $a volume $2 rdacarrier
504 $a Includes bibliographical references and index.
700 1 $a Schäffer, Andreas, $e editor.
700 1 $a Brink, Paul van den, $e editor.
700 1 $a Heimbach, Fred, $e editor.
700 1 $a Hoy, Simon P., $e editor.
700 1 $a Jong, Frank M.W. de $q (Frank Marinus Wijnand), $d 1959- $e editor.
700 1 $a Rombke, Jorg, $e editor.
700 1 $a Roß-Nickoll, Martina, $e editor.
700 1 $a Souza, José M. P. $q (José Maria Pacheco), $e editor.
711 2 $a SETAC-Europe Workshop PERAS $d (2007 : $c Coimbra, Portugal)

or

245 00 $a Semi-field methods for the environmental risk assessment of pesticides in soil : $b SETAC Workshop PERAS, Coimbra, Portugal / $c [edited by] Andreas Schaeffer [and seven others].
260 $a Boca Raton, FL : $b CRC Press, $c [2011], ©2011.
300 $a xxxviii, 105 pages : $b illustration ; $c 25 cm
336 $a text $2 rdacontent
337 $a unmediated $2 rdamedia
338 $a volume $2 rdacarrier
504 $a Includes bibliographical references and index.

700 1 $a Schäffer, Andreas, $e editor.
711 2 $a SETAC-Europe Workshop PERAS $d (2007 : $c Coimbra, Portugal)

Note on the record:

245 00	The names of all the editors were recorded in the statement of responsibility. The names of editors do not need to be included in a statement of responsibility to justify inclusion of 7XX fields in the bibliographic record.
700	Access points for all the editors
700 $e	The relationship designator from RDA appendix I in the 700 field is cataloger's judgment
or 245	Alternative— If a single statement of responsibility names more than three persons, families, or corporate bodies performing the same function, or with the same degree of responsibility, omit all but the first of each group of such persons, families, or bodies. Indicate the omission by summarizing what has been omitted in the language and script preferred by the agency preparing the description. (RDA 2.4.1.5) [Edited by] Andreas Schaeffer [and seven others]
700 1	Authorized access point for the first editor only

EXAMPLE 6

001 692015378
040 $a DNLM/DLC$erda$cDLC$dYDX$dBTCTA$dNLM$dYDXCP $dCDX$dOHS
020 $a 9781609137144 (pbk.)
100 1 $a Yamada, Thoru, $d 1940-, $e author
245 10 $a Practical guide for clinical neurophysiologic testing : $b EP, LTM, IOM, PSG, and NCV / $c Thoru Yamada, MD, Professor, Department of Neurology, University of Iowa, Iowa City, Iowa ; Elizabeth Meng, BA, R.EEG/EP T., Surprise, Arizona.
260 $a Philadelphia : $b Wolters Kluwer Health/Lippincott Williams & Wilkins Health, $c [2011], ©2011.
300 $a x, 292 pages : $b illustrations ; $c 28 cm
336 $a text $2 rdacontent
337 $a unmediated $2 rdamedia
338 $a volume $2 rdacarrier
520 $a "This book provides advanced content that begins where the "Practical Guide for Clinical Neurophysiologic Testing: EEG"

ends. This advanced guide, more geared to Neurology fellows than to electroneurodiagnostic technologists, discusses evoked potentials, including visual, brainstem auditory, and somatosensory EPs. The author covers intraoperative neurophysiologic monitoring, epilepsy monitoring, long-term bedside EEG monitoring, and sleep studies"—Provided by publisher.

505 0 $a Evoked potentials -- Principles of evoked potentials -- Visual evoked potentials -- Brainstem auditory evoked potentials and auditory evoked potentials -- Somatosensory evoked potentials -- Intraoperative neurophysiologic monitoring -- Introduction and recording technology -- EEG monitoring for carotid endarterectomy -- Spinal cord monitoring -- Long-term EEG monitoring -- Diagnostic video-EEG monitoring for epilepsy and spells: indications, application, and interpretation -- Invasive video EEG monitoring in epilepsy surgery candidates: indications, technique, and interpretation -- Long-term bedside EEG monitoring for acutely ill patients (LTM/cEEG) -- Sleep studies -- Sleep physiology and pathology -- Technology of poly-somnography -- Sleep apnea and related conditions -- Evaluating narcolepsy and related conditions -- Parasomnias -- Nerve conduction studies -- Nerve conduction studies.

700 1 $a Meng, Elizabeth, $e author.

787 0 $i Related to (work): $a Yamada, Tōru, 1940- $t Practical guide for clinical neurophysiologic testing : EEG. $d Philadelphia, PA : Lippincott Williams & Wilkins, ©2010 $z9780781778619 $w (DLC) 2009024851 $w (OCoLC) 403363500

Note on the record:

245 $c	Transcribe a statement of responsibility in the form in which it appears on the source of information (RDA 2.4.1.4)
787 0 $i	The $i is used for Relationship Designator to present related work.

PLACE OF PUBLICATION, PUBLISHER, AND DATE OF PUBLICATION

EXAMPLE 7

LEADER 00000nam 2200000I i 4500
001 50219184
008 020723s1999 za b 000 0 eng d

040 $a INU$cINU$dOSU$erda
043 $a f-za—
100 1 $a Matenga, C. R. $q (Crispin R.), $e author.
245 10 $a Livelihoods from solid waste in Lusaka City : $b challenges and opportunities : a survey research report / $c by C.R. Matenga and S.L. Muyakwa.
260 $a [place of publication not identified] : $b [publisher not identified], $c [1999?] $e [Lusaka]
300 $a xv, 97 leaves ; $c 28 cm
336 $a text $2 rdacontent
337 $a unmediated $2 rdamedia
338 $a volume $2 rdacarrier
500 $a "July 1999."
500 $a "Funded by Pilot Environmental Fund, Environmental Support Programme (ESP), Ministry of Environment and Natural Resources"—Cover.
700 1 $a Muyakwa, Stephen L., $e author.
776 08 $i Online version: $a Matenga, C. R. (Crispin R.) $t Livelihoods from solid waste in Lusaka City. $d [Lusaka? : s.n., 1999] $w (OCoLC)654284582

Note on the record:

260 $a	Place of publication not identified.
260 $b	Publisher not identified.
260 $c	Probable date.
260 $e	Place of manufacture was found on the verso of title page.
700 10	For a work by two or more persons, families, or corporate bodies having the same responsibility for creating the work, the authorized access point will be under the first creator (100) having principal responsibility, if indicated. If the principal responsibility cannot be determined, record the first name of the creator that appears on the source of information. Use appendix I to choose one or more appropriate terms representing the person, family, or corporate body to indicate the nature of the relationship.
776 08	Information about the other available physical forms.
776 $i	Designation of a relationship between the resource described in the 776 field and the resource described in the 1xx/245 of the record.

ACCOMPANYING MATERIALS

EXAMPLE 8

001 316058624
007 c $b 0 $e g
010 $a 2010042001
040 $a DLC$erda$cDLC$dYDX$dBTCTA$dYDXCP$dVP@$d CDX$dBWX$dOCLCQ
020 $a 1555706681 (alk. paper)
020 $a 9781555706685 (alk. paper)
100 1 $a Weber, Mary Beth, $e author.
245 10 $a Describing electronic, digital, and other media using AACR2 and RDA : $b a how-to-do-it manual and CD-ROM for librarians / $c Mary Beth Weber, Fay Angela Austin.
260 $a New York : $b Neal-Schuman Publishers, $c [2011], ©2011.
300 $a xviii, 301 pages : $b illustrations ; $c 28 cm. + $e 1 CD-ROM (4 3/4 in.)
336 $a text $2 rdacontent
337 $a unmediated $2 rdamedia
337 $a computer $2 rdamedia
338 $a volume $2 rdacarrier
338 $a computer disc $2 rdacarrier
490 1 $a How-to-do-it manuals ; $v 168
505 0 $a Essential background—Cartographic resources—Sound recordings—Videos—Electronic resources—Electronic integrating resources—Microforms—Multimedia kits and mixed materials.
700 1 $a Austin, Fay Angela, $e author.
830 0 $a How-to-do-it manuals for libraries ; $v no. 168.

or

300 $a xviii, 301 pages : $b illustrations ; $c 28 cm.
300 $a 1 CD-ROM (4 3/4 in.)

or

300 $a xviii, 301 pages : $b illustrations ; $c 28 cm.
500 $a Accompanied by 1 CD-ROM (4 3/4 in.)

Note on the record:

300 $e	It includes 1 CD-ROM as an accompanied material. Create multiple 300 fields—one for the extent and the other for the accompanying materials. or—Give a note for the accompanying material.
337	Notice the multiple 337 fields to address the inclusion of the accompanying materials.
338	Notice the multiple 338 fields to address the inclusion of the accompanying materials. Use the name of a carrier type from RDA 3.3.1.3, unless it is a booklet or some other material not on that list.

PREFERRED TITLE OF THE WORK, AUTHORIZED ACCESS POINTS, AND INDICATED RELATIONSHIPS

Compilation of Works

EXAMPLE 9

Compilation of Works by Different Creators with a Collective Title

001 61115544
010 $a 2005020590
040 $a DLC$cDLC$dBAKER$dBTCTA$dTXHLC$erda
020 $a 1585476986 (lib. bdg. : alk. paper)
020 $a 9781585476985 (lib. bdg. : alk. paper)
245 04 $a The golden West : $b three classic novels / $c edited by Jon Tuska
250 $a Large print edition.
260 $a Thorndike, ME. : $b Center Point Publishing, $c 2006.
300 $a 365 pages ; $c 23 cm
336 $a text $2 rdacontent
337 $a unmediated $2 rdamedia
338 $a volume $2 rdacarrier
505 0 $a Tappan's burro / by Zane Grey—Jargan / by Max Brand—The trail to Crazy Man / by Louis L'Amour.
520 $a Brings us the best short novels written by the world's most popular writers of the traditional Western story.
700 1 $a Tuska, Jon, $e editor.
700 12 $a Grey, Zane, $d 1872-1939. $t Tappan's burro.
700 12 $a Brand, Max, $d 1892-1944. $t Jargan.
700 12 $a L'Amour, Louis, $d 1908-1988. $t Trail to Crazy Man.

Note on the record:

245	The preferred title of the compilation
505 0	The content of the compilation
700 12	If more than one work is embodied in the manifestation, only the predominant or first named work is required ("Work Manifested" RDA 17.8). LC's policy is to give analytical authorized point for predominant or first work in the compilation when it represents a substantial part of the resource. Other access points are cataloger's judgment. MARC 700 field, 2nd indicator "2" (item contains work) indicates relationship; otherwise, use "contains (work)" relationship designator.

EXAMPLE 10

Compilation of Two Works by the Same Creator without Collective Title

LEADER 00000pam 2200000 i 4500
001 42603182
008 990923s2000 inuab b 000 1 eng
010 $a 99048766
040 $a DLC$cDLC$erda
100 1 $a Poe, Edgar Allan, $d 1809-1849, $e author.
240 10 $a Short stories. $k Selections
245 10 $a Thirty-two stories / $c Edgar Allan Poe ; edited, with introductions and notes by Stuart Levine and Susan F. Levine
246 3 $a 32 stories
260 $a Indianapolis, Indiana : $b Hackett Pub. Co., $c [2000], ©2000.
300 $a xii, 385 pages : $b illustrations, maps ; $c 23 cm
336 $a text $2 rdacontent
337 $a unmediated $2 rdamedia
338 $a volume $2 rdacarrier
505 00 $t Metzengerstein -- $t The Duc De L'Omelette -- $t MS. found in a Bottle—$t The assignation -- $t Shadow -- $t Silence -- $t Ligeia -- $t How to write a Blackwood article -- $t A predicament -- $t The fall of the house of Usher -- $t William Wilson -- $t The man of the crowd -- $t The murders in the rue Morgue -- $t A descent into the Maelstrom -- $t Eleonora -- $t The masque of the red death -- $t The pit and the pendulum -- $t The domain of Arnheim -- $t The tell-tale heart -- $t The gold-bug -- $t The black cat -- $t The purloined letter -- $t The balloon-hoax -- $t The literary life of Thingum Bob, Esq -- $t Some words with a mummy -- $t The power of words -- $t The imp of the perverse -- $t The facts

in the case of M. Valdemar -- $t The cask of amontillado -- $t Mellonta Tauta -- $t Hop-frog -- $t Von Kempelen and his discovery.
700 1 $a Levine, Stuart, $e editor.
700 1 $a Levine, Susan F. $q (Susan Fleming), $e editor.
700 12 $a Poe, Edgar Allan, $d 1809-1849. $t Metzengerstein.
700 12 $a Poe, Edgar Allan, $d 1809-1849. $t Duc De L'Omelette.
700 12 $a Poe, Edgar Allan, $d 1809-1849. $t MS. Found in a bottle.
700 12 $a Poe, Edgar Allan, $d 1809-1849. $t Assignation.
700 12 $a Poe, Edgar Allan, $d 1809-1849. $t Shadow.
700 12 $a Poe, Edgar Allan, $d 1809-1849. $t Silence.
700 12 $a Poe, Edgar Allan, $d 1809-1849. $t Ligeia.
700 12 $a Poe, Edgar Allan, $d 1809-1849. $t How to write a Blackwood article.
700 12 $a Poe, Edgar Allan, $d 1809-1849. $t Predicament.
700 12 $a Poe, Edgar Allan, $d 1809-1849. $t Fall of the house of Usher.
700 12 $a Poe, Edgar Allan, $d 1809-1849. $t William Wilson.
700 12 $a Poe, Edgar Allan, $d 1809-1849. $t Man of the crowd.
700 12 $a Poe, Edgar Allan, $d 1809-1849. $t Murders in the Rue Morgue.
700 12 $a Poe, Edgar Allan, $d 1809-1849. $t Descent into the Maelstrom.
700 12 $a Poe, Edgar Allan, $d 1809-1849. $t Eleonora.
700 12 $a Poe, Edgar Allan, $d 1809-1849. $t Masque of the red death.
700 12 $a Poe, Edgar Allan, $d 1809-1849. $t Pit and the pendulum.
700 12 $a Poe, Edgar Allan, $d 1809-1849. $t Domain of Arnheim.
700 12 $a Poe, Edgar Allan, $d 1809-1849. $t Tell-tale heart.
700 12 $a Poe, Edgar Allan, $d 1809-1849. $t Gold-bug.
700 12 $a Poe, Edgar Allan, $d 1809-1849. $t Black cat.
700 12 $a Poe, Edgar Allan, $d 1809-1849. $t Purloined letter.
700 12 $a Poe, Edgar Allan, $d 1809-1849. $t Balloon-hoax.
700 12 $a Poe, Edgar Allan, $d 1809-1849. $t Literary life of Thingum Bob, Esq.
700 12 $a Poe, Edgar Allan, $d 1809-1849. $t Some words with a mummy.
700 12 $a Poe, Edgar Allan, $d 1809-1849. $t Power of words.
700 12 $a Poe, Edgar Allan, $d 1809-1849. $t Imp of the perverse.
700 12 $a Poe, Edgar Allan, $d 1809-1849. $t Facts in the case of M. Valdemar.
700 12 $a Poe, Edgar Allan, $d 1809-1849. $t Cask of Amontillado.
700 12 $a Poe, Edgar Allan, $d 1809-1849. $t Mellonta Tauta.

700 12 $a Poe, Edgar Allan, $d 1809-1849. $t Hop-frog.
700 12 $a Poe, Edgar Allan, $d 1809-1849. $t Von Kempelen and his discovery.

or

LEADER 00000pam 2200000 i 4500
001 42603182
008 990923s2000 inuab b 000 1 eng
010 $a 99048766
040 $a DLC$cDLC$erda
100 1 $a Poe, Edgar Allan, $d 1809-1849, $e author.
240 10 $a Short stories. $k Selections
245 10 $a Thirty-two stories / $c Edgar Allan Poe ; edited, with introductions and notes by Stuart Levine and Susan F. Levine.
246 3 $a 32 stories
260 $a Indianapolis, Indiana : $b Hackett Pub. Co., $c [2000], ©2000.
300 $a xii, 385 pages : $b illustrations, maps ; $c 23 cm
336 $a text $2 rdacontent
337 $a unmediated $2 rdamedia
338 $a volume $2 rdacarrier
505 00 $t Metzengerstein -- $t The Duc De L'Omelette -- $t MS. found in a Bottle -- $t The assignation -- $t Shadow -- $t Silence -- $t Ligeia -- $t How to write a Blackwood article -- $t A predicament -- $t The fall of the house of Usher -- $t William Wilson -- $t The man of the crowd -- $t The murders in the rue Morgue -- $t A descent into the Maelstrom -- $t Eleonora -- $t The masque of the red death -- $t The pit and the pendulum -- $t The domain of Arnheim -- $t The tell-tale heart -- $t The gold-bug -- $t The black cat -- $t The purloined letter -- $t The balloon-hoax -- $t The literary life of Thingum Bob, Esq -- $t Some words with a mummy -- $t The power of words -- $t The imp of the perverse -- $t The facts in the case of M. Valdemar -- $t The cask of amontillado -- $t Mellonta Tauta -- $t Hop-frog -- $t Von Kempelen and his discovery.
700 1 $a Levine, Stuart, $e editor.
700 1 $a Levine, Susan, $e editor. Levine, Susan F. $q (Susan Fleming), $e editor.
700 12 $a Poe, Edgar Allan, $d 1809-1849. $t Metzengerstein.

Note on the record:

240 10	Conventional collective title is used as the preferred title.
260	Publisher's name on source of information is abbreviated.
260 $c	Date of publication is taken from other source; copyright date is on the verso of the title page. Both dates will be recorded.
260 $c	The copyright date is recorded proceeded with the appropriate symbol.
505 0	Content note of the work—give a contents note in a 505 ("no limit on number of works in contents note unless burdensome").
700 12	If more than one work is embodied in the manifestation, only the predominant or first named work is required ("Work Manifested" RDA 17.8). LC's policy is to give analytical authorized point for predominant or first work in compilation when it represents a substantial part of the resource. Other access points are cataloger's judgment. MARC 700 field 2nd indicator "2" (item contains work) indicates relationship; otherwise, use "contains (work)" relationship designator.

EXAMPLE 11

Compilation of Two Works in the Same Form by the Same Author

LEADER 00000cam 2200000 i 4500
001 7903996
008 821019s1981 laua b 000 0 eng
010 $a 81050422 //r89
020 $z 0916242121 : $c $10.95
040 $a DLC$cDLC$dMTU$erda
100 1 $a Faulkner, William, $d 1897-1962, $e author.
240 10 $a Poems. $k Selections. $f 1981
245 10 $a Helen, a courtship ; and, Mississippi poems / $c by William Faulkner ; introductory essays by Carvel Collins and Joseph Blotner.
260 $a New Orleans, Louisiana : $b Tulane University, $c [1981], ©1981.
300 $a 165 pages : $b illustration ; $c 22 cm
336 $a text $2 rdacontent
337 $a unmediated $2 rdamedia
338 $a volume $2 rdacarrier
530 $a Also issued online.
700 1 $a Collins, Carvel, $d 1912-1990.

700 1 $a Blotner, Joseph, $d 1923-
700 12 $a Faulkner, William, $d 1897-1962. $t Helen, a courtship.
700 12 $a Faulkner, William, $d 1897-1962. $t Mississippi poems.
776 08 $i Online version: $a Faulkner, William, 1897-1962. $s Helen, a courtship. $t Helen, a courtship ; and, Mississippi poems. $d New Orleans, La. : Tulane University ; Oxford, MS : Yoknapatawpha Press, c1981 $w (OCoLC)563029449

Note on the record:

240 10	Conventional collective title is used as the preferred title.
240 10 $f	Date of work is given in subfield $f.
700 12	If more than one work is embodied in the manifestation, only the predominant or first named work is required ("Work Manifested" RDA 17.8). LC's policy is to give analytical authorized point for predominant or first work in compilation when it represents a substantial part of the resource. Other access points are cataloger's judgment. MARC 700 field 2nd indicator "2" (item contains work) indicates relationship; otherwise, use "contains (work)" relationship designator.
776 08	Information about the other available physical forms.
776 08 $i	Designation of a relationship between the resource described in the 776 field and the resource described in the 1xx/245 of the record.

Electronic Version of the Above Work

LEADER 00000cam 2200000 i 4500
001 7903996
008 821019s1981 laua b 000 0 eng
010 $a 81050422 //r89
020 $z 0916242121 : $c $10.95
040 $a DLC$cDLC$dMTU$erda
100 1 $a Faulkner, William, $d 1897-1962, $e author.
240 10 $a Poems. $k Selections. $f 1981
245 10 $a Helen, a courtship ; and, Mississippi poems / $c by William Faulkner ; introductory essays by Carvel Collins and Joseph Blotner.
260 $a New Orleans, Louisiana : $b Tulane University ; $a Oxford, MS : $b Yoknapatawpha Press, $c [1981], ©1981.
300 $a 1 online resource (165 pages) : $b text file, PDF
336 $a text $2 rdacontent

337 $a computer $2 rdamedia
338 $a online resource $2 rdacarrier
500 $a Errata slip inserted.
700 1 $a Collins, Carvel, $d 1912-1990.
700 1 $a by Blotner, Joseph, $d 1923-
700 12 $a Faulkner, William, $d 1897-1962. $t Helen, a courtship.
700 12 $a Faulkner, William, $d 1897-1962. $t Mississippi poems.
776 08 $i print version: Faulkner, William, 1897-1962. $t Helen, a courtship ; and, Mississippi poems. $d New Orleans, La. : Tulane University ; Oxford, MS : Yoknapatawpha Press, c1981 $w (OCoLC)563029449.

Note on the record:

776 08	When the carrier of the work is not the same as carrier of original, use MARC 21 field 776.
776 08 $i	The $i indicates the relationship between the print and the electronic version of the work.

EXAMPLE 12

001 48493548
010 $a 2001006801
040 $a DLC$cDLC$dOCLCQ$dBAKER$dBTCTA$dOCLCG$d TXBXL$erda
020 $a 076422591X (pbk.)
020 $a 9780764225918 (pbk.)
100 1 $a MacDonald, George, $d 1824-1905, $e author.
240 10 $a Novels. $k Selections
245 14 $a The curate of Glaston : $b three dramatic novels from Scotland's beloved storyteller / $c George MacDonald ; edited by Michael Phillips.
260 $a Minneapolis : $b Bethany House, $c [2002]
300 $a 187, 209, 218 pages ; $c 23 cm
336 $a text $2 rdacontent
337 $a unmediated $2 rdamedia
338 $a volume $2 rdacarrier
505 0 $a The curate's awakening—The lady's confession—The baron's apprenticeship.
700 12 $a MacDonald, George, $d 1824-1905. $t Curate's awakening.
700 12 $a MacDonald, George, $d 1824-1905. $t Lady's confession.
700 12 $a MacDonald, George, $d 1824-1905. $t Baron's apprenticeship.
700 1 $a Phillips, Michael R., $d 1946-, $e editor.

Note on the record:

240 10	Conventional collective title is used as the preferred title.
505	Give a contents note in a 505 ("no limit on number of works in contents note unless burdensome").
700 12	If more than one work is embodied in the manifestation, only the predominant or first named work is required ("Work Manifested" RDA 17.8). LC's policy is to give analytical authorized point for predominant or first work in compilation when it represents a substantial part of the resource. Other access points are cataloger's judgment. MARC 700 field 2nd indicator "2" (item contains work) indicates relationship; otherwise, use "contains (work)" relationship designator.

EXAMPLE 13

001 707969546
010 $a 2011021562
040 $a DLC$beng$cDLC$dYDX$dBTCTA$dUKMGB$dYDXCP $dJAO$dBWX$erda
020 $a 9780765329769
020 $a 076532976X
100 1 $a Kelton, Elmer, $e author.
245 10 $a Three novels / $c by Elmer Kelton ; Introduction by Dale Walker.
250 $a First edition.
260 $a New York : $b Forge, $c 2011.
300 $a 496 pages ; $c 22 cm
336 $a text $2 rdacontent
337 $a unmediated $2 rdamedia
338 $a volume $2 rdacarrier
505 0 $a Joe Pepper—Long way to Texas—Eyes of the hawk.
700 1 $a Walker, Dale L.
700 12 $a Kelton, Elmer. $t Joe Pepper.
700 12 $a Kelton, Elmer. $t Long way to Texas.
700 12 $a Kelton, Elmer. $t Eyes of the hawk.

Note on the record:

240 10	Conventional collective title is used as the preferred title.
505	Give a contents note in a 505 ("no limit on number of works in contents note unless burdensome").
700 12	If more than one work is embodied in the manifestation, only the predominant or first named work is required ("Work Manifested" RDA 17.8). LC's policy is to give analytical authorized point for predominant or first work in compilation when it represents a substantial part of the resource. Other access points are cataloger's judgment. MARC 700 field 2nd indicator "2" (item contains work) indicates relationship; otherwise, use "contains (work)" relationship designator.

EXAMPLE 14

Compilation of Works by Different Creators with No Collective Title

LEADER 00000cam 2200000I i 4500
001 39667739
008 980810s1998 enk 000 0 eng d
020 $a 184002027X
020 $a 9781840020274
040 $a UBY$erda$beng$cUBY$dBAKER$dYDXCP$dOCLCG$d B9K$dNLE$dOCLCQ
245 00 $a Riders to the sea ; $b The shadow of the glen / $c J.M. Synge. Purgatory / W.B. Yeats.
260 $a London : $b Oberon Books, $c 1998.
300 $a 67 pages ; $c 21 cm
336 $a text $2 rdacontent
337 $a unmediated $2 rdamedia
338 $a volume $2 rdacarrier
500 $a Includes an introduction, The living and the dead : Synge and Yeats, by Declan Kiberd, and a director's note by John Crowley.
520 $a These three one-act plays are unified by a thematic thread—death—and the refusal of the dead to leave the living alone.
505 0 $a Riders to the sea / J.M. Synge --The shadow of the glen / J.M. Synge --Purgatory / W.B. Yeats.
700 12 $a Synge, J. M. $q (John Millington), $d 1871-1909. $t Riders to the sea.
700 12 $a Synge, J. M. $q (John Millington), $d 1871-1909. $t Shadow of the glen.
700 12 $a Yeats, W. B. $q (William Butler), $d 1865-1939. $t Purgatory.

Two works by different creators

Note on the record:

245 00	Two works by different creators. Compilation of works by different creators is not named as a whole. Cataloger can choose to devise a title proper (RDA 2.3.2.9 "Resource lacking a collective title")
505	Give a contents note in a 505 ("no limit on number of works in contents note unless burdensome").
700 12	If more than one work is embodied in the manifestation, only the predominant or first named work is required ("Work Manifested" RDA 17.8). LC's policy is to give analytical authorized point for predominant or first work in compilation when it represents a substantial part of the resource. Other access points are cataloger's judgment. MARC 700 field2nd indicator "2" (item contains work) indicates relationship; otherwise, use "contains (work)" relationship designator.

EXAMPLE 15

Compilation of Works by Different Creators with a Collective Title

LEADER 00000nam 2200000 i 4500
001 23731760
008 910412s1991 nyua j b 000 0 eng
010 $a 91018425
020 $a 0820415545 (alk. paper)
040 $a DLC$cDLC$dOSU$erda
245 00 $a Eight plays for youth : $b varied theatrical experiences for stage and study / $c edited by Christian H. Moe and R. Eugene Jackson.
260 $a New York : $b P. Lang, $c [1991], ©1991.
300 $a xxv, 367 pages : $b illustrations ; $c 24 cm.
336 $a text $2 rdacontent
337 $a unmediated $2 rdamedia
338 $a volume $2 rdacarrier,
490 1 $a American university studies. Series XXVI, Theatre arts ; $v volume 8
505 0 $a Little red riding wolf / by R. Eugene Jackson -- The fabulous fable factory / by Joseph Robinette and Thomas Tierney --Tom Sawyer / by Christian H. Moe and Cameron Garbutt -- Second chance / by Lou Furman -- Alice's adventures in Podland / by Kaarin S. Johnston -- A new age is dawning / by Will Huddleston -- The incredible jungle journey of Fenda Maria / by Jack Stokes --The Jack tales / by R. Rex Stephenson.
700 1 $a Moe, Christian Hollis, $d 1929- $e editor.

700 1 $a Jackson, R. Eugene, $e editor.
700 12 $a Jackson, R. Eugene. $t Little red riding wolf.
700 12 $a Robinette, Joseph. $t Fabulous fable factory.
700 12 $a Tierney, Thomas, $d 1942- $t Fabulous fable factory.
700 12 $a Moe, Christian Hollis, $d 1929- $t Tom Sawyer.
700 12 $a Garbutt, Cameron W. $t Tom Sawyer.
700 12 $a Furman, Lou, $d 1944- $t Second chance.
700 12 $a Johnston, Kaarin S., $d 1950- $t Alice's adventures in Podland.
700 12 $a Huddleston, Will. $t New age is dawning.
700 12 $a Stokes, Jack. $t Incredible jungle journey of Fenda Maria.
700 12 $a Stephenson, R. Rex. $t Jack tales.
830 0 $a American university studies. $n Series XXVI. $p Theatre arts ; $v v. 8.

Note on the record:

245 00	The collective title of the compilation.
505	Give a contents note in a 505 ("no limit on number of works in contents note unless burdensome").
700 1	Editors of the compilation
700 12	If more than one work is embodied in the manifestation, only the predominant or first named work is required ("Work Manifested" RDA 17.8). LC's policy is to give analytical authorized point for predominant or first work in compilation when it represents a substantial part of the resource. Other access points are cataloger's judgment. MARC 700 field 2nd indicator "2" (item contains work) indicates relationship; otherwise, use "contains (work)" relationship designator.

EXPRESSIONS

EXAMPLE 16

Resource With One Expression

LEADER 00001369cam a22003498i 450
001 764404903
008 101124t20112011enk b 001 0 eng
020 $a 9780199777594 (hardcover : alkaline paper)
040 $a DLC$erda$cDLC$dYDX$dYDXCP$dCDX$dBWX$dVVC
041 1 $a eng $h mar

100 1 $a Ḍhere, Rāmacandra Cintāmaṇa, $d 1930-
240 10 $a Śrīviṭṭhala, eka mahāsamanvaya. $l English
245 14 $a The rise of a folk god : $b Viṭṭhal of Pandharpur / $c by Ramchandra Chintaman here ; translated by Anne Feldhaus.
260 $a Oxford ; $a New York : $b OXFORD UNIVERSITY PRESS, $c [2011], ©2011.
300 $a xvii, 350 pages : $b illustrations, map ; $c 24 cm.
336 $a text $2 rdacontent
337 $a unmediated $2 rdamedia
338 $a volume $2 rdacarrier
490 1 $a South Asia research
546 $a Includes translation from Marathi.
700 1 $a Feldhaus, Anne, $e translator.
830 0 $a South Asia research (New York, N.Y.)

Note on the record:

041 1	This resource is an English translation
240 10	Preferred title is the title of the original text + $l for the Language of the expression.
260 $a	Only first place of publication is required.
546	In this field, record the language of the content, a different element than language of expression.

EXAMPLE 17

Resource Has One Expression in More Than One Language

LEADER 00000cam 2200409 i 4500
001 294887613
008 081229s2009 gw a 000 1 eng c
020 $a 9783832793074
020 $a 3832793070
040 $a BTCTA$cBTCTA$dYDXCP$dGSE$dSINLB$dOSU$d UtOrBLW$erda
041 0 $a eng $a ger $a fre $a spa $a ita
245 00 $a Garden & outdoor design / $c [editor: Haike Falkenberg]
246 3 $a Garden and outdoor design
260 $a Kempen : $b teNeues Pub. Group, $c [2009], ©2009.
300 $a 222 pages : $b chiefly colored illustrations ; $c 20 cm
336 $a text $2 rdacontent
337 $a unmediated $2 rdamedia
338 $a volume $2 rdacarrier

500 $a Includes index.
505 0 $a Furniture -- Practical and necessary -- Decoration.
546 $a Text in English, German, French, Spanish and Italian.
700 1 $a Falkenberg, Haike, $e editor.

Note on the record:

041 1 and 546	Use this field for resources with single expression other than translations and the Bible. The cataloging agency has the option of creating access points for the expression with the language names(s) in MARC 21 field 7xx or to give the language(s) of that single expression in the 041/546 fields in the bibliographic record.
245 $c	Editor information was taken from outside the resource.

EXAMPLE 18

LEADER 00000cam 2200397I i 4500
001 437298944
008 090922s2010 maua bd 001 0 eng
010 $a 2009039499
020 $a 9781592535958
020 $a 159253595X
040 $a DLC$cDLC$dBTCTA$dCP$dYDXCP$dBWX$dCDX $dVP@$dOSU$dUtOrBLW$erda
041 0 $a eng $a fre $a ger $a ita $a spa
100 1 $a Wolf, Peter J., $e author.
245 10 $a Graphic design = $b Le language du graphisme / $c Peter J. Wolf.
246 31 $a Language du graphisme
260 $a Beverly, Mass. : $b Rockport Publishers, $c [date of publication not identified], ©2010.
300 $a 431 pages : $b illustrations (chiefly color) ; $c 27 cm
336 $a text $2 rdacontent
337 $a unmediated $2 rdamedia
338 $a volume $2 rdacarrier
500 $a "A visual directory for terms of global design."
546 $a Text in English, French, German, Italian, and Spanish.
700 12 $a Wolf, Peter J., $e author. $t Graphic design. $l English.
700 12 $a Wolf, Peter J., $e author. $t Graphic design. $l French.
700 12 $a Wolf, Peter J., $e author. $t Graphic design. $l German.
700 12 $a Wolf, Peter J., $e author. $t Graphic design. $l Italian.
700 12 $a Wolf, Peter J., $e author. $t Graphic design. $l Spanish.

Note on the record:

041	Language of the content.
546	The cataloging agency has the option of creating access points for the expression with the language names(s) in MARC 21 field 700 subfield $l or to give the language(s) of that single expression in the 041/546 fields in the bibliographic record.
260 $c	Date of publication is not available.
260 $c	Copyright date is on the verso of the title page and is recorded preceded with the appropriate symbol.
700 12	A compilation of expressions in different languages—provided an authorized access point for each expression in the resource. Only the predominant or first-named expression is a core requirement ("Expression manifested" RDA 17.10). LC's policy is to give analytical authorized access point for predominant or first expression in the compilation when it represents a substantial part of the resource. Other access points are cataloger's judgment. If more than one work is embodied in the manifestation, only the predominant or first named work is required ("Work Manifested" RDA 17.8). MARC 700 field 2nd indicator "2" (item contains work) indicates relationship; otherwise, use "contains (work)" relationship designator.

EXAMPLE 19

Two or more expressions in the same manifestation (original language and translation into other languages)

LEADER 00000cam 22005298 i 4500
001 610869909
008 100624s2011 onc j 000 0 spa
010 $a 2010024913
020 $a 9780778785798 (pbk.)
020 $a 0778785793 (pbk.)
040 $a DLC$cDLC$dBTCTA$dNLC$erda
041 1 $a spa $a eng $h eng
100 1 $a Kalman, Bobbie, $e author.
240 10 $a Arms and legs, fingers and toes. $l Spanish & English
245 10 $a Arms and legs, fingers and toes = $b Brazos, piernas y dedos / $c Bobbie Kalman.
246 31 $a Brazos, piernas y dedos

260 $a St. Catharines, Ontario : $b Crabtree Pub., $c [2011], ©2011.
300 $a 16 pages : $b illustrations ; $c 21 cm.
336 $a text $2 rdacontent
337 $a unmediated $2 rdamedia
338 $a volume $2 rdacarrier
490 1 $a My world, Level B = Mi mundo, Nivel B
530 $a Issued also in an electronic format.
546 $a Text in English and Spanish.
700 12 $a Kalman, Bobbie, $e author. $t Arms and legs, fingers and toes. $l English.
700 12 $a Kalman, Bobbie, $e author. $t Arms and legs, fingers and toes. $l Spanish.
800 1 $a Kalman, Bobbie. $t My world. $p Bobbie Kalman's leveled readers. $n Level B.

Note on the record:

041 and 546	Language of the content. The cataloging agency has the option of creating access points for the expression with the language names(s) in MARC 21 field 700 subfield $l or to give the language(s) of that single expression in the 041/546 fields in the bibliographic record.
490	Other Title Information of Series in More Than One Language or Script (RDA 2.12.4.4)
700 12 $l	Provided an authorized access point for each expression in the resource. Only the predominant or first-named expression is a core requirement ("Expression manifested" RDA 17.10). LC's policy is to give analytical authorized access point for predominant or first expression in the compilation when it represents a substantial part of the resource. Other access points are cataloger's judgment. MARC 700 field 2nd indicator "2" (item contains work) indicates relationship; otherwise, use "contains (work)" relationship designator.

EXAMPLE 20

LEADER 01567cam a22003495 i 450
001 669990297
040 $a DLC$beng$cDLC$erda
040 1 $a eng$akor$hkor
100 1 $a Yi, Sŏng-bok, $d 1952-
245 10 $a I heard life calling me : $b poems of Yi Sŏng-bok / $c translators, Hye-jin Juhn, George Sidney.

260 $a Ithaca, New York : $b East Asia Program, Cornell University, $c [2010]
300 $a xii, 280 pages ; 22 cm.
336 $a text $2 rdacontent
337 $a unmediated $2 rdamedia
338 $a volume $2 rdacarrier
490 0 $a Cornell East Asia series, $x 1050-2955 ; $v 145
546 $a Poems in Korean with English translation on facing pages; preface and appendixes in English
500 $a Translation of: Twinggunŭn tol ŭn ŏnje cham kkaenŭn'ga (When does a rolling stone awaken), originally published in 1980, and Namhae Kŭmsan (South sea, silk mountain), originally published in 1986
700 1 $a Juhn, Hye-jin.
700 1 $a Sidney, George.
700 12 $a Yi, Sŏng-bok, $d 1952- $t Twinggunŭn tol ŭn ŏnje cham kkaenŭn'ga. $l Korean. $k Selections.
700 12 $a Yi, Sŏng-bok, $d 1952- $t Twinggunŭn tol ŭn ŏnje cham kkaenŭn'ga. $l English. $k Selections.
700 12 $a Yi, Sŏng-bok, $d 1952- $t Namhae Kŭmsan. $l Korean. $k Selections.
700 12 $a Yi, Sŏng-bok, $d 1952- $t Namhae Kŭmsan. $l English. $k Selections.
830 0 $a Cornell University East Asia papers.

Note on the record:

041	Language of the content.
546	The cataloging agency has the option of creating access points for the expression with the language names(s) in MARC 21 field 700 subfield $l or to give the language(s) of that single expression in the 041/546 fields in the bibliographic record.
700 12 $l	If more than one work is embodied in the manifestation, only the predominant or first named work is required ("Work Manifested" RDA 17.8). LC's policy is to give analytical authorized point for predominant or first work in compilation when it represents a substantial part of the resource. Other access points are cataloger's judgment. MARC 700 field 2nd indicator "2" (item contains work) indicates relationship; otherwise, use "contains (work)" relationship designator.

EXAMPLE 21

LEADER 00000nam 2200000 i 4500
001 1812782
008 750913s1975 mtu b 000 0 eng
010 $a 75-30775
020 $a 0891300430
035 $a 2283301
040 $a DLC$cDLC$dOSU$erda
041 0 $a eng $a gre $a heb
043 $a e-gr—
245 04 $a The book of Baruch : $b also called I Baruch : (Greek and Hebrew) / $c edited, reconstructed, and translated by Emanuel Tov.
260 $a Missoula, Mont. : $b Published by Scholars Press for the Society of Biblical Literature, $c [date of publication not identified], ©1975.
300 $a v, 51 pages ; $c 24 cm.
336 $a text $2 rdacontent
337 $a unmediated $2 rdamedia
338 $a volume $2 rdacarrier
490 1 $a Texts and translations ; $v 8. $a Pseudepigrapha series ; $v 6
500 $a Based on I. Tov's thesis, Hebrew University, Jerusalem, 1973.
546 $a English, Greek, and Hebrew.
504 $a Includes bibliographical references: (page 9)
730 02 $a Bible. $p Apocrypha. $s Baruch. $l English. $f 1975.
730 02 $a Bible. $p Apocrypha. $s Baruch. $l Hebrew. $f 1975.
730 02 $a Bible. $p Apocrypha. $s Baruch. $l Greek. $f 1975.
700 10 $a Tov, Emanuel, $e editor, $e translator.
830 0 $a Texts and translations ; $v no. 8.
830 0 $a Texts and translations. $p Pseudepigrapha series.

Note on the record:

041	In this field, record the language of the content.
546	The cataloging agency has the option of creating access points for the expression with the language names(s) in subfield $l or to give the language(s) of that single expression in the 041/546 fields in the bibliographic record.
260 $c	Date of publication is not available. Copyright date is on the verso of the title page and is recorded preceded with the appropriate symbol.

730 $l	Provided an authorized access point for each expression in the resource—only the predominant or first-named expression is a core requirement ("Expression Manifested" RDA 17.10). LC's policy is to give analytical authorized access point for predominant or first expression in the compilation when it represents a substantial part of the resource. Other access points are cataloger's judgment.
730 $f	Date of the expression.

EXAMPLE 22

Parallel Text in English and Spanish

LEADER 00000cam 2200373I i 4500
001 694569946
003 OCoLC
005 20110103125631.0
008 101230s2011 maua j 000 1 eng d
020 $a 9780763650414
020 $a 0763650412
035 $a (OCoLC)694569946
040 $a JPL$cJPL$dJPL$erda
041 1 $a eng $a spa $h eng
100 1 $a Patricelli, Leslie, $e author.
245 14 $a The birthday box = $b Mi caja de cumpleaños / $c Leslie Patricelli.
246 31 $a Mi caja de cumpleaños
250 $a First bilingual edition.
260 $a Cambridge, Mass : $b Candlewick Press, $c 2011.
300 $a 1 volume (unnumbered) : $b color illustrations ; $c 18 cm
336 $a text $2 rdacontent
337 $a unmediated $2 rdamedia
338 $a volume $2 rdacarrier
500 $a On board pages.
520 $a An imaginative young child has a wonderful time playing with a box he receives for his birthday.
546 $a Parallel text in English and Spanish.
700 12 $a Patricelli, Leslie, $e author. $t Birthday box. $l English.
700 12 $a Patricelli, Leslie, $e author. $t Birthday box. $l Spanish.

Note on the record:

041 1	Language of the content
546	The cataloging agency has the option of creating access points for the expression with the language names(s) in MARC 21 field 700 subfield $l or to give the language(s) of that single expression in the 041/546 fields in the bibliographic record.
246	Parallel title is not a core element.
250	On source of information "first bilingual edition."
245	Parallel text in English and Spanish.
300	The work is not numbered.
700 12	• A compilation of work in different languages—provided an authorized access point for each expression in the resource. Only the predominant or first-named expression is a core requirement ("Expression Manifested" RDA 17.10). • LC's policy is to give analytical authorized access point for predominant or first expression in the compilation when it represents a substantial part of the resource. Other access points are cataloger's judgment. • MARC 2nd indicator "2" (item contains work) indicates relationship; otherwise, use "contains (work)" relationship designator.

EXAMPLE 23

Compilation of Translations in the Same Language by a Single Creator

LEADER 00000cam 2200445 i 4500
001 301888752
008 090217s2009 enk b 000 1 eng
010 $a 2009005387
020 $a 9780199238552 $c (pbk. : acid-free paper)
020 $a 0199238553
040 $a DLC$cDLC$dYDX$dBTCTA$dYDXCP$dUKM$dCDX$erda
041 1 $a eng $h ger
100 1 $a Kafka, Franz, $d 1883-1924, $e author.
240 10 $a Short stories. $l English. $k Selections
245 14 $a The metamorphosis and other stories / $c Franz Kafka ; translated by Joyce Crick ; with an introduction and notes by Ritchie Robertson.
260 $a Oxford : $b Oxford University Press, $c 2009.
300 $a xviii, 146 pages ; $c 20 cm.
336 $a text $2 rdacontent
337 $a unmediated $2 rdamedia
338 $a volume $2 rdacarrier
490 1 $a Oxford world's classics

505 0 $a Meditation --The judgment --The metamorphosis -- In the penal colony --Letter to his father.
546 $a Translated from the German.
700 12 $a Kafka, Franz, $d 1883-1924. $t Urteil. $l English.
700 12 $a Kafka, Franz, $d 1883-1924. $t Verwandlung. $l English.
700 12 $a Kafka, Franz, $d 1883-1924. $t Strafkolonie. $l English.
700 12 $a Kafka, Franz, $d 1883-1924. $t Brief an den Vater. $l English.
700 1 $a Crick, Joyce, $e translator.
830 0 $a Oxford world's classics (Oxford University Press)

Note on the record:

041 1	The Language of content.
240 10	Conventional collective title for the expression. Cataloging agency could choose not to include 240 in addition to the MARC 2 field 700.
505 0	Content note of the compilation.
546	The language of content.
700 12	Expression manifested is a core element, if there is more than one expression of the work manifested. If more than one expression is embodied in the manifestation, only the predominant or first named expression manifested is required ("Expression Manifested" 17.10). LC's policy is to give analytical authorized access point for predominant or first expression in the compilation when it represents a substantial part of the resource. Other access points are cataloger's judgment. MARC 700 field 2nd indicator "2" (item contains work) indicates relationship; otherwise, use "contains (work)" relationship designator.

RELATED WORK

EXAMPLE 24

LEADER 00000cam 2200565Ii 4500
001 692015378
010 $a 2010051087
040 $a DNLM/DLC$erda$cDLC$dYDX$dBTCTA$dNLM$dYDXCP $dCDX$dOHS
100 1 $a Yamada, Thoru, $d 1940- $e author
245 10 $a Practical guide for clinical neurophysiologic testing : $b EP, LTM, IOM, PSG, and NCS / $c Thoru Yamada, MD, FAASM, FACNS, Professor, Department of Neurology, Chief, Division of Clinical Electrophysiology, University of Iowa Roy J. and Lucille

A. Carver College of Medicine, Iowa City, Iowa ; Elizabeth Meng, BA, R.EEG/EP T., EEG Technologist, Department of Neurology, Maryvale Hospital, Phoenix, Arizona.

260 $a Philadelphia : $b Wolters Kluwer Health/Lippincott Williams & Wilkins Health, $c [2011], ©2011.

300 $a x, 292 pages : $b illustrations ; $c 28 cm

336 $a text $2 rdacontent

337 $a unmediated $2 rdamedia

338 $a volume $2 rdacarrier

520 $a "This book provides advanced content that begins where the "Practical Guide for Clinical Neurophysiologic Testing: EEG" ends. This advanced guide, more geared to neurology fellows than to electroneurodiagnostic technologists, discusses evoked potentials, including visual, brainstem auditory, and somatosensory EPs. The author covers intraoperative neurophysiologic monitoring, epilepsy monitoring, long-term bedside EEG monitoring, and sleep studies"—Provided by publisher.

505 0 $a Evoked potentials -- Principles of evoked potentials -- Visual evoked potentials -- Brainstem auditory evoked potentials and auditory evoked potentials -- Somatosensory evoked potentials -- Intraoperative neurophysiologic monitoring -- Introduction and recording technology -- EEG monitoring for carotid endarterectomy -- Spinal cord monitoring -- Long-term EEG monitoring -- Diagnostic video-EEG monitoring for epilepsy and spells: indications, application, and interpretation -- Invasive video EEG monitoring in epilepsy surgery candidates: indications, technique, and interpretation -- Long-term bedside EEG monitoring for acutely ill patients (LTM/cEEG) -- Sleep studies -- Sleep physiology and pathology -- Technology of polysomnography -- Sleep apnea and related conditions -- Evaluating narcolepsy and related conditions -- Parasomnias -- Nerve conduction studies -- Nerve conduction studies.

700 1 $a Meng, Elizabeth, $e author.

787 0 $i Related to (work): $a Yamada, Tōru, 1940- $t Practical guide for clinical neurophysiologic testing. $d Philadelphia, PA : Lippincott Williams & Wilkins, c2010 $z 9780781778619 $w (DLC) 2009024851 $w (OCoLC)403363500

Note on the record:

787 0 $i	This book is related to another work by the same author: "Practical guide for clinical neurophysiologic testing." The MARC 21 field 787 $i provides information about a related work when the relationship does *not* fit any of the other 76x–78x fields. The $w is the related work record control number.

TREATIES

EXAMPLE 25

Bilateral Treaty

LEADER 00000cam 2200000 i 4500
001 20998636
008 881019s1987 dcu f000 0 eng
010 $a 88601273
040 $a DLC$cDLC$dOCL$dWOO$erda
043 $a n-us—$ae-ur—
086 $a S 1.131:25
086 $a S 1.131:25
110 1 $a United States.
240 10 $a Treaties, etc. $g Soviet Union, $d 1987 December 8
245 10 $a Treaty between the United States of America and the Union of Soviet Socialist Republics on the elimination of their intermediate-range and shorter-range missiles.
260 $a Washington, D.C. : $b U.S. Department of State, Bureau of Public Affairs, Office of Public Communication Editorial Division, $c [1987]
300 $a 56 pages ; $c 28 cm.
336 $a text $2 rdacontent
337 $a unmediated $2 rdamedia
338 $a volume $2 rdacarrier
490 1 $a Selected documents ; $v number 25
500 $a Cover title.
505 0 $a The Treaty -- Memorandum of understanding regarding the establishment of the data base for the Treaty -- Protocol on procedures governing the elimination of the missile systems subject to the Treaty -- Protocol regarding inspections relating to the Treaty.
500 $a "December 1987."
710 1 $a Soviet Union.
830 0 $a Department of State publication ; $v 9555.
830 0 $a Selected documents (United States. Department of State. Bureau of Public Affairs) ; $v n. 25.

Note on the record:

110 1	The first signatory is a core element as creator.
240 10 $a	"Treaties, etc." is the preferred title.
240 10 $g	The second signatory is also a core element that has been added in MARC 21 field 240 $g.
240 10 $d	Month in access point is not abbreviated.
260 $b	On the source of information : "Department." Do not abbreviate.
490 1	On the source of information "number."
710 1	Cataloger's decision to include or not include separate access point for the second signatory.

EXAMPLE 26

Multilateral Treaty

LEADER 00000cam 2200385I i 4500
001 60374288
006 m d
007 cr bn $3 00auaba
008 050514s1926 enkb s f000 0 eng d
037 $a 98-088 $bLLMC
040 $a LLMC2$cLLMC2$dOCL$dLLMC2$erda
041 0 $a eng $a fre
043 $a a-tu—$aa-iq—
110 1 $a Great Britain.
240 10 $a Treaties, etc. $d 1926 June 5
245 10 $a Treaty between the United Kingdom and Iraq and Turkey regarding the settlement of the frontier between Turkey and Iraq : $b together with notes exchanged, Angora, June 5, 1926 : with a map.
260 $a London : $b H.M. Stationery Office, $c 1926.
300 $a 14 pages : $b map ; $c 25 cm.
336 $a text $2 rdacontent
337 $a unmediated $2 rdamedia
338 $a volume $2 rdacarrier
490 1 $a Cmd. ; $v 2679
500 $a "Turkey number 1 (1926)."
500 $a "Ratifications have not yet been exchanged."
546 $a French and English in parallel columns.
710 1 $a Iraq.

710 1 $a Turkey.
830 0 $a Cmd. (Great Britain. Parliament) ; $v 2679.

Note on the record:

110 1	Treaties are recorded under the first country mentioned, regardless of number of signatories or alphabetical order.
710 1	Cataloger's decision to include or not include separate access point for the second and third signatory.

BIBLE AND PREFERRED TITLE

EXAMPLE 27

Records for Old Testament and New Testament

LEADER 00000nam 2200000 i 4500
001 7273090
008 810220s1979 yu fh b 000 0 sccm
010 $a 81-454454
035 $a 3036618
040 $a DLC$cDLC$dm.c.$dOSU$erda
041 0 $a scc $a chu $b eng
130 0 $a Bible. $p New Testament. $p Acts. $l Church Slavic. $s Matičin apostol. $f 1979
245 10 $a Matičin apostol : $b XIII vek / $c priredili Radmila Kovačević, Dimitrije E. Stefanović ; uvod i opis rukopisa napisao Dimitrije Bogdanović ; urednik Pavle Ivić.
246 1 $a Apostolos of Matica srpska
260 $a Beograd : $b Srpska akademija nauka i umetnosti, $c 1979.
300 $a 361 pages, 3 leaves of plates : $b illustrations ; $c 28 cm.
336 $a text $2 rdacontent
337 $a unmediated $2 rdamedia
338 $a volume $2 rdacarrier
490 1 $a Zbornik za istoriju, jezik i književnost srpskog naroda : 1. odeljenje ; $v knj. 29
500 $a Added title page: The Apostolos of Matica srpska.
500 $a Prefatory matter in Serbo-Croatian (Cyrillic).
500 $a Text is a transcription of the original manuscript, deposited in Biblioteka Matice srpske in Novi Sad, sig. RR 184.
500 $a Summary in English.
700 1 $a Kovačević, Radmila.

700 1 $a Stefanović, Dimitrije E.
700 1 $a Bogdanović, Dimitrije.
710 2 $a Matica srpska (Novi Sad, Serbia). $b Biblioteka. $k Manuscript. $n RR 184.
830 0 $a Zbornik za istoriju, jezik i književnost srpskog naroda. $n I odeljenje ; $v knj. 29.

Note on the record:

130 0	The abbreviations "O.T." and "N.T." are spelled out as "Old Testament" and "New Testament" when included in authorized access points.
130 0 $f	Date of the work.
490 1	Transcribe a title of the series as it appears on the source of information (RDA 2.12.4.4 and 2.3.2.4)
700 10	Authorized access points for contributors.

EXAMPLE 28

LEADER 00000cam 2200493 i 4500
001 746099448
006 m d
007 $b o $d m $e g
008 110809t20112011vau q 000 0 eng c
040 $a STF$erda$beng$cSTF
041 1 $a eng $a lat $a grc $a heb
245 00 $a BibleWorks 9 : $b software for Biblical exegesis and research.
246 3 $a BibleWorks nine
246 3 $a Bible works 9
246 3 $a Bible works nine
246 1 $i Title on disc labels: $a Software for Biblical exegesis and research
250 $a v. 1.0.
260 $a Norfolk, VA : $b BibleWorks LLV, $c [2011], ©2011.
300 $a 3 computer discs : $b DVD-ROM ; $c 4 3/4 in. + $e 1 booklet (16 p. : illustrations ; 21 cm.)
336 $a text $2 rdacontent
337 $a computer $2 rdamedia
338 $a computer disc $2 rdacarrier
500 $a Title from container.
500 $a Accompanying booklet is quick-start guide.

520 $a Bible Works is an electronic Bible concordance and morphological analysis program. It includes texts of the Hebrew Old Testament, Greek Old Testament and New Testament in a wide range of English and modern foreign language texts. It also has Bible dictionaries and other aids.
538 $a System requirements: Windows XP/Vista/7; 1024x768 display; minimum 512 MB RAM; 1 GB hard drive space free (20 GB for full install); DVD drive; Internet Explorer version 7; sound card; internet connection for updates.
730 02 $a Bible. $p Old Testament. $l Hebrew. $f 2011.
730 02 $a Bible. $p Old Testament. $l Greek. $f 2011.
730 02 $a Bible. $p New Testament. $l Greek. $f 2011.
730 02 $a Bible. $p Old Testament. $l English. $f 2011.
730 02 $a Bible. $p Old Testament. $l Latin. $f 2011.

Note on the record:

040 1	Language of the content is in Hebrew, Greek , Latin, and English.
245	The preferred title is the title of the manifestation.
250	Notice that the edition statement was recorded as it is found on the source of information.
300 $e	The accompanying material was recorded in 300 $e and was recorded in 500 as a note. There are three options to record the accompanying materials. Add another 300 field for the accompanying materials; use $e in 300 field, or add the accompanying materials in a note.
730 02 $a	Authorized access point for each separate expression in the resource; only the first one is required.
730 02 $f	Date of the expression.
730 02 $l	Language of the expression.

EXAMPLE 29

LEADER 01866cam a2200421 i 450
001 706031846
008 110608s2011 sz b 001 0 eng c
040 $a QCL$beng$cQCL$dIBV$dERASP$erda$dCGU$dTZT$dUBY$dAUXAM$dOCLCA$dYDXCP$dOHX
020 $a 9782600014458
020 $a 2600014454
041 0 $a lat $a eng
100 1 $a Buchanan, George, $d 1506-1582, $e author.

245 10 $a Poetic paraphrase of the Psalms of David = $b Psalmorum Davidis paraphrasis poetica / $c George Buchanan ; edited, Translated, and provided with introduction and commentary by Roger P.H. Green.
246 3 $a Psalmorum Davidis paraphrasis poetica
260 $a Genève : $b Librairie Droz, $c 2011.
300 $a 640 pages ; $c 25 cm.
336 $a text $2 rdacontent
337 $a unmediated $2 rdamedia
338 $a volume $2 rdacarrier
490 1 $a Travaux d'humanisme et Renaissance, $x 0082-6081 ; $v no CDLXXVI
546 $a Text in Latin with parallel English translation; preface, introduction and commentary in English.
700 12 $a Buchanan, George, $d 1506-1582. $t Psalmorum Davidis paraphrasis poetica. $l English $s (Green)
700 12 $a Buchanan, George, $d 1506-1582. $t Psalmorum Davidis paraphrasis poetica. $l Latin $s (Green)
700 1 $a Green, Roger $q (Roger P. H.), $e editor, $e translator.
730 0 $a Bible. $p Psalms.
830 0 $a Travaux d'humanisme et Renaissance ; $v no 476.

Note on the record:

490 1	Notice the ISSN and the numbering with the series is recorded as it appears on the source on information.
700 12	• If more than one expression is embodied in the manifestation, only the predominant or first named expression manifested is required ("Expression Manifested" 17.10). • LC's policy is to give analytical authorized access point for predominant or first expression in the compilation when it represents a substantial part of the resource. Other access points are cataloger's judgment. • MARC 700 field 2nd indicator "2" (item contains work) indicates relationship; otherwise, use "contains (work)" relationship designator.
700 12 $l	The subfield $l has the language of each separate expression.
700 12 $s	Other Distinguishing Characteristic of the Expression.
730 0	The name of the Testament is omitted in the preferred title for individual books or groups of books.

SERIALS

EXAMPLE 30

LEADER 00000ngma 2200000 i 4500
001 1783887
008 741112d19701972enkmrz$ $uuua$eng$
022 $a 0022-3689
040 $a AMH$cAMH$dOCLCQ$dOH1$erda
210 0 $a J. phys., A Proc. Phys. Soc., Gen.
222 0 $a Journal of physics. A, Proceedings of the Physical Society, General
245 00 $a Journal of physics. $n A, $p General physics.
260 $a [London] : $b Institute of Physics, $c ©1970-1972.
300 $a 3 volumes ; $c 25 cm
310 $a Monthly, $b 1972.
321 $a Six numbers a year, $b 1970-71.
336 $a text $2 rdacontent
337 $a unmediated $2 rdamedia
338 $a volume $2 rdacarrier
362 0 $a Began with: volumes 3-5; January 1970-December.
550 $a Volumes for 1969-January 1971 published by the Institute of Physics and the Physical Society; March 1971- by the Institute of Physics, in association with the American Institute of Physics.
710 2 $a Institute of Physics (Great Britain) $e publisher
710 2 $a Institute of Physics and the Physical Society, $e publisher
710 2 $a American Institute of Physics, $e publisher
780 00 $a Journal of physics. A, General physics (Proceedings of the Physical Society)$x0022-3689$w(DLC)sn 94015712$w (OCoLC)4128703.
785 00 $t Journal of physics. A, Mathematical, nuclear and general $x0301-0015$w(DLC) 73643054$w(OCoLC)1786366.

Terms and months are transcribed as they are on the source of information.

Note on the record:

245 00	Record title as it appears on the sources of information including capitalization. Or follow appendix "A" for capitalization.
260 $c	Copyright date is not required if date of publication has been supplied; it is given here as an additional element.
300 $c	Is not core element. General instruction at 3.5.1.3 instructs catalogers to record centimeters using metric symbol "cm." An alternative to this instruction allows for recording dimensions in a system of measure preferred by cataloging agencies.

321, 362, 550	Terms and months are transcribed as they are on the source of information.
362	Giving numbering information in a formatted 362 (362 0) or an unformatted 362 (362 1) is permitted. No abbreviation in 362 field.
550	Issuing body note.
710 2	Location of corporate body's headquarters (Great Britain).
780 00	MARC coding 780 00 is RDA relationship "continues." No need for RDA relationship designators.
785 00	MARC coding 785 00 is RDA relationship "continued by."
$x and w	Identifiers are part of a structured description and are NOT used alone.

EXAMPLE 31

LEADER 01411cas a2200433 i 450
001 764633740
008 111130c20119999nyumr p 6 0 a0eng
010 $a 2011207119
040 $a DLC$cDLC$erda
022 0 $a 2164-8557 $2 1
130 0 $a Green Lantern (New York, N.Y. : 2011)
222 0 $a Green Lantern $b (New York, N.Y. 2011)
245 10 $a Green Lantern.
260 $a New York, NY : $b DC Comics, $c 2011-
300 $a numbers : $b chiefly color illustrations ; $c 26 cm
310 $a Monthly
336 $a still image $2 rdacontent
336 $a text $2 rdacontent
337 $a unmediated $2 rdamedia
338 $a volume $2 rdacarrier
362 0 $a 1 (November 2011)-
500 $a Title from indicia.
588 $a Latest issue consulted: 2 (December 2011).

Note on the record:

222 0	Serial Key title. The subfield "$b" is for qualifying information.
130 0	Preferred title of the serial. It includes place of the work and date of the work as a qualifier to differentiate works. Use subfield "$a" for both the title proper and the parenthetical qualifier.
588	If description is not based on first issue or part of serial, RDA 2.20.13.3 instructs to give a note identifying the issue or part used as the basis of the identification. RDA 2.20.13.3.1 instructs to make a note identifying the latest issue or part consulted in preparing the description.

EXAMPLE 32

LEADER 02274cas a2200505 i 450
001 760903440
010 $a 2011214985
040 $a DLC$cDLC$erda$dDLC
022 $a 2146-0264
041 0 $a tur $a eng
245 00 $a Anadolu Üniversitesi bilim ve teknoloji dergisi. $n C, $p Yaşam bilimleri ve biyoteknoloji = $b Anadolu University journal of science and technology. $n C, $p Life sciences and biotechnology.
246 11 $a Anadolu University journal of science and technology. $n C, $p Life sciences and biotechnology
246 13 $a Yaşam bilimleri ve biyoteknoloji
246 13 $a Life sciences and biotechnology
260 $a Eskişehir : $b Anadolu Üniversitesi, $c 2011-
300 $a volumes ; $c 29 cm.
310 $a Two issues yearly
336 $a text $2 rdacontent
337 $a unmediated $2 rdamedia
338 $a volume $2 rdacarrier
362 1 $a Began with cilt 1, sayı 1 (Şubat 2011).
490 0 $a Anadolu Üniversitesi yayınları
530 $a Also issued in electronic format.
546 $a Turkish and English; summaries in both languages.
588 $a Description based on: Cilt 1, sayı 1 (Şubat 2011); title from title page.
588 $a Latest issue consulted: Cilt 1, sayı 2 (Ağustos 2011).
710 2 $a Anadolu Üniversitesi.

776 08 $i Online version:: $t Anadolu Üniversitesi bilim ve teknoloji dergisi. C, Yaşam bilimleri ve biyoteknoloji eğitimi (Online) $x 2146-0213 $w (OCoLC)757850627
780 01 $t Anadolu Üniversitesi bilim ve teknoloji dergisi $x 1302-3160 $w (DLC) 2009212662 $w (OCoLC)234594019
856 41 $u http://btd.anadolu.edu.tr/index.php/BTDC/index

Note on the record:

588	If description is not based on first issue or part of serial, RDA 2.20.13.3 instructs to give a note identifying the issue or part used as the basis of the identification. RDA 2.20.13.3.1 instructs to make a note identifying the latest issue or part consulted in preparing the description.
776 08	Carrier of reproduction is not the same as carrier of original: use MARC 776. Provide relationship to the electronic version.
780 01	MARC coding 780 01 is RDA relationship "Continues in part." No need for RDA relationship designators.
856 41	MARC coding 865 41 is RDA relationship to the "Version of resource."

EXAMPLE 33

001 757847734
040 $a STF$erda$beng$cSTF
022 $a 2212-0335
041 0 $a eng $a fre
245 00 $a EYE international catalogue
246 18 $a EYE international film catalogue
260 $a Amsterdam : $b EYE Film Institute Netherlands, $c [2011]-
300 $a volumes : $b color illustrations ; $c 22 cm
310 $a Annual
336 $a text $2 rdacontent
337 $a unmediated $2 rdamedia
338 $a volume $2 rdacarrier
362 1 $a Began with 2011.
546 $a English, with film descriptions in English and French.
588 $a Description based on: 2011; title from title page.
710 2 $a EYE Film Instituut Nederland, $e issuing body.
780 00 $t Holland film $x 1385-0504

Note on the record:

260 $c	Beginning publication date supplied.
780 00	MARC coding 780 00 is RDA relationship "continues." No need for RDA relationship designators.

EXAMPLE 34

001 712624600
010 $a 2011208511
040 $a EQO$cEQO$erda$dNRC$dUKMGB$dCUS$dDLC
022 $a 2042-9738 $y 2042-9746
245 00 $a IET electrical systems in transportation.
246 30 $a Institute of Engineering and Technology electrical systems in transportation
246 1 $i At head of title: $a IET Journals
260 $a [United Kingdom] : $b Institute of Engineering and Technology, $c 2011-
300 $a Volume : $b illustrations ; $c 30 cm
310 $a Quarterly
336 $a text $b txt $2 rdacontent
337 $a unmediated $b n $2 rdamedia
338 $a volume $b nc $2 rdacarrier
362 1 $a Began with: Volume 1, issue 1 (March 2011).
530 $a Also issued online.
588 $a Description based on: Volume 1, issue 1 (March 2011); title from cover.
588 $a Latest issue consulted: Volume 1, issue 2 (June 2011).
710 2 $a Institution of Engineering and Technology, $e issuing body.
776 08 $i Online version: $t IET electrical systems in transportation $x 2042-9746 $w (DLC) 2011261048 $w (OCoLC)723082276 VIDOECATSSET

Note on the record:

260 $a	It is recommended to supply a probable place of publication when the place is not identified on the source of information. In this case, the probable place of publication is recorded in square brackets.
776 08	Carrier of reproduction is not the same as carrier of original: use MARC 776 to provide relationship to the electronic version.

EXAMPLE 35

Electronic Serial

LEADER 00000cas 2200000I i 4500
001 add 37664074
007 c $b r $d m $e n $f u
040 $a F#A$erda$cF#A$dOCL$dOCLCQ$dOCL$dGUA$dPFM$d SERSO$dCLU$dOCLCQ$dUKMGB
222 2 $a SCJ. Scandinavian cardiovascular journal $b (Online)
245 00 $a Scandinavian cardiovascular journal.
246 1 $a Scand Cardiovasc J
246 1 $a SCJ
260 $a [England] : $b Taylor & Francis, $c ©1990-
310 $a Six numbers a year
336 $a text $2 rdacontent
337 $a computer $2 rdamedia
338 $a online resource $2 rdacarrier
362 1 $a Began with volume 31, number 1 (1997).
515 $a Some numbers issued in combined form.
525 $a Has supplements.
550 $a Official organ of the Scandinavian Association for Thoracic Surgery ; and also the Swedish Society of Thoracic Surgeons and the Norwegian Cardiothoracic Surgery Society, 2010-
550 $a Endorsed by: Swedish Heart Association, 2010-
588 $a Description based on: Volume 31, number 1 (1997); title from contents screen (informa healthcare, viewed November 9, 2010).
588 $a Latest issue consulted: Volume 44, number 4 (2010) (viewed November 9, 2010).
710 2 $a Scandinavian Association for Thoracic Surgery, $e issuing body
710 2 $a Svensk thoraxkirurgisk förening, $e issuing body.
710 2 $a Norsk thoraxkirurgisk forening, $e issuing body.
710 2 $a Svenska hjärtförbundet, $e endorsing body.
770 08 $i Supplement (work): $t Scandinavian cardiovascular journal. Supplement $x 1401-7458 $w (DLC)sn 97039293 $w (OCoLC)247450129
776 08 $i Issued also in print: $t Scandinavian cardiovascular journal $x 1401-7431 $w (DLC)sn 97001726 $w (OCoLC)36869381
780 00 $t Scandinavian journal of thoracic and cardiovascular surgery $w (DLC) 2009247835 $w (OCoLC)319154748
856 40 $u http://informahealthcare.com/loi/cdv

The source had volume and number spelled out. Transcribe as they are on the source of information.

Note on the record:

260 $b	Publisher information was recorded as it appears on the source of information including "&."
260 $c	Date of publication not found in any resources. The copyright date is recorded proceeded with the appropriate symbol.
362 1	The source had volume and number spelled out. Transcribe as they are on the source of information. Giving numbering information in an unformatted 362 (362 1) is permitted.
550	Note referring to current and former issuing bodies.
710 $e	Relationships designation.
710s	Use the preferred languages for the issuing bodies (Svensk thoraxkirurgisk förening used instead of Swedish Association for Thoracic Surgery ; Norsk thoraxkirurgisk forening used instead of Norwegian Cardiothoracic Surgery Society; and Svenska hjärtförbundet used instead of Swedish Heart Association. See RDA 11.8.1.3 "Record the language or languages the body uses in its communications using an appropriate term or terms in the language preferred by the agency creating the data.")
770	This field indicates the relationship to the supplements.
780 00	MARC tag number and indicators show relationship of this title to the earlier title. No relationship designator is needed.

VISUAL MATERIALS

EXAMPLE 36

LEADER 00000cgm 2200409I i 4500
001 698747245
007 vf cbaho$
008 110128s1996 bl 060 vlpor d
040 $a OSU$cOSU$dOSU$dUtOrBLW$erda
245 00 $a Pantanal : $b Corumbá - Mato Grosso do Sul - Brasil / $c Jorciney Benites.
246 1 $i Title on cassette label : $a Pantanal sul Mato-grossense
246 30 $a Pantanal
260 $a Corumbá : $b JB Video Produções, $c [1996?]
300 $a 1 videocassette (60 min.) : $b sound, color ; $c 1/2 in.
336 $a two-dimensional moving image $2 rdacontent
337 $a video $2 rdamedia.
338 $a videocassette $2 rdacarrier.

500 $a Title from container.
538 $a VHS format.
700 1 $a Benites, Jorciney, $e producer.
710 2 $a JB Video Produções , $e production company.

Note on the record:

260 $c	Date of publication is in question.
300	Abbreviations for measurements of duration (RDA B.5.3) should be used. For example, min. (for minutes), sec.(for seconds), and in. (for inches)
336, 337, 338	Content type; media type and; carrier type for videocassette.
538	System requirements.
700 1	Access point for the production company.
700 1 $e	Relationship designators for the producer from appendix I.
710 2 $e	Relationship designators for the corporate body from appendix I.

EXAMPLE 37

001 727067696
007 v $b d $d c $e v $f a $g i $h z $i m
040 $a STF$beng$cSTF$erda$dOCLCA$dTEF$dOCLCA
024 1 $a 883316288849
046 $k 1963
245 00 $a Sunday in New York / $c Metro-Goldwyn-Mayer presents a Seven Arts production; screen play, Norman Krasna ; produced by Everett Freeman ; directed by Peter Tewksbury.
250 $a Remastered edition.
257 $a United States.
260 $a [Place of publication not identified] : $b [publisher not identified] ; $a Burbank, CA : $b Distributed by Warner Home Video, $c [2011], ©2011.
300 $a 1 videodisc (NTSC, 105 min.) : $b DVD video, Recorded DVD, sound, color ; $c 4 3/4 in.
336 $a two-dimensional moving image $2 rdacontent
337 $a video $2 rdamedia
338 $a videodisc $2 rdacarrier
380 $a Motion picture.
490 1 $a Archive collection
538 $a DVD, all regions, full screen (1.33:1) presentation; Dolby Digital mono.

511 1 $a Cliff Robertson, Jane Fonda, Rod Taylor, Robert Culp, Jo Morrow, Jim Backus, Peter Nero.
508 $a Director of photography, Leo Tover; music, Peter Nero; editor, Fredric Steinkamp.
500 $a Originally produced in the United States as a motion picture in 1963.
500 $a Based on Norman Krasna's play of the same title.
520 $a A sophisticated comedy concerning a young Albany girl's romantic misadventures with a man who she meets one rainy Sunday in New York. Complications result from the appearance of her airline-pilot brother and her home-town beau.
500 $a Includes trailer.
700 1 $a Krasna, Norman, $e screenwriter.
700 1 $a Freeman, Everett, $e film producer.
700 1 $a Tewksbury, Peter, $d 1924- $e film director.
700 1 $a Robertson, Cliff, $d 1923-2011, $e actor.
700 1 $a Fonda, Jane, $d 1937- $e actor.
700 1 $a Taylor, Rod, $d 1929- $e actor.
700 1 $a Culp, Robert, $d 1930-2010, $e actor.
700 1 $a Morrow, Jo, $d 1939- $e actor.
700 1 $a Backus, Jim, $e actor.
700 1 $a Nero, Peter, $d 1934- $e actor.
700 1 $i Motion picture adaptation of (work): $a Krasna, Norman, $e author. $t Sunday in New York.
710 2 $a Metro-Goldwyn-Mayer, $e presenter.
710 2 $a Seven Arts Productions, $e production company.
830 0 $a Archive collection.

Note on the record:

046 $k	The date or beginning of the date range on which a resource has been created when it is **not** more appropriately recorded in another field.
250	Edition statement recorded as it appears on the source of information.
257	Country of producing entity.
380	Form of work -- A term expressing the class or genre of the work.
700 1 $i	Designation of a relationship between the resource described in the 7xx field and the resource described in the 1xx/245 of the record.

EXAMPLE 38

001 721317074
007 v $b d $d c $e v $f a $g i $h z $i u
040 $a STF$beng$cSTF$erda$dSTF$dIWA$dOCLCA$dOCLCQ$d OCLCA$dINU$dVOC
024 3 $a 0797734486995
041 1 $a eng $j eng $j spa
046 $k 2010
245 00 $a Sex in an epidemic / $c producer/director/editor, Jean Carlomusto.
257 $a United States.
260 $a [New York, New York] : $b Outcast Films , $c [2011], ©2011.
300 $a 1 videodisc (61 min.) : $b sound, color with black and white sequences ; $c 4 3/4 in.
336 $a two-dimensional moving image $2 rdacontent
337 $a video $2 rdamedia
338 $a videodisc $2 rdacarrier
380 $a Motion picture.
538 $a DVD ; NTSC, region 1, Full screen 1.33:1.
546 $a In English; optional subtitles in Spanish.
546 $a Closed-captioned for the hearing-impaired.
500 $a Originally produced in the United States as a motion picture in 2010.
500 $a Extras include deleted scenes.
511 0 $a With Michael Shernoff, Richard Berkowitz, Larry Kramer, Rodger McFarlane, Cynthia Gomez, George Bellinger, Jr., Kenyon Farrow, Maxine Wolfe, Waheedah Shabazz El.
508 $a Music, Sam Sutton; production company, Sunyata Films.
505 0 $a Rare cancer NYC-- Birth of safer sex-- Political disease -- Women, AIDS, & activism -- Politics of prevention -- Preaching abstinence -- Prevention today -- Prevention justice -- Bonus scenes : Closing the baths ; Safe sex becomes safer ; How Magali got involved ; HIV Law Project Women's Group.
700 1 $a Carlomusto, Jean, $e film director, $e film editor, $e film producer.
700 1 $a Kramer, Larry, $e interviewee.
700 1 $a Shernoff, Michael, $d 1951-2008, $e interviewee.
700 1 $a White, Edmund, $d 1940- $e interviewee.
700 1 $a McFarlane, Rodger, $e interviewee.
700 1 $a Gómez, Cynthia A, $e interviewee.
700 1 $a Berkowitz, Richard, $d 1955- $e interviewee.
700 1 $a Wolfe, Maxine, $e interviewee.

700 1 $a Bellinger, George, $d 1955- $e interviewee.
700 1 $a Farrow, Kenyon, $e interviewee.
700 1 $a Sutton, Sam, $e composer.
710 2 $a Outcast Films, $e film distributor.
710 2 $a Sunyata Films, $e production company.

Note on the record:

046 $k	The date or beginning of the date range on which a resource has been created when it is not more appropriately recorded in another field.
250	Edition statement recorded as it appears on the source of information.
257	Country of producing entity.
380	Form of work.
700 10	Authorized access points for the contributors.
700 10 $e	Relationships designation for the authorized access points.

EXAMPLE 39

001 742060332
007 v $b d $d c $e v $f a $g i $h z $i m
040 $a STF$beng$cSTF$erda$dSTF$dTEF
024 1 $a 883316331231
046 $k 1963
245 04 $a The wheeler dealers / $c Metro-Goldwyn-Mayer presents ; a Filmways picture ; screenplay by George J.W. Goodman, Ira Wallach ; produced by Martin Ransohoff ; directed by Arthur Hiller.
250 $a Remastered edition.
257 $a United States.
260 $a [Place of publication not identified] : $b [publisher not identified] ; $a Burbank, CA : $b Distributed by Warner Home Video, $c [2011], ©2011.
300 $a 1 videodisc (NTSC, 105 min.) : $b DVD video, Recorded DVD, sound, color ; $c 4 3/4 in.
336 $a two-dimensional moving image $2 rdacontent
337 $a video $2 rdamedia
338 $a videodisc $2 rdacarrier
380 $a Motion picture.
490 1 $a Archive collection
538 $a All regions.

500 $a Originally produced in the United States as a motion picture in 1963.
500 $a Includes trailer.
511 1 $a James Garner, Lee Remick, Phil Harris, Chill Wills, Jim Backus, Louis Nye, John Astin, Elliott Reid, Patricia Crowley
508 $a Director of photography, Charles Lang; film editor, Tom McAdoo; music, De Vol.
500 $a Based on a novel by George J.W. Goodman.
500 $a Mono, widescreen 2.4:1.
521 8 $a Not rated.
700 1 $a Garner, James, $e act.
700 1 $a Remick, Lee, $e act.
700 1 $a Harris, Phil, $d 1904-1995, $e act.
700 1 $a Wills, Chill, $d 1902-1978, $e act.
700 1 $a Backus, Jim, $e act.
700 1 $a Nye, Louis, $e act.
700 1 $a Astin, John, $e act.
700 1 $a Reid, Elliott, $d 1920- $e act.
700 1 $a Crowley, Pat, $d 1933- $e act.
700 1 $a Hiller, Arthur, $e film director.
700 1 $a Ransohoff, Martin, $e film producer.
700 1 $i Motion picture adaptation of (work): $a Goodman, George J. W., $d 1930- $e author $t Wheeler dealers.
700 1 $a Goodman, George J. W., $d 1930- $e screenwriter.
700 1 $a Wallach, Ira, $d 1913-1995, $e screenwriter.
710 2 $a Metro-Goldwyn-Mayer, $e presenter.
710 2 $a Filmways Pictures, $e production company.
830 0 $a Archive collection.

Note on the record:

046 $k	The date or beginning of the date range on which a resource has been created when it is *not* more appropriately recorded in another field.
257	Country of producing entity.
380	Form of work.
538	Regional encoding—record the regional encoding if it is considered to be important for identification or selection.

EXAMPLE 40

LEADER 00000cgm 2200577I i 4500
001 707840717
007 vd cvaizu
008 110319p20101988nju074 vllat d
020 $a 9780769790510
020 $a 0769790518
024 1 $a 032031456495
040 $a OSU$cOSU$dOSU$dUtOrBLW$erda
100 1 $a Pärt, Arvo, $e composer.
245 10 $a St. John Passion / $c Arvo Pärt ; a Christopher Swann production in association with RM ARTS and Channel 4.
260 $a West Long Branch, NJ : $b Distributed by Kultur International Films, $c [2010]
300 $a 1 videodisc (74 minutes) : $b sound, color ; $c 12 cm
336 $a two-dimensional moving image $2 rdacontent
337 $a video $2 rdamedia
338 $a videodisc $2 rdacarrier
538 $a Region 1, NTSC; 4:3 full screen; LPCM sound.
500 $a Insert with chapter index.
508 $a Produced and directed by Christopher Swann.
511 0 $a Hilliard Ensemble (solo voices and instruments) ; Western Wind Choir ; Paul Hillier, conductor.
518 $a Performed in Durham Cathedral 1982.
520 $a Taken from chapters eighteen and nineteen of the Gospel according to St. John, the piece is sung in Latin and includes an introduction.
538 $a DVD format.
546 $a Sung in Latin with English subtitles.
700 1 $a Hillier, Paul, $e conductor.
700 1 $a Swann, Christopher, $e producer, $e director.
700 12 $a Pärt, Arvo. $t Johannespassion.
710 2 $a Hilliard Ensemble, $e performer.
710 2 $a Western Wind Chamber Choir, $e performer.
710 2 $a RM Arts (Firm), $e production company.
710 2 $a Channel Four (Great Britain), $e production company.
710 2 $a Kultur International Films, $e distributor.

Note on the record:

336, 337, 338	Content type; media type and; carrier type for videodisc.
538	Regional encoding—record the regional encoding if it is considered to be important for identification or selection.
538	System requirement
546	Language of the content
700 1	Access point for producers, conductor, and performers
710 2 ( )	"Channel Four (Great Britain)", shows the corporate body Headquarter location in parenthesis.

MAPS

EXAMPLE 41

LEADER 00000cem 2200000I i 4500
001 34783224
005 19970811085239.0
007 ajucanun
008 960524s1991 mnub ea 0 eng d
034 1 $a a$b19008000$dW0300000$eE0600000$fN0400000 $gS0300000
040 $a ALM$cALM$dOCL$dMIA$erda
043 $a f———
052 $a 8200
110 2 $a American Teaching Aids (Firm), $e cartographer.
245 10 $a Africa / $c American Teaching Aids ; designed by Naturally Graphics ; topography illustrated by Duane Barnhart.
246 1 $i Title on lesson plan: $a Map of Africa
255 $a Scale [approximately 1:19,008,000] $c (W 30°—E 60°/N 40°—S 30°)
260 $a Minneapolis, MN : $b ATA ; $a Asheville, N.C. : $b Poster Education [distributor], $c 1991.
300 $a 1 map : $b color; $c 54 x 56 cm.
336 $a cartographic image $2 rdacontent
337 $a sheet $2 rdamedia
338 $a cartographic image $2 rdacarrier
490 1 $a Lesson plan ; $v no. 284
490 1 $a Continents chart series ; $v ATA8278
500 $a Activities written by Patricia Rowe Gilkerson.

500 $a Designed as a part of Poster Education's unit plan on Africa, set no. AF9.
500 $a Lesson plan published by Poster Education in 1995.
500 $a Lesson plan follows National Geography Standards.
500 $a Includes statistical data.
500 $a Teacher's guide and reproducible geography activity sheets on verso.
700 1 $a Gilkerson, Patricia Rowe.
700 1 $a Barnhart, Duane C.
710 2 $a Naturally Graphics (Firm), $e cartographer.
710 2 $a Poster Education (Firm), $e cartographer.
830 0 $a Lesson plan ; $v no. 284.
830 0 $a Continents chart series ; $v ATA8278.

Note on the record:

110 2 $e	Designators to indicate relationships between a resource and persons, families, and corporate bodies associated with a resource are given in RDA appendix I.
336, 337, 338	Content type; media type and; carrier type for map.
255	The scale of the map.
710 2 ( )	Corporate body's headquarters location.
710 2 $e	Designators to indicate relationships between a resource and persons, families, and corporate bodies associated with a resource are given in RDA appendix I.

GLOBE

EXAMPLE 42

LEADER 00000nem 2200385I i 4500
001 663101735
007 d $b c $d c $e e $f u
008 100909s2010 gw bcgj d 0 eng d
034 1 $a a$b20000000
040 $a OSU$cOSU$dUtOrBLW$erda
049 $a OSUU
110 2 $a Columbus Globes GmbH, $e printer.
245 14 $a The Earth / $c Geo-Institut Columbus GmbH.
246 1 $i Also known as : $a Extreme raised relief classroom floor globe
255 $a Scale approximately 1:20,000,000.

260 $a Porta Westfalica, Germany : $b Geo-Institute Columbus GmbH ; $a Seattle, WA : $b [Distributed by] 1-World Globes & Maps, $c [2010?]
300 $a 1 globe : $b colored, raised relief on chrome plated steel stand ; $c 64 cm in diameter
336 $a cartographic three-dimensional form $2 rdacontent
337 $a unmediated $2 rdamedia
338 $a object $2 rdacarrier
500 $a Title and legend on meridian ring.
500 $a Raised-relief floor globe produced from vacuum-formed vinyl on hard foam.
500 $a Relief of landmass and ocean bottom shown by vinyl raised relief, shading, gradient tints, and spot heights.
520 2 $a A three-dimensional raised relief globe mounted on chrome plated steel pedestal with a 5-caster base supporting a plastic horizon ring. Adjustable in height from 47-51 inches with gyroscopic ability.
710 2 $a 1-World Globes & Maps, $e distributor.

Note on the record:

255	Approximately is spelled-out.
300 $c	The measurement is by the "diameter."
336, 337, 338	Notice the recording of the content type; media type, and carrier type for "globe."

SOUND RECORDING

EXAMPLE 43

001 744963951
006 m c
007 s $b d $d f $e s $f n $g $h n $i n $j m $k m $l n $m e $n d
007 c $b o $d c $e g $f a $g --- $h a $i u $j u $k m
040 $a CGU$beng$cCGU$erda$dUBY
041 1 $d fre $d eng
100 1 $a Hamasyan, Tigran, $d 1987- $e composer, $e performer.
245 10 $a Tigran Hamasyan / $c Tigran Hamasyan.
260 $a [Paris] : $b Jazz Magazine Jazzman : $b NEMM & Cie., $c [2011], ℗2011.
300 $a 1 audio disc : $b digital, CD audio, stereo ; $c 4 3/4 in.
336 $a performed music $2 rdacontent

336 $a two-dimensional moving image $2 rdacontent
337 $a audio $2 rdamedia
337 $a computer $2 rdamedia
338 $a audio disc $2 rdacarrier
511 0 $a Tigran Hamasyan, piano.
500 $a Issued with: Jazz magazine jazzman, no 628 (2011).
500 $a Enhance compact disc.
500 $a Disc includes video file.
538 $a System requirements: software to play MPEG4 video file.
505 0 $a The sky is cloudy (inédit) (1:59) -- Rain shadow ; What the waves brought (Tigran Hamasyan live à Summertime, présenté par Elsa Boublil sur France Inter) (10:49).
505 8 $a Video file: Session #01 : Looking for the block / Tigran Hamasyan ; réalisé par Jeremiah (5:30).
730 0 $a Jazz magazine jazzman, $n no 628.

Note on the record:

100	Multiple relationship designations.
336, 337, 338	Multiple content type; media type, and carrier type to address the accompanying materials.
500	Accompanying materials can be recorded in MARC 21 500 field as a note.
730 $a	Preferred title for a musical work.
730 0 $n	A numeric designation that is added to the preferred title for a musical work. It is a serial number, opus number, or thematic index number assigned to a musical work by a composer, publisher, or a musicologist.

EXAMPLE 44

001 706125882
006 m h
007 s ǂb d ǂd f ǂe m ǂf n ǂg g ǂh n ǂi n ǂj m ǂk m ǂl n ǂm e ǂn e
007 c ǂb o ǂd n ǂe g ǂf s
040 $a STFǂbengǂcSTFǂerdaǂdSTFǂdOCLCA
245 00 $a Harry James : ǂb Stanford Memorial Hall 1955.
246 30 $a Stanford Memorial Hall 1955
246 1 $a ǂi Title from container: ǂa Harry James at Stanford Memorial Hall in 1955
260 $a [U.S.] : ǂb [Roy A. Long], ǂc [2007]
300 $a 1 audio disc : ǂb WAV ; ǂc 4 3/4 in.
300 $a 1 computer disc : ǂb CD-ROM, WAV ; ǂc 4 3/4 in.

336 $a performed music ǂ2 rdacontent
337 $a audio ǂ2 rdamedia
337 $a computer ǂ2 rdamedia
338 $a audio disc ǂ2 rdacarrier
338 $a computer disc ǂ2 rdacarrier
511 0 $a Harry James with the Harry James Orchestra.
500 $a "This CD is a custom-made copy of an archival recording from our collection"--CD sleeve.
518 $o Recorded live by Roy A. Long ǂd 1955 ǂp Stanford, California.
538 $a Requires software to play WAV files.
500 $a Complete contents not known; listing created through listening.
505 1 $a Don't be that way -- Sleepy lagoon -- Midnight sun – That's all -- Stardust -- In a sentimental mood -- [unknown] [Ellington tune?] -- Hold my hand (vocal) -- Caravan -- [unknown] -- Young man with a horn -- [unknown] – Roll'em -- Body and soul (vocal) -- [unknown] [High noon? ; Friendly persuasion?] -- [unknown] (Buddy Rich, drums?) -- Embraceable you --
Trumpet blues -- Two o'clock jump).
700 1 $a James, Harry, ǂd 1916-1983, ǂe instrumentalist.
700 2 $a Harry James Orchestra, ǂe instrumentalist.

Note on the record:

260 $a	If the country, state, province, etc., of publication is known, supply that name
260 $c	If the date of publication is not identified, supply a probable date
300	Describe accompanying materials in MARC 21 field 300 $e *or* in a second 300 field, whichever seems most appropriate. *or* in a 500 note In this record the accompany materials were described in a second 300 MARC 21 tag.
337s and 338s	Multiple media type and Carrier type to records accompany materials.
518	Date/time and place of an event note
511	Participant or performer note

EXAMPLE 45

LEADER 00000cjm 2200000 i 4500

001 689075126

007 s $b d $d b $e s $f m $g e $h n $i n $j m $l l $m u $n e

040 $a EMU$beng$cEMU$erda

041 1 rus $e rus $e ger $g eng $g rus

245 00 $a Tikhie stranit͡sy = $b Whispering pages.

246 31 $a Whispering pages

260 $a [Russia] : $b Severnyĭ fond : $b Eskom Film, $c [between 1994 and 2000?]

300 $a 1 sound disc : $b analog, 33 1/3 rpm, stereo ; $c 12 in.

336 $a performed music $a spoken word $a sounds $2 rdacontent

337 $a audio $2 rdamedia

338 $a audio disc $2 rdacarrier

500 $a Soundtrack of the motion picture Tikhie stranit͡sy, directed by Aleksandr Sokurov and released in 1994.

546 $a In Russian with notes on container in Russian and English. Container includes libretto Kindertotenlieder in German and Russian.

511 0 $a Aleksandr Cherednik and Ekaterina [that is, Elizaveta] Korolëva, cast ; Lina Mkrtchi͡an, contralto ; Mariinsky Opera and Ballet House Orchestra ; Al′girdas Paulavichi͡us, conductor.

500 $a The soundtrack consists chiefly of Gustav Mahler's Kindertotenlieder presented in fragmented sections, and interspersed with some dialogue and background noises.

518 $a Recorded at the Lenfil′m Studio.

700 1 $a Cherednik, Aleksandr.

700 1 $a Korolëva, Elizaveta.

700 1 $a Mkrtchyan, Lina.

700 1 $a Paulavichi͡us, Al′girdas.

700 1 $i adaptation of (work) $a Mahler, Gustav, $d 1860-1911. $t Kindertotenlieder.

710 2 $a Mariinskiæi teatr (1991-). $b Orkestr.

730 0 $i Soundtrack of (work) $a Tikhie stranit͡sy.

Note on the record:

245 00	Parallel title.
260 $c	Probable range of dates.
511 0	Participant or Performer Note
518	Place of recording.
700 10	Relationship to original work "Adaptation of" in $i.

EXAMPLE 46

LEADER 00000cim 2200373i 4500
001 123944967
007 s $b d $d f $e s $f n $g g $h n $i n $j m $k m $l n $m e $n d
010 $a 2007569990
040 $a DLC$erda$beng$cDLC
024 1 $a 880364187827
028 02 $a AJ-1003 $b AntonJazz
033 0 $a 20031028 $b 4364 $c E66
245 00 $a holiday time / $c ANTON SCHWARTZ.
260 $a Oakland, CA, USA : $b AntonJazz, $c [2003?], ℗2003.
300 $a 1 compact disc : $b digital, optical, 1.4 m/s ; $c 4 3/4 in.
306 $a 002732
336 $a performed music $2 rdacontent
337 $a audio $2 rdamedia
338 $a audio disc $2 rdacarrier
500 $a Principally jazz arrangements by Anton Schwartz of Christmas standards.
511 1 $a Anton Schwartz, tenor sax ; Art Hirahara, piano ; John Wiitala, bass ; Tim Bulkley, drums.
518 $a Recorded $d on 2003 October 28, $p at Spark Studios, Emeryville, California.
500 $a HDCD encoded.
505 00 $t Jingle Bells / $r J.S. Pierpont $g (5:37) -- $t Winter Wonderland / $r R. Smith & $r F. Bernard $g (3:57) -- $t The Christmas Song / $r M. Torme & $r R. Wells -- $t Sleigh Ride / $r L. Anderson $g (4:33) -- $t In the Wee Small Hours of the Morning / $r D. Mann & $r B. Hilliard $g (7:20).
700 1 $a Schwartz, Anton, $d 1967- $e arranger, $e performer.
700 1 $a Hirahara, Art, $e performer.
700 1 $a Wiitala, John, $e performer.
700 1 $a Bulkley, Tim, $e performer.
700 12 $a Pierpont, James, $d 1822-1893. $t Jingle Bells; $o arranged.

Note on the record:

033 0	Date and time of an event.
306	Playing time.
511 1	Participant or Performer Note.
700 1$e $e	Multiple designators to indicate relationships between a resource and persons with a resource are given in RDA appendix I.
700 1	Access points for performers.

EXAMPLE 47

LEADER 02600cjm a2200481 i 450
001 690470551
007 s $b d $d f $e s $f n $g g $h n $i n $j m $k m $l n $m e $n d
040 $a DLC$beng$cDLC$erda
245 00 $a 14 DURANGUENSES Corazón acústico.
246 1 $i Title on container: $a 14 DURANGUENSES de Corazón acústico
246 3 $a Catorce DURANGUENSES de Corazón acústico
260 $a Woodland Hills, CA : $b Disa Records, $c [2009?], ℗2008
300 $a 1 compact disc : $b digital, optical, 1.4 m/s ; $c 4 3/4 in.
336 $a performed music $2 rdacontent
337 $a audio $2 rdamedia
338 $a audio disc $2 rdacarrier
500 $a Duranguense love songs and ballads.
546 $a Sung in Spanish.
511 0 $a Grupo Montéz de Durango (1st, 8th works); K-Paz de la Sierra (2nd, 9th, 13th works); Patrulla 81 (3rd, 10th works); Brazeros Musical de Durango (4th work); Los Creadorez del Pasito Duranguense (5th work); Los Horóscopos de Durango (6th, 12th works); La Autoridad de la Sierra (7th work); Isabela (11th work); Alacranes Musical (14th work).
530 $a Available also in MP3 digital audio format, downloadable as complete album or as individual tracks, from various online music vendors.
500 $a Compilation of selections previously issued 2004-2008.
505 0 $a Como en los buenos tiempos -- Si tú te fueras de mí -- Como me haces falta --Ando buscando un amor -- Que lástima -- Dos locos --Todo cambió -- Bachata rosa -- Te juro que te amo -- Eres divina -- A quién --Mi amor por tí --Y acquí estoy --Por tu amor.
710 22 $a Grupo Montéz de Durango, $e composer. $t Como en los buenos tiempos.
710 2 $a Grupo Montéz de Durango, $e performer.
710 2 $a K-Paz de la Sierra (Musical group), $e performer.
710 2 $a Patrulla 81 (Musical group), $e performer
710 2 $a Brazeros Musical de Durango (Musical group), $e performer.
710 2 $a Creadorez del Pasito Duranguense de Alfredo Ramírez (Musical group), $e performer.
710 2 $a Horóscopos de Durango (Musical group), $e performer.
710 2 $a Autoridad de la Sierra (Musical group), $e performer.
700 0 $a Isabela $c (Musician), $e performer.
710 2 $a Alacranes Musical, $e performer.

Note on the record:

245	Title is recorded as it is on the source of information. Notice that it is in capital letters.
260 $c	Probable year. Copyright date is record's copyright date, preceded with the appropriate symbol.
546	Language of content.
511	Participant or performer note.
500	Note to show relationships to other compilation of selections that was previously issued in 2004-2008.
700 1 $c	Forename and the $c is for title associated with a name.
710	Corporate body authorized access points.

COMPILATIONS OF MUSICAL WORKS

EXAMPLE 48

001 801675419
007 s $b d $d f $e s $f n $g g $h n $i n $j m $k m $l n $m e $n d
040 $a BKX$beng$cBKX$erda
041 1 $g ger $g fre $g eng $m ger $m eng
100 1 $a Krommer, Franz, $d 1759-1831, $e composer.
240 1 $a Concertos. $k Selections
245 10 $a Clarinet concertos / $c Krommer.
260 $a Thun, Switzerland : $b Claves Records, $c [2012]
300 $a 1 CD (70 min., 19 sec.) : $b digital, stereo ; $c 4 3/4 in.
336 $a performed music $2 rdacontent
337 $a audio $2 rdamedia
338 $a audio disc $2 rdacarrier
381 $a Selections
382 $b clarinet $n 1 $a chamber orchestra
382 $b clarinet $n 2 $a chamber orchestra
383 $b op. 36 $b op. 86 $b op. 35
500 $a Title from spine.
500 $a Op. 86 originally for flute and orchestra, arr. by Joseph Küffner.
511 1 $a Thomas Friedli, Antony Pay (op. 35), clarinets ; English Chamber Orchestra ; Antony Pay, conductor.
518 $a Recorded at Henry Wood Hall, London, September 1985.
500 $a Originally released in 1986.

500 $a Program notes in English and German by Verena Weibel-Trachsler with French translation in container insert.
505 0 $a Clarinet concerto in E-flat major, op. 36 -- Clarinet concerto in E minor, op. 86 -- Concerto for two clarinets in E-flat major, op. 35.
700 1 $a Friedli, Thomas, $d 1946- $e instrumentalist.
700 1 $a Pay, Antony, $e instrumentalist, $e conductor.
700 1 $a Küffner, Joseph, $d 1776-1856, $e arranger.
700 12 $a Krommer, Franz, $d 1759-1831. $t Concertos, $m clarinet, orchestra, $n op. 36, $r E♭ major.
700 12 $a Krommer, Franz, $d 1759-1831. $t Concertos, $m flute, orchestra, $n op. 86, $r E minor; $o arr.
700 12 $a Krommer, Franz, $d 1759-1831. $t Concertos, $m clarinets (2), orchestra, $n op. 35, $r E♭ major.
710 2 $a English Chamber Orchestra, $e performer.

Note on the record:

240	Use a term chosen by the cataloger if the compilation contains the complete works in a single form.
381	"Any characteristic that is not accommodated in a special field that serves to characterize a work or expression. Examples are an issuing body, arranged statement of music, version, or a geographic term. May be used to differentiate a work from another work with the same title." Definition is from MARC Formats for Bibliographic Data.
382	Multiple medium of performance (RDA 6.15)-- A term that indicates the instrumental, vocal, and/or other medium of performance . It is a core element for musical works that may be recorded as separate element, as additions to access points or as both, to differentiate a musical work from another work with the same name.
383	"A serial number, opus number, or thematic index number assigned to a musical work by the composer, publisher, or a musicologist. May be used to differentiate a musical work from another with the same title." Definition is from MARC Formats for Bibliographic Data.

MUSIC SCORE

EXAMPLE 49

LEADER 00000cam 2200617 i 4500
001 704353100
040 $a CGU$beng$cCGU$erda
100 1 $a Bremner, Robert, $d died 1789, $e arranger.

245 14 $a The songs in The gentle shepherd / $c adapted for the guitar by Robert Bremner.
260 $a [Place of publication not identified] : $b [publisher not identified], $c [date of publication not identified] $e ([Edinburgh] : $f [National Library of Scotland], $g [2011?])
300 $a 1 score (17 leaves) ; $c 21 x 30 cm
336 $a notated music $2 rdacontent
337 $a unmediated $2 rdamedia
338 $a volume $2 rdacarrier
500 $a Songs from the ballad opera The gentle shepherd by Allan Ramsay, transcribed for solo guitar.
546 $a Music includes lyrics of songs in English.
534 $p Photocopy of: $c Edinburgh : Sold at his music shop, [1759.]. $n Original held by the $l National Library of Scotland. $n Date of publication from NLS public catalog, accessed 25 February 2011.
546 $b staff notation.
500 $a Production information determined from acquisition records.
700 1 $i musical arrangement of (work): $a Ramsay, Allan, $d 1686-1758. $t Gentle shepherd.

Note on the record:

260 $a	Place of publication not identified.
260 $b	Publisher not identified.
260 $e	Manufacture information.
534	Original Version Note.
700 1 $i	Relationship information to another work.

EXAMPLE 50

001 676869564
040 $a DLC$beng$cDLC$erda$dDLC
245 00 $a Seven muses : $b a contemporary anthology for flute and piano.
246 3 $a 7 muses
260 $a [United States?] : $b Theodore Presser Company, $c [2010?]
300 $a 1 score (56 pages) + 1 part (19 pages) ; $c 31 cm.
336 $a notated music $2 rdacontent
337 $a unmediated $2 rdamedia
338 $a volume $2 rdacarrier
490 0 $a Flute music by women composers

505 0 $a Demon's dance from Medieval suite / Katherine Hoover -- Movement II from Sonata / Lita Grier -- Movement I from Concerto for flute, strings, and percussion / Melinda Wagner -- Vignette / Eugénie R. Rocherolle--Movement III from The golden flute / Chen Yi -- Movement II from Concerto for flute and orchestra / Ellen Taaffe Zwilich -- Pastorale / Germain Tailleferre.
700 1 $a Hoover, Katherine, $d 1937- $t Medieval suite. $p Demon's dance
700 1 $a Rocherolle, Eugénie R. $t Vignette.
700 1 $a Tailleferre, Germaine, $d 1892-1983. $t Pastorales, $m flute, piano.

Note on the record:

260 $a	If the place of publication is uncertain, indicate its probable place of publication by a question mark.
260 $c	Probable date of publication.
700s	When the compilation is not complete, identify each of the works in the compilation separately.
700 $m	Numeric designation. Provide as many numeric designations as available.

EXAMPLE 51

001 701014749
040 $a OHX$beng$cOHX$erda$dCGU$dDLC
100 1 $a Saint-Saëns, Camille, $d 1835-1921.
240 10 $a Suites, $m violoncello, piano, $n op. 16, $r D minor
245 10 $a Suite for violoncello and piano = $b für Violoncello und Klavier, opus 16 : original version = Originalfassung / $c Camille Saint-Saens ; herausgegeben von = edited by Maria Kliegel.
246 31 $a Suite für Violoncello und Klavier
246 31 $a Originalfassung
260 $a Mainz : $b Schott, $c [2010], ©2010.
300 $a 1 score (43 pages) and 1 part (17 pages) ; $c 31 cm.
336 $a notated music $2 rdacontent
337 $a unmediated $2 rdamedia
338 $a volume $2 rdacarrier
490 1 $a Cello library = Cello-Bibliothek
546 $b Staff notation.
700 1 $a Kliegel, Maria, $e editor.
830 0 $a Cello Bibliothek.

Note on the record:

240 10 $m, $n, $r	[$m] Numeric Designation (RDA 6.16)[$n]and Key (RDA 6.17)[$r] are core elements for musical works that may be recorded as separate elements, as additions to access points or as both to differentiate a musical work from another work with the same name.
245 10 $b	Multiple parallel titles.

EXAMPLE 52

001 713182143
040 $a TDF$beng$cTDF$erda$dCGU$dOHX$dNUI
100 1 $a Adler, Samuel, $d 1928- $e composer.
245 10 $a Festival fanfare and dance : $b for brass ensemble and timpani / $c Samuel Adler.
260 $a [King of Prussia, PA] : $b Theodore Presser Company, $c [2011], ©2011.
300 $a 1 score (20 pages) ; $c 28 cm
306 $a 000800
336 $a notated music $2 rdacontent
337 $a unmediated $2 rdamedia
338 $a volume $2 rdacarrier
500 $a For 3 trumpets, 3 horns, 2 trombones, tuba, and timpani.
500 $a Cover title.
500 $a "August 31, 2009"—at end.
546 $b Staff notation.
500 $a "Transposed score"— replace by Caption.
500 $a Duration: approximately 8 min.

Note on the record:

306	Playing time.
546 $b	Form of musical notation—record the form of musical notation used to express the musical content of the resource.

EXAMPLE 53

001 768165723
040 $a OHX$erda$beng$cOHX$dDLC$dTDF$dCGU$dSTF
020 $a 9783890074801
020 $a 3890074804
041 0 $g ger $g eng $m ger
100 1 $a Beethoven, Ludwig van, $d 1770-1827, $e composer.

240 10 $a Romances, $m violin, orchestra, $n op. 50, $r F major
245 10 $a Romanze F-Dur für Violine und Orchester, op. 50 : $b Faksimile nach dem Autograph der Library of Congress, Washington / $c Ludwig van Beethoven ; mit einem Kommentar von Stefan Drees.
250 $a Facsimile edition.
260 $a Laaber : $b Laaber-Verlag, $c [2011], ©2011.
300 $a 1 score (12, 24 pages) : $b color facsimiles ; $c 25 x 31 cm.
336 $a notated music $2 rdacontent
337 $a unmediated $2 rdamedia
338 $a volume $2 rdacarrier
490 1 $a Meisterwerke der Musik im Faksimile ; $v Band 20
500 $a Color facsimile of autograph manuscript held by the Library of Congress, ML30.8b.B4 op. 50 Case.
546 $a Introduction in German with English translation (pages [5]-12).
700 1 $a Drees, Stefan, $d 1966- $e writer of added commentary.
710 2 $i Reproduction of (item) : $a Library of Congress. $k Manuscript. $n ML30.8b .B4 op. 50 Case.
830 0 $a Meisterwerke der Musik im Faksimile ; $v Bd. 20.

Note on the record:

240 10 $m,n,r	Medium of performance, numeric designation of the musical work, and the key.
710 2 $i	Related item—it is a core LC element for reproductions when it is important to identify the specific item that was reproduced.

EXAMPLE 54

001 793653629
040 $a VGM$erda$cVGM
100 1 $a Bach, Johann Christoph Friedrich, $d 1732-1795, $e composer.
240 10 $a Sonatas, $m keyboard instrument, flute, violin, $n W. VII, 7, $r C major.
245 10 $a Sonate für Flöte, Violine und konzertierendes Cembalo (Klavier), C-Dur = $b for flute, violin and obbligato harpsichord (piano), C major / $c Johann Christoph Friedrich Bach ; Edited by Frank Nagel.
260 $a Mainz : $b Schott ; $b Distributed in North and South America exclusively by Hal Leonard, $c [between 2000 and 2010], ©1970.

300 $a 1 score (24 pages) + 2 parts ; $c 31 cm.
336 $a notated music $2 rdacontent
337 $a unmediated $2 rdamedia
338 $a volume $2 rdacarrier
382 $a harpsichord $a flute $a violin
382 $a piano $a flute $a violin
384 $a C major
491 0 $a Antiqua $v 9
500 $a Distributor information from label on page 4 of cover.
546 $b Staff notation.
700 1 $a Nagel, Frank, $e editor.

Note on the record:

240 10 $m,n,r	Medium of performance, numeric designation of the musical work, and the key.
382	Multiple medium of performance (RDA 6.15)-- A term that indicates the instrumental, vocal, and/or other medium of performance. It is a core element for musical works that may be *recorded as separate elements, as additions to access points or as both*, to differentiate a musical work from another work with the same name.
384	The Key (RDA 6.17) --The pitch name and the mode (e.g., major or minor). It is a core elements for musical works that may be recorded as separate elements, as additions to access points or as both, to differentiate a musical work from another work with the same name.

LIBRETTOS

EXAMPLE 55

LEADER 02796cjm a2200553 i 450
001 690470610
007 s $b d $d f $e s $f n $g g $h n $i n $j z $k m $l n $m e $n d
010 $a 2010619295
040 $a DLC$erda$beng$cDLC
033 0 $a 19770319 $b 3804 $c N4
033 0 $a 20080119 $b 3804 $c N4
041 $d ita $d eng
100 1 $a Puccini, Giacomo, $d 1858-1924.
245 13 $a La Bohème / c Giacomo Puccini.
260 $a [New York] : $b Toll Brothers-Metropolitan Opera International Radio Network, $c [2008]

300 $a 3 compact discs (2 hrs., 28 min., 27 sec.) : $b digital, optical, 1.4 m/s ; $c 4 3/4 in.
306 $a 022827
336 $a performed music $2 rdacontent
337 $a audio $2 rdamedia
338 $a audio disc $2 rdacarrier
500 $a Radio broadcast of opera in 4 acts.
500 $a Music by Giacomo Puccini; libretto by Luigi Illica and Giuseppe Giacosa, based on Scènes de la vie de bohème by Henri Murger.
546 $a Sung in Italian; announcements, interviews, and features in English.
511 0 $a Cast: Renata Scotto, Luciano Pavarotti, Maralin Niska, Ingvar Wixell, Allan Monk, Paul Plishka, and various singers; Metropolitan Opera Orchestra and Chorus, James Levine, conductor; Margaret Juntwait, host
518 $a Originally broadcast on 1977 March 19, from the Metropolitan Opera House, New York; re-broadcast 2008 January 19, over the Toll Brothers-Metropolitan Opera International Radio Network
500 $a Recordable compact discs.
500 $a Includes interviews with various singers and Metropolitan Opera staff, most of which concern Pavarotti's famous performances at the Metropolitan Opera, and other excerpts of historical performances; recordings include breaks for local station identifications.
700 1 $a Illica, Luigi, $d 1857-1919, $e librettist.
700 1 $a Giacosa, Giuseppe, $d 1847-1906, $e librettist.
700 1 $a Scotto, Renata, $d 1934- $e performer.
700 1 $a Pavarotti, Luciano, $d 1935-2007, $e performer.
700 1 $a Niska, Maralin, $d 1930- $e performer.
700 1 $a Wixell, Ingvar, $d 1931- $e performer.
700 1 $a Monk, Allan, $d 1942- $e performer.
700 1 $a Plishka, Paul, $d 1941- $e performer.
700 1 $a Levine, James, $d 1943- $e conductor.
700 1 $a Juntwait, Margaret, $e host.
700 1 $i Libretto for (work) $a Murger, Henri, $d 1822-1861. $t Scènes de la vie de Bohème.
710 2 $a Metropolitan Opera (New York, N.Y.), $e performer.

Note on the record:

033 0	Date/Time and Place of an Event, and it is repeatable.
041	Language of the content and it is recorded also in the 546 field.
306	Playing time.
511 0	A note about the participants, players, narrators, presenters or performers.
518	Date/Time and Place of an Event Note.
700s	Record all the participants with $e "Relationship designation."
700 1 $i	See appendix J.2.5 to use the phrase $i Libretto for (work), in order to provide an access point for the libretto, which is a related work to the musical work. If the composer is mentioned in the libretto, an access point may be made for the composer.

EXAMPLE 56

001 810775676
010 $a2012564221
040 $a DLC‡erda‡beng‡cDLC‡dOSU
100 1 $a Jennens, Charles, ‡d 1700-1773, ‡e librettist.
245 10 $a Messiah : ‡b an oratorio : as it is performed at the Theatre Royal in the Hay-market / ‡c set to music by Mr. Handel.
260 $a London : ‡b [publisher not identified], ‡c [1769]
300 $a 16 pages ; ‡c 19 cm
336 $a text ‡2 rdacontent
337 $a unmediated ‡2 rdamedia
338 $a volume ‡2 rdacarrier
500 $a Title from cover.
500 $a Libretto compiled by Charles Jennens from the Bible and the Prayer Book Psalter; cf. Grove music online.
541 $c Purchased; ‡a Simon Beattie; ‡d July 11, 2012.
700 1 $i Libretto for (work): ‡a Handel, George Frideric, ‡d 1685-1759. ‡t Messiah.

Note on the record:

100 $e	Librettist is a relationship designator for an author of a libretto of an opera or other stage work, or an oratorio. (RDA appendix I)
245 $c	Statement of responsibility is transcribed in the form in which it appears on the source of information. (RDA 2.4.1.4) If a noun or noun phrase occurs with a statement of responsibility, treat the noun or noun phrase as part of the statement of responsibility. (RDA 2.4.1.8)
541 $c	Source of acquisition.
700 $i	Relationship information to other work.

INTEGRATED RESOURCES—LOOSE-LEAF

EXAMPLE 57

LEADER 00000cam 2200517 i 4500
001 74447042
010 $a 2010217962 $z 2006933602
040 $a SLL$beng$cSLL$dSLL$dOCLCQ$dDLC$erda
020 $a 1575894149 (loose-leaf)
020 $a 9781575894140 (loose-leaf)
043 $a n-us-ma
245 00 $a Child welfare practice in Massachusetts / $c editor, Amy M. Karp [and 16 others].
260 $a Boston, MA : $b MCLE, $c 2006-
300 $a volumes (loose-leaf) : $b illustrations, forms ; $c 27 cm + $e 1 CD-ROM (4 3/4 in.)
336 $3 book $a text $2 rdacontent
336 $3 computer disc $a text $2 rdacontent
337 $3 book $a unmediated $2 rdamedia
337 $3 computer disc $a computer $2 rdamedia
338 $3 book $a volume $2 rdacarrier
338 $3 computer disc $a computer disc $2 rdacarrier
500 $a "2070218B01"—Title page verso.
500 $a CD-ROM contains forms and documents in PDF and Word format.
538 $a System requirements for CD-ROM: desktop computer with CD-ROM drive; Adobe Acrobat; word processing software capable of reading Word documents.
588 $a Description based on: 1st supplement 2009.
700 1 $a Karp, Amy M.
710 $a Massachusetts Containing Legal Education, Inc. (1982-)

Note on the record:

245 00 $c	In the statement of responsibility, the name of first editor was recorded and the number of other editors was included in brackets.
300 $e	Accompanying materials.
336, 337, 338 $3	Notice the use of $3 "Materials specified" in 336, 337, 338. Multiple 336,337,338 for the related work "accompanying material."
500	Note on the content of the accompanying materials.
538	System requirements.

COMPUTER FILE

EXAMPLE 58

LEADER 03034cmm a2200517 i 450
001 624618368
007 c $b o $d c $e g $f a
007 a $b j $d c $e a $f n $g z $h n
040 $a DLC$beng$cDLC$erda
245 00 $a Red dead redemption / $c Rockstar Games presents.
250 $a PlayStation 3.
260 $a New York, New York : $b Rockstar Games, $c [2010], ©2010.
300 $a 1 computer disc : $b sound, color ; $c 4 3/4 in. +$e 1 instruction manual (24 pages : illustrations ; 13 X 16 cm) + 1 map (50 X 78 cm folded to 13 X 16 cm)
336 $a two-dimensional moving image $a text $a cartographic image $2 rdacontent
337 $a computer $a unmediated $2 rdamedia
338 $a computer disc $2 rdacarrier
338 $a volume $2 rdacarrier
338 $a sheet $2 rdacarrier
380 $a Video game
500 $a Game features: third-person 3D shooter; open-world action-adventure in the Wild West; play as a dangerous outlaw trying to make good; bring an old partner back to justice, dead or alive; missions of six-gun shootouts and stealthy sabotage; travel the land on horseback, by stagecoach, or ride the railroads.
500 $a PlayStation Network features: multiplayer; leaderboards; lobbies/matchmaking ; invite in game; voice chat; add-on content ; PlayStation home; trophies.

500	$a Sources used: Internet movie database WWW site, viewed November 15, 2010; Allgame WWW site, viewed November 30, 2010; Copyright staff catalog.
520	$a "America, 1911. The Wild West is dying. When federal agents threaten his family, former outlaw John Marsten is forced to pick up his guns again and hunt down the gang of criminals he once called friends. Experience an epic fight for survival across the sprawling expanses of the American West and Mexico, as John Marsten struggles to bury his blood-stained past, one man at a time"--Container.
538	$a System requirements: PlayStation 3; 600 MB hard drive space ; HD video output 720p ; Dualshock 3 controller; broadband
538	$a Blu-ray Disc; wide screen
538	$a Blu-ray Disc; region 1; wide screen.
710 2	$a Rockstar Games (Firm), $e video game developer, $e publisher
710 2	$a Copyright Collection (Library of Congress) $5 DLC

Note on the record:

250	Edition on the source "PlayStation 3"
300 $e	Accompanying materials.
336	Content of the computer file includes three categories: moving image (for the computer file), text (for the manual) and cartographic image (for the map).
338	Carrier type was repeated to present the carrier of the accompanying materials as well as the computer file.
	Form of the work.
380	System requirements.
538	The third MARC 21 tag "538" is used for regional encoding.
710	The second MARC 21 710 field included item specific information "Copyright Collection (Library of Congress").

SIMULTANEOUS PUBLICATION— DIFFERENT TITLES IN SAME LANGUAGE

"If the work is published simultaneously in the same language under different titles, choose the title proper of the first resource received as the preferred title" (RDA 6.2.2.4).

EXAMPLE 59

United States edition was received first:

100 10 $a Penny, Louise.
245 12 $a A rule against murder / $c by Louise Penny.
250 $a first U.S. edition.
260 $a New York : ǂb Minotaur Books, ǂc 2009.
300 $a viii, 322 pages ; ǂc 25 cm

Note on the record:

245	The preferred title will be based on the title proper of the manifestation first received. In this case, the United States edition was received first in the library and the title proper was recorded in MARC 21 tag 245.

EXAMPLE 60

The UK edition was received later:

100 10 $a Penny, Louise.
240 10 $a Rule against murder
245 14 $a The murder stone / $c by Louise Penny.
260 $a London : $b Headline, $c 2008.
300 $a viii, 312 pages ; ǂc 24 cm

Note on the record:

240	The UK edition is received later. Create a new record and use the preferred title for the US edition in MARC 21 tag 240.
245	Record the proper title for the UK edition in MARC tag 245.

EXAMPLE 61

The UK edition was received first:

100 10 $a Penny, Louise.
245 14 $a The murder stone / $c by Louise Penny.
260 $a London : $b Headline, $c 2008.
300 $a viii, 312 pages ; ǂc 24 cm

Note on the record:

245	The preferred title will be based on the title proper of the manifestation first received. In this case, the UK edition was received first in the library and the title proper was recorded in MARC 21 tag 245.

EXAMPLE 62

The US edition was received later:

100 10 $a Penny, Louise.
240 10 $a Murder stone
245 12 $a A rule against murder / $c by Louise Penny.
250 $a first U.S. edition.
260 $a New York : ǂb Minotaur Books, ǂc 2009.
300 $a viii, 322 pages ; ǂc 25 cm.

Note on the record:

240	The US edition is received later. Create a new record and use the preferred title for the UK edition in MARC 21 tag 240.
245	Record the proper title for the US edition in MARC tag 245.

II. AUTHORITY RECORDS

Some of the following examples were updated to include only the new RDA fields for authority records. However, the records continue to be coded based on AACR2. These records were created as part of the RDA test for headings, which are used in bibliographic records created following RDA guidelines and the Library of Congress Policy Statements. In this case, you will find the new authorized access points in MARC 21 field 700 first indicator 1 and second indicator 4. Some RDA headings are the same as those in AACR2, but some have changed.

EXAMPLE 1

000 00591cz a2200181n 450
001 8451440
005 20101026064256.0
008 101021n$ azannaabn $n aaa c
010 $a no2010171522
035 $a (OCoLC)oca08663815
040 $a UPB$beng$cUPB$erda$dUPB
046 $f 18861002 $g 19150317
100 1 $a Girard, Louis, $d 1886-1915

370 $b Souain-Perthes-lès-Hurlus, France
374 $a soldier
375 $a male
377 $a fre
670 $a Fusillés pour l'exemple, 2002: $b page 4 of cover (Louis Girard) page 59 (né le 2 octobre 1886) front cover (fusillé le 17 mars 1915 à Souain)

Note on the record:

008 10	Descriptive cataloging rules, use "z" for other rule
040 $e	Description conventions "rda"
046 $f and $g	Special coded dates. $f is birth date and $g is death date. Notice that the year, month and day are included in 046
370	Associated place
374	Occupation
375	Gender
377	Associated language

EXAMPLE 2

000 00870cz a2200193n 450
001 8478939
005 20110209062924.0
008 101118n$ azannaabn $a ana c
010 $a no2010188360
035 $a (OCoLC)oca08691108
040 $a UPB$beng$cUPB$erda$dWaU
046 $s 2007
110 2 $a Bowler Press
370 $e North Vancouver, B.C.
371 $a 53 Bewicke Ave $b North Vancouver $c BC $e V7M 3B6 $d Canada $m print@thebowlerpress.ca $u www.thebowlerpress.ca/
372 $a Fine press printing
500 1 $w r $i Founder: $a Morrison, Jarrett $q (Jarrett Stephen), $d 1973-
670 $a The importance of being earnest, MMVIII, 2008, ©2008 : $b title page (The Bowler Press) title page verso (located in North Vancouver, B.C.)
670 $a The Bowler Press website, 18 November 2010 $b (printer of fine press editions; founded by Jarrett Morrison in 2007) $u www.thebowlerpress.ca/

Note on the record:

040 $e	Description conventions "rda."
046 $s	Special coded dates: start period (start date for period of activity).
370	Associated place.
371	Address. Notice here the $u for the Uniform Resource Identifier.
372	Field of activity.

EXAMPLE 3

000 01974cz a2200265n 450
001 6230224
005 20110906082608.0
008 040422n$ acannaabn $n aaa
010 $a n 2004073151
035 $a (OCoLC)oca06331362
040 $a DLC$beng$cDLC$dUPB$dDLC
046 $f 1939
100 1 $a Schechter, Joel
370 $c U.S.
371 $a University of Southern California, Health Sciences Campus, BMT 306, M/C 9112 $b Los Angeles $c California $e 90089-9112
372 $a cell structure and organization $a endocrinology/metabolism $a vision research $a immunology $s 1968
372 $a cell biology $a neurobiology
373 $a University of Southern California $s 1969
374 $a professor $a dean
670 $a Histology, c2003 : $b disc label (Joel Schechter)
670 $a Sinauer Associates, Inc., Publishers Website, Apr. 22, 2004 : $b Histology page (Joel E. Schechter, Keck School of Medicine of the University of Southern California)
670 $a University of Southern California, Faculty directory, via WWW, 29 November 2010 $b (PIBBS Research Faculty, Joel E. Schechter, professor, Cell & Neurobiology, Keck School of Medicine; office: BMT 306, mail code, 9112 HSC; education, MA 1963 Medical Illustration—Johns Hopkins University, Baltimore, Maryland; PhD 1968 Anatomy—University of California, Los Angeles; postdoctoral research fellowship: 1968-1969—University of California, Los Angeles; started at USC: 1969; research topics: cell structure & organization, endocrinology/metabolism, vision research, immunology)

faculty, staff and affiliate directory (Joel Schechter, professor of cell and neurobiology assistant dean of student affairs and of the basic science curriculum; address: University of Southern California, Health Sciences Campus, BMT 306, M/C 9112, Los Angeles, CA 90089-9112)
670 $a Call to Joel Schechter, 29 November 2010 $b (confirmed middle initial, birth year 1939)
700 14 $a Schechter, Joel $q (Joel E.), $d 1939-

Note on the record:

008 10	Descriptive cataloging rules, "a" for AACR2 rule.
040	Description conventions is not RDA—this record was updated to include RDA files, but the not the instructions.
046 $f	Special coded dates: Birth date.
370	Associated place.
372	Field of activity (notice the multiple 372 to indicate multiple fields of activity).
373	Affiliation.
374	Occupation.
700 14	This field includes the authorized access point for the person based on RDA instructions.

EXAMPLE 4

000 02364cz a2200433n 450
001 4260561
005 20111222074837.0
008 820429n$ acannaabn $a aaa
010 $a n 82045212 $z no 2008102404
035 $a (OCoLC)oca00742198
040 $a DLC$beng$cDLC$dDLC$dOCoLC$dUPB$dDLC$dUPB$d Uk$dP$dUPB
046 $f 19330923
100 1 $a Wilson, William A. $q (William Albert), $d 1933-
370 $e Logan, Utah $e Provo, Utah
372 $a Folklore
372 $a English language and literature
373 $a Brigham Young University
373 $a BYU Folklore Archives

373 $a Charles Redd Center for Western Studies
373 $a American Folklore Society
373 $a Utah State University
373 $a Association for Mormon Letters
373 $a Fife Folklore Conference
374 $a Mormon folklorist
374 $a University professor
374 $a University administrator
374 $a Author
374 $a Editor
400 1 $w nne $a Wilson, William Albert
400 1 $a Wilson, Bert, $d 1933-
670 $a His Folklore and nationalism in modern Finland, c1976.
670 $a His Folklore and nationalism in modern Finland, 1974 : $b vita (b. 9/23/53)
670 $a What's true in Mormon history : the contribution of folklore to Mormon studies, 2008: $b t.p.(William A. Wilson) p.4 cover (William A. "Bert" Wilson)
670 $a Mormon Literature & Creative Arts, website viewed 1 March 2011 $b (William A. Wilson; also known as William A. (Bert) Wilson; emeritus professor of English at Brigham Young University; chair of the BYU English Department; director of the BYU Folklore Archives; editor of Western Folklore; executive board American Folklore Society; president Utah Folklore Society; published widely on folklore and nationalism in Finland to folklore of Mormons; director Charles Redd Center for Western Studies at Brigham Young University; former director of Folklore Program at Utah State University; developed Fife Folklore Conference; past president of the Association for Mormon Letters)
670 $a PeopleSearch, website viewed 1 March 2011 $b (William Albert Wilson, age 77, previous cities Provo, UT and Logan, UT)
670 $a Phone call to author, 1 March 2011 $b (Birthdate: September 23, 1933)
670 $a UPB files, Mar. 1, 2011 $b (Wilson, William Albert, b. 1933)

Note on the record:

008 10	Descriptive cataloging rules, "a" for AACR2 rule.
046 $f	Special coded dates: $f is Birth date (Notice that the year, month and day are included in 046).
370	Associated place.
372	Field of activity (notice the multiple 372 to indicate multiple fields of activity)
373	Affiliation (notice the multiple 373 to indicate multiple affiliations)
374	Occupation (notice the multiple 374 to indicate multiple occupations)

EXAMPLE 5

000 03485cz a2200613n 450
001 1894546
005 20110823091408.0
008 800604n$ acannaabn $b aaa
010 $a n 79107741 $z no 98056029 $z no 98056518 $z no 98006061 $z no 00058310
035 $a (OCoLC)oca00339691
040 $a DLC$beng$cDLC$dDLC$dICRL$dInU$dDLC$dPPi-MA$d DLC$dOCoLC$dUPB-Mu$dDLC
046 $f 17701217 $g 18270326
053 0 $a ML410.B4 $c Biography (General)
053 0 $a ML410.B42 $c Biography (Criticism)
100 1 $a Beethoven, Ludwig van, $d 1770-1827
370 $a Bonn, Germany $b Vienna, Austria $c Germany
372 $a music
374 $a composer $a pianist
375 $a male
377 $a ger
400 1 $a Bīt'hūfin, $d 1770-1827
400 1 $a Beethoven, L. van $q (Ludwig), $d 1770-1827
400 1 $a Van Beethoven, Ludwig, $d 1770-1827
400 1 $a Beethoven, Louis van, $d 1770-1827
400 1 $a Beethoven, Ludvig van, $d 1770-1827
400 1 $a Bethovenas, L., $d 1770-1827
400 1 $a Betkhoven, L͡iudvig van, $d 1770-1827
400 1 $a Beṭhoṿn, Ludṿig ṿan, $d 1770-1827
400 1 $a Beethoven, Ludwik van, $d 1770-1827
400 1 $a Betkhoven, L. van $q (L͡iudvig), $d 1770-1827
400 1 $a Bētōven, Rūtovihhi van, $d 1770-1827

400 1 $a בטהובן
400 1 $a בעטהאָוון, לודוויג ואון
400 1 $a ルートビッヒベートベン, $d 1770-1827
400 1 $a 贝多芬, $d 1770-1827
667 $a Machine-derived non-Latin script reference project.
667 $a Non-Latin script references not evaluated.
667 $a Thematic-index numbers for works without opus numbers are from Kinsky, G. Das Werk Beethovens, e.g., [Variations, piano, WoO 80, C minor]. If Kinsky and opus numbers are not available, use numbers from Hess, W. Verzeichnis der nicht in der Gesamtausgabe veröffentlichen Werke Ludwig van Beethovens, e.g., [Minuets, string quartet, H. 33, A ♭ major]
670 $a His Symphonie no 2 en ré majeur, op. 36 [SR] 197-? : $b labels (L. v. Beethoven)
670 $a His Deux préludes par tous les 12. tons majeurs, between 1814 and 1828 : $b t.p. (Louis van Beethoven)
670 $a His Sonata in A-flat major, op. 110 (1821) for piano [SR] p1980 : $b label (Ludvig van Beethoven)
670 $a Bach, J.S. Sonata nr. 1 violončelei ir fortepijonui G-dur, BWV 1927 [SR] 1978? : $b label (L. Bethovenas)
670 $a His Symphony no. 3 in E flat major, op. 55 [SR] p1984 : $b label (Ludwig van Beethoven) notes inserted (L͡iudvig van Betkhoven)
670 $a Fiszbin, K. A Yidisher bliḳ oyf Beṭhoyn, 1984 : $b p. 21 (Ludṿig ṿan Beṭhoyn [part. voc.])
670 $a Łobaczewska, S. Beethoven, 1984 : $b p. 7 (. . . Ludwika van Beethovena)
670 $a His Sonata no. 29 . . . 1993? : $b labels (L. van Betkhoven)
670 $a His Sonata for piano and violoncello no. 5 in D major, op. 102, no. 2, 197- : $b label (Ludwig van Beethoven) container (Rūtovihhi van Bētōven)
670 $a New Grove $b (Beethoven, Ludwig van; b. Bonn, baptized Dec. 17, 1770, d. Mar. 26, 1827, Vienna; German composer)
670 $a MGG $b (Beethoven, Ludwig van; b. Dec. 16 or 17, 1770 (baptized Dec. 17))
670 $a Baker, 8th ed. $b (Beethoven, Ludwig van; b. Dec. 15 or 16, 1770 (baptized Dec. 17))
670 $a Beethoven compendium, 1992 : $b p. 12 (b. Dec. 16, 1770; there is still slight doubt about the precise date)
700 14 $a Beethoven, Ludwig van, $d 1770-1827

Note on the record:

008 10	Descriptive cataloging rules, “a” for AACR2 rule.
046	Special coded dates. $f is birth date and $g is death date. Notice that the year, month and day are included in 046.
370	Associated place.
372	Field of activity.
374	Occupation.
375	Gender.
377	Associated language.
700 14	This field includes the authorized access point for the person based on RDA instructions.

EXAMPLE 6

```
000    03375cz a2200673n 450
001    955335
005    20111108074826.0
008    790418n$ acannaabn $b aaa
010    $a n 79021164 $z sh 89001267 $z no 98029431
035    $a (OCoLC)oca00254964
040    $a DLC$beng$cDLC$dDLC$dMdU$dDLC$dInU$dDLC$d
       PPiU$dDLC$dOCoLC$dInU$dOCoLC$dICU$dOCoLC$dUPB
046    $f 18351130 $g 19100421
053 0  $a PS1300 $b PS1348
100 1  $a Twain, Mark, $d 1835-1910
370    $a Florida, Mo. $b Redding, Conn. $c Hannibal, Mo.
374    $a writer
374    $a lecturer
375    $a male
377    $a eng
400 1  $a Tvėn, Mark, $d 1835-1910
400 1  $a Tuėĭn, Mark, $d 1835-1910
400 1  $a Tuwayn, Mārk, $d 1835-1910
400 1  $a Twayn, Mārk, $d 1835-1910
400 1  $a T‘u-wen, Ma-k‘o, $d 1835-1910
400 1  $a Tven, M. $q (Mark), $d 1835-1910
400 1  $a Alden, Jean François, $d 1835-1910
400 1  $a Touen, Makū, $d 1835-1910
400 1  $a Twain, Marek, $d 1835-1910
```

400 0 $a Make Tuwen, $d 1835-1910
400 1 $a Tuwen, Make, $d 1835-1910
400 0 $a Make Teviin, $d 1835-1910
400 1 $a Твен, Марк, $d 1835-1910
400 1 $a טבן_, מרק, $d 1835-1910
400 1 $a טוויין, מארק, $d 1835-1910
400 1 $a טוויין, מרק, $d 1835-1910
400 1 $a טווין, מארק, $d 1835-1910
400 1 $a טווין, מרק, $d 1835-1910
400 1 $a טווען, מארק, $d 1835-1910
400 1 $a טוין, מרק, $d 1835-1910
400 1 $a טווען, מארק, $d 1835-1910
400 1 $a טוויין, מארק, $d 1835-1910
400 1 $a 馬克吐温, $d 1835-1910
500 1 $w nnnc $a Clemens, Samuel Langhorne, $d 1835-1910
500 1 $w nnnc $a Snodgrass, Quintus Curtius, $d 1835-1910
500 1 $w nnnc $a Conte, Louis de, $d 1835-1910
667 $a Machine-derived non-Latin script reference project.
667 $a Non-Latin script references not evaluated.
663 $a For works of this author written under other names, search also under $b Clemens, Samuel Langhorne, 1835-1910, $b Snodgrass, Quintus Curtius, 1835-1910 $b Louis de Conte, 1835-1910
670 $a Geviksman, V. A. Prints͡ i nishchiĭ, 1984 : $b t.p. (M. Tvena)
670 $a His Makū Touen tanpenshū, 1961.
670 $a His Personal recollections of Joan of Arc, 1923 : $b v. 1-2, t.p. (the Sieur Louis de Conte; Jean François Alden) spine (Mark Twain)
670 $a DAB, 1930 : $b (Clemens, Samuel Langhorne, 1835-1910; better known under pseud. Mark Twain; also used name Quintus Curtius Snodgrass)
670 $a Mark Twain's personal recollections of Joan of Arc, 1997 : $b CIP t.p. (Sieur Louis de Conte) p. vii (Sieur Louis de Conte shared . . . initials with Samuel L. Clemens)
670 $a Przygody Huck'a, 1912 : $b t.p. (Marek Twain)
670 $a Alda-bar ȯnggelegsen erin caġ, 1985 : $b v. 1, t.p. (Make Teveiin) colophon (Make Tuwen)
670 $a Wikipedia, via WWW, Oct. 18, 2011 $b (b. November 30, 1835 in Florida, Missouri; grew up in Hannibal, Missouri; d. April 21, 1910 in Redding, Connecticut; a writer and lecturer; wrote in genres of fiction, historical fiction, children's literature, non-fiction, travel literature, satire, essay, philosophical literature, social commentary, literary criticism)

Note on the record:

008 10	Descriptive cataloging rules, "a" for AACR2 rule
046	Special coded dates. $f is birth date and $g is death date. Notice that the year, month and day are included in 046.
370	Associated place.
374	Occupation (notice multiple fields of occupation).
375	Gender.
377	Associated language.

EXAMPLE 7

000 00996cz a2200277n 450
001 2221999
005 20120105074754.0
008 951122n$ acannaabn $a aaa c
010 $a no 95055361
035 $a (OCoLC)oca03961488
040 $a VtMiM-Mu$beng$cVtMiM-Mu$dPPi-MA$dDLC$dUPB $d IEN
046 $f 19650828
053 0 $a ML420.T953 $c Biography
100 1 $a Twain, Shania
370 $a Windsor, Ont.
372 $a Country Music
374 $a Singer
375 $a female
400 1 $a Twain, Eilleen
400 1 $a Edwards, Eilleen
670 $a Twain, S. The woman in me [SR] p1995 : $b label (Shania Twain)
670 $a Contemporary musicians, v. 17 $b (Twain, Shania; b. Eileen Twain, Aug. 28, 1965, Windsor, Ont.)
670 $a Her Website, Nov. 13, 2000 $b (b. Eilleen Edwards, Aug. 28, 1965, Windsor, Ont.; changed name 1991 to Shania)
670 $a Her Beginnings, 1989-1990 $b (album cover (from AMG Website): Eilleen Shania [larger type] Twain)

Note on the record:

008 10	Descriptive cataloging rules, "a" for AACR2 rule
046 $f	Special coded dates. $f is birth date. Notice that the year, month and day are included in 046.
370	Associated place.
372	Field of activity.
374	Occupation.
375	Gender.

EXAMPLE 8

010 $a no2010162260
040 $a UPB$beng$cUPB$erda$dDLC
130 0 $a Bible. $p Pentateuch. $l Greek
670 $a On conditionals in the Greek Pentateuch, ©2010.

Note on the record:

130 0 $p	The name of the Testament is omitted in the preferred title for individual books or groups of books.
130 0 $l	Language of Expression.

EXAMPLE 9

010 $a no2010162297
040 $a UPB$beng$cUPB$erda
130 0 $a Doctrine and Covenants. $l English. $f 1946
670 $a The Doctrine and Covenants of the Church of Jesus Christ of Latter-day Saints, 1946.

Note on the record:

130 0	For works created before 1501, choose the title or form of title in the original language by which the work is identified in modern sources as the preferred title.
130 0 $l	Language of the expression
130 0 $f	Date of expression. It is core if needed to differentiate an expression of a work from another expression of the same work.

EXAMPLE 10

010 $a no2010161608
040 $a UPB$beng$cUPB$erda$dDLC
100 0 $a Ctesias, $d active 5th century B.C. $t Persica
670 $a Ctesias' History of Persia, 2010.

Note on the record:

100 0 $d	Date associated with the person—If specific years of activity cannot be established, record the century or centuries in which the person was active.
100 0 $t	Referred title of the work.

EXAMPLE 11

010 $a no2010161857
040 $a UPB$beng$cUPB$erda$dUPB
100 1 $a Findlay, Andrew $c (Film editor)
670 $a András Schiff at the Royal Academy of Music, London, c2007: $b credits (Editor, Andrew Findlay)
670 $a Andrew Findlay—film and video editing, via WWW, 24 June 2010 $b (Curriculum Vitae, Bristol-based professional broadcast film, video and non-linear editor)

Note on the record:

100 1 $c	Field of activity—is a field of endeavour, area of expertise, etc., in which a person is engaged or was engaged.

EXAMPLE 12

010 $a no2010161882
040 $a UPB$beng$cUPB$dUk$erda$dUk
111 2 $a Foro Bicentenario Latinoamericano
411 2 $a Foro Bicentenario
667 $a Individual instances (e.g., Foro Bicentenario 2004) not to be established
670 $a La construcción de las memorias nacionales, c2008 : $b t.p. (Foro Bicentenario Latinoamericano 2006)
670 $a América Latina mira al bicentenario, 2004 : $b t.p. (Foro Bicentenario 2004) p. 7 (held in Santiago, Chile, Nov. 9, 2004)
670 $a Migración, integración, identidad, c2008 : $b t.p. (Foro Bicentenario, 2008) p. 12 (first Foro Bicentenario was held 11 Nov. 2003 Chile)

Note on the record:

667	Cataloger note—is an annotation that might be helpful to those using or revising the authorized access point representing a person, family, or corporate body, or creating an authorized access point representing a related person, family, or corporate body.

EXAMPLE 13

010 $a no2010160513
040 $a UPB$beng$cUPB$erda$dUPB
130 0 $a Bible. $p New Testament. $l Greek
667 $a DESCRIPTIVE USAGE: Bible authorized access points used in descriptive portions of the record are analytical, i.e., they need to contain data elements in RDA 6.30.3.2 as applicable.
670 $a The Greek imperative mood in the New Testament, [2010]

Note on the record:

130 0 $l	Language of the expression.
667	Cataloger note—is an annotation that might be helpful to those using or revising the authorized access point representing a person, family, or corporate body, or creating an authorized access point representing a related person, family, or corporate body.

EXAMPLE 14

010 $a no2010160519 $z no 2010172236
040 $a UPB$beng$cUPB$dDLC$erda
130 0 $a Bible. $p Old Testament. $l Hebrew. $f 1968
430 0 $a Torah Nevi'im u-Khetuvim
670 $a Torah Nevi'im u-Khetuvim, 1968 or 1969.

Note on the record:

130 0 $l	Language of the expression.
130 0 $f	Date of expression. It is core if needed to differentiate an expression of a work from another expression of the same work.

CHAPTER NINE

CHECKLISTS

I. CHECKLIST FOR COPY CATALOGERS

This checklist was created to help copy catalogers identify the RDA records from OCLC.

- To identify RDA records, look for:

  Fixed field

  LEADER/18 value "i" (ISBD),
  040 $a ____ $b eng $c ____ $e rda
  100 $e Relationship designators, $e
  110 $e Relationship designators, $e
  111 $e Relationship designators, $e
  245 $a Title transcribed as found (you might see the title transcribed as found on the title page, e.g., uppercases and typos in title)

245	$a Spelling is not corrected in the title (No [sic], i.e., or $h)
254	$a Capitalized words in the title as they appear on the title page
245	$c Statement of responsibility might be longer to include all authors, editors, illustrators, etc., as they appear on the title page, or, the first author [and three other authors]. No more "Rule of Three."
246	$i Title read: the correct spelling.
240	$a Conventional title ("conventional title" + "Selections"), 240 10 Works. Selections.
260	$a No [S.L.]
260	$a Might include [place of publication not identified]
260	$b No [s.n.]
260	$b Might include [publisher not identified]
260	$c Copyright symbol (©) and phonogram symbol (℗) might be present
300	No abbreviations
336	Content type
337	Media type
338	Carrier type
250	$a Transcribed as found on the source (e.g., no abbreviation is used unless the edition statement was abbreviated on the source of information)
505	Content note for the compilation
546	Language note
7xx	$e Relationship designators in MARC 21 field 7xx $e or $j (e.g., author, composer, issuing body, etc.)
7xx	Many 7xx fields for each work, if the work is a compilation

- Tips for cataloging serials:

245	Correct typo in serial title *Do not supply other title information (e.g., no $b [proceedings])*
246	Later title proper (RDA 2.3.8)
362	Numbering of serials elements (RDA 2.6)
260	Place of publication (RDA 2.8.2)
260	$b Publisher's information
300	Transcribe volume, number, year and month as on the resource (RDA 3.2)
300	$c dimensions (RDA 3.4)
310	Frequency—no abbreviation (RDA 3.14)
588	Note on issue or part used as the basis for identification (RDA 2.30.13)
500	Note on change in carrier characteristics (RDA 3.22.6)
772	Related works (RDA 25.1)

780 Related works (RDA 25.1)
785 Related works (RDA 25.1)
787 Related manifestations and items (RDA 27.1, 28.1)
775 Related expressions and manifestations (RDA 26.1)
776 Related expressions and manifestations

II. CHECKLIST FOR ORIGINAL CATALOGERS

This checklist for creating RDA records is based on the LC's RDA records checklist (Creating LC Practice Records for the RDA Test). However, each library needs to decide which RDA elements they will need for their collection. The following list is not comprehensive, but it is a starting point.

Pre-cataloging decisions:

- What is the mode of issuance of your resource: a single part monograph, a multipart monograph, an integrating resource, or a serial? (RDA 2.1 and 2.13) (see chapter 6)
- Determine if you should create a new description or add information to the existing record. (consult RDA 1.6) (see chapter 6)
- Decide on the language and scripts of your record. According to your agency's preference, you can record elements in the same language and script as in the source, in a transliterated form instead, or in both forms. (RDA 1.4) (see chapter 5)
- Decide if you are making a comprehensive description (RDA 2.1.2) or an analytical description. (RDA 2.1.3) (see chapter 5)
- Determine your preferred source of information based on the type of resource. (RDA 2.2) (see chapter 5)
- If there is no title in the book, transcribe one from (in order of preference): (a) accompanying material, (b) a container, (c) another published description of the book, or (d) any other available source. Explain in a note that the title was devised. (RDA 2.2.4 and 2.20.2.3) (see chapter 5)

A. TRANSCRIBING THE ELEMENTS OF DESCRIPTION (RDA 1.7) (See Chapter 5)

CAPITALIZATION (RDA 1.7.2)

Transcribe exactly what is on the resource (or retain what is supplied from a digital source) or adjust the capitalization according to RDA appendix A.

ABBREVIATIONS (RDA 1.7.8)

Consult RDA appendix B for the use of abbreviations in the elements.

INACCURACIES (RDA 1.7.9)

Transcribe an element as it appears on the source; transcribe an inaccuracy or a misspelled word unless the instructions for a specific element indicate otherwise.

PUNCTUATION (RDA 1.7.3)

Supply ISBD punctuation between elements and between areas. Consult RDA appendix D for punctuation.

Accents and other diacritical marks (RDA 1.7.4)

SYMBOLS (RDA 1.7.5)

Replace symbols and other characters, etc., that cannot be reproduced by the facilities available, with a description of the symbol. Make an explanatory note if necessary.

SPACING OF INITIALS AND LETTERS (RDA 1.7.6)

If separate letters or initials appear on the source of information without full stops between them, transcribe the letters without spaces between them, regardless of spacing on the source.

SQUARE BRACKETS

When adjacent elements within one area are to be enclosed in square brackets, enclose each in its own set of square brackets.

B. RECORDING THE ELEMENTS IN BIBLIOGRAPHIC RECORDS

(For specific elements used for specific materials see chapter 6)

- Identifier for the manifestation (RDA 2.15) (MARC 21 fields 020, 022, 024, 027, 028, 030, 074, 086)
- Title proper (RDA 2.3.2) (MARC 21 field 245) (see chapter 5, "Title Proper")
- Parallel title proper (RDA 2.3.3) (MARC 21 field 245) (see chapter 5, "Parallel Title Proper")
- Other title information (RDA 2.3.4) (MARC 21 field 245) (see chapter 5, "Other Title Information")
- Statement of responsibility relating to title proper (RDA 2.4.2) (MARC 21 field 245) (see chapter 5, "Statement of Responsibility")

  (Only the first is required. Cataloger's judgment is required to determine how many access points will be needed.)
- Variant title (RDA 2.3.6) (MARC 21 field 246)

  (Note that in RDA, variant titles are not *core elements. They may be recorded, but they are not required.)*
- Designation of edition (RDA 2.5.2) (MARC 21 field 250) (see chapter 5, "Edition Statement")

- Publication statement (RDA 2.8–2.11) (MARC 21 field 260 $a, $b, $c) (see chapter 5 "Publication Information")
  (Only the first place of publication recorded is required; only the first publisher's name recorded is required.)
- Copyright date (RDA 2.11) (MARC 21 field 260 $c) (see chapter 5, "Copyright Date")
  (Only required if date of publication and date of distribution are not identified.)
- Extent of resource (RDA 3.4) (MARC 21 field 300) (see chapter 6, "Extent")
- Illustrative content (RDA 7.15) (MARC 21 field 300 $b) (see chapter 5, "Illustrative Content")
- Dimensions (RDA 3.5) (MARC 21 filed 300 $c) (see chapter 5, "Dimensions")
- Accompanied materials (RDA 27.1) (MARC 21 field 300 $e) (see chapter 5 "Accompanied Materials")
- Content type (RDA 6.9) (MARC 21 field 336) (see chapters 2 and 5, "Content Type")
- Media type (RDA 3.2) (MARC 21 field 337) (see chapters 2 and 5, "Media Type")
- Carrier type (RDA 3.3) (MARC 21 field 338) (see chapters 2 and 5, "Carrier Type")
- Series statement (RDA 2.12 and 2.12.9) (MARC 21 field 490) (see chapter 5, "Series Statement")

Uniform Resource Locator (URL) (RDA 4.6) (MARC 21 field 856 $u) (see chapter 5, "Providing Acquisition and Access Information")

- Language of the content (RDA 7.12) (MARC 21 field 041, 546) (see chapter 5, "Language of the Content")
- Script of the content (RDA 7.13.2) (MARC 21 field 546) (see chapter 5 "Script of the Content")
- Notes (RDA 2.20.2) (MARC 21 field 500) (see chapter 5, "Notes")

C. AUTHORIZED ACCESS POINTS (MARC FIELDS 1XX–130, 240, 7XX–730, 760–787)

1. ELEMENTS IN THE AUTHORIZED ACCESS POINT TO IDENTIFY THE WORK OR EXPRESSION (AACR2 MAIN ENTRY)

Authorized access point for a work (RDA 6.27.1)

Preferred title (RDA 6.2) (MARC 21 130, 245, 100–111 $t) (see chapter 6)

Other elements for works if needed to break conflict

Form of work (RDA 6.3) (MARC 21: added to preferred title)

Date of work (RDA 6.4) (MARC 21: added to preferred title)

Place of origin of the work (RDA 6.5) (MARC 21: added to preferred title)
Other distinguishing characteristic of the work (RDA 6.6)
Compilations (RDA 6.2.2) (see chapter 6)
Authorized access point for musical work (see chapter 6)
Preferred title (RDA 6.2) (MARC 21 130, 245, 100–111 $t)
Medium of performance (RDA 6.15) (MARC 21 $m in authorized access point)
Numeric designation of a musical work (RDA 6.16) (MARC 21 $n in authorized access point)
Key (RDA 6.17) (MARC 21 $r in authorized access point)

Authorized access point for legal work (see chapter 6)
Preferred title (RDA 6.19.2) (MARC 21 130, 245, 100–111 $t)

Authorized access point for religious work (see chapter 6)
Preferred title (RDA 6.23.2) (MARC 130, 245, 100–111 $t)

Authorized access point for an expression (RDA 6.27.3) = authorized access point for the work plus one or more of the following additions:
Content type (RDA 6.9) (MARC 21: $h in authorized access point)
Date of expression (RDA 6.10) (MARC 21 $f in authorized access point)
Language of expression (RDA 6.11) (MARC 21 $l in authorized access point)
Other distinguishing characteristic for the expression (RDA 6.12) (MARC 21: various subfields)

2. CREATOR (RDA 19.2) (MARC 21 100–111). (See Chapter 6)

If creator is a person

Authorized access point for a person (RDA 9.19)
Preferred name is the base of the access point (RDA 9.2.2) (MARC 21 100 or 700)
Additional elements for differentiation (use as needed)
Date associated with the person
Date of birth (RDA 9.3.2) (MARC 21 100 $d or 700 $d)
Date of death (RDA 9.3.3) (MARC 21 100 $d or 700 $d)
Period of activity of the person (RDA 9.3.4) (MARC 21 100 $d or 100 $d)
Title of the person (RDA 9.4) (MARC 21 100 $c or 700 $c)
Other designation associated with the person (RDA 9.6) (MARC 21 21100 $c or 700 $c)
Field of activity of the person (RDA 9.15) (MARC 100 $c or 700 $c)
Profession or occupation (RDA 9.16) (MARC 21 100 $c or 700 $c)
Fuller form of name (RDA 9.5) (MARC 21 100 $q or 700 $q)

If creator is a family

Authorized access point for a family (RDA 10.10)

Preferred name is the base of the authorized access point) (RDA 10.2.2) (MARC 21100 3# or 700 3#)

Additions to the preferred name of family

Type of family (RDA 10.3)

Date associated with the family (RDA 10.4) (MARC 21 100 $d or 700 $d)

Place associated with the family (RDA 10.5) (MARC 21100 $c or 700 $c)

Prominent member of the family (RDA 10.6) (MARC 21 100 $g or 700 $g)

If creator is a corporate body

Authorized access point for a corporate body (RDA 11.13)

Preferred name is the base of the authorized access point (RDA 11.2.2) (MARC 21 110/111 or 710/711)

If the corporate body is not a conference, add information from the following list as needed to break conflict:

Other designation associated with the corporate body (RDA 11.7) (MARC 21 110 or 710)

Place associated with the corporate body (RDA 11.3) (MARC 21 110 or 710 $c)

Location of headquarters (RDA 11.3.3) (MARC 21 110 or 710)

Date of establishment (RDA 11.4.3) (MARC 21 110 or 710 $d)

Date of termination (RDA 11.4.4) (MARC 21 110 or 710 $d)

Associated institution (RDA 11.5) (MARC 21 110 or 710 $u)

If the corporate body is a conference, exhibition, etc., add information from the following list as needed to break conflict:

Other designation associated with the corporate body (RDA 11.7) (MARC 21 111 or 711)

Number of a conference, etc. (RDA 11.6) (MARC 21 110 or 710 $n)

Location of conference, etc. (RDA 11.5) (MARC 21 111 $c or 711 $c)

Date of a conference, etc., (RDA 11.4.2) (MARC 21 111 $d or 711 $d)

D. RELATIONSHIPS OTHER THAN THOSE NAMED ABOVE

CONTRIBUTOR (RDA 20.2) (MARC 21 7XX)
(See Chapter 7)

RELATED WORK (RDA 25.1) (MARC 21 505, 7XX)
(See Chapter 6, "Recording Relationships")

RELATED EXPRESSION (RDA 26.1) (MARC 21 505, 7XX)
(See Chapter 6, "Recording Relationships")

RELATED MANIFESTATION (RDA 27.1) (MARC 21 500, 760–787)
(See Chapter 5, "Recording Relationships")

RELATED ITEM (RDA 28.1) (MARC 21 500, 760–787)
(See Chapter 5, "Recording Relationships")

III. CHECKLIST FOR AUTHORITY CONTROL

This checklist will assist catalogers in establishing a new authority record based on RDA or identifying existing RDA records in the OCLC/LC Authority File.

008/10 Descriptive cataloging rules; use "z" for other rule
040 $e (R) Description conventions; use "rda"
046 Special Coded Dates (Repeatable)
  $f is Birth date
  $g is Death date
  $k Beginning or single date created (Date of expression)
  $u the source can be given in subfield $u in the 046 and 37X fields or can be given in a single 670 field:

1xx $d Dates in the preferred name

- Months are not abbreviated (RDA 9.3.2.3)
- "cent." becomes "century" (RDA 9.19.1.5)
- "ca." becomes "approximately" (RDA 9.3.1.3)
- "fl." becomes "active" or possibly "flourished" (RDA 9.19.1.5)
- No restrictions on using "active" or "flourished" in modern times (RDA 9.19.1.5)
- "b." and "d." become "born" and "died" or a hyphen before or after the year (RDA 9.19.1.3)
- Words such as "Jr.," "IV" are part of the preferred name, given after the forename(s) in languages other than Portuguese (RDA 9.2.2.9.5);

the term is given in MARC subfield $c. For names in Portuguese, the terms are part of the surnames.

Other distinguishing characteristics of the expression of a musical work
$o "arr." becomes "arranged" (RDA 6.18.1.4)
- "acc." becomes "accompanied" (RDA 6.15.1.12)
- "unacc." becomes "unaccompanied" (RDA 6.15.1.12)

Identifying person (Persons include fictitious entities)
- Distinctive families are established as NARs in LC/NAF and used as creators and contributors in bibliographic records (RDA 8.1.2)
- Fictitious entities that are presented as having responsibility for a work are listed as creators and contributors in bibliographic records (RDA 8.1.2 and 9.0). The preferred name is recorded according to the guidelines in RDA 9.2.2 for the type of name (given names, names containing surnames, etc.); RDA 9.2.2.22 covers this example.

There is no instruction in RDA to delete a frequency word (e.g., "Biennial") from the name of the conference.

Preferred title for the Bible (RDA 6.23.2.9)
- For the Old Testament, record *Old Testament* as a subdivision of the preferred title for the Bible.
- For the New Testament, record *New Testament* as a subdivision of the preferred title for the Bible.

Books of Bible (RDA 6.23.2.9.2)
- For books of the Catholic or Protestant canon, record the brief citation form of the Authorized Version as a subdivision of the preferred title for the Bible.

New MARC Fields

336 Content type
370 Associated place
371 Address
372 Field of activity
373 Affiliation
374 Occupation
375 Gender
376 Family information
377 Associated language
380 Form of work
381 Other distinguishing characteristic of work or expression
382 Medium of performance
383 Numeric designation of a musical work
384 Key

REFERENCE

"Creating LC Practice Records for the RDA Test." Accessed September 29, 2012.

BIBLIOGRAPHY

American Library Association. *Anglo-American Cataloguing Rules*, Second Edition. 2002 revision. www.aacr2.org.

Argus, C., and C. Todd. "Implementation, Documentation and Training: What Happens Now?" Presented at the Australian Committee on Cataloging Seminar, RDA: The Next Generation Cataloguing Standard, Sydney, October 24, 2008. www.nla.gov.au/lis/stndrds/grps/acoc/papers2008.html.

Australian Committee on Cataloguing. "RDA: Resource Description and Access." 2008. www.nla.gov.au/lis/stndrds/grps/acoc/rda.html. Includes presentations and articles, information about the RDA electronic discussion list, and various other resources.

Berdinka, Susan. "Some Thoughts about FRBR—It Is a Beautiful Thing." *Thoughts on Technical Librarianship* October 30, 2010.

Berners-Lee, Tim, James Hendler, and Ora Lassila. "The Semantic Web: A New Form of Web Content That Is Meaningful to Computers Will Unleash a Revolution of New Possibilities." *Scientific American* 284, no. 5 (May 2001): 34–43.

Block, Rick."RDA: Cataloging Code for the 21st Century?" Paper presented at Columbia University, New York, NY, December 9, 2009.

Bloss, Marjorie E. "Testing RDA at Dominican University's Graduate School of Library and Information Science: The Students' Perspectives." *Cataloging and Classification Quarterly* 49, no. 7/8 (2011): 582–99.

Calhoun, Karen. "The Changing Nature of the Catalog and Its Integration with Other Discovery Tools." Final Report prepared for the Library of Congress. Washington, DC: Library of Congress, March 17, 2006. www.loc.gov/catdir/calhoun-report-final.pdf.

Chapman, Ann. "RDA: A New International Standard." *Ariadne* 49, no. 2 (2006). www.ariadne.ac.uk/issue49/chapman.

Chew Chiat Naun. "Next Generation OPACs: A Cataloging Viewpoint." *Cataloging and Classification Quarterly* 48, no. 4 (2010): 330–42.

———. *RDA Vocabularies for a Twenty-First-Century Data Environment.* Chicago: ALA Techsource, 2010.

Coyle, Karen. *Understanding the Semantic Web: Bibliographic Data and Metadata.* Chicago: ALA Techsource, 2010.

Coyle, Karen, and Diane Hillman. "Resource Description and Access (RDA): Cataloging Rules for the 20th Century." *D-Lib Magazine* 13, no. 1/2 (2007). www.dlib.org/dlib/january07/coyle/01coyle.html.

Delsey, Tom. "AACR2 Versus RDA." Presentation given at the Canadian Library Association Pre-Conference, May 29, 2009. http://tsig.wikispaces.com/file/view/AACR2_versus_RDA.pdf.

Dunsire, Gordon. "Distinguishing Content from Carrier: The RDA/ONIX Framework for Resources Categorization." *D-Lib Magazine* 13, no.1/2, 2007. http://eprints.rclis.org/bitstream/10760/13412/1/3.pdf.

———. "UNIMARC, RDA and the Semantic Web." 2009. www.5.nlc.gov.cn/newen/fl/iflanlc/iclc/IFLAds/201012/P020101210594440572365.pdf.

Gorman, Michael. *The Enduring Library.* Chicago: American Library Association, 2003.

———. "RDA: The Coming Cataloging Debacle." 2007. www.slc.bc.ca/rda1007.pdf.

———. "Technical Services: Past, Present, Future." Paper presented at the Association of Library and Information Science Education Annual Conference, Boston, MA, January 15, 2010.

Gradmann, Stefan. (2005). "rdfs:frbr—Towards an Implementation Model for Library Catalogs Using Semantic Web Technology." In *Functional Requirements for Bibliographic Records (FRBR): Hype or Cure-All?* Edited by Patrick Le Boeuf. Binghamton, NY: Haworth, 2005.

Hitchens, Alison, and Ellen Symons. "Preparing Catalogers for RDA Training." *Cataloging and Classification Quarterly* 47, no. 8 (2009): 691–707.

Hoffman, Gretchen L. "Meeting Users' Needs in Cataloging: What Is the Right Thing to Do?" *Cataloging and Classification Quarterly* 47, no. 8 (2009): 631–41.

Huthwaite, Anne. "RDA: History and Background." Presented at the Australian Committee on Cataloging Seminar, RDA: The Next Generation Cataloguing Standard, Sydney, October 24, 2008. www.nla.gov.au/lis/stndrds/grps/acoc/papers2008.html.

International Federation of Library Associations and Institutions Study Group on the Functional Requirements for Bibliographic Records. *Functional Requirements for Bibliographic Records.* The Hague, Netherlands: IFLA, 1997.

———. "Statement of International Cataloguing Principles." Paper presented at the IFLA Meeting of Experts on International Cataloguing Code (IME ICC), February 2009. www.ifla.org/VII/s13/icp/ICP-2009_en.pdf.

Joint Steering Committee for the Development of RDA. "A Brief History of AACR." www.rda-jsc.org/history.html.

———. "JSC/RDA/Complete Examples (Bibliographic)" Revised 17 June 2010. Available at www.rda-jsc.org/docs/6JSC_RDA_Complete_Examples_(Bibliographic)_revised.pdf.

———. "A New Organization for RDA." www.rda-jsc.org/rda-new-org.html.

———. "Presentations on RDA." www.rda-jsc.org/rdapresentations.html.

———. "Resource Description and Access: A Prospectus." October 28, 2008. www.rda-jsc.org/docs/5rdaprospectusrev6.pdf.

Kiorgaard, Deirdre, and Ebe Kartus. "A Rose by Any Other Name?: From AACR2 to Resource Description and Access." 2006. www.valaconf.org.au/vala2006/papers2006/83_Kartus_Final.pdf.

Lewis, Peter R. "Preface." *Anglo-American Cataloguing Rules,* Second Edition. Chicago: American Library Association, 1978.

Library of Congress. "Examples for RDA—Compared to AACR2 (Work in Progress)." Prepared for the Special Libraries Association Conference, June 16, 2009. www.sla.org/PDFs/SLA2009/2009_rdaexamples.pdf.

———. "New RDA Examples from LC." www.loc.gov/catdir/cpso/RDAtest/rdaexamples.html.

Library of Congress Bibliographic Control Research Group. Testing Resource Description and Access (RDA). "About the U.S. National Libraries Test Plan for RDA." www.loc.gov/bibliographic-future/rda/about.html.

———. "Final Report and Recommendations." www.loc.gov/bibliographic-future/rda.

———. "Testing Resource Description and Access (RDA)." www.loc.gov/bibliographic-future/rda/.

Library of Congress Network Development and MARC Standards Office. "RDA in MARC." January 2010. www.loc.gov/marc/RDAinMARC29.html.

Library of Congress Working Group on the Future of Bibliographic Control. "On the Record: Report of the Library of Congress Working Group on the Future of Bibliographic Control." January 9, 2008. www.loc.gov/bibliographic-future/news/lcwg-ontherecord-jan08-final.pdf.

Marshall, Catherine C., and Frank M. Shipman. "Which Semantic Web?" Paper presented at the Association for Computing Machinery 14th Conference on Hypertext and Hypermedia, Nottingham, England, August 2003.

Medeiros, Norm. "The Catalog's Last Stand." *OCLC Systems and Services* 23, no. 3 (2007): 235–37.

Miller, Liz, and Diane Zabel. "Resource Description and Access (RDA)." *Reference and User Services Quarterly* 50, no. 3: 216–22. http://lsc5521catmanualsp2012.wikispaces.com/file/view/RDA+Intro_2011_mod+12.pdf.

"NCSU RDA Practice Bibliographic Record: DVD." https://staff.lib.ncsu.edu/confluence/download/attachments/17600159/DVD-1-Emma-MARC21-RDA-Record.pdf?version=2&modificationDate=1285272928000.

Needleman, Mark. "The Resource Description and Access Standard." *Serials Review* 34, no. 2 (2008): 233–34.

ODLIS: Online Dictionary for Library and Information Science, s.v. "cooperative cataloging."

Oliver, Chris. *Introducing RDA: A Guide to the Basics*. Chicago: American Library Association, 2010.

Patton, Glenn. "An Introduction to FRAD. Getting Ready for RDA and FRBR: What You Need to Know." Presentation given at the American Library Association Annual Conference, June 2008. http://presentations.ala.org/images/c/c5/Frad_ala_200806_color.pdf.

Piepenburg, Scott. "Re: RDA a 'Done Deal' at ALA," online posting, AUTOCAT. May 19, 2010. autocat@listserv.syr.edu.

Pin-Shan Chen, Peter. "The Entity-Relationship Model: Toward a Unified View of Data." *ACM Transactions on Database Systems* 1, no. 1 (1976): 9–36.

RDA Toolkit. A webinar demonstration of RDA Toolkit is available at www.rdatoolkit.org/training/guidedtour.

Riva, Pat. "Introducing Functional Requirements for Bibliographic Records and Related IFLA Developments." *ASIS&T Bulletin* Aug./Sept. 2007.

"Sample RDA Records in OCLC." City University of New York. New York, NY. http://cunycataloging.pbworks.com/w/page/32018740/Sample-RDA-records-in-OCLC.

Schiff, Adam. "Changes from AACR2 to RDA: A Comparison of Examples." Paper presented at the British Columbia Library Association Conference, Penticton, BC, Canada, April 27, 2010.

Seikel, Michele. "No More Romanizing: The Attempt to Be Less Anglocentric in RDA." *Cataloging and Classification Quarterly* 47, no. 8 (2009): 741–48.

Singer, Ross. "Linked Library Data Now!" *Journal of Electronic Resources Librarianship* 21, no. 2 (2009): 114–26.

Taylor, Arlene G. *Wynar's Introduction to Cataloging and Classification* 9th ed. Westport, CT: Libraries Unlimited, 2004.

———. ed. *Understanding FRBR: What It Is and How It Will Affect Our Retrieval Tools.* Westport, CT: Libraries Unlimited, 2007.

Taylor, Wendy, and Helen Williams. "Report on CILIP's Executive Briefings on Resource Description and Access, held at CILIP on 23 March, 2010, and repeated at the Bloomsbury Hotel on 30 March, 2010." www.ariadne.ac.uk/issue63/rda-briefing-rpt.

Tillett, Barbara B. "Catalog It Once for All: A History of Cooperative Cataloging in the United States Prior to 1967." In *Cooperative Cataloging: Past, Present, and Future.* Edited by Barry B. Baker. New York: Haworth, 1993.

———. "Keeping Libraries Relevant in the Semantic Web with RDA; Resource Description and Access." *JLIS.IT* 2, no. 2 (2011).

———. "Resource Description and Access: Background/Overview." Webcast. May 15, 2008.

———. "Resource Description and Access: Overview: History, Principles, Conceptual Models," Paper presented at the IFLA Satellite Meeting on RDA, Quebec, August 8, 2008. Available at www.collectionscanada.gc.ca/jsc/docs/iflasatellite-20080808-tillett.pdf www.rda-jsc.org/docs/iflasatellite-20080808-tillett.pdf.

———. *What Is FRBR?: A Conceptual Model for the Bibliographic Universe.* Washington, DC: Library of Congress Cataloging Distribution Service, 2007.

INDEX

A

B

D

S

T